From Death Row to Freedom

D1520837

UNIVERSITY PRESS OF FLORIDA

Florida A&M University, Tallahassee
Florida Atlantic University, Boca Raton
Florida Gulf Coast University, Ft. Myers
Florida International University, Miami
Florida State University, Tallahassee
New College of Florida, Sarasota
University of Central Florida, Orlando
University of Florida, Gainesville
University of North Florida, Jacksonville
University of South Florida, Tampa
University of West Florida, Pensacola

FROM DEATH ROW TO FREEDOM

The Struggle for Racial Justice in the Pitts-Lee Case

PHILLIP A. HUBBART

University Press of Florida

Gainesville · Tallahassee · Tampa · Boca Raton

Pensacola · Orlando · Miami · Jacksonville · Ft. Myers · Sarasota

Publication of this work made possible by a Sustaining the Humanities through the American Rescue Plan grant from the National Endowment for the Humanities.

28 27 26 25 24 23   6 5 4 3 2 1

Library of Congress Cataloging-in-Publication Data
Names: Hubbart, Phillip A., author.
Title: From death row to freedom : the struggle for racial justice in the Pitts-Lee case / Phillip A. Hubbart.
Description: 1. | Gainesvile : University Press of Florida, [2023] | Includes bibliographical references and index.
Identifiers: LCCN 2022050111 (print) | LCCN 2022050112 (ebook) | ISBN 9780813069722 (hardback) | ISBN 9780813080130 (paperback) | ISBN 9780813070483 (pdf) | ISBN 9780813072838 (ebook)
Subjects: LCSH: Pitts, Freddie Lee—Trials, litigation, etc. | Lee, Wilbert—Trials, litigation, etc. | Judicial error—Florida—Case studies. | Trials (Murder)—Florida. | False imprisonment—Florida—Case studies. | Capital punishment—Florida—Case studies. | Criminal justice, Administration of—Florida. | BISAC: HISTORY / African American & Black | SOCIAL SCIENCE / Ethnic Studies / American / African American & Black Studies
Classification: LCC KF224.P53 H83 2023 (print) | LCC KF224.P53 (ebook) | DDC 345.759/0211—dc23/eng/20230103
LC record available at https://lccn.loc.gov/2022050111
LC ebook record available at https://lccn.loc.gov/2022050112

The University Press of Florida is the scholarly publishing agency for the State University System of Florida, comprising Florida A&M University, Florida Atlantic University, Florida Gulf Coast University, Florida International University, Florida State University, New College of Florida, University of Central Florida, University of Florida, University of North Florida, University of South Florida, and University of West Florida.

University Press of Florida
2046 NE Waldo Road
Suite 2100
Gainesville, FL 32609
http://upress.ufl.edu

This book is dedicated to Gene Miller (1928–2005), a Pulitzer Prize–winning journalist for the *Miami Herald,* one of the great reporters of his generation, and the person most responsible for correcting the miscarriage of justice this book chronicles. Miller's masterful attention to detail, his skillful writing, and his fierce devotion to justice are legendary. His colleagues at the *Miami Herald* called him "the soul and conscience of the newsroom."

I will never reject, from any consideration personal to myself, the cause of the defenseless or the oppressed.

Attorney Oath of Admission to the Florida Bar

The enormity of the injustice done to the Petitioners in this case is almost beyond belief. That such an event could happen in this country in this day and age is a reminder to all of us that injustice of enormous magnitude is still very much among us. No evasions, no rationalizations, no highly skilled legal argument can quite obscure this simple truth.

Phillip A. Hubbart
Pitts/Lee Certiorari Petition
United States Supreme Court
May 1, 1975

It would have been easy to come out [of prison] feeling all whites were racists and that the entire legal system was bad. But really, in the end, it was white people and the system that eventually saw justice was done.

Freddie Pitts
Ebony
September 1983

Contents

Prologue

On the night of July 31, 1963, at the height of the civil rights crisis in the South, two white filling station attendants were held up at gunpoint at a gas station outside a small southern town in the Florida Panhandle. The attendants were kidnapped from the station and were found murdered several days later in the countryside. About $100 in cash was stolen from the station.

Two young Black men, Freddie Pitts and Wilbert Lee, were soon arrested for this crime. They were interrogated by local police at all hours of the day and night, subjected to police threats and beatings, were represented by a court-appointed lawyer who cooperated with the police, and were so intimidated that they confessed and pled guilty to the crimes, even though they were entirely innocent. In short order, they were convicted and sentenced to death.

After twelve years of protracted legal proceedings and wrangling at the highest levels of state government, Pitts and Lee were eventually cleared of the charges against them and walked out of prison as free men. The crime for which they were convicted had, in fact, been committed by a white man—a total stranger to Pitts and Lee, but a man well known to the local police.

This book is my insider's account of that case. I was one of the defense lawyers for these two men, having joined the defense team two years after their original convictions. We defense lawyers, however, were not primarily responsible for Pitts and Lee's ultimate vindication. That distinction belongs to a Pulitzer Prize–winning journalist, a private polygraph examiner, an attorney general, and a governor—inspired, in turn, by a pair of courageous men who refused to be victims and fought back.

This is a compelling murder case. But more important, it is also a piece of history that deserves to be remembered. It is a piece of Florida history.

It is a piece of southern history. And ultimately, it is a piece of American history. Thus, my reason for writing this book: to record the central events of this case as the story unfolded over a period of twelve years.

The historic significance of the case is plain. It is emblematic of the civil rights era of the 1960s. Indeed, to isolate the case from this turbulent era is to profoundly misunderstand what happened. This was not a time when isolated and unconnected Black Americans such as Pitts and Lee could stand up for their rights in the segregated South without incurring the anger and sometimes the violence of powerful white people. And Pitts and Lee did in fact face terrible threats and violence during their ordeal in August 1963, eventually surrendering to this relentless terror.

Indeed, the South back then was defiant in protecting its Jim Crow segregated society in which Black Americans were treated as second-class citizens. Civil rights organizations were challenging this deeply unjust system, and there was widespread southern resistance. White Citizens Councils—the "respectable" alternative to the Ku Klux Klan—sprang up all over the South to fight what they saw as "outside agitators." Old North-South hatreds bubbled to the surface.[1]

On January 14, 1963, Alabama governor George Wallace spoke for many white southerners when he was sworn in as governor. He announced in his inaugural address: "I draw a line in the dust and toss the gauntlet before the feet of tyranny and I say segregation now, segregation tomorrow, segregation forever."[2]

Several months later, in the spring of 1963, civil rights groups launched massive demonstrations against white-only lunch counters and other segregated facilities in Birmingham, Alabama. The police response was to arrest thousands of demonstrators, supported by police dogs and high-pressure fire hoses. The media coverage of the event went nationwide.[3]

On June 11, 1963, Governor Wallace stood in the entrance to the University of Alabama in Tuscaloosa in an attempt to block the admission of two young Black students despite a federal court order that directed that they be admitted. Federal marshals were required to enforce this order and to ensure the proper registration of these students.[4]

That evening at 8 p.m., President John F. Kennedy spoke to the nation in a groundbreaking civil rights address. He said, "We are confronted primarily with a moral issue. It is as old as the Scriptures and as clear as the American Constitution."[5] A few hours later, civil rights activist Medgar Evers was shot and killed in Jackson, Mississippi. He soon became one of the martyred heroes of the civil rights movement.[6]

The following month, on July 18, 1963, sixteen young Black youths were arrested for staging a peaceful sit-in protest at a whites-only lunch counter at a pharmacy in St. Augustine, Florida. This protest was part of a national campaign to desegregate lunch counters in business establishments all over the South that had begun on February 1, 1960, in Greensboro, North Carolina. Four of the St. Augustine protesters, who were juveniles, were convicted of "delinquency" (which was not a crime) in a county court and were sentenced to state juvenile reform schools. A firestorm of protest ensued. Similar sit-in demonstrations were conducted in the city on an almost daily basis throughout July, August, and September 1963. On Labor Day in September 1963, a mass demonstration followed in the town plaza, resulting in a violent police reaction in which arrests were made using police dogs, nightsticks, and cattle prods.[7]

Meanwhile, on August 16, 1963, the local chapter of the NAACP in Pensacola, Florida, issued a sweeping series of requests of the city designed to immediately desegregate all public institutions and many private businesses in the city and to require those institutions to hire Black employees. Tense negotiations followed with the biracial committee the city had set up to deal with its racial problems. The committee proposed a less drastic integration plan that would have been voluntary, but the city council and county commission ultimately refused to adopt it. [8]

As the crisis deepened, members of the Ku Klux Klan bombed the 16th Street Baptist Church in Birmingham, Alabama, on September 15, 1963, killing four little Black girls. This tragedy was widely covered by the national media and the ensuing impact shook the nation.[9]

Still fixed in the memory of many white southerners were the Freedom Rides in which civil rights demonstrators rode Greyhound and Trailway buses throughout the segregated South in 1961–1962. These young people were protesting the white-only waiting rooms and restaurants at interstate bus stations. Local police allowed crowds of white thugs and members of the Ku Klux Klan to viciously attack these riders—some with baseball bats, lead pipes, and chains—as the riders arrived by bus in cities such as Anniston, Birmingham, and Montgomery, Alabama. In Anniston, the mob set the riders' Greyhound bus on fire and destroyed it. [10]

In the midst of this crisis, on July 31, 1963, the double robbery/kidnap/murders in this case took place. In a mindless rush to judgment, four weeks later, on August 28, 1963, Pitts and Lee were sentenced to death for these murders and sent to death row. The local deputy sheriff who was in charge of the initial investigation later said that Pitts and Lee's case was handled in this rapid fashion "due to the black movement that was just beginning to get started in the Florida Panhandle area"—there having been "an incident" in Pensacola just prior to their arrest.[11]

No credible defense could possibly have been mounted for these men in such a steamroller atmosphere, and none was. Meanwhile, the white man who committed these crimes escaped from the area the morning after the murders, fled to Fort Lauderdale, and soon committed another murder that was strikingly similar to the murders he had committed outside Port St. Joe.

And on the very day Pitts and Lee were sentenced to death, August 28, 1963, Martin Luther King Jr. was giving his historic "I Have a Dream" speech at the foot of the Lincoln Memorial. The speech was the high point of the peaceful three-day march on Washington, DC, involving some 250,000 demonstrators to celebrate brotherhood, to protest racism, and to lobby Congress for civil rights legislation.[12] It is one of the supreme ironies of this case, as Dr. King's dream for this country as spoken that day in the nation's capital stood in stark contrast to the simultaneous nightmare that Pitts and Lee were living through in the Florida Panhandle.

THE MURDER CONVICTIONS
(1963-1964)

1

Introduction

The End of the Ordeal

On September 19, 1975, I walked into a large gymnasium-like room at Florida State Prison at Raiford, Florida, with my two co-counsel, Irwin Block and Maurice Rosen. Waiting for us at a long press table were Freddie Pitts and Wilbert Lee, our two Black clients for the past decade. Their twelve-year ordeal behind prison bars, nine of them on death row, was coming to an end. Governor Reubin Askew and the Florida Cabinet had just pardoned the two men, based on the ground that they were innocent of a 1963 robbery, kidnap, and murder of two white gas station attendants—a crime that a white man who was unknown to Pitts and Lee had committed alone.

Assembled that day in this crowded room was the national press. The room was jammed with eighty-one members of the press, including eighteen television camera crews and sixteen still photographers. They were waiting to film, photograph, and interview Pitts and Lee about how it felt to be totally exonerated. The place was filled with the deafening noise of loud voices and the clattering of heavy equipment.[1]

We sat down at the press table with our clients, and suddenly for a few seconds everything fell silent. But then the TV cameras focused, the still cameras clicked, and the questions poured forth. We were on national television. It was almost surreal. I was a 38-year-old public defender and had never experienced anything like it.

In the audience was Gene Miller, a reporter for the *Miami Herald*. He had investigated and reported on this case for nearly nine years, eventually winning a Pulitzer Prize in the process.[2] He had also written a book about the case, aptly entitled *Invitation to a Lynching*.[3] Without his legwork, his reporting, and most of all his book, this pardon would never have happened.

Absent from this event was the private lie detector examiner who broke the case wide open, former City of Miami homicide detective Warren Holmes. This was not surprising, as Holmes always shunned the limelight. Hired by Broward County law enforcement officials in a related murder case arising out of Fort Lauderdale, Holmes had obtained a detailed and stunning confession from Curtis Adams, the white man who had murdered the two gas station attendants. Significantly, two Broward County police detectives had earlier developed a trail of evidence that implicated Adams in these murders. Adams's former girlfriend later corroborated the confession to Holmes and Adams repeated it to the Broward County Sheriff's Office, the Florida attorney general, counsel to the Florida governor, and other members of the Florida Cabinet.

Adams even led Broward County police to the exact spot in the country outside Port St. Joe, Florida, where he had shot and killed the two gas station attendants after kidnapping them from their station. It was the precise spot where local police had found the bodies of the two men, laid out full length on the ground, as Adams's confession had stated. Moreover, the findings in the autopsy reports on the victims' bodies proved consistent with Adams's confession and inconsistent with the confessions Pitts and Lee had made.

When the press interview was over and the pardon had been officially filed at 12:03 p.m. in the state capital, Pitts and Lee walked out of prison as free men. Both reacted with a surprising degree of goodwill, although they had plenty to be angry about.

Pitts was from Mobile, Alabama. At the time of his arrest, he was a 19-year-old private in the United States Army stationed on maneuvers outside Port St. Joe. He had no prior criminal record. As Pitts walked out of prison that day, he was asked whether he was bitter. "I think I have a certain degree of bitterness," he said, "but animosity and hatred . . . no." He then added with a touch of sardonic humor: "I've had enough of this hotel," he said. "They have very poor accommodations."[4]

Lee was a 28-year-old resident of Port St. Joe at the time of his arrest, an odd jobs worker with a minor criminal record, including being a passenger in a stolen car. He was simply overjoyed at his release: "I've got my prison clothes off, and I've got my free world clothes on," he said, "and gee baby, I feel like a Philadelphia lawyer."[5]

As Pitts and Lee made their way to the cars that would take them away from prison, the defense team and Gene Miller followed along. Behind

Miller's glasses were tears, and he said in a soft voice, "God, this is a beautiful, beautiful sight."[6]

After a short ride to the airport, we were all whisked away in a commercial airlines flight out of Gainesville, Florida. When we landed at the Miami International Airport, the media and a huge crowd of well-wishers greeted us. Pitts and Lee stepped up to the cameras and microphones while we defense lawyers ducked out, leaving our clients to enjoy their great moment. Characteristically, Miller also ducked out with us.

Later that evening there was an emotional celebratory dinner at the Miami Herald building in downtown Miami. Everyone connected with the case was there. Although much of the dinner remains a blur to me now, I do remember rising to say that Pitts and Lee's long ordeal and their ultimate triumph was "a tribute to the strength and endurance of the human spirit." I still believe that.

The next day, we were front page news in the *Miami Herald*.[7] We were also the second-most-reported story in the country, eclipsed only by the continuing news coverage of the sensational FBI arrest on September 18, 1975, of William Randolph Hearst's granddaughter, Patty Hearst, for federal bank robbery.[8]

*　　*　　*

The pardon itself, however, had been a long time in the making. Governor Reubin Askew later said that he spent more time on this issue than he had on any other issue during his eight years in office, some eighteen months of investigation. He read transcripts, studied court papers, and interviewed witnesses. He was a lawyer by training and pored over every detail.

He read Gene Miller's book *Invitation to a Lynching*, which laid out the case in full. In fact, Miller had written the book with Governor Askew in mind as its sole reader. He even sent the book's page proofs to Askew before the book was published. Miller refused to publicize the book when it was released. He didn't want anyone to think he was making any money from this case.

Toward the end of his inquiries, Askew arranged an interview with me at a motel in Miami where he was staying in connection with some unrelated state business. I was the elected public defender in Miami, and Askew had previously appointed me to represent Pitts and Lee outside my circuit.

We sat together in the pool area at the governor's motel with no one else around. Askew knew the case thoroughly and had probably made up his mind. We covered a lot of ground, but basically all he wanted to know was my personal opinion on whether the men I represented were innocent. I told him I had no doubt whatever.

As an aside, Askew expressed concern about a group that was picketing his office in Tallahassee with signs attacking his handling of the case. He wanted to know whether we defense lawyers were connected with these people, whom he regarded as left-wing radicals. I assured him that we had no knowledge of this group and thoroughly disapproved of their tactics, as we were lawyers, not political activists. He seemed satisfied and the conversation soon turned to other matters and eventually concluded.

Askew was an extremely able, highly respected political moderate from Pensacola, located in the Florida Panhandle.[9] He was familiar with some of the law enforcement and prosecutorial officials involved in this case and knew what they were capable of. I think that knowledge may have had a lot to do with his ultimate decision to grant the pardon, although we will never really know, as he always kept personalities out of the matter and looked to the facts alone.

On September 10, 1975, Governor Askew spoke at an emotionally charged meeting of the Florida Cabinet in Tallahassee that was heavily covered by the media. He analyzed the case in some detail and concluded:

> I cannot categorically state who murdered Grover Floyd and Jesse Burkett. But there is more than enough evidence for me to seriously question the guilt of Pitts and Lee. This evidence, in fact, points to their innocence. I am sufficiently convinced that they are innocent to warrant the action I take today. I am persuaded that the ends of justice require me to seek freedom and a full pardon for these two men.[10]

At the same cabinet meeting, Attorney General Robert Shevin also spoke in favor of the pardon. Shevin had previously filed in court a "confession of error" when the case reached the Florida Supreme Court in 1971, which paved the way for a new trial—a temporary victory, as it turned out.

But this extraordinary court filing and Shevin's approval of the pardon were highly unpopular in North Florida, particularly in the Florida Panhandle. These actions doomed Shevin's later run for governor in 1978 to succeed Askew. He lost this race in the Democratic Party runoff primary to state senator Bob Graham who later served two terms as governor and three terms in the US Senate. Shevin never again ran for statewide public office, as his political career was effectively over. Askew and Shevin will always remain for me the heroes of this case, along with Miller and Holmes.

The next day, September 11, 1975, Governor Askew signed an executive order granting a full pardon to Pitts and Lee, subject to the approval of three members of the Florida Cabinet. Under Florida's constitution, the governor does not have the unilateral power to issue a pardon. Such a pardon requires a majority vote of the Florida Cabinet, which then consisted of six other members, plus the vote of the governor. On that same day, Attorney General Robert Shevin also signed the pardon.

In the tense few days that followed, two other cabinet members individually came to the governor's office and signed the pardon—State Treasurer Phil Ashler and Commissioner of Education Ralph Turlington. Those were enough signatures to make the pardon official.

I had flown to the state capital in Tallahassee immediately after I learned of Askew's initial announcement, and I was there when Turlington and Ashler signed the pardon. In the next few days, I talked to two other Florida Cabinet members: Gerald Lewis, the state comptroller, and Bruce Smathers, the secretary of state. Although their signatures were not legally necessary, we thought it would be a good idea if they, too, signed the pardon to show the cabinet's near-unanimous support for this action.

But unfortunately, I was unable to persuade them. Both men wanted another lie detector test of Pitts and Lee. We declined. The evidence of innocence was overwhelming, Pitts and Lee had already passed numerous lie detector tests, and the pardon was official without their signatures.

Both cabinet members, however, were sympathetic, particularly Lewis, who even offered to help Pitts and Lee get a job. They just felt they needed more time to study the case. Only Doyle Conner, the Florida commissioner of agriculture, was adamantly against the pardon. He was from North Florida near the Florida Panhandle, where the pardon was unpopular.[11]

Immediately after Turlington had signed the pardon, a small group of reporters sought me out for a brief press conference. I was asked about my reaction to the pardon and, feeling emotionally exhausted, I replied: "I have a bittersweet sense of great joy and yet underlying sorrow. Joy at this incredible victory after 12 hard, long years, and sorrow that it did not come sooner. Words cannot possibly express the debt of gratitude we owe to Governor Reubin Askew, without whose leadership and troubled conscience we would not be in this position today." The last question the press asked was how long I had worked on the case. There was a noticeable hush in the room and no more questions when I replied, "Ten years."

I had previously filed a petition for certiorari in the US Supreme Court on May 1, 1975, to review Pitts and Lee's Florida convictions. The pardon, however, set aside those convictions, rendering them void. Accordingly, the court had no alternative but to dismiss this petition, which it did eventually, as the underlying conviction had been erased by the pardon. Thus, I never got a chance to argue Pitts and Lee's case before the High Court, although I like to think we would have won the case there. Still, the pardon was infinitely better as it freed these men entirely of the charges against them. The best the court could have given them was a new trial.

* * *

The final vindication for Pitts and Lee came in April 1998 when the Florida legislature, with Governor Lawton Chiles's signature, awarded them $500,000 apiece for their twelve years of wrongful imprisonment. A small atonement, I think, for one of the worst injustices in American history. But at least it was some sort of apology. Also, Pitts was eventually given an honorable discharge from the army and his dishonorable discharge was rescinded.

After their release from prison, Pitts and Lee lived productive and exemplary lives. They both moved to the Miami area, where Pitts worked as a long-distance trucker. Lee was hired as a rehabilitation officer for the Miami-Dade County jail. After over thirty years of gainful employment, they both retired.

On October 17, 2018, at the age of 83, Wilbert Lee passed away in Miami. I was honored to speak at his memorial service. Freddie Pitts, who was nine years younger than Lee, died in Miami on September 2, 2020, at the age of 76. Sadly, there was no memorial service for Pitts; he passed in obscurity.

Curtis Adams, the real murderer in this case, died in prison on January 19, 1991, while serving a life sentence for a remarkably similar gas station robbery, kidnapping, and murder.[12] He committed that crime in Fort Lauderdale sixteen days after he had committed virtually the same type of crime in the Florida Panhandle and then fled the area to avoid arrest.

* * *

In the face of all this, basic questions arise. What happened in this case that led to this incredible injustice? How could Pitts and Lee be sent to death row for a crime that the evidence overwhelmingly shows was committed by another man who was well known to the police and who Pitts and Lee did not know? And why did it take nine years for these men to be released from prison after this evidence of innocence was revealed to the local authorities? This book tries to answer these questions.

The story of how it all happened is both gripping and at times astounding. It may even seem on occasion to be the product of a screenwriter's imagination. But I can assure the reader that the events recounted in this book actually happened.

During this time, the case led me into the most important experience of my professional career, one that changed my life forever and has haunted me to this day. I have never really gotten over it. I'm convinced that if Pitts and Lee had been white and the murdered gas station attendants had been Black instead of the other way around, this injustice would never have happened. Race made all the difference.

As Americans, we have much in our history to be proud of, much that is inspiring, much to celebrate. But there are also disgraceful incidents in our past that we as a nation must face. This case is one of those shameful episodes. There is no minimizing it; there is no way to justify or rationalize it. We have to confront and remember times like this if we are to make any progress as a nation in the painful struggle for racial reconciliation. James Baldwin put it best: "Not everything that is faced can be changed; but nothing will change until it is faced."[13]

Fortunately, this case is also a story of redemption, as the forces of justice in our system finally awakened and tried to rectify what had been done to Pitts and Lee. I am proud to have played a small role in this long fight.

As Freddie Pitts reflected in 1983 after his release from prison, "It would have been easy to come out [of prison] feeling all whites were racists and that the entire legal system was bad. But really, in the end, it was white people and the system that eventually saw justice was done."[14] A magnanimous insight, I think, for a man who went through twelve years of hell convicted for a crime another man committed.

This book lays out the entire case as it unfolded in Port St. Joe, Panama City, Wewahitchka, Winter Haven, Fort Lauderdale, Key West, Chattahoochee, Raiford, Miami, Clearwater, Marianna, and Tallahassee. It lasted over twelve years. Three gruesome murders were committed. And a host of people were caught up in a tangled web of events that followed.

Organizing all of this information into a coherent whole and recounting how this appalling miscarriage of justice occurred during the civil rights era of the 1960s is the central mission of this book.

2

Curtis Adams and the Port St. Joe/Fort Lauderdale Murders

On the night of July 31, 1963, Jesse Burkett and Grover Floyd, two white filling station attendants, were working at Skip's Mo Jo Service Station on Highway 98 in a hamlet called Highland View just across the bridge from the town of Port St. Joe, Florida. Both men were longtime local residents of the area.

Port St. Joe is located at the eastern end of the Florida Panhandle, on the Gulf of Mexico. The town back then had a total population of approximately 4,000.[1] The St. Joe Paper Company was the main business in the area. Located on the Gulf side of Highway 98 on the outskirts of Port St. Joe, it had a sprawling factory yard with smokestacks that spewed an acrid sulfuric odor that drifted over the town. Across the highway was the Black section of town, known as "The Quarters."

Jesse Burkett went to work that night in the early evening hours. The 54-year-old, the older of the two attendants, was a retired Air Force sergeant with heart trouble. He was tall and slim and chewed tobacco. Grover Floyd, aged 28, worked part-time that night and came to the station later in the evening. He sometimes worked for the state road department. He was stout, weighing about 240 pounds.

The gas station was old and nondescript, a bit run down. It was the only 24-hour filling station in the area. It had four gasoline pumps elevated on a concrete island and an outside telephone booth located under a Coca-Cola sign. Inside the wooden shack of an office was a men's bathroom, an old desk, a cash register that sat on top of the desk, and a loaded .38-caliber revolver in a slot in the desk under the cash register.[2] Outside the office was a women's bathroom with a sign painted in red that stated "White Ladies Only."

Deputy Sheriff Wayne White lived in the white section of Port St. Joe. He was the chief investigator for the Gulf County Sheriff's Office. The elected sheriff, Byrd Parker, was elderly and no longer took much of an active role in what little crime investigation was necessary in the county. White knew many of the people in town, including the two attendants at the Mo Jo station.

Across town in the Black section near the paper factory, Wilbert Lee and his wife Ella Mae lived in a two-room wooden shack with a back porch on an unpaved road. The house, which had no electricity and no telephone, was illuminated only by a Coleman lantern. Lee, aged 28, was bright but only partially literate. He had left school after the sixth grade and could barely read or write. He worked at an assortment of odd jobs in the area. His nickname was Slingshot.

Freddie Pitts was a 19-year-old private in the United States Army stationed on maneuvers outside Port St. Joe. He and his fellow soldiers were living in tents at the army camp. At times, Pitts got a pass from his army duties and went into town to do errands and visit friends. When he did so, he drove a 1958 Ford borrowed from a fellow soldier, Private Dupree McMath. Despite having only an eighth-grade education, Pitts was quite literate and articulate.

That night, Wilbert Lee had a party at his house with a number of Black guests, including Freddie Pitts. The two knew each other slightly. They were both affable and easygoing young men. Several other people joined the party that night, including three other Black soldiers from Pitts's unit. It was a fun party with soul food, drink, and song.

One of the guests who later joined the party was Willie Mae Lee, a 19-year-old Black resident of Port St. Joe who was no relation to Wilbert or Ella Mae Lee. She lived in a modest residence in the Black section of town with her sister, her brother-in-law, and her young daughter, whom her sister was raising. Willie Mae was not married and had a seventh-grade education.

Curtis Adams lived in an upstairs apartment in the white section of Port St. Joe with his girlfriend Mary Jean Akins and her two small children. Curtis and Mary Jean did not know Freddie Pitts or Wilbert Lee; they were complete strangers. But the lives of all these people would soon be enmeshed in a web of events that would unfold that night and change their lives forever. Curtis Adams would be the prime mover of these events and Mary Jean Akins the prime witness.

* * *

Adams was a quiet-spoken, wiry white man of medium build, in his early 30s, a longtime resident of Port St. Joe. When he could find work, Adams did a variety of odd jobs, including construction work and commercial fishing. Adams was on parole for the 1956 armed robbery of a filling station in Panama City, Florida, a crime for which he had received a ten-year prison sentence. He had just been released from prison the year before.

Mary Jean Akins, his girlfriend, was a thin, quiet-spoken white woman in her mid- to late 20s. She worked in town as a telephone operator for the St. Joe Telephone and Telegraph Company. She had two young children with her husband Lavern, who was serving a prison sentence at Florida State Prison for stealing farm livestock. She had a sad look about her and resembled a woman who, despite her youth, had seen her share of hard times. Her nickname was Billie. She was attracted to Adams because he was quiet and gentle and treated her well. "I felt for him," she would later tell Gene Miller. "Whenever somebody's real good to you, you have concern for him."[3]

Her relationship with Adams was in sharp contrast to life with her estranged husband Lavern, who drank heavily, had a violent temper, and beat her up regularly when he was drunk. She had filed for divorce from him but had never followed through. He would later drink himself to death after he was released from prison. Mary Jean was used to living around men who stole whenever they wanted and dreaded what would happen if they ever got caught. She was also pregnant by Adams.

Because they feared notoriety because of their cohabitation in the small town of Port St. Joe, Adams and Mary Jean decided to leave the area and live in Fort Lauderdale, where they would be more anonymous. Mary Jean resigned her position with St. Joe Telephone and Telegraph, and canceled their telephone and electric service. They packed up on July 31, 1963, and planned to leave town the next morning.[4] But they didn't have enough money to make the trip or to live on. Adams said he had an idea where he could get some cash and Mary Jean braced herself for what was to happen.

Adams left their apartment late that night, armed with a .25-caliber Beretta automatic pistol. He told Mary Jean that he intended to rob a small business in the area. He drove off in Mary Jean's 1960 two-door white Ford and went to the Mo Jo station, arriving there in the early morning hours of August 1, 1963.[5] When he pulled in, Grover Floyd and Jesse Burkett came out and waited on him. No one else was in the station. Adams asked the attendants to fill his car up with gas, which they did, and Adams walked into the station office. About that time another car pulled up.[6]

Freddie Pitts and Wilbert Lee were in this car along with Wilbert's wife, Ella Mae Lee; Ella Mae's sister Dorothy Martin; and Private Roland Jones. Pitts was driving a 1958 Ford that he had earlier borrowed from a fellow soldier. They had all come from the party at Wilbert Lee's house.[7]

Because Wilbert Lee had no telephone in his house, he had come to the Mo Jo station to use the pay phone there to make a long-distance call to a cousin concerning a death in the family and an upcoming funeral in Apalachicola, Florida. It was the only reason for their trip to the station. The others had just come along for the ride. Willie Mae Lee had arrived at the station earlier and soon joined the group.[8]

When Adams saw the carload of Black people pull in, he quickly hid in the men's bathroom inside the station to avoid being seen and latched the door from the inside. He soon heard an argument going on between Floyd and Burkett and the Black people but couldn't quite make out what it was about. Someone tried to get into the bathroom where he was but couldn't do so because he had locked the door.[9]

Unbeknown to Adams, the argument was over the use of the women's white-only bathroom. Dorothy Martin wanted to use the facilities and Floyd and Burkett wouldn't let her. Martin was upset and told them, "Where I come from everyone uses the same damn bathroom." She was from Pensacola and was visiting Wilbert Lee and his wife for a few days.[10]

When the argument died down, Adams opened the bathroom door slightly, but seeing another customer in the station, he immediately closed the door. About five minutes later, he cracked the door open again. This time he saw a truck loaded with two 55-gallon drums and retreated once again into the bathroom.[11]

It was a strange experience for Adams. He had not counted on such complications. He couldn't do what he planned with all those people around, and he couldn't leave the station and come back later because a customer might identify him as he left. So he nervously waited in the bathroom for everyone to leave.

Aubrey Branch, a 15-year-old white teenager, and his white teenage companion Billy Versiga were the occupants of the truck that Adams had seen. They were filling up the truck's gasoline drums in preparation for a fishing trip they were about to make. Both Branch and Versiga were aware of the argument that Dorothy Martin was having with the attendants. They also noticed Pitts's car.[12]

In the meantime, Wilbert Lee completed his long-distance call in the telephone booth beneath the Coca-Cola sign near the station, and Martin eventually had to relieve herself in the weeds near the station.[13] Their mission completed and the phone call made, Pitts and Lee drove off with their companions and soon learned of the argument over the white-only ladies bathroom. They had not overheard the argument at the station. After a short detour, they returned to the party at Lee's house.[14]

After the party was over, Wilbert and his wife Ella Mae went to bed and were home together the rest of the night. Dorothy Martin retired as well in a separate bed in the same bedroom.[15] Freddie Pitts and Willie Mae Lee eventually drove off together in his car for a lover's tryst and were together for the rest of the night.[16]

During the evening, Pitts's car broke down. At the time, they were in a Black section of the county a few miles from Port St. Joe in an area known as Kenny's Quarters. Willie Mae Lee knew Henry Hogue, an elderly local resident known as Mr. Red, who lived in Kenny's Quarters. She and Pitts walked to Hogue's house, woke him up, and asked for his help. Hogue gave them a push with his car.[17]

Hogue was quite certain that only Pitts and Willie Mae Lee were there that night and that no one was in the back seat of the car. The police would later claim that that wasn't so, that Wilbert Lee was hiding there. But Hogue was positive no one was in the back seat, that Lee wasn't there.[18] Indeed, he wasn't. He was home in bed with his wife.

Later that night the car broke down again; this time it was overheated. Pitts pulled into a Pure Oil gas station on Highway 98 and filled the radiator with water. About that time, Aubrey Branch and Billy Versiga drove by in their truck on the way to their fishing trip and recognized the car as the one they had seen at the Mo Jo station earlier in the evening.[19]

Pitts eventually took Willie Mae home and went back to his army camp just before dawn. They were amorous with each other that night but had different stories about whether they had had sex. Both had been drinking on and off during the evening.[20]

Meanwhile, back at the Mo Jo station, when everything finally settled down and all the customers had left, Adams tried to get out of the bathroom. But this time he couldn't. The attendants had locked the door from the outside so no one could get in. Adams rattled on the door until the attendants let him out.[21] The attendants then told Adams about the argument with the Black people and they all had a good laugh over the incident. Adams was their friend and neighbor; they called him by his nickname

Boo.[22] But Grover Floyd and Jesse Burkett could not possibly have known what Curtis Adams was about to do next.

*   *   *

In the early morning hours of August 1, while it was still dark, Adams returned to his apartment in Port St. Joe. Mary Jean Akins was waiting for him.[23] Adams had always said that he would never leave any witnesses in the robberies he committed, but that was empty talk. He had never killed anyone and Mary Jean had never taken him seriously. This time, however, it was for real. Adams told Mary Jean that he had robbed the local Mo Jo station as planned but had had to kill the two attendants. He had forced them at gunpoint to drive her car into a wooded area in the country, where he shot them both with a .38-caliber revolver he had stolen from beneath the desk in the station.

Mary Jean was stunned. Here is her account of what happened as reported by *Miami Herald* reporter Gene Miller. This is the substance of what she later testified at the 1972 trial of Pitts and Lee in Marianna, Florida.

> He [Adams] returned maybe about 2 or 3 AM. I don't know the exact time. I'd left the TV on and the station had gone off the air, and I was dozing on the couch. He came up the stairs—we lived upstairs—and he had mud on his shoes and he went straight to the bathroom and started cleaning his shoes.
>
> And he seemed to be rather shaken up and I asked him what was the matter, and he said he had to kill them. I asked him who and he said the two that were at the station.
>
> * * *
>
> He started scraping the clay, it looked dried, off his shoes and he tore up a pad of some kind, one of those little charge pads that they usually have in a station or a grocery store. He tore it up and flushed it down the commode. . . . And he went through the money to see if there was anything that might be identified. He had about a hundred dollars. I'm not sure how much it was.
>
> I thought to myself, Lord have mercy, this little bit for two people to have lost their lives.
>
> Later on he got the lights turned out so there wouldn't be lights burning in the house at that time in the morning for somebody to notice, you know. It rained, and he said it would wash away the tracks. I was frightened.

We were in bed and I thought to myself, well if he would do that to [these] people, what in the world would he do to me?[24]

Mary Jean knew that Adams stole from time to time and she had worried about what would happen if he ever got caught. But this was murder. Maybe she was all wrong about Adams. Maybe he wasn't the gentle and reserved man she had been drawn to, so unlike the drunken, violent husband she had left. Maybe Adams was hiding something beneath that quiet exterior, something sinister, something threatening. "Maybe" was not the right word. Mary Jean lay in bed as the terror of the night sank in.

The next morning, on August 1, 1963, around 8:00 a.m., Curtis Adams left Port St. Joe with Mary Jean and her two small children and headed for Fort Lauderdale. En route, they planned to stay the night in Winter Haven, where one of Mary Jean's sisters lived.[25] Winter Haven is about 350 miles southeast of Port St. Joe, not far from where Disney World is now located. Fort Lauderdale is about 150 miles farther south, along the east coast of Florida, just north of Miami. Adams drove Mary Jean's white Ford on the trip, the car he had used the previous night when he had gone to the Mo Jo station.

Before they left Port St. Joe, Mary Jean noticed something unusual. The door on the driver's side of her car was covered with black stains. She asked Adams what that was. Adams said it must have come from the chewing tobacco that Jesse Burkett had spit out the window while he was forced to drive her car into the country that night. Mary Jean got a washrag she had used on her baby's face and wiped the door clean of the tobacco stains.[26]

That evening when they arrived in Winter Haven, Curtis Adams retired for the night with Mary Jean at her sister's house. By then, the enormity of what he had done hit him. Adams had no moral qualms about committing robberies or even murder. But this was different. He had known Grover Floyd and Jesse Burkett personally and he liked them. They had begged for their lives. They had promised that they would never identify him. They would make up a story. But Curtis had killed them anyway. He couldn't leave any witnesses.[27]

For hours, Adams shook from head to toe as he lay in bed, causing even the bed to shake. Mary Jean reported:

It was that night that Curtis started getting the shakes. He lay there and shook so hard the bed shook. It wasn't just nervous; his whole body was shaking. I think it lasted possibly a good hour or two. And he said it wasn't the fact that he had killed somebody, it was the fact that he had known the men so well. That was the first time I realized that he knew them so well.[28]

Adams then told Mary Jean in detail about the events of the previous night.

He said whenever he got there, there was a car that drove up right behind him. He'd got out and went into the restroom before anyone saw him. It was some colored people and I don't know whether they bought gas or what, but they had tried to use the restroom and the two white men in the station told them it was out of order. They made some smart remark about something and they messed around a little bit and they finally left.

Curtis said that the two men laughed about it afterwards because they didn't want the colored people using the restroom. And then he went in the station and he said he wanted what money they had. And the old man kept talking to him, trying to talk him out [of it]. He [Adams] said whenever he got the money, he got a gun from the station there and flashlight. I don't remember whether he put the two men in the front seat and him in the back. But anyway, he told them where to go—out on the road to Wewahitchka.

They turned back in there somewhere and he took them back there. And he said the old man kept begging him don't kill him because he wouldn't tell a soul, that he'd even make up a story or do anything just to keep him from killing them. The old man, from what I understand, he had a heart attack, and he begged for his life, but he killed both of them.[29]

Adams didn't sleep that night and for several nights thereafter. For the first month, he thought about the murders all the time. And he started drinking more and more to block it all from his memory, to the point where he was drinking a fifth of whiskey every day.[30]

The next morning, Mary Jean panicked. She got in her car with her two children and drove to another sister's home in Perry, Florida, over 200 miles to the north, leaving Adams behind. She was desperate to escape from him.[31]

But when she got there, she realized her sister in Winter Haven would have no idea what had happened to her. So she telephoned her sister. Unfortunately, Adams was still there. He got on the telephone and told her to stay where she was until he caught up with her or he would kill her sister and her husband in Winter Haven. He still had his Beretta automatic pistol and she knew he was capable of murder.[32]

Terrified that this might happen if she continued to run, Mary Jean stayed in Perry until Adams arrived along with her sister and her husband from Winter Haven. They all then returned to Winter Haven.[33] Adams, Mary Jean and her two children then continued on their trip to the Fort Lauderdale area and stayed in a trailer park in Dania for a few weeks.

*　　*　　*

From that day forward, Mary Jean lived in constant fear of Adams. As she explained:

> I wanted him to get caught, but I didn't want to be the one who said anything. I was very much afraid of him. He'd always said that if I ever told anybody, if I ever got smart and tried to go to the police or anything, he would say that when he done it, I was with him—and he'd kill me when he got loose.[34]

On August 16, 1963—sixteen days after he had committed the robbery, kidnap, and murder of Grover Floyd and Jesse Burkett—Adams once again left the residence where he and Mary Jean lived late at night. He was armed with his Beretta automatic pistol. He said he needed to commit another robbery to get more money to live on and drove off in Mary Jean's car.

Later that night, Adams returned to their trailer and told Mary Jean that he had held up a service station in the area and had had to kill the attendant. He had forced the attendant at gunpoint to drive the car into a wooded area in the country where Adams shot the attendant, just like he had done sixteen days earlier when he robbed and murdered Floyd and Burkett.

As Mary Jean explained: "He came back after midnight and he told me that he had killed this man and I didn't know until the next day that it was this Shamrock station. He said he couldn't afford to leave any witnesses and it was some time before they found the body."[35]

This time, however, Adams didn't shake that night from head to toe like he did after killing Floyd and Burkett. Instead, he calmly went to bed. Adams was used to murder by then, and anyway, the attendant Floyd McFarland was a total stranger and meant nothing to Adams. Over a week later, Floyd McFarland's body was discovered hidden in the woods.

Reeling from all these horrifying murders, Mary Jean finally found an excuse to separate from Adams without arousing his suspicions. She was by now many months pregnant by Adams and needed to prepare herself for giving birth. He understood this. So shortly after the McFarland murder, they vacated their trailer in Dania and went back to North Florida to make arrangements for Mary Jean's childbirth.

On their way out of town, they passed by the place in the country where Adams had shot and killed McFarland. Mary Jean recalled: "A couple or three days later that weekend we started back to my sister's house in Winter Haven and from the car on the highway he pointed to where the body was. But I didn't see it. That was maybe a week before anyone found it."[36] Adams eventually left Mary Jean in the care of another sister in Carrabelle, Florida, near Port St. Joe. He went on to Key West. They never lived together again.

In the meantime, the community in Port St. Joe was rocked with the police investigation of the Floyd-Burkett murders. Pitts and Lee were swept into that investigation and ultimately would pay the price for the murders Curtis Adams had committed.

3

The Port St. Joe Interrogations

On August 1, 1963, in the early morning hours before daylight, a passing truck driver pulled into the all-night Mo Jo station on Highway 98, just outside Port St. Joe, Florida. He got out and looked around. The station was open, all the lights were on, but no one was there. He telephoned the Gulf County Sheriff's Office and told them about this odd sight.[1]

Gulf County Deputy Sheriff Jimmy Barfield was sent to investigate. He arrived at the station around 4:30–5:00 a.m. After investigating the place for a short time, Barfield called his office and asked that the chief investigator, Deputy Sheriff Wayne White, be sent to the station.[2]

Soon thereafter, White arrived along with Richard Skipper, the station's owner, who had also been called. Together they looked through the station. The cash register drawer was empty, and according to Skipper about $100 in cash was missing. Also gone was the station's .38-caliber revolver.[3]

It was all quite strange. White was puzzled. What had happened to the attendants? He talked it over with Skipper. Not to worry, they thought. Maybe the attendants had just taken the missing cash and gone off on a drunken spree. They both knew these men well. But when the men could not be found in the area, White began to suspect that the station had been robbed and the attendants kidnapped—maybe even murdered. Soon he became convinced of this, even before the bodies of Floyd and Burkett were discovered.

For the next four days, August 1 to August 4, White worked around the clock without any sleep, investigating this case. Murder was a virtually unknown crime in Gulf County and he could not afford to leave it unsolved. It was his first criminal homicide case—the most important case that he had ever been involved in. He was extremely anxious to solve it.[4]

Moreover, White needed help. Gulf County had few full-time deputies. So White notified the Florida Sheriffs Bureau in Tallahassee to send him some backup assistance, which included a lie detector examiner. Later, a forensic evidence team from the bureau would conduct an investigation. White also asked the adjoining and much larger Bay County Sheriff's Office in Panama City for help. Gulf and Bay Counties were in the same judicial circuit, and the police in both counties would sometimes help one another on cases.

*   *   *

In short order, White sought out and interviewed Aubrey Branch and Billy Versiga, the two white teenagers who were in the station that night. White learned from them that they had seen a carload of Black people while there and had witnessed an argument over the use of the station's white-only women's bathroom. They identified several of the Black people in attendance. They also identified Freddie Pitts's car.[5]

Given the tense racial atmosphere that existed in the South at that time, a white deputy sheriff like Wayne White might well have been alarmed. Racial segregation was under attack throughout the South during this time, there was widespread southern resistance to this movement, and many white southerners feared a possible violent reaction from Black people. Indeed, 1963 was a particularly racially turbulent year that included the massive March on Washington on August 28 and the Ku Klux Klan bombing of the 16th Street Baptist Church in Birmingham, Alabama, on September 15.

Prior to learning of the racial incident at the Mo Jo station, however, Wayne White had an entirely different take on this case. For a short time, he, in fact, considered Curtis Adams to be the prime suspect in this robbery, kidnap, and murder, and for good reason. Adams had a record for armed robbery and was the only person living in Gulf County with such a record. White knew Adams quite well and considered him entirely capable of robbing and murdering Floyd and Burkett. White would disclose all this years later in a conversation he had with a fellow law enforcement officer from Fort Lauderdale.[6]

But whatever initial suspicions White may have had of Curtis Adams in August 1963 were banished once he learned of the racially charged argument at the Mo Jo station. He interpreted this argument as a motive for murder and decided to pursue it.

White never sought out or questioned Curtis Adams, who was still in town preparing to leave the area for Fort Lauderdale. Instead, White decided to round up all the Black people who were in the Mo Jo station that night, jail them, question them, and give them lie detector tests. Included in this dragnet were the alibi witnesses for Pitts and Lee and other Black people he thought might be connected with the case.

This decision turned out to be a fateful one from which there would be no turning back—not then, not ever. The same contorted reasoning would soon be adopted by the entire white power structure in the area, including other police officials and the local prosecutor.

To White and the other authorities, this was a Black-on-white killing. Nothing, absolutely nothing could ever dissuade them from that conclusion. The longer the investigation continued, the more convinced White and others became that they were right. Later revelations about the case didn't move them. Curtis Adams was not involved; he was white. It had to be one of the Black people who were in the Mo Jo station that night—and eventually that became Pitts and Lee.

*   *   *

White encountered no difficulty locating these people. They were all living in town and cooperated fully with the police. None of them made any effort to escape the area, as Curtis Adams had done. They were always on hand whenever White wanted to see them. Some of these people even came to the police station voluntarily once they received word that White wanted to question them.

In this cooperative but tense fashion, the police arrested all the Black people who were at the Mo Jo station that night: Freddie Pitts, Wilbert Lee, Ella Mae Lee, Dorothy Martin, Willie Mae Lee, and Roland Jones. Ella Mae Lee, Wilbert's wife, could account for Wilbert's whereabouts for most of the evening in question. Dorothy Martin, as Ella Mae's sister, could give similar testimony. Willie Mae Lee and Pitts were each other's alibi for that night. And Jones was an army private stationed with Pitts outside Port St. Joe. To the police, all were suspects and all were held in jail for weeks.

It never occurred to White that it was only Dorothy Martin who had had the argument with the Mo Jo station attendants. Everyone else was at most merely a witness to the incident—including the white people who were also in the station that night but were never treated as suspects. Indeed, Wilbert Lee was busy making his phone call when all this happened.

But White made no such distinctions. He lumped all the Black people in the station that night as "involved" in the incident. All those arrests were blatantly illegal, as there was not a shred of evidence (much less probable cause) to believe that any of these people had robbed or murdered the two filling station attendants. Moreover, White never obtained a court order that would have allowed him to hold any of these people in custody as a material witness. They were held all without a charge for nearly a month and were not released until Pitts and Lee were sentenced to death. Ironically, as it turned out, Dorothy Martin, the only Black person who had argued with the attendants, was never charged with their murders.

The police also detained and questioned other Black people, including Lambson Smith, Henry Hogue, Regina Thomas, and Thomasina Stallworth. Even though none of these people had gone to the Mo Jo station that night, White suspected that they had some knowledge of the case. Various other Black residents were also picked up and briefly questioned.

Lambson Smith was in the army and had attended Wilbert Lee's party that night. For a while, he was even charged with the murders, although he was later released. Henry Hogue had given Pitts a push when Pitts's car stalled that night. Regina Thomas was a local resident who had been at Lee's party. Thomasina Stallworth was a local resident who had occasionally dated Pitts. She was held in jail for nearly three weeks without being charged with a crime. The police continually questioned her at night, accused her of lying when she denied any knowledge of any robbery or murder, and threatened to throw her to "the boys" or put her in a death cell when she maintained her innocence.[7] When she was finally released, she got on a bus for Jacksonville, vowing never to return to Port St. Joe.[8]

All of this is not surprising, as Black people in the South had been treated as second-class citizens with little or no rights for nearly a century. Many white law enforcement agencies regularly conducted illegal dragnet arrests and brutal police interrogations of poor Black people, particularly in high-profile cases. A prime example is the infamous Quincy Five case in Florida, which unfolded over the period 1970–1973. This case involved the murder of a white Leon County deputy sheriff during a grocery store robbery in the Panhandle town of Quincy. In a frenzy to solve the crime and avenge the death of a fellow deputy sheriff, white officers of the Leon County Sheriff's Office engaged in a flurry of arrests, followed by prolonged, threat-filled, extremely violent police interrogations of five young Black men, later known the Quincy Five.

This led to a tangled tale of false confessions, shaky eyewitness identifications, wrongful convictions, a death sentence, an appellate court reversal, a jury acquittal, ruined lives, and finally dropped charges. This ultimate exoneration happened after three unrelated men from Jacksonville, Florida were later indicted and convicted of the robbery/murder at the Quincy grocery store. This conviction was based on fingerprint evidence from the crime scene that showed that these three men had committed the crime, not the Quincy Five defendants.[9] The parallels with the Pitts-Lee case are striking.

*   *   *

On the morning of August 1, 1963, Freddie Pitts and fellow soldier Lambson Smith got a pass from their army duties and went by car into Port St. Joe to wash their clothes at a laundromat.[10] On the way, Pitts stopped by the Mo Jo station, where he frequently did business, to get some gas for his car. While there, he saw and talked to the station owner, Richard Skipper. Pitts had met Skipper the day before when Skipper had helped Pitts fix a broken water hose in his car and had cashed Pitts's army check as payment. It had been a friendly encounter; Skipper testified at the 1972 trial in Marianna that Pitts was "polite" throughout this meeting.[11]

From Skipper, Pitts learned for the first time that the station had been robbed and that the attendants were missing.[12] Skipper seemed baffled about what had happened. He showed Pitts the cash register and said that money was missing from the till. Pitts expressed concern, but the matter was left at that. Pitts then got some gas at the station and left to do his laundry.[13]

Later in the day, Pitts went for relaxation to a local hangout for Black youths. While there, Deputy Sheriff Jimmy Barfield arrived and asked Pitts if he had been at the Mo Jo station the night before. Pitts said he had and explained about cashing his check with Skipper earlier in the day, then returning later so Wilbert Lee could make his telephone call. Barfield then asked Pitts to follow him to the Mo Jo station, which Pitts did.[14]

Barfield got there first and was talking to Skipper when Pitts arrived. Barfield asked Pitts if there had been an argument involving the Black people who were there about the use of a white-only women's bathroom. Pitts said: "I heard about it after we left." Barfield pointedly replied, "Well, I asked you that to see what you were going to say."[15] The police already had that information. Barfield had asked the question to see if Pitts would lie about the incident. But Pitts told the truth.

Later that afternoon, Pitts learned that Wayne White wanted to talk to everyone who had been at the station that night. Pitts was told to pick up those people and bring them to the police station in Port St. Joe.[16] Pitts drove off in his car, picked up Wilbert Lee at his house, and looked for and picked up Willie Mae Lee. Pitts then went to the police station with Wilbert and Willie Mae.[17] No one was there. They waited a while, but when no one showed up, they went back to the Mo Jo station looking for White. White wasn't there either, but Skipper was. Lee talked to Skipper, explaining how he had been at the station that night to make a telephone call.[18] After a while, Skipper told them to go back to the police station, which they did. Once again no one showed up, so eventually everyone went home and Pitts returned to his army camp for the night.[19]

Around 11:00 p.m., while at his home, Lee received word from his cousin that Wayne White had been to the house earlier looking for him. So Lee went into town, located White, and told him that he had gone to the Mo Jo station the previous night to make a telephone call concerning an upcoming funeral. He also told White that he would be leaving town the next morning for nearby Apalachicola to attend this funeral but said he would be back in the afternoon if White needed to see him again. Lee then went home for the night.[20] Again, Wilbert Lee was acting as a good citizen trying to be helpful to the police.

I've always thought it rather odd for so-called murderers to be looking for the police so that they could be questioned for the murders that they supposedly committed or witnessed. To the contrary, this conduct tends to show that Pitts and Lee were entirely innocent.

But all of that soon changed. Early the next morning, August 2, 1963, Wayne White went to Lee's home and told Lee to come with him. So Lee got dressed and went with White to the police station.[21] Upon their arrival, White—seemingly out of the blue—accused Lee of lying, and said a lie detector man from Tallahassee would soon be there to give him a polygraph test. According to Lee, White said: "Well, you're a damn liar. You killed two white men. I'm going to lock your ass up till the lie detector man comes over here." Lee, utterly bewildered and frightened, was then placed in a holding cell. He knew full well what it meant for a Black man to be accused of murdering a white man in the South.[22]

Later that afternoon, Freddie Pitts got weekend leave from his army duties and went into town to visit Thomasina Stallworth at her house. They had been dating off and on and planned to go to New Orleans for the weekend.[23] Soon thereafter, Wayne White finally contacted Pitts, took him to the police station, and questioned him briefly. Pitts explained that he had been at the Mo Jo station that night, had learned later about Dorothy Martin's argument with the attendants, but had no knowledge about the attendants' disappearance. White seemed satisfied and released him.[24]

Around 5:00 p.m. that day, as Pitts was returning to his army camp, Barfield pulled him over and told him that a lie detector man wanted to run some tests on him at the Port St. Joe police station—and on one of his fellow soldiers, Roland Jones.[25] Pitts drove to the army camp to get Jones. Barfield followed and informed Pitts's superiors about what was happening. Pitts then drove himself and Jones to the police station in Port St. Joe. When they arrived, the police thoroughly searched Pitts's car, which was illegal as they had no probable cause to believe that the car contained contraband or any evidence of a crime. The police found nothing incriminating.[26]

Tellingly, none of the white people who were in the Mo Jo station the night of the murders were ever arrested, interrogated at the police station, or given lie detector tests.

*　*　*

The stage was then set for the police to run polygraph tests on all the Black people who White had rounded up that day. Under settled law throughout the country, the results of polygraph or lie detector tests have long been inadmissible in court. One of the major reasons for this exclusion is that the polygraph's value largely depends on the ability of the polygraph examiner to ask the right questions, to correctly evaluate the results obtained, and to properly size up their subjects. In other words, polygraph examinations are highly subjective. A good polygraph examiner can often get reliable results, while a poor one can get false results. Nonetheless, the police sometimes use the polygraph as a technique for questioning crime suspects.

Waiting at the Port St. Joe police station was Joe Townsend, a polygraph examiner from the Florida Sheriffs Bureau. He was there in response to White's request for investigative help. Townsend was a recent hire of the bureau and soon became a central part of the police interrogation team in this case. He would run numerous polygraph tests on suspects followed by long interrogation sessions with the intention of getting a confession out of one or more of the suspects instead of serving as an expert adviser to the police. His methods were controversial.

Three months earlier, at the age of 46, Townsend had retired from the United States Air Force as a polygraph examiner. He did so in the wake of a scandal. He had extracted a false confession from Gerald Anderson, an airman who was accused and later convicted of murder. Townsend had run polygraph tests on Anderson, accused him of lying, and obtained a confession. Anderson was eventually cleared, released from prison, and given an honorable discharge.[27]

Later, in 1970 Townsend became involved in two other similar cases. In the Quincy Five murder case, he extracted false confessions from two of the five defendants after running prolonged lie detector tests on them and accusing them of lying. All of the Quincy Five defendants were eventually cleared and released. That same year in Auburndale, Florida, Townsend also got a questionable confession of rape out of Jesse O. Roberts, a Black 15-year-old youth with an IQ of 50. The state dropped the rape charge after the jury at trial hung 11 to 1 for acquittal. Roberts had an ironclad alibi. Six teachers at a school for developmentally challenged children testified that Roberts was in class at the time of the crime.[28]

At the station house, White immediately briefed Townsend on the case. Central to this briefing was the racially charged argument in the Mo Jo station. In his report, Townsend stated that during Pitts and Lee's stop with their group at the Mo Jo station earlier in the evening of July 31, 1963, "two of the females (in the group) engaged in a violent argument with Mr. Burkett over the use of the ladies restroom."[29]

Townsend then proceeded to run a series of polygraph tests on all of the assembled Black suspects. The tests started at 12:45 p.m. on August 2, 1963, and lasted an astounding fifteen and a quarter straight hours—until 4:00 a.m. August 3, 1963, the next morning. White lined up the suspects and Townsend ran multiple tests.[30] This ordeal—unprofessional by any standards—took place in a cramped room on the second floor of the police station. It was an exhausting experience for everyone.

Wilbert Lee was the first to be examined. Next came Roland Jones, Freddie Pitts, Lambson Smith, Ella Mae Lee, and Willie Mae Lee. Some were tested multiple times, and all were interrogated at length. Townsend's major inquiry centered on the whereabouts of the missing gas station attendants and what had happened to them. The bodies of Floyd and Burkett had not yet been discovered. White had correctly surmised that they might have been killed.

Townsend asked: "Do you know where Mr. Burkett is now? Do you know what happened to Mr. Burkett? Did you rob Mr. Burkett last Wednesday night? Regarding Mr. Burkett's disappearance, are you deliberately holding back any information about that?"[31]

All of the Black people who were tested told the truth. They denied any knowledge of what had happened to the two station attendants. But Townsend cleared only Roland Jones and Lambson Smith; he accused everyone else of lying. Even though Lambson Smith was cleared, he was not released. He was questioned further, held for the murders, cleared again, and eventually released as the police flailed about in search of someone to charge.

According to Townsend's written report, the examination of Wilbert Lee began around 12:30 p.m. and lasted two hours.[32] After three or four polygraph tests, Townsend concluded that Lee had lied, confronted Lee with this conclusion, and accused him of the murders. Here is Lee's account of what happened:

> So that afternoon a man comes with a polygraph test and during the time he is giving it to me, he told me I'm lyin'. He says "You done it! You done it! You done it!"
> When I had done nothing.[33]
> He told me that when the machine is running longways like this, say I was telling a big lie. When they run short like that, I was telling a little lie.
> I told him I never went to school for that, sir, I didn't know anything about that, but I was innocent. Which I was telling the truth. I was innocent.[34]

White then arrested Lee for further investigation and placed him in a holding cell. All of Lee's prior cooperation with White meant nothing. He was dirt poor. He had no lawyer. He was alone and at the mercy of the police.

The examination of Freddie Pitts began at 4:40 p.m. and ended at 7:30 p.m. Townsend tested him over and over.[35] This was an unusual polygraph practice; one or two such tests were generally the norm.

Here is the testimony Pitts gave at the September 1968 hearing in Port St. Joe about what happened during those examinations:

> I agreed to take the test, because I wanted to clear this up, because I didn't have anything to do with it, and I was under the impression that this would clear me. . . .
> Mr. Townsend showed me a slip of paper, which I read which was saying that this was voluntary and that no one forced me to take the test and it was my own will to take the test. I signed the paper.[36]

Townsend then ran a prolonged series of lie detector tests. During these tests, Pitts repeatedly said he had no knowledge of a robbery or murder of the two gas station attendants and did not know where they were at that time. Townsend, however, would have none of this and concluded that Pitts was lying.[37]

Pitts's account continues:

> After the first test he [Townsend] didn't say too much. He said, "I'm
> going to run another test," and after he ran another test he said "You
> are not leveling with me. You are not telling all you know."
> And then he divides [*sic*] another level questions that he thought
> of to ask me and then he just kept on like this. And finally he told me.
> "Well, you are not telling me the truth, you know something about
> this, and you have knowledge of this matter." . . . I told him I did not
> know anything about it. . . .
> After a time—I don't know just how long—he went to the door and
> he called Chief Deputy White. . . . He told him I had knowledge of
> this crime, that I knew something and that I wasn't telling the truth.
> . . .
> Wayne White, the chief deputy, took a seat there and he sit there
> and listened while Mr. Townsend ran about three, maybe four more
> tests on me. . . . Then afterwards, Mr. Townsend said I was lying, that
> I knew about the crime.[38]

* * *

Upon hearing Townsend's pronouncement, White acted immediately. He
handcuffed Pitts, took him outside the station, and placed him in the back
seat of his patrol car. Seated next to Pitts was Deputy Sheriff George Kittrell
of the adjoining Bay County Sheriff's Office from Panama City. Kittrell was
stocky, pink-faced, hard-eyed, and slow of speech. He was also a friend of
the missing Jesse Burkett and had volunteered to help find him.

White accused Pitts of the murders, demanded that Pitts lead them to
the bodies of Floyd and Burkett that night, and drove his patrol car into the
countryside. Kittrell did most of the questioning. Pitts protested that he had
no idea where the attendants were. It was a brutal, all-night ride that lasted
until dawn—approximately ten to eleven hours. Like Lee, Pitts knew full
well what it meant for a Black man to be accused of murdering a white man
in the South. His only hope was that the army would somehow rescue him
from this nightmare.

Here is Freddie Pitts's sworn testimony at the 1972 trial in Marianna,
Florida:

> They took me out looking for the bodies of the two men that were
> missing from the station and they began questioning me about the

location of the bodies. I told them "I don't know anything about it, I didn't have anything to do with it. I don't know where the bodies are." And Deputy Kittrell was sitting to my left in the rear seat, began to beat me with a slapjack.

Q. Would you describe what it is?

A. It's a jack, it's a blackjack actually. It's about this long and it fits right in the hand (indicating). It's curved to fit in the hand and it has something, it flares out at the other end and has a, looks like a ball of some kind inside it.

Q. Was it covered with leather?

A. Yes, sir.

Q. Do you know how many times he beat you?

A. No, sir. I don't.

Q. What happened during the beatings?

A. Well after he began to beat on me, I tried to cover it up and I did something like this to duck the licks (indicating) and he began to beat me in the back of the head and I just lost track of how many times he hit me or how many times I lost consciousness and the whole night after that was just a blur and confusion and I just can't recall the exact way things happened, just how things went during that time.

Q. Do you have any memory of whether or not they stopped at the Skipper Station?

A. Well, I woke up or I came to or regained consciousness or however you want to say it and on one occasion we were at Skipper's Mo Jo Station. . . . Mr. Skipper asked me, "N——r, what did you do with those two men?" And I said "I didn't do anything with them," or something to that effect, and Mr. Skipper, Mr. Kittrell said "Well, damn it, you're going to tell us before the night is out."

Q. Anything happen after that, what was he doing when he said that?

A. He was fixing to strike me again and I don't remember what happened after that.

Q. Do you recall, do you know how long this went on?

A. No, sir, I don't have any idea.[39]

At the 1972 trial of Pitts and Lee, Wayne White testified that they drove by the Mo Jo station during this all-night ride and saw Richard Skipper. Skipper asked if Pitts had told them anything about the killings. When

White indicated no, Skipper said "let him get his damned gun and he'd tell him." But before Skipper could do anything, they drove off.[40]

This brutal ride, full of violence and threats, continued as White drove through the Gulf County countryside until daybreak. Pitts was continually hounded to lead them to the bodies and constantly struck on the head with the blackjack Kittrell wielded.

But when no bodies were ever found, when this ride proved entirely futile, White finally gave up and returned to the Port St. Joe police station. As he later testified, the search was abandoned because "I didn't think Pitts was familiar with where we were going."[41]

George Kittrell never denied this beating under oath at any time in court during this case. He was never even called by the state as a witness in any of the many postconviction and new trial proceedings in the case. He was present at the some of these hearings, but he always sat alone in the hallway outside the courtroom apart from everyone else. No one apparently wanted much to do with him.

After this long ride, Kittrell was later seen at the Bay County Jail in Panama City with a cast on his right hand. Wayne White claimed he had accidentally slammed his patrol door on Kittrell's hand.[42] But one of Kittrell's fellow officers had a different version of what had caused this injury. D. L. Barron, the chief of detectives at the Panama City Police Department, joked that Kittrell "had run in with some hard-headed n——s in town." He made this statement at the Bay County Jail in the presence of Kittrell and Sergeant Bruce Potts, an army CID (Criminal Investigation Division) investigator who was there trying to see Pitts.[43]

As for Wayne White, he would never admit that anyone had ever laid a hand on Pitts. Although he was not called by the state at the 1972 trial to deny Pitts's account of this horrific ride, he observed the police code of silence. In deposition, White categorically claimed that he never saw anyone strike Pitts or Lee at any time during the investigation.[44]

But when Pitts was returned to the police station in Port St. Joe, he was semi-conscious. His head was throbbing from the many blackjack blows he had received, and his swollen physical condition was observed, as will be revealed later, by many people over the ensuing week, including two army CID investigators.

Indeed, throughout the month of August 1963, Pitts was in a continual state of fear about what would happen next. He never fully recovered from his injuries during this period or from the memory of them. He was a Black man charged with murdering two white men in the South during the fever pitch of the civil rights movement in the country. He was totally isolated with no money and no lawyer. He desperately hoped that the army would hear of his plight and rescue him from this terrible ordeal. But that was a forlorn hope. Pitts was now in the hands of the civilian authorities over which the army had no jurisdiction.

4

The Panama City Interrogations

After returning to Port St. Joe, White decided to move all the Black people he had in custody to the nearby Bay County Jail in Panama City. That jail was much larger and more secure, and there, White would have the assistance of the Bay County Sheriff's Office and the Panama City Police Department to help him investigate the case. Both agencies had plenty of experience investigating murder cases. This was White's first criminal homicide case, and he was more than happy to hand over the main responsibility for investigating the case to more experienced hands.

But more important, as White testified at the 1972 trial in Marianna, he was afraid that Pitts and Lee might be lynched from the small and less secure Port St. Joe jail if he didn't make the move. "Tensions in the Gulf County community were running pretty high," he later told army CID investigator Sergeant Donald Hoag.[1] White was particularly worried, he said, that "the family of the victims" might do the lynching. He was also aware of a racial problem in town at the time of the incident.[2]

Lynching has a long and infamous history in the South, and in Florida in particular. Florida had the second highest rate of lynching per capita of all the southern states (i.e., the former Confederate states plus Kentucky) for the period 1880 to 1940. Only Mississippi had a higher rate.[3] White could not be too careful.

So on August 3, 1963, Pitts and Lee were transported in White's patrol car to the Bay County Jail. Robert Sidwell, a news reporter, a friend of Wayne White, and an honorary deputy sheriff, volunteered to do the driving. He was the owner of a local radio station.[4] Before they left, according to Pitts, White got in the back seat of the patrol car where Pitts was being held. White crossed his arms in front of him with a gun openly displayed in his right hand and said to Pitts, "When Lee get into this car, when Slingshot get into this car, don't open your goddamn mouth."[5]

Immediately thereafter, Lee was removed from the jail and placed in the back seat of the patrol car with Pitts. According to Lee, one of the police officers told him, "We have to get [you] away from here because the mob crowd come, so the mob was coming—and he get us to Panama City and put us in that jail."[6] Robert Sidwell later stated, "It was a pretty well known fact that it [the move] was for their own safety. There was some apprehension in the community about their safety."[7]

*   *   *

Meanwhile, in the early morning hours of August 3, 1963, the bodies of Floyd and Burkett were discovered in a wooded area of the county where Curtis Adams had killed them. A local resident, Ludie Gaston, was fishing in a canal with her sister when they saw one of the bodies lying flat on the ground, partially hidden in a nearby clearing amid some trees and underbrush. At first Gaston thought the man might be sleeping off a drunk, but when the two women looked closer, they saw large flies buzzing around the body. This man was obviously dead.[8]

Gaston and her sister hurried to a fire tower about three miles away and told the watchman on duty what they had seen. The watchman then called the Gulf County Sheriff's Office, and Sheriff Byrd Parker and Deputy Sheriff James Graves arrived around 8:00 a.m.[9] Wayne White arrived on the scene later.[10]

The dead bodies had been lying in the woods for over two days. Each body had a bullet hole in the head but no other injuries. The corpses were badly decomposed and the smell was overwhelming. The news spread quickly, and soon a number of spectators in pickup trucks showed up at the scene. Maggots swarmed all over the dead flesh. Some spectators threw up.[11]

According to Graves's testimony at the 1972 trial in Marianna, the two bodies were discovered stretched out full length on the ground in a V arrangement, which Graves visually demonstrated at trial, with the two heads pointing toward each other "maybe about three feet apart."[12]

At the time, the *Star*, the Port St. Joe weekly newspaper, ran a story on the murders that confirms this testimony:

According to investigators, the two men [Floyd and Burkett] had been shot in the head at such an angle as to indicate that they had been forced to kneel or lie down before they were shot. Each was shot one time in the head.

Sheriff Parker said the two men had no bruises or injuries other than the gunshot wounds.[13]

No police photographs were taken of the bodies as they were found in the woods. A news photograph, however, appeared in the *Star* of Wayne White pointing to some weeds in the woods where the bodies had been found.[14] An ambulance was ordered, and the bodies were taken to the W. P. Comforter Funeral Home in Port St. Joe.

Dr. C. W. Ketchum, a pathologist at Tallahassee Memorial Hospital, was immediately summoned, and that day conducted a limited autopsy on the two bodies at the request of State Attorney J. Frank Adams. Ketchum conducted this autopsy in a shed behind the funeral home. He confined his examination to the removal of the bullets from each victim's head, as Adams had requested. Ketchum was surprised at this request, as he was accustomed to conducting full autopsies of the entire body in criminal homicide cases. But he followed Adams's instructions and confined his autopsy to the victim's heads.[15]

On August 4, 1963, a day later, Ketchum filed two autopsy reports stating that each man had died as a result of a single bullet wound to the back and side of the head that fatally penetrated the brain, "fired from a .38 caliber gun." This was the same type of gun—a .38-caliber revolver—that Curtis Adams had stolen from the Mo Jo station to commit the killings.

According to Ketchum's reports, the fatal bullet had entered Floyd's head to the left of the midline toward the rear portion of the skull and had exited near the right ear. The fatal bullet had entered Burkett's head in the right temporal area above the right ear and had no exit wound. Ketchum had removed bullet fragments on the left side of Burkett's head and turned them over to the police.[16]

As will be revealed later, this forensic evidence and these physical observations fully supported Curtis Adams's confessions and contradicted both Pitts and Lee's false and involuntary confessions and Willie Mae Lee's police statements and trial testimony.

*   *   *

All of the Black prisoners who "failed" to pass Townsend's polygraph tests in the Port St. Joe jail were transported to the Bay County Jail in Panama City for further questioning. So was Lambson Smith, even though Townsend had cleared him. The stage was set for a series of relay police interrogation sessions and lie detector tests that lasted for nearly a week, from August 3 to August 8, 1963. During this time, the police flailed around in their efforts to wrap up the case as fast as they could. They were under enormous pressure to do so. Murder was a virtually unknown crime in Gulf County and people expected the police to bring the criminals to justice without delay.

Moreover, the civil rights movement was heating up in the Florida Panhandle and the police could not afford to let this case drag on. In nearby Pensacola, a political fight was raging between the local NAACP and the city council over whether area theaters, drive-ins, golf courses, bowling alleys, public pools, medical facilities, and beaches should be integrated immediately.[17] The Floyd/Burkett killings in Port St. Joe rocked the local community and added to this unrest. Many white southerners feared a Black backlash during this time of upheaval. Things had to be brought under control fast.

At this point, the Bay County sheriff, M. J. "Doc" Daffin, stepped forward to take charge of the case. He was clearly the man for the job. He was a World War II combat veteran, he had been elected to multiple terms as sheriff of Bay County since 1952, and he was a powerful political figure in the Florida Panhandle. When I took Daffin's deposition years later, I was impressed with his dominating personality. He portrayed himself as a "good old country boy" with a down-home southern drawl that no doubt helped his political popularity, but he was also shrewd and quick witted.[18] Daffin was assisted by D. L. Barron, the chief of detectives of the Panama City Police Department, and officers from both departments. His other important assistant was Joe Townsend, who had traveled to Panama City to continue his relentless polygraph work.

Townsend set up shop in a room at the Bay County Jail and proceeded to conduct virtually nonstop polygraph tests on all the Black suspects they had in custody in an effort to break them down and get them to confess, much as he had done in the Air Force's Gerald Anderson case and would later do in the Quincy Five case. He was not just serving as an expert adviser to the police; he had become a police interrogator. But he wasn't making much progress. Something was needed to break open the case.

So Daffin had Willie Mae taken out of her cell and brought to an interrogation room at the Bay County Jail, where he began to question her. Willie Mae continued—truthfully—to deny that she knew anything about the robbery or murders. She told Daffin that she had been at the Mo Jo station on the night in question with Pitts and Lee and others, that they had all left and gone back to Wilbert Lee's party, that she and Pitts had left that party together that evening, and that they were in each other's company in Pitts's car for the rest of the night and never went back to the Mo Jo station.

But Daffin and the other police officers kept accusing her of lying, insisting that she knew about the murders and that she was involved. She was threatened with the electric chair for being an accomplice to the crime. No one from the community had stepped forward to help her. She had no money to hire a lawyer. Nor was there any public defender system to protect her. She was at the mercy of the police.

Daffin later testified at the September 1968 hearing on the defendants' motion to vacate the convictions of Pitts and Lee that he questioned Willie Mae Lee day and night, that he never charged her with a crime, that he never got a court order to hold her in custody as a material witness, that he nonetheless kept her in jail until Pitts and Lee were sentenced to death (a period of 25 days), and that he knew of no law that permitted him to do so.[19] In other words, Daffin conceded that Willie Mae Lee was illegally in custody during the entire time that he and others interrogated her.

Given all this coercive pressure, it is not surprising that she ultimately gave in and told the story that Daffin and the other police interrogators wanted to hear. She said that she returned to the Mo Jo station a second time that night with Pitts, who then committed the robbery and murders with another man who was hidden in the back seat of Pitts's car. This was of course not what happened.

Here is Willie Mae Lee's February 2, 1968, sworn statement to State Attorney J. Frank Adams and Florida Attorney General Investigator S. R. DeWitt about why she told this story. She said:

A. 'Cause I was scared. And tired of all the questioning.
Q. You were scared and tired of all the questioning. Why were you scared Billie?
A. 'Cause . . . Mr. Kittrell and them questioning me and hollering at me, and told me to tell the damn truth, that I wasn't telling the truth.
Q. Did anyone tell you that if you didn't tell them, that you stood a chance of going to the electric chair?
A. Yes.
Q. Who told you that Billie?
A. They say . . . I stood a chance of going to the electric chair and that I was just as involved as they were.
Q. And who told you that?

A. I don't remember. It was one of the men in the . . . in the questioning.[20]

But to everyone's surprise, Willie Mae named Lambson Smith, not Wilbert Lee, as the second killer, the man she said was hidden in the back seat of Pitts's car. Smith had already been cleared by Townsend in Port St. Joe. He was still being held in jail but he wasn't even a suspect. But that was not a problem for the police. Townsend had just made a mistake. The police would now concentrate on Smith.

Because Wilbert Lee was no longer a suspect, the police released him and his wife Ella Mae and transported them back to Port St. Joe. In compliance with Daffin's order, Lee remained in Port St. Joe so that the police could later deliver his written statement to him for his signature. This was a statement in which Lee denied any knowledge of the murders.

It is one of many ironies in this case that in spite of the terror that had earlier been visited upon him, Lee remained available to the police at all times and made no effort to flee the area. As Lee later testified, "I hadn't done anything to run away from Port St. Joe."[21]

*　　*　　*

Meanwhile, in order to conclude the case, the police called upon J. Frank Adams for assistance. Adams was the state attorney for the Fourteenth Judicial Circuit of Florida, which covered a number of adjoining counties, including Gulf and Bay Counties. Adams came to the Bay County Jail to take a statement from Willie Mae Lee that was to formalize the oral confession Willie Mae had previously given to Daffin. Wayne White, Assistant State Attorney William E. Harris, and a stenographer were also present. Willie Mae Lee was frightened but ready to tell her story.

At the outset, J. Frank Adams tried to reassure her.

Q. You're not scared are you?
A. Yes.
Q. Now don't be afraid of us. We just want to ask you a few questions. There is no need for you to be afraid.[22]

He then asked her to raise her right hand, swore her in to tell the truth, and asked her a series of questions. Willie Mae then tried her best to tell the most persuasive story she could.

Part of it was the truth, and Willie Mae had no trouble recounting that part. She had been at the Mo Jo station that night and had left the station with Pitts and Lee to return to the party at Lee's house. Later she had left the party with Pitts, they had driven around in an apparent romantic tryst, and their car had stalled outside Port St. Joe. A local resident, Henry Hogue, gave them a push to get the car started.[23]

After that, she had to lie; she had to link Pitts and Lambson Smith to the murders. So she repeated what she had told Daffin. Smith had been hidden all along in the back seat of Pitts's car. Smith had suddenly risen up out of this seat with a handkerchief or scarf hiding part of his face like a bandanna and had revealed himself.[24] That part of the story was bizarre on its face. Why would Smith be there in the first place? If he and Pitts were intent on this crime all along, why was he concealed in the back seat with this weird bandanna disguise? And who was he hiding from? It didn't make much sense.

But more to the point, Henry Hogue directly contradicted her account. Hogue testified at the 1972 trial that he saw no one in the car he pushed that night other than Pitts and Willie Mae.[25] This was a vital piece of evidence that the police never pursued when they questioned Hogue during the investigation. To the white police, Hogue was an old man. What did he know? He could safely be ignored—and he was.

Willie Mae continued. She said Pitts and Smith took her back to the Mo Jo station, where they robbed and kidnapped the two attendants, took them all by car into the country, marched the attendants out of the car into the woods at gunpoint, leaving her behind, and apparently killed them outside her presence—although she heard no shots. Smith had a gun, she said, and Pitts did not. She also said that she wailed and cried during the whole incident and was an unwilling witness to everything. After it was over, she said, Pitts told her to "keep her damned mouth shut" or she would lose her little girl.[26]

It was quite a performance. But, unfortunately for the police, Willie Mae's story soon imploded. When Lambson Smith was questioned further at the Bay County Jail, he handled himself quite well and refused to confess. He was a high school graduate from Chicago. He politely explained he had never gone to the Mo Jo station that night, that he had been at Wilbert Lee's house at the party all night, and that he hadn't left until the next morning. He had a number of alibi witnesses from the party to back him up.[27]

Eventually Daffin and the other officers were forced to rethink everything. Smith apparently was not one of the killers. They had Pitts, but they needed a second killer to close the case. They couldn't believe that one

Black man could kidnap two white men and kill them single-handedly. He needed an accomplice. So Daffin had Townsend run another polygraph test on Willie Mae. During this test, Townsend got her to substitute Wilbert Lee for Lambson Smith—which, after a little prodding, she was perfectly willing to do.[28]

J. Frank Adams was then summoned to the Bay County Jail to take a new statement from Willie Mae, which he proceeded to do accompanied by one of his assistants and a stenographer. At the outset, however, Adams had to deal with the pesky problem of Lambson Smith. He asked Willie Mae why she had earlier told him under oath that Smith was one of the killers. Willie Mae didn't have much of an answer, but she tried her best. "I was forced to," she said. "After Sheriff Daffin asked me about Smitty and I told him no and he kept asking me and Wilbert Lee's wife said he were and I got confused and then I said he was involved."[29]

This was an incoherent, convoluted "reason" if there ever was one. But J. Frank Adams and the police instantly understood. They took this statement to mean that Wilbert Lee's wife, Ella Mae, had pressured Willie Mae to name Smith instead of Wilbert Lee. The police had Ella Mae in jail together with Willie Mae—they had contact with each other. In order to protect her husband, Ella Mae had "forced" Willie Mae to lie. Willie Mae's later explanations became even more explicit to reflect this version of what happened, and that was the narrative the authorities told themselves to excuse their lapse with Lambson Smith.

Satisfied with her answer, Adams then swore Willie Mae in and took a second written statement from her. It generally followed the statement she had earlier given to him, substituting Wilbert Lee for Lambson Smith. She also punched her story up a bit by adding some imaginary details.[30] In this version, Pitts was armed with a gun and used it to viciously hit Floyd in the head:

Q. [By Mr. Adams] Who had the gun?
A. Freddie Pitts.
Q. Where did he have the gun?
A. He had the gun in his hand. He must have asked him to call Mr. Floyd over there. Freddie hit him with the gun up side of the head and he was bleeding. . . . Freddie rushed over there and hit him with the pistol right up there (witness indicates victim was hit over the right eye). Mr. Floyd fell up against the car.[31]

In her earlier version, Willie Mae had said that Pitts was unarmed, that Lambson Smith had the gun, and that no one was hit at the station. In the latest version, her hearing had also improved. She had now heard the killers fire three or four shots in the woods while she remained in the car; in the earlier version, she had heard no gunshots.[32]

Willie Mae also gave an entirely different reason why she had named Smith instead of Wilbert Lee in her initial statement to J. Frank Adams. And it had nothing to do with being "forced" by Ella Mae Lee to tell this story. As Townsend later reported, Willie Mae told him she had named Lambson Smith instead of Wilbert Lee because "Lee was related to her and she was mad at Smith for being in bed with Regina Thomas on the night of July 31, 1963."[33]

But this supposed jealousy reason for accusing Lambson Smith and a family reason for protecting Wilbert Lee made no sense and was promptly dropped. Wilbert Lee was not related to Willie Mae and she and Smith were never romantically involved. It was just an unfortunate lapse from Willie Mae that the police could safely ignore, which they did.

*   *   *

After all these readjustments in Willie Mae's story had been accomplished, Wilbert Lee had to be rearrested. The police went back to Port St. Joe, where Lee was waiting for them to deliver his exonerating statement for his signature, and he was brought back to the Bay County Jail. Lee's desperate hope for freedom during this time was smashed. It had lasted only a few days. And his great fear returned about what the police would do to him next.

Wilbert's wife, Ella Mae Lee, was also returned to the Bay County Jail as a "material witness." Lee's fears about what they would to do to her added to his sense of dread. Lambson Smith was still being held but was eventually released, having narrowly escaped his brief nightmare. Everything seemed to be coming together nicely for the police. The case was well on its way to being "solved."

But still, Willie Mae might be seen as a compromised witness because she had a motive to lie to extricate herself from any criminal involvement. Her sworn written statement to the state attorney blaming Lambson Smith also undermined her credibility.

Again not a problem for the prosecution. Her statement about Lambson Smith was simply buried in the state attorney's files and was not revealed to the outside world until years later, when the defense lawyers finally got a copy. Significantly, in 1971, the Florida Supreme Court upheld a circuit court order granting a new trial to Pitts and Lee based on the state's suppression of this evidence.

Willie Mae told her story with such conviction that the police felt that any local white jury would believe her. She had the intelligence, the nerve, and the daring to pull it off, despite the many contradictions and holes in her account.

Although Willie Mae was not charged with the Floyd-Burkett murders or with any other crime, the police couldn't afford to release her and subpoena her for later court proceedings like a normal witness. If they did that, she might have second thoughts. They couldn't afford to have their star witness change her story again or, worse yet, disappear. To make sure that she told her story right and stayed in the area, the police kept her in jail as a "material witness" until Pitts and Lee had been sentenced to death, although they never obtained a court order allowing them to do so. They also worked on her story during this time so that it became more detailed and seemed more credible. She was always under police control and did what they wanted.

At this point, there was only one thing left for the police to do. To wrap up the case, Daffin needed a confession from Pitts and Lee that would align with Willie Mae's "straightened-out" story. This could be done, the police thought, by having Willie Mae repeat her new story in Pitts and Lee's presence, interrogating Pitts and Lee afterward, and getting them to agree with Willie Mae's coerced account.

In the end, the state's entire case consisted entirely of false confessions from Willie Mae Lee, Freddie Pitts, and Wilbert Lee. The state had no forensic or physical evidence whatever.

5

The Army CID Investigation

While the police were interrogating their Black prisoners at the Bay County Jail, two outsiders soon appeared who would eventually rock the entire police investigation. They never intended to do this; they cooperated fully with the local police. But in fact, they undermined the credibility of the case the police were building against Pitts and Lee. They also exposed the racist and unprofessional conduct the police were engaged in.

In most criminal cases, police officers conduct their interrogations and investigations in secret. No outsiders are allowed to observe or interfere. If there is a later dispute over whether the police physically or mentally mistreated a particular prisoner, the prisoner's account is almost always rejected as biased and the police account is accepted by courts and juries. But this case was different. Credible outsiders became involved who had no axe to grind.

The US Army assigned Sergeant Bruce Potts and Sergeant Donald Hoag, two white Criminal Investigation Division (CID) investigators from Fort Rucker, Alabama, to determine the whereabouts and status of Private E-2 Freddie Pitts and Specialist 4 Lambson Smith. Both Pitts and Smith had been stationed outside Port St. Joe and were now in police custody.

Sergeant Potts was born in Kentucky, was raised in Pensacola, Florida, and considered Huntsville, Alabama, his home. He had a decided southern accent. Sergeant Hoag was a northerner who was originally from Ohio.[1] Both men had extensive experience in the army investigating homicide, rape, assault, and other criminal cases. Potts was 31 and had served for thirteen years in the army, eight years as a criminal investigator. He had a friendly manner and got along well with people. Hoag's manner was more cautious and by the book. He was 37 and had seventeen years of service in the army, five as a criminal investigator. They both had extensive experience testifying for the army in courts-martial against accused soldiers.[2]

The mission of the army investigators was to locate Pitts and Smith, determine their current status, take a statement from both soldiers, and file a report. It was a routine assignment. The army always defers to the civilian authorities in matters of this nature for whatever disposition these authorities decide to make. After that, depending on their investigator's report, the army may court-martial the soldiers involved and impose whatever penalty is deemed necessary. It's all very impersonal; army bureaucracy in action. As Sergeant Potts testified at the September 1968 hearing in Port St. Joe:

> To put it in the vernacular of the street, Pitts was a small spoke in the U.S. Army, the Big Picture as they say, and I was there to do a very small, minor job. I was told to see if I could interview Pitts. Not to repudiate a confession, not to corroborate, substantiate or anything else. To see if we could get a written statement from this man to include in the report. These were the instructions we were sent back down by our provost marshal. . . . We were not lawyers for this man, sir. . . .
>
> It's hard for me to explain verbally, sitting here saying it, but the man [Pitts] was a number to me. I do have feelings, Counselor, don't get me wrong, but to me the man was a job to do.[3]

The army investigators headed to the Bay County Jail in Panama City where Pitts and Smith were located, arriving there in the late afternoon of August 3.[4] Upon their arrival, they asked to look at the booking ledger, which they were allowed to do, but could find no entry for either Pitts or Smith. That was odd. Their official information was that these soldiers had been in this jail for at least a day or two. They should have been booked by now. But never mind; all they needed to do was to get a statement from these men and leave.[5]

Focusing on their assignment, they were directed upstairs at the jail to a police officer who could provide some information. They soon found Deputy Sheriff George Kittrell, who gave them a brief rundown on the case. Yes, he said, Pitts and Smith were in the jail; they were both charged with murder. The facts of the case were briefly outlined. Everything was being wrapped up. The police had the right people.[6]

Potts and Hoag were then introduced to Sheriff Daffin, who was in charge of the investigation. Daffin confirmed what Kittrell had told them and said that the case would be concluded that night. Fine, they said, they'd just like to interview Pitts and Smith briefly for a small statement, get out of there that evening, and return to Fort Rucker.[7] It was all very friendly. They were all law enforcement officials, military and civilians talking the same language with the same outlook. Sergeant Potts with his southern accent no doubt cemented that relationship.

But there was a slight holdup. As Daffin explained, this was a Gulf County case, and therefore he, as the sheriff of Bay County, had no jurisdiction to allow them to interview the two soldiers. Gulf County Sheriff Byrd Parker would need to be contacted to authorize such an interview.[8] This seemed perfectly reasonable. As military men, Potts and Hoag understood the necessity of going through channels. They could wait for the proper authorization.

With time to kill, they drove to the army camp outside Port St. Joe where Pitts and Smith had been stationed. They introduced themselves, conducted a few interviews, and looked around the camp. Soon they returned to the Bay County Jail to see if the necessary clearance had come through for them to conduct their interviews. But no clearance had been received. They were told to return the next day.[9]

Unhurried and unconcerned, they were used to occasional delays of this nature. In the meantime, they decided to help the police investigation by finding some evidence against the two soldiers if they could. They would include these findings in their own report, and what they found might be relevant in any future court-martial proceedings against Pitts and Smith.

That evening they went back to the Port St. Joe army camp, where they interviewed twelve to fifteen soldiers late into the night. In the process, they took statements from Privates Roland Jones and Roosevelt Bowie. These soldiers, however, were alibi witnesses for Smith. They stated that they had been at Wilbert Lee's party on the night in question with Smith and other soldiers, that Smith was a part of the party throughout the evening, and that they returned to the army camp with Smith and the other soldiers when the party was over. That information was the first sign that something might be awry with this case.[10]

Potts and Hoag further asked the first sergeant at the camp to collect all of Pitts and Smith's personal property and bring the items to the supply tent. After thoroughly examining the soldiers' equipment, clothing, and shoes, they found nothing incriminating. No mud, sand, or blood that might link the soldiers to the scene of the crime. No torn clothing that might indicate a struggle. No knife, bullets, or gun. To be certain, however, the army investigators impounded both soldiers' duffle bags, which were full of clothes and other items, to give to the police for later analysis at a crime lab.[11] When they were finished, Potts and Hoag retired for the night at nearby Tyndall Air Force Base outside Panama City. It had been a long day's work.

* * *

The next morning, Sunday, August 4, at 7:00 a.m., the army investigators returned to the Bay County Jail, but once again they were denied permission to see Pitts and Smith.[12] They first met with Gulf County Deputy Sheriff Wayne White, who told them they would have to talk to Sheriff Daffin, who was controlling this investigation. But when they talked to Daffin, they were told this was a Gulf County case and they would have to talk to Gulf County Sheriff Byrd Parker. But when they contacted Sheriff Parker, he told them that the prisoners were outside his jurisdiction and they would have to talk to Daffin. As Sergeant Potts put it later, "We were given the runaround."[13]

After that, every day from August 5 to August 7, 1963, both army investigators politely sought permission to interview Pitts—and each time the police refused. On August 5, 1963, however, Potts and Hoag were allowed to interview Lambson Smith because, as Daffin told them, they had "the wrong n——r." But they still couldn't see Pitts.[14] During this delay, Potts and Hoag briefly returned to Fort Rucker, made a verbal report to their superiors, and obtained permission to return to Panama City to continue their investigation.[15]

By this time, Potts and Hoag had become extremely suspicious. Never in their experience had local police ever refused to allow them to interview soldiers the police had in custody for this length of time and with such foolish excuses.[16] What was going on? Why couldn't they see Pitts? All they wanted was a short statement from him. Something strange was going on, something the police didn't want them to see.

Still, they dared not confront the police with their concerns. If they did, they might get thrown out of the Bay County Jail for interfering with the police investigation. Potts and Hoag were there at the sufferance of the local authorities, so they tried their best to remain on good terms with all the local law enforcement personnel. Potts even emphasized his southern accent ever so slightly when he spoke. Casually, they attempted to find out as much about the case as they could without being critical of anyone. It was a delicate situation.

They had learned from the weather bureau at Tyndall Air Force Base that it had rained heavily on the night of July 31 and the morning of August 1. Whoever killed the two attendants in the wooded area that night would likely have traces of mud on their shoes and clothing.[17] Exactly. Like the mud that Curtis Adams had on his shoes and had to scrape off when he returned to his apartment immediately after murdering the two attendants.

But they could find no mud on the belongings of Pitts and Smith. Still, a crime lab analysis of their property might reveal some trace amount that would match the scene of the crime. So they gave Pitts's and Smith's duffle bags stuffed with clothing and other items to Wayne White for that purpose. A possible lead, they said.[18]

Also, Potts and Hoag offhandedly inquired whether any physical evidence had been discovered that might link these soldiers to the crime. Had the murder weapon been found? Were any footprints or tire tracks found at the scene? If so, plaster casts might be taken of the prints and tracks. But no, White said, they had no weapon, no physical evidence. Instead, he said, they had a confession from an "eyewitness," Willie Mae Lee. White and others outlined that story.[19]

But to Potts and Hoag, the story didn't make much sense. As Potts explained to White:

> You know, it don't seem right that these two white guys would let these two colored guys force them into a car and take them out and murder them.
>
> It seems to me that if two colored people are gonna hold up a filling station like that with two white people, if they were going to kill them, they'd kill them right there at the filling station.
>
> I was born and raised in the South, and I just don't believe that two white people would go out and get in a car voluntarily.[20]

He had a point. It did seem out of character for the times—particularly given the tense racial atmosphere that then existed in the South. For generations, Black people had had an ingrained fear of southern white men, who generally regarded all Blacks as children and "uppity" Blacks with contempt. If two Black men in the South had committed this robbery and were intent on murder, they most likely would never have considered kidnapping their intended victims. Such an attempt would almost certainly have resulted in stubborn resistance. It would be best for them to shoot the attendants at the station. That's what Sergeant Potts tried to express to the police in ever-so-gentle terms.

On the other hand, if a *white* man had committed this crime, this kidnapping scenario seemed far more likely, particularly if the criminal was someone the attendants knew well—someone like Curtis Adams, the real murderer in the case. The attendants would have gotten in the criminal's car when ordered to do so, called on their long friendship with their assailant, and tried to talk him out of shooting them.

Potts even asked the local police if there was anyone living in Gulf County with a criminal background who might be capable of this crime. In fact, there was: Curtis Adams, the only man in the area with a record for armed robbery, the very crime under investigation. But the police put them off and ignored Adams.[21] In Deputy Sheriff Wayne White's mind, this was a Black-on-white killing, Curtis Adams was white and not involved, and nothing could ever persuade him otherwise.

*　　*　　*

As the week dragged on, Potts and Hoag became more and more appalled at the way the police were conducting their investigation. While they were in a small room at the Bay County Jail soon after they arrived, the army investigators were introduced to Joe Townsend, who was conducting lie detector tests on all the Black prisoners the police had arrested. According to Potts, Townsend ran so many tests on these people that a huge amount of graph paper from the polygraph machine overflowed onto the desk where Townsend was working and into a nearby wastebasket.

This was highly unprofessional. Polygraph examiners routinely retain their polygraph charts as a record of their work for later use in reviewing their findings and filing reports. But Townsend was throwing his polygraph charts away and seemed intent on getting confessions instead of assessing the truthfulness of the subjects he was testing.

"I was standing right next to where [Townsend] had his machine," Potts recalled, "and there was quite a large amount of [used] graph paper around the desk, in the trash can, just an enormous amount of it laying around."[22] "He had enough tape running there he could have run a whole Army regiment on."[23] "I can't quote him verbatim, but he said, in effect, that 'the whole carload of n——s were in on this and every one of them was guilty. Everyone knew something about this.'"[24]

Many law enforcement officers involved in the case frequently used the abusive n-word. Although this racially divisive speech was officially forbidden in the army, Potts and Hoag were hardened military investigators and could tolerate this behavior in civilian authorities to a certain extent—but not when the racism interfered with an objective pursuit of the facts.

Here is Sergeant Potts's testimony at the 1972 trial in Marianna, Florida, which reveals one of the methods the police liked to use when questioning

Black witnesses, particularly women. My co-counsel Irwin Block did the questioning:

Q. Would you tell us please sir what conversations you had with Mr. White and what if anything you did with him?
A. We had several conversations with Mr. White and also accompanied him on his trip to Port St. Joe from Bay County Jail, and from Port St. Joe we accompanied him on to Wewahitchka to the Gulf County Jail.
Q. May I ask you, did Mr. White say anything to you about the method of interrogating black witnesses?
A. Yes sir, he did.
Q. What did he tell you?
A. He said: "The only way to get these n——s down here to tell you what you want to hear is to threaten them to shave their head off and electrocute them."[25]

The police had other methods that were equally abusive for questioning Black witnesses. Two incidents in particular stand out. Both army investigators witnessed these events and testified to them at the March 1972 trial in Marianna.

The first incident involved an elderly Black man named Robert Jennings. White claimed that Jennings was a bootlegger who had supplied the liquor for the party Wilbert Lee had held on the night of the murders. White arrested Jennings and took him to the Port St. Joe jail.[26]

Here is Sergeant Hoag's testimony about what happened next:

At the Port St. Joe jail the three of us were in there with Jennings—Potts, Wayne White and myself . . . and [White] addressed [Robert] Jennings, he [said], "n——r, you talk—you tell me what I want to hear."

* * *

And at this time there was a grate, as I believe a cold air return, it had a screw or two missing from it and he pointed to it and said "If you don't tell me what I want to hear, you're going to wind up through that return."[27]

Sergeant Potts testified to the same incident:

[White] said, "Preacher, you're going to tell me what I want to know and you're going to tell me the truth just exactly what I want to hear and if you don't I'm going to ram your head down that ventilator shaft, you understand what I talking about." The Preacher said "Yes, sir."[28]

White then demanded to know who was at Wilbert Lee's party on the night in question. But despite White's repeated questioning, all a "confused" and "incoherent" Jennings could remember was that there were soldiers and other people at a party across the street from where he lived, but he didn't know their names.[29] White eventually gave up and released Jennings.

The second incident involved an illiterate Black 14-year-old girl named Regina Mae Thomas. White questioned her at the Gulf County Jail in Wewahitchka. She was an alibi witness for Wilbert Lee—something White didn't want to hear.[30] This is Sergeant Hoag's testimony at the March 1972 trial in Marianna, about how White tried to get Regina Mae to change her story:

> During the questioning of this girl, Regina Mae, Deputy White had a black scarf, I don't know where he got it from, he had the scarf that women normally wear on their head, he made the remark to Regina Mae that this scarf was used in the murder incident and robbery incident and he would take the scarf and sort of flick it in her face, and as he did, she would get hysterical and scream out.
>
> Q. How did he refer to her when he started the questioning?
> * * *
>
> A. Well, he called her different names, he called her "n——r" and "Regina" and "Regina Mae." He made some remark about she had [an] illegitimate child and if he didn't get to the truth of the matter, he'd see that this child be taken away from her.[31]

Sergeant Potts corroborated this account in the March 1972 trial testimony in Marianna.[32] But White couldn't get Regina Mae to change her story. All she would do was cry. So he transported her to the Bay County Jail in Panama City and turned her over to Sheriff Duffin, who proceeded to "straighten" her out.

The entire incident made a huge impression on Sergeant Potts. He included it in his official CID report that he filed with the army on August 19, 1963, while the occurrence was still fresh in his mind.

> On 6 August 1963, Rita [sic] Mae Thomas was interviewed and she stated that she had seen Willie Mae Lee and Pitts leave in Pitts's car for the woods to make love and that she was in the house with Smith.

Thomas further stated that Wilbur [*sic*] Lee was in the house all night and was still in the house when Pitts came back about 0500 hours.

Thomas was taken to the Bay County Jail by White and talked to Daffin for about 20 minutes. Daffin then called Hoag, I, and White into the room and Thomas had changed her story. . . . She is illiterate and appeared to have been scared when telling her second story.[33]

As Sheriff Daffin explained to everyone at the time, "You just don't know how to talk to these n——s around here."[34]

In essence, Potts and Hoag, two objective and highly qualified investigators, were eyewitnesses to the racist and unprofessional methods the police employed in handling this case. This conduct called into question the integrity of the entire law enforcement investigation. Still, the army investigators made no comment. They had to interview and get a statement from Freddie Pitts before they returned to Fort Rucker and they needed the good will of the police to accomplish this task. So for the moment they kept quiet.

6

A Court Hearing

From August 2 to August 9, 1963, the police interrogations continued at the Bay County Jail. Pitts and Lee were questioned by the Gulf County, Bay County, and Panama City police at all hours of the day and night. They were subjected to a constant series of lie detector tests and relay interrogations in an effort to get them to confess. They were accused of lying and confronted with Willie Mae Lee, who repeated her false accusations in their presence. But through it all, Pitts and Lee refused to confess.

Pitts was so beaten up, he couldn't keep track of the days. Adding to his confusion were the continual interrogations he was subjected to. As he later testified, "I was constantly brought out of my cell, questioned by Sheriff Daffin."[1]

Lee had a better memory of his ordeal. Here is his account of one all-night interrogation session. At the 1972 trial in Marianna, Lee testified:

Q. All right. The second time they took you over to the Bay County Jail, that night do you remember getting any sleep at all?
A. No, sir. I didn't get any sleep from that afternoon after arriving there approximately three o'clock—from there on I was under interrogation.
Q. How long did they question you?
* * *

A. I was questioned somewhere around three o'clock in the afternoon until midnight and then they changed shifts on me until daylight that morning. I was falling away from the desk and the table.[2]

The state called no witness at trial to deny this testimony.

Pitts and Lee had no one in the community to come forward and rescue them—no friends or relatives, no public defender system, no lawyer to stand up for their rights and stop this abuse with a habeas corpus petition in court.

Pitts and Lee finally got some relief from this ordeal, but it proved to be of little help to them. On August 7, after nearly a week of interrogation, they were handcuffed and brought in separate cars to Wewahitchka, which was then the county seat of Gulf County, for a brief court hearing. Lambson Smith, who had still not been released, was also taken with them.[3]

Circuit Judge W. L. Fitzpatrick, the eventual trial judge in this case, had gotten word that the defendants had been in custody for a week without a first appearance hearing in violation of Florida law. Section 901.23 of the *Official Florida Statutes* for 1963 required that a law enforcement officer who makes an arrest without a warrant "shall *without unnecessary delay* take the person arrested to the nearest and most accessible magistrate in the county in which the arrest occurs . . . and shall make before the magis-trate a complaint, which shall set forth the facts concerning the offense for which the person was arrested."

Fitzpatrick contacted David Gaskin, the only lawyer in Wewahitchka, and asked him to represent Pitts, Lee, and Smith at this hearing at which, as was later arranged, County Judge Sam Husband would preside. As allowed by Florida law at the time, Husband was not a lawyer. He had run a used-car lot before his election to the bench.[4] By way of contrast, circuit judges were required to be lawyers. Gaskin no doubt accepted this assignment reluctantly. No lawyer in the area was eager to get involved in this case. Gaskin had a small-town law practice at the time that primarily involved criminal cases and some probate work.[5]

When Pitts, Lee, and Smith arrived in the courtroom at Wewahitchka, David Gaskin briefly interviewed them in the open courtroom. Everyone was standing and the three defendants were handcuffed. Gaskin did not ask for a private room to interview the three men and he did not discuss the facts of the case with them. Armed deputies looked on a short distance away.[6] The interview was rushed and unprofessional. It is standard professional practice that lawyer-client interviews be conducted in a private room a reasonable time in advance of any appearance in court, not in an open courtroom just minutes before a court hearing with people looking on.

According to both Pitts's and Lee's testimony at the 1968 hearing in Port St. Joe on our motion to vacate the defendants' convictions, Gaskin did not identify himself at all. He just approached them and started talking. They assumed he was a court official of some kind and they had no idea he was a lawyer, much less their lawyer.[7] Lee also testified that this unidentified man "asked me could I hire an attorney and I told him no. He said if you can't hire one, well the Court will appoint one. . . . So he told me I didn't have to say anything to the judge. And after that he says, 'Well, how do you all plead?' So we all immediately almost said not guilty. Then he turned us loose and went back in front of the judge."[8]

On August 14, 1968, at my request, Gaskin sent me a letter relating his version of this interview. I had telephoned him previously. By that time, it was well known that defense counsel were attempting to reopen the case. On August 8, 1968, I had also sent Gaskin a number of perfectly readable army CID reports that Bruce Potts and Donald Hoag had filed in August 1963 that supported Pitts and Lee's innocence. "After reading these reports," I wrote, "you can well understand why there is something radically wrong with this case."[9] But Gaskin refused to read these reports at any length because, he said, they were illegible, although he never asked for better copies. Obviously, he wasn't interested.[10]

In his August 14 letter to me, Gaskin stated he had told the three defendants at the outset of the interview that "I had been appointed to represent them at this arraignment."[11] But he failed to indicate who had appointed him or even that he was a lawyer. Gaskin further stated that the mood of Pitts and Lee that day was "rather jovial," that they were quite "friendly" with the police officers in court, and that Pitts or Lee or both of them wanted "to enter a plea of guilty and ask the court for mercy."[12] Only Lambson Smith, Gaskin said, seemed to be worried about anything and wanted to plead not guilty. In Gaskin's version, Pitts and Lee, on the other hand, were carefree and ready to be sentenced.[13]

I was shocked when I first read this portion of the letter. No person in their right mind who has been charged with a capital offense would have acted that way in these circumstances—eager to plead guilty to a capital offense for which they could be sentenced to death and in the process be "jovial" about it all.

Understandably, Pitts and Lee denied this account. They maintained that they were frightened and were in no "jovial" mood at this hearing. They stood in handcuffs in full view of everyone, charged with a capital crime with full knowledge they could be sentenced to death. They had just gone through a week of grueling police interrogation, had not confessed to the police or to anyone else, and had steadfastly maintained their innocence. At no time did they suddenly change their minds, become "jovial," and tell Gaskin that they wanted to plead guilty and throw themselves on the mercy of the court. Indeed, when they returned to the Bay County Jail after this hearing, they continued to maintain their innocence to the police for several more days.

Pitts was all beaten up and could barely talk. But Gaskin said in his letter that he noticed no signs of such a beating and claimed that Pitts and Lee stated that they had not been mistreated, something both men emphatically deny.[14] Gaskin knew many of the police officers in this case, including Wayne White and Sheriff Daffin. He was also acquainted with George Kittrell, the officer who had administered the merciless beating to Pitts.[15]

After the interview, all three defendants were taken in handcuffs before Judge Husband, who had been waiting on the bench during the interview. Gaskin stood before the judge and announced that the defendants wanted to plead not guilty and waive any preliminary hearing.[16] Gaskin stated in his letter to me that all three defendants "approved my entering a plea of not guilty and waiving preliminary hearing subject to the right to ask for a preliminary hearing at any time prior to a grand jury indictment."[17]

Under Florida law at the time, a preliminary hearing was a separate proceeding that a defendant in a criminal case was entitled to before an indictment or information was filed. At such a hearing, the state was required to present testimony and evidence establishing "probable cause" that the defendant had committed the crime for which he or she was charged. If no probable cause was shown, the defendant was entitled to be released.[18]

A criminal defendant who asks for a preliminary hearing has nothing to lose and everything to gain. Even if the magistrate finds probable cause and the defendant is committed to custody, the defendant is able to find out the strength or weakness of the state's case and later obtain a transcript of the testimony of each witness to use against the witness at trial in case the witness changes his or her testimony in any material respect. Conversely, a defendant who waives a preliminary hearing, as Gaskin advised, gains nothing.

Gaskin, however, had not been appointed for such a formal proceeding and was not prepared to conduct one. Nor did he ask, as he should have, for one to be scheduled later. So he waived the preliminary hearing and none was held. Although they were legally entitled to one, Pitts and Lee had no idea what a preliminary hearing was and neither Gaskin nor the judge made that clear to them. Gaskin claimed in his letter that he had told Pitts and Lee that they could ask for a preliminary hearing later "at any time prior to the grand jury indictment."[19] But this statement is inaccurate. Gaskin waived the preliminary hearing and consequently Pitts and Lee lost the legal right to have one conducted thereafter.

Following a brief inquiry, the judge accepted the defendants' plea of not guilty and their waiver of a preliminary hearing. He then bound the defendants over to the circuit court for further proceedings and the first appearance hearing was adjourned.

After the hearing, all three defendants were placed together in the same jail cell in the courthouse and were given lunch. This is Wilbert Lee's account of that incident:

> When they brought lunch, Pitts complained that he could hardly eat. So he told us, say, look, and feel his head. Felt his head, he had several knots around the side, and his jaw was swollen, and he opened his mouth, and [I] looked inside his mouth and it was all swollen up. He said he had been beaten up. . . . He said it was a law enforcement officer whupped him up.[20]

Here is Lambson Smith's account of the same incident:

> I asked Pitts . . . how did he mix me up in this, and I didn't get a reply. He just looked at me. He didn't say anything. . . . I was shocked when I saw him because he looked like he hadn't had anything to eat or any sleep. His face seemed to be swollen up. He looked like he hadn't washed up or anything. . . . Oh, his eyes were red and his eyes seemed to be swollen a little. . . . Across his forehead was swollen, had a couple of knots or bumps on his forehead."[21]

Pitts and Lee were then returned to the Bay County Jail in Panama City for further police interrogations. Lambson Smith was also returned to the Bay County Jail and was not released until the Gulf County Grand Jury declined to indict him about two weeks later.

Gaskin had given the three defendants some hurried and abstract advisements on their constitutional right to remain silent, but he had not recommended that they should exercise that right in any way. In particular, he did not advise Pitts and Lee to stop talking to the police about the case without a lawyer present.[22] That is standard defense lawyer advice in criminal cases of this nature, particularly first-degree murder cases. If Gaskin had done so and Pitts and Lee had followed that advice, the police might never have gotten any confessions out of them.

But Gaskin displayed no desire to interfere with the police investigation. His role in the case was limited and temporary. He was only there for the first appearance hearing, nothing more. At the September 1968 hearing in Port St. Joe, Gaskin made that perfectly clear in his testimony. I did the questioning.

Q. You were not aware, of course, since you were through with the case, that the Defendants were then interrogated after the Court hearing?

A. No sir, I was—

Q. Had you been aware of it, you might have done something about it, is that right, sir?

A. Well, I was no longer counsel.

Q. I understand.

A. I was just a member of the bar back then and I would be intruding on something that—I had to have authority, either from the Defendants or from the Courts.[23]

No doubt Gaskin did not think that he was doing anything wrong or unprofessional. This was the way things were done in that area in criminal prosecutions where the defendants were Black and poor and the case was notorious. No one expected a vigorous defense of such people. Most lawyers and judges in the area would have regarded Gaskin's conduct as entirely appropriate.

However, a growing number of people in the country were appalled at this system. Innocent people like Pitts and Lee got ground up in it. White people with plenty of money to hire first-rate criminal lawyers were not treated this way. But change was in the air, and much of this system would be rolled back in the 1960s and 1970s. But in 1963, the voices that advocated this change were the Don Quixotes of the day.

7

Pitts and Lee Confess

After returning to the Bay County Jail, Pitts and Lee continued to hold out and refused to confess. After a day or two of more interrogations, however, they finally broke down and signed written confessions that the police had prepared. It was the only thing they could do that would end their ordeal.

On August 8, 1963, at 1:10 p.m., Freddie Pitts signed his confession after basically parroting the story the police fed to him, largely tracking the story the "witness" Willie Mae Lee had recited in his presence, although with some important discrepancies.[1]

But what happened next sent the police into a fury. The army CID investigators, Sergeant Bruce Potts and Sergeant Donald Hoag, were finally allowed to see Pitts after a week of police refusals. The interview took place in a private room at the Bay County Jail. Pitts's commanding officer, Lieutenant Thomas Arata, was also present.

This is Sergeant Potts's account of what happened when it was still fresh in his mind. This account is contained in an official CID report that Potts filed eleven days later with the United States Army:

> On 8 August 1963, Daffin informed Hoag and I that Pitts had confessed and had stated that Wilbur [sic] Lee and Willie Mae Lee had shot and killed the two men.
>
> At 1645 hours [4:45 p.m.], Hoag and I were permitted to interview Pitts. During the interview with Pitts, Daffin removed Pitts from the room every 10 minutes to find out what story he was telling us.
>
> Pitts was examined by myself and Lt. Arata. Pitts had three or four lumps or knots on the right side of his head, his right jaw was swollen and he had trouble talking. His left eye was bloodshot and watering. Pitts said he could not eat his food as his teeth were loose and his jaw hurt. Pitts stated that the night he was picked up was a complete blank

to him and that he had signed a confession as he was told by Daffin and White that they would get him out of the mess he was in.

Pitts' mental and physical condition was very poor and it became apparent while talking to him why the Civil Law Enforcement Officials had refused to let him be interviewed sooner.[2]

Sergeant Potts elaborated on this account when he testified at the 1972 trial in Marianna:

Q. And tell us what you saw when you first saw Freddie Pitts?

A. Freddie Pitts was brought into the room by Sheriff Daffin and as he walked into the room he was moving very slow and he appeared to be in, I would say, physical strain or stress. He took his time trying to sit down in the chair.

He was very slow about it and several times he appeared to favor his ribs or his stomach, and after he sat down into the chair, I took a look . . . at his physical being and I could observe that his lip was swollen, up at the right side of his jaw where it hinges was swollen. I could see he had knots on his head.

Q. Have you in your experience of criminal investigation seen people who were beaten?

A. Yes sir.

Q. What is that opinion?

A. In my opinion he had been severely beaten.[3]

Sergeant Hoag gave corroborating testimony at the March 1972 trial in Marianna:

[Pitts] appeared like he was under duress. He walked slowly, shuffling and just looked tired and beat up. . . . I looked at his eyes and I could see his eyes were bloodshot and watery. . . . He made mention about his jaw hurting, he put his hand on his jaw, and said "Oh, his jaw" . . . that his ribs hurt and his eyes were burning and that he had bumps on his head. . . . I place[d] my hand on the top of his head and in the back area of his head and I could feel what I believed to be knots in this area of his head. . . . I was of the opinion that he was beaten or mistreated.[4]

None of this testimony by Sergeants Potts and Hoag was ever denied by any police witness at the 1972 trial in Marianna.

After these physical observations had been noted, Sergeant Potts followed standard army CID procedure for questioning suspects. He advised Pitts of his rights under the Military Code of Justice and of his right to remain silent under the Fifth Amendment to the US Constitution.

Sergeant Hoag then spoke up and explained to Pitts that if he was guilty of these murders he might as well tell them. Pitts had already confessed to the police and wouldn't be putting himself in any further jeopardy by telling the army investigators the truth.[5] At that point, Pitts let out "a big sigh of relief—like you let the air out of a balloon—and said 'I'm glad to see somebody from the Army.'"[6] As he would tell us later, Pitts thought the army had come to rescue him. Hoag continued: "I want you to level with us, tell us the truth." Pitts replied that he hadn't committed the murders. Then why did you confess to the police? Hoag asked. "I'm afraid for my life," Pitts replied. "If I didn't do that, I don't know if I could even get to trial or not."[7]

Pitts then related in detail what had happened on the night in question. He repudiated his police confession, he said that he had been beaten and terrorized into making it, and he explained that he had never returned to the Mo Jo station after visiting it once that evening. He told Potts and Hoag that he had been with Willie Mae Lee for the balance of the night and that he had no knowledge of the Floyd-Burkett murders.

There was a typewriter in the room and the army investigators used it to prepare a statement on a standard army form containing Pitts's account of what happened that night. Pitts swore to the statement and signed it. It was later filed with the army as part of the official CID investigative report on the case.

At the end of this statement, Sergeant Potts asked point blank:

Q. Do you [Pitts] know anything about the robbery or murder that took place at Port St. Joe, Florida, on 1 August, 1963?
A. Only what I have learned while being here and what Skipper told Smith and I on the morning of 1 August 1963. . . .
Q. Did you murder the men who work at the Mo Jo Station?
A. No.
Q. Do you know who murdered the men at the Mo Jo Station?
A. No.
Q. Did you tell the authorities at jail you were involved in this crime?
A. Yes.
Q. Why?

A. I was beaten and I don't know what is going on. My head is hurting.

Q. Are you clear in mind as to what you are telling me?

A. Yes. I am not under pressure and people are not feeding me a lot of words.

Q. Is this statement the truth, the whole truth, and nothing but the truth?

A. Yes.[8]

During the forty minutes of this interview, Sheriff Daffin pulled Pitts out of the room three or four times to ask him what he was telling the army investigators.[9] Although Daffin couldn't get a straight answer, he must have known full well what was taking place. Daffin's entire case was in danger of falling apart. But he had no choice. He had to let Potts and Hoag see his beaten-up prisoner. He couldn't put them off any longer.

When the army investigators had finished and were leaving the room, Daffin pressed Hoag to tell him what had happened. Hoag answered that Pitts had retracted his confession. Here is Sergeant Hoag's testimony at the September 1968 hearing in Port St. Joe about what happened next:

Right after that, Sheriff Daffin . . . went over to the room Mr. Townsend was at and said to Townsend, "He's denying everything that he said previously." And I don't remember the exact words Townsend yelled, but he said "Jesus," something like that.[10]

Sergeant Potts added in a statement he later gave to Warren Holmes:

It seemed like it was mass confusion went on there in that jail for a while . . . and it appeared that we were—we were sitting on a hot seat there, so the best thing for us to do was to gently fade out of the picture, and we did.

Q. Did they ever in essence order you out of station?

A. No, but it was gradually reaching that point.[11]

Potts and Hoag left the jail in a rush and went back to Fort Rucker to file their reports.

Pitts then turned to Sheriff Daffin and said he wanted a lawyer. The army investigators had advised Pitts to make this request. Daffin was outraged. "Let me tell you one goddamn thing," he roared. "These Army men haven't got anything to do with it. You're in the hands of the civilian authorities, and they got nothing to do with it."[12] Sheriff Daffin was right, and it was beginning to sink in for Pitts. The army had no power to save him. He returned to his jail cell full of fear as to what would happen next.

* * *

Despite the apparent collapse of their case, the police soon regrouped from this momentary setback. Forget the army. They had nothing to do with the case. The police had Willie Mae's confession. They had Pitts's confession. So what if the army had taken a sworn retraction statement from Pitts? So what if Willie Mae had made a sworn statement implicating Lambson Smith? Both statements would never be seen in court anyway and were buried. All they needed was a confession from Wilbert Lee and the case would be wrapped up. But Lee had been stubborn. For over a week, he had continually refused to confess. Now, however, it was time to get tough. The police had heard enough.

That same day, in the evening of August 8, 1963, Lee was taken out of his cell and interrogated by a room full of police officers, including Daffin, White, and Barron, and other officers Lee did not recognize.

Lee had a vivid memory of the night. His wife Ella Mae was still in jail and the police used her as a weapon to break him down. Lee was also threatened and beaten. Here is what Lee said about what happened that night when he testified at the 1972 trial in Marianna—an account that was never denied by any state witness at that trial:

Q. Did the police at any time while you were in custody . . . did they physically mistreat you at any time?
A. Yes, there came a time that did happen.
Q. All right, would you tell us about that.
A. During the interrogation, I was brought downstairs one night and as I was entering the room it was statements made to me by one police officer, said, "you're going to talk tonight," and as we entered the room and started asking me questions and I didn't know anything about what he was talking about and at that time, well, I was slapped up the side of the head with a black jack or slap jack two or three times.
Q. Did anybody make any threats to you or anyone else in your presence?
A. Yes, that did happen after I was slapped up side of the head two or three times with this slap jack, and as you say didn't come across with what they were trying to get worked up to, well that's when they

brought my wife in and they tried to make my wife tell me that I left the house and she broke down and started to cry and hollering and was going on.

And Mr. Daffin said, "Get her ass out of here, take her out." And when they take her out, then one of the officers there, I don't know his name, he mentioned, he mentioned that "If you don't confess and cooperate, we're going to take your wife and shave her hair off and electrocute her."[13]

Lee did not recognize the men who beat him that night and who brutally threatened his wife, but no doubt they were police officers from the Bay County Sheriff's Office or the Panama City Police Department, officers Lee would not have known.

Faced with this unspeakable terror, Wilbert Lee capitulated. On August 9, 1963, at 1:30 in the morning, he signed a written confession the police had prepared containing the story they wanted to hear. It was a story the police had pounded into him, a story Willie Mae Lee had recited in his presence.

"What broke me was not the beatings," Wilbert Lee said many years later. "It was when they told me: 'Boy, let me tell you one thing: If you don't cooperate with us, we're going to shave the hair off your n——r wife's head and execute her.' I didn't want my wife to die."[14]

Unlike Pitts's confession, however, Lee's confession states that Pitts shot Floyd and Burkett four times after Lee had struck both victims with a tire jack. Pitts's confession, in contrast, denies that he shot the attendants at all or was even present when that happened. Pitts's confession says that Lee and Willie Mae took the victims into the woods while he remained in his car, after which he heard two shots. But that scenario was soon abandoned. Within a week, the police got Pitts to agree with Lee's confession that Pitts had fired four fatal shots.[15]

After a week of constant interrogations, the police finally had what they needed. They had their confessions from Pitts and Lee. They had their confession from Willie Mae Lee. There were conflicts among these statements, but they would soon be ironed out. To their great relief, the case was now "solved." Lee returned to his jail cell to await the terrifying events that would unfold in the days ahead.

*   *   *

Still, the police had a problem. Not an insurmountable one, not one that would threaten their case, but one they'd rather not have. The police never discovered any physical evidence to support the defendants' confessions or otherwise link Pitts and Lee to the murders. They tried to find such evidence during their investigation without success. And what evidence they did uncover contradicted those confessions.

The police never found the gun they say Pitts used to kill the attendants. Pitts said in his confession that he threw the gun away near a canal at "the White City Bridge."[16] But the police couldn't find this supposed gun at that location when they searched for it. They took Pitts with them to help them find it at that spot and at various other places in the county, but they never came up with the gun. Pitts couldn't lead them to it. Small wonder.

Further, Lee's confession says that he "whammed the hell" out of both the attendants with an iron "jack handle," causing them to fall to the ground, following which Pitts fired his gun "four times" into both victims.[17] But the police never found this "jack handle" despite their many efforts to locate it that included a thorough search of Pitts's car.

Meanwhile, a formal forensic investigation was conducted at the request of the police. The Florida Sheriffs Bureau in Tallahassee processed and analyzed all the physical evidence the police had gathered for examination, but nothing incriminating was ever found.

On August 6, 1963, Special Agent James F. Kelly with the Florida Sheriffs Bureau's Mobile Crime Unit came to Wewahitchka. When he arrived, he met Wayne White, who showed him a car parked in back of the sheriff's office. It was the car Pitts had driven on the night in question.[18] Agent Kelly processed the car for possible evidence. He took soil samples from the floor mat under the front seat and from under the fenders of the car. He also took into custody various items of clothing he found in the trunk and on the front seat. Because the car had been sitting in the hot sun for several days outside the sheriff's office, Kelly decided it was not suitable for processing for latent fingerprints.[19]

The police also gave Agent Kelly several key items of evidence: a paper bag containing shoes that belonged to Freddie Pitts and Lambson Smith, a bag of clothing that belonged to Freddie Pitts, and a soil sample taken from the crime scene where the bodies had been found. Kelly, however, never received any of the clothing Lee had been wearing when he was arrested—clothing the police had taken from him. Also, the police never took any plaster casts of tire tracks and footprints at the crime scene, even though Sergeant Potts and Sergeant Hoag had urged them to do so.[20]

The crime laboratory at the Florida Sheriffs Bureau later examined the evidence Agent Kelly had obtained. Their findings are contained in a report the bureau later filed with the Gulf County Circuit Court in Wewahitchka. The report gives the results of a comparison of the shoes belonging to Freddie Pitts and Lambson Smith (Exhibits 2-A and 2-B) with the soil samples taken from the area where the bodies were discovered (Exhibit 2-C). Here is the crime laboratory's finding after making that comparison:

> These shoes (Exhibits 2-A & 2-B) were examined and it was not possible to demonstrate the presence of blood on their surfaces. A small amount of sand in and on these shoes were found to be generally dissimilar to the samples contained in Exhibit 2-C. However, this may be due to contamination by accumulation.[21]

This was not a conclusive finding, but nonetheless a significant indication that Pitts and Smith had never been at the scene of these murders. The laboratory made numerous other findings about the rest of the evidentiary items they examined but found nothing that linked Pitts or Lee to the murders of Floyd and Burkett.

Agent Kelly was not happy with the way the police handled the forensic end of the case. He thought the police had displayed little interest in the subject and had rushed him to complete his work.[22]

Still, the police had everything they needed. Granted, it would have been helpful to find the gun and jack handle they say were used to smash and kill the two attendants. And it would have been nice to get some favorable findings from the Florida Sheriffs Bureau. But none of that was essential. They had their confessions from Pitts, Lee, and Willie Mae Lee. That was enough to satisfy any local all-white jury who would hear this case. As for any evidence that contradicted their case, including the autopsy report, the forensic findings, and Sheriff Parker's findings at the crime scene—all of that was either ignored or buried.

Only one minor thing remained to be done. Pitts and Lee's confessions needed to be cleaned up. The inconsistencies between the two statements had to be ironed out, and the sordid details that had led to the extraction of the two confessions needed to be buried. Again, this was not a problem. The police would soon get help from a local defense lawyer who displayed no desire to challenge the police investigation of this case.

8

The Initial Trial Court Proceedings

On August 12, 1963, Freddie Pitts, Wilbert Lee, and Lambson Smith appeared before Circuit Judge W. L. Fitzpatrick in Wewahitchka, Florida. The purpose of the hearing was to determine whether the court should appoint a lawyer to represent these defendants at trial or whether they would hire their own counsel.

Although Willie Mae Lee had long since retracted her initial statement blaming Lambson Smith for the Floyd-Burkett murders, the police had not yet released Smith, and for that reason he was included in this hearing.

Fitzpatrick was shocked when he first saw Pitts and Lee on August 12. Here is the judge's account of what happened that day as given in a deposition he gave me on January 31, 1972. What makes this testimony so riveting is that the judge volunteered it at the close of the deposition:

> I can see those two (2) men [Pitts and Lee] sitting across from that desk right now just as plain as I did then. And one reason for that is their color—I've never seen colored people that color before; I've never seen a dead colored person.
>
> Q. Pardon me?
>
> A. I say I've never seen a corpse, a dead corpse colored person; but their color was horrible—they looked awful. I felt deep sympathy for anybody that looked like that or felt like I know they felt because of the way they looked. They looked so frightened; the color was drained out of their face. I saw that at that point, I think that's the first time—I know that's the first time they had been before me, and when I sentenced them the same color, and it's a terrible thing to look at, it's horrible.
>
> * * *
>
> While I was talking to them you could see that look on their face—it was terrible, like I was going to kill them myself. I guess they were afraid of me. I don't know.[1]

This description captures exactly how Pitts and Lee looked at the court hearings they appeared at that month—including, as Fitzpatrick said, the day they were sentenced to death, August 28. A great deal of blood had been drained from their faces that left a shocking, white-like pallor to their facial skin. They looked like zombies, like living corpses, and Pitts's face was still swollen and cut from the severe beating he had received from the police.

Although Pitts and Lee have no recollection of this, Fitzpatrick testified that he had a private meeting in his chambers with both men before the August 12 hearing to determine whether they had been mistreated by the police. He said other matters were discussed at this conference, but he couldn't remember if he actually broached the question of police brutality.[2]

As a result, Judge Fitzpatrick made no judicial determination in this or any other proceeding about whether Pitts and Lee had been brutalized by the police over the previous week. If such a finding had been made, the state's case might have fallen apart and the defendants might eventually have been released—no doubt to the outrage of the local community. We will never know, but perhaps that was what Judge Fitzpatrick feared might happen if he looked too closely into what the police had done to these men.

The judge was a fine jurist with decent instincts, but he was also a man of his times. Addressing the three Black defendants before him, he said: "You *boys* have been held in Bay County because of a lack of facilities in the Gulf County Jail. Do you *boys* have any objection to being retained in the Bay County Jail?"[3]

Lee was 28 years old. Pitts and Smith were enlisted men in the United States Army. They were hardly "boys." They were young men. But many white southerners addressed Black men that way. The South in the 1960s was a white supremacist society and had been for centuries, stretching back to the days of slavery. Times were changing, but the custom of whites referring to adult Blacks paternalistically as children persisted. For centuries, when a white southerner called a Black man a "boy," it was both meant and interpreted as a racial putdown.

*   *   *

In open court, the judge asked the three defendants whether they intended to hire a lawyer. Lambson Smith indicated that he would, but Pitts and Lee said that they had no money to employ counsel and requested that the court appoint a lawyer to represent them. Fitzpatrick then appointed W. Fred Turner as their attorney. Turner was in court at the time and accepted the assignment. "Mr. Turner," Fitzpatrick announced, "has just made history in a càse in Panama City and is one of the finest criminal lawyers in this circuit, if not the finest."[4] Understandably, Pitts and Lee were impressed. And from that point on, they placed their complete trust in Mr. Turner to defend and save them from the peril they were in. As it turned out, this trust would lead to their ultimate downfall.

Fitzpatrick then addressed indirectly a matter that no doubt was troubling him. With Mr. Turner standing at their side, the judge asked Pitts and Lee "if they have any complaints to register."[5] It was the closest the judge came that day to addressing the horror before him. But perhaps he knew that Turner would likely intervene and end the inquiry. And, according to Wilbert Lee, that's exactly what happened. When Lee tried to answer the judge's question, Turner raised his hand and prevented it.[6] Noticing this, the judge asked: "Would you like to confer with them?" to which Turner replied "Yes sir."[7] A private conference ensued in which Lee said he wanted to tell the judge how he and his wife had been mistreated by the police. But Turner said "don't make any accusations" and said that "he would take care of that [later], it might hurt the case."[8] Turner then advised the judge that his clients had nothing to bring to the attention of the court. The matter was then dropped.[9]

The attending police were no doubt relieved. The sordid details of how they had treated Pitts and Lee since being arrested would not be aired. And if all went well with Turner as defense counsel, none of that brutal affair would ever be revealed in court.

Like David Gaskin before him, Fred Turner was no Atticus Finch, Harper Lee's heroic attorney in *To Kill a Mockingbird*. Turner had to live and practice law in that area. He could not afford to be seen as a civil rights advocate, as someone who stood up for Black rights in the segregated South. And this case, in my opinion, required just that—something that would have made him a pariah in Gulf and Bay Counties. The police could therefore count on Turner to be most cooperative with them and not challenge their case.

Turner had been practicing law in the Fourteenth Judicial Circuit ever since he had been admitted to the Florida Bar in October 1948. It was a small legal community with a clubby atmosphere. Among other things, he knew the state attorney, J. Frank Adams, and played golf with Judge Fitzpatrick.[10] Three circuit judges, including Fitzpatrick, recommended that Turner be reinstated to practice law in the federal court after he had been readmitted to the Florida Bar following his conviction and prison sentence for failure to file federal income taxes in 1952–1953—a crime that was seen at the time as only an unfortunate lapse in judgment.[11] Turner had also known one of the murder victims in this case, Jesse Burkett, and had represented him on a criminal charge of pandering.[12] Today we would call that a conflict of interest, but back then in a community of that size, it represented a minor technicality.

Turner was also famous, as Fitzpatrick had said. His fame was based on his association with *Gideon v. Wainwright,* a US Supreme Court case.[13] Clarence Gideon had been convicted in Panama City of burglary without benefit of a lawyer, as he had no money to hire one. On appeal, the Court in this landmark case reversed the conviction and held that the Sixth and Fourteenth Amendments to the Constitution guaranteed a right to defense counsel in all felony cases, and that if a defendant such as Gideon had no money to hire counsel, the court was required to appoint one. At that time, Turner did not represent Gideon. But when the matter was sent back to Panama City for a retrial, Turner was appointed as trial counsel and won the case before a local jury.

Clarence Gideon, however, was white. He had been charged with a nonviolent felony, and the case had no racial overtones. A vigorous defense of the case was considered socially acceptable. The Pitts-Lee case, on the other hand, was a racially charged, Black-on-white murder prosecution in which well-liked people had been brutally killed. It was a toxic case that no lawyer in the area wanted to be involved in. In those times and in this case, any serious defense of Pitts and Lee by a local lawyer was out of the question.

* * *

Once Turner was in the case, the stage was set for the police to obtain a new, sanitized version of the confessions they had previously extracted from Pitts and Lee. Those confessions, tainted as they were with the brutality and threats that accompanied them, needed to be buried. Also, important conflicts between the two confessions had to be ironed out. So on or about August 14, 1963, Sheriff Daffin arranged for a new interrogation session of Pitts and Lee at the Bay County Jail. Significantly, Fred Turner was a participant in this interrogation session.

Willie Mae Lee, who was in jail, was taken out of her cell and brought down for this session. The police had earlier forced her into falsely confessing to these murders and had used her as a weapon for breaking down Pitts and Lee. In exchange, she was never prosecuted.

Here is Sheriff Daffin's testimony as to what happened that day, which he gave at the August 28, 1963, trial of this case in Wewahitchka. State Attorney

J. Frank Adams did the questioning and called Pitts and Lee "boys." Daffin referred to Wilbert Lee as "Slingshot," his nickname, rather than his proper name.

> So we brought Willie Mae and Slingshot together and Slingshot wanted to deny it and Willie Mae said, "Slingshot, you know this story that I am giving is true. You know that's the way it happened. It's no use for you to set there and deny it," and pretty soon he did admit it.
>
> And then Freddie came down and he was obstinate about admitting it, and we brought Slingshot back down with Willie Mae and let them tell the whole story about how it happened and then after a while he admitted it was the truth, what they were saying.
>
> * * *
>
> Q. Was the conversation between you and these two boys and Willie Mae free and voluntary?
> A. Yes and after they had been appointed an attorney.
> Q. What did they tell you in connection with the death of Mr. Burkett—you say they had been appointed an attorney?
> A. Yes sir.
> Q. Was he present when the conversation was held?
> A. Yes, sir. He was.[14]

According to Pitts and Lee, Turner actively participated in this interrogation. Here is Freddie Pitts's testimony at the September 1968 hearing in Port St. Joe on our motion to set aside the defendants' convictions:

> The next time I saw Mr. Turner, I was brought down into a room. . . . Mr. Turner was in the room, Sheriff Daffin, Doc Barron, Wilbert Lee, and Willie Mae Lee. . . . I was made to sit between Willie Mae Lee and Wilbert Lee and listen to what she was saying.
> Q. And what was she saying?
> A. That Wilbert and I had taken her without her consent out to the Mo-Jo Station, that she had seen—after we got to the station Wilbert rose up in the back seat with a scarf over his face and we had taken these men out—. . .
> Q. When she got through with her story, what, if anything, did you say?
> A. I denied it and told them I didn't have anything to do with it.
> Q. And how long did this go on?

A. I don't know just how long it went on, but I kept telling them that I didn't know anything about it, that what Willie Mae was saying was wrong, I did not know anything about the murders of these two men. . . .

Q. And what did they keep saying to you?

A. They kept telling me that I may as well confess, that Wilbert and Willie Mae had confessed in this thing and was telling the truth and I may as well go ahead and tell the truth. . . .

Q. And what, if anything, did Mr. Turner say to you?

A. After a while Mr. Turner said, "Well, Willie Mae is telling her story, Wilbert has confessed to it and unless you confess I'm going to have to tell the judge there is a conflict in your story and I can't handle your case." . . .

Q. And how did you feel when Mr. Turner, your lawyer, made that statement to you?

A. I don't know exactly how I felt. I mean, I didn't know what to think, I didn't know what to do.

Q. And what did you do?

A. I sat there for a while thinking, and after a while I said, "All right, I did it."[15]

At the same hearing, Wilbert Lee testified to an identical account of this meeting with Sheriff Daffin, Willie Mae Lee, Freddie Pitts, and Fred Turner. In particular, Lee testified:

A. At that time I was to set and listen what she had to say. So when Willie Mae Lee started to tell her story, well I started protesting my innocence and it led from word to word. So Mr. Turner and Mr. Daffin, they shouted at me and told me to shut my damn mouth and shut up and listen, so I just sat there and listened.[16]

Lee testified that he broke down during this session and confessed and that he witnessed Pitts confess after they brought Pitts down and made him listen to Willie Mae Lee's story.[17] Lee further testified to Turner's threat to withdraw as Pitts's attorney unless Pitts confessed: "I believe then at that point that's where Mr. Turner told [Pitts] that he couldn't represent him because I had confessed."[18]

A single consistent, albeit false, account of what had happened the night of the murders was then hammered out in which Pitts and Lee would agree to Willie Mae Lee's story. Under this new version, the conflict between Pitts and Lee's earlier confessions about who shot Floyd and Burkett was cleared up. It was now Pitts who shot both men. Pitts's prior confession that Willie Mae Lee and Wilbert Lee had done the killing was buried. They now had one consistent account of Pitts and Lee's confessions—an account that Sheriff Daffin could later testify to when the case came to trial on August 28, 1963.[19]

Understandably, Pitts and Lee were devastated by this encounter. But they placed their complete trust in Turner's assurances that this was the best way to proceed in order to save their lives. Judge Fitzpatrick had pronounced Turner the best criminal lawyer in the area, as indeed he was. They were also deathly frightened about what might happen if they did not cooperate with the police and Mr. Turner. They did what they were told.

At that point, the police finally had what they wanted: sanitized and consistent confessions from Pitts and Lee and Willie Mae Lee. The police were ready for trial. Based on this evidence, an all-white jury was certain to convict Pitts and Lee and send them to death row. And that's exactly what happened.

In my experience, police confessions obtained with the defendant's lawyer present occur only where the defendant gets something in exchange for the confession—namely, a lenient sentence in a plea deal or total immunity from prosecution. Pitts and Lee got neither.

When Turner had interviewed Pitts and Lee at the Bay County Jail, Pitts had related his innocence in considerable detail, the police beating he had received, and the participation of the Army CID sergeants. Lee had similarly related his defenses. Turner had recorded their statements on a Dictaphone that he brought to the interview. But all of that was now irrelevant. Pitts and Lee had said they were guilty and that was the end of it.[20]

Instead, Turner readied himself to plead both men guilty to first-degree murder at the arraignment three days later. In the interim, he made no effort to seek a plea deal with J. Frank Adams in which his clients would receive sentences of life imprisonment in exchange for their guilty pleas. That was the usual practice of defense lawyers when pleading guilty to a capital crime, but not in this case. Turner planned to plead Pitts and Lee guilty "straight up" and throw them on the mercy of the court.[21]

David Gaskin had said that that was the course Pitts and Lee were eager to adopt at the first appearance hearing, and that would also be Turner's story.[22] Pitts and Lee, Turner said, wanted to plead guilty. That was their idea, not his, and who was he to stand in their way?[23] No doubt many in the local white community would entirely approve. Turner might even be seen as public spirited because he was helping the police bring two guilty men to justice. Indeed, Turner soon gained local fame because of this case and later was elected as a circuit judge in the area.

But from a constitutional point of view, his conduct was an outrage and a shocking breach of professional ethics. Turner was supposed to be Pitts and Lee's lawyer and defend them, not act like a prosecutor and help convict them. The US Supreme Court had so held in the Gideon case, of which Turner was well aware.

It therefore came as no surprise that in later years Turner tried to distance himself from the interrogation session in which his clients had confessed to the police. On February 28, 1968, I took Turner's deposition in connection with a postconviction motion we had filed in 1966 that sought to vacate Pitts and Lee's original convictions. Here is Turner's testimony at that deposition, in which he vacillated between being certain that he wasn't present during the interrogation session, on the one hand, to having no recollection of the event, on the other:

I can say this with all the accuracy in the world. At no time did I discuss the case with them [Pitts and Lee] in the presence of any other law enforcement officer, *of which I am aware right now. I don't recall any time.*

* * *

Q. I take it you have read the trial transcript of the mercy trial, August 28?

A. No sir. I have not read the trial transcript. I've never had a copy of the trial transcript.[24]

* * *

Q. Would it refresh your memory if I were to show you the testimony of Sheriff Daffin at the trial?

A. Yes, mm-hm, it would help.

Q. Particularly the second and third pages.

* OFF THE RECORD *

A. Now what is your question?

Q. My question is, did you ever attend an interrogation session with your clients, Pitts and Lee, and with Sheriff Daffin, and D. L. Barron, the Chief of Detectives in Panama City, in your presence?

A. No, sir, I don't recall any such—any such occasion that the sheriff was talking about.

* * *

Q. You have no recollection at all concerning this interrogation of sheriff—that Sheriff Daffin testified to at the trial?
A. No, I do not.[25]

But on February 2, 1968, when I took Daffin's deposition, there was no waffling on this issue. In that deposition, Daffin had reiterated his August 1963 trial testimony that Turner was indeed present during the interrogation session in question. In referring to this session, Daffin could not have been any clearer:

Q. And are you absolutely certain that Fred Turner was there?
A. I'm positive he was there, yes sir. I know he was.
Q. The reason I'm asking[,] Sheriff, is that Mr. Turner testified yesterday he wasn't there.
A. Well, he was, I don't care.[26]

Later in September 1968, at the hearing on our motion to vacate Pitts and Lee's convictions in Port St. Joe, Turner's memory improved. Here is Turner's testimony which he gave in court at an evidentiary hearing on our motion to vacate the defendants' convictions. Irwin Block, my co-counsel, did the questioning.

Q. Mr. Turner, prior to the plea of guilty did you discuss the facts of this case with the Defendants in the presence of the Sheriff?
A. Well now it's hard to say. I don't believe so.
* * *
Now it could have happened after I notified the Sheriff of our intention to plead. That at some time we were together and discussing the plea, that could have happened. But I know to what you have reference Mr. Block. But I doubt that even that happened. I say it could have, but I doubt it very seriously. . . . That's the best I—I don't recall, Mr. Block, discussing the facts of this case in front of these defendants with any of these law enforcement officers.
* * *
Q. (Mr. Block continuing) May I ask you sir, if at the trial Sheriff Daffin testified to a conversation he had with the Defendants in your presence?
A. Yes.
Q. Did you object to it?
A. Did I object to his testimony?

Q. Yes.

A. No.[27]

Indeed, there was no reason for Turner to object to Daffin's testimony. In Turner's account, Pitts and Lee had confessed in his presence after Willie Mae Lee had been brought down from the jail, as Sheriff Daffin had testified.[28] The only information Daffin added was that he had also been there and had done the questioning. Turner accepted these details at trial.

The police were no doubt delighted about all of these events. Turner was being totally cooperative with them. He had helped them get the confessions they needed. And he was neither challenging their investigation nor preparing a defense. Their entire case against Pitts and Lee was moving ahead as planned to a swift resolution and a death sentence. Although certain formalities had to be observed—a grand jury indictment, an immediate guilty plea, and a sentencing hearing—the outcome was never in doubt.

9

The Death Sentence

On August 15, 1963, with Judge Fitzpatrick presiding, eighteen white residents of Gulf County were selected in court and sworn in as members of the Gulf County Grand Jury.[1] These jurors were chosen from a list of eligible voters called a venire.[2] But eligible Black voters in Gulf County—who constituted 14.4 percent of the entire voting population of the county—were systematically excluded from this process. Indeed, the jury service cards used in the county at that time indicated "col" whenever the juror was Black, so officials knew which voters to exclude from jury service.

At an evidentiary hearing on our motion to dismiss this indictment during the new trial proceedings in 1971–1972, I asked George Core:

Q. You have been the Clerk of this Court since 1948, is that correct?
A. Yes, sir.
Q. And in your . . . memory, Mr. Core, has any Negro ever served on the Grand Jury in Gulf County prior to August 15, 1963?
A. No, sir.[3]

Later, Core sent a letter to the court correcting his testimony. He had remembered, he said, that one Black juror had served on the Gulf County Grand Jury in 1959.[4]

From a pool containing 14.4 percent of eligible Black jurors in Gulf County, it is mathematically impossible for only one Black juror in fifteen years to have been randomly selected for grand jury service without regard to race, as constitutionally required. Racial discrimination was blatant.

Nonetheless, on August 16, 1963, this illegally constituted grand jury heard testimony in the Pitts-Lee case. Witnesses were called to establish the murders. Willie Mae Lee was brought over from her jail cell to testify to her false confession. Based on this testimony, the grand jury that day indicted Pitts and Lee for the first-degree murders of Grover Floyd and Jesse Burkett.

Shortly thereafter, State Attorney J. Frank Adams filed a motion with the circuit court asking that the grand jury testimony be typed up because he needed "to determine whether perjury was committed before the grand jury."[5] Adams later testified in postconviction proceedings conducted in Port St. Joe in September 1968 that the only witness he suspected of perjury at this hearing was Willie Mae Lee, his chief witness.

This is J. Frank Adams's testimony in that hearing before the Gulf County Circuit Court. I had to drag this detail out of him in court, as he was most reluctant to admit what he had done.

Q. Mr. Adams, let me show you page 321 of the original court file in this case and ask you whether or not this is a motion which you filed in August 1963, with respect to the testimony given before the grand jury.

A. Yes sir, my signature.

Q. And in this motion I believe you stated that you suspected perjury had been committed in this case before the grand jury?

A. Yes, sir.

* * *

Q. Well, whom did you suspect of committing perjury before the grand jury?

A. I don't recall right now who I had that charge leveled against, who I was thinking about at the time, but I do know there was some changes being made in some of the statements that was given from the time I first heard it until it came before the grand jury.

Q. The only witness's testimony that was typed up in this case, was it not, was Willie Mae Lee's?

A. That's right.

Q. Would it be a fair statement then that you suspected Willie Mae Lee of perjury in this case?

A. Willie Mae had made two statements at that time. First one about Lambson Smith—

Q. One which she blamed Lambson Smith and Freddie Pitts.

A. And that's the one I was thinking about at the time.

Q. She testified before the grand jury in this case, right?

A. Yes.

Q. Which is a matter of court record now.

A. Yes.

Q. Been typed up and disclosed to both sides.

A. Yes.

Q. And in the grand jury testimony didn't she blame Freddie Pitts and Wilbert Lee for the murders?

A. Yes.

Q. And you suspected that that might be perjurious, is that correct?

A. Which one was perjury? She had sworn to the first statement?

* * *

Q. In your petition, Mr. Adams, did you not state that you needed a copy of the grand jury testimony in the case to determine "whether or not perjury was committed before the grand jury"? So you suspected that Willie Mae Lee was committing perjury before the grand jury when she blamed these murders on Wilbert Lee and Freddie Lee Pitts.

A. Not necessarily. I suspected that she had lied the first time or the second time, one. I didn't have it centered on either one.

Q. Well, now, in your petition didn't you say that you suspected perjury before the grand jury, not in your office, but before the grand jury?

A. Does the petition say that?

Q. I believe it does. (Exhibiting to witness)

A. (Witness examining) That is my signature.

Q. Did you suspect any other witness of perjury in this case besides Willie Mae Lee? The answer is no?

A. The answer is no. I didn't have anybody in mind.[6]

How a prosecutor could rightly secure an indictment and later a conviction based on perjurious testimony, particularly the perjury of his primary witness, is something Adams has never been able to explain. A prosecution attorney's highest ethical duty is not to convict but to see that justice is done. Indeed, it has long been the law that a criminal conviction in a state court based on the state's knowing use of perjured testimony renders the conviction invalid under the Fourteenth Amendment to the US Constitution.[7]

The specter of a perjury prosecution no doubt loomed large in Willie Mae Lee's mind. She had to know that if she ever withdrew her false testimony against Pitts and Lee she would be in serious trouble and would likely go to prison. That has always been the state's implied threat against Willie Mae Lee, the threat that kept her in line for as long as this case played out.

More important, the grand jury did not receive all the relevant evidence in the case. They did not hear the testimony of the two army CID investigators, Bruce Potts and Donald Hoag. These investigators were prepared to testify that Pitts had been beaten by the police, that Pitts had retracted his police confession and made a full exonerating statement to them, and that their investigation had shown that Pitts and Lee were innocent.

In fact, they traveled ninety-seven miles to Wewahitchka from Fort Rucker on their own time to give this testimony before the grand jury. But when they arrived, they learned that the grand jury had already met and had indicted Pitts and Lee. In an earlier phone call, Wayne White had given them the wrong date for the grand jury hearing, which they suspected was done intentionally.[8]

On August 17, 1963, the day after the indictments were returned, Judge Fitzpatrick dismissed the charges based on a technical flaw in the language of the indictments. However, the grand jury promptly met again the same day, and based on the testimony they had previously heard, reindicted Pitts and Lee for the same crimes but without this language flaw.

Although Turner had filed a motion to dismiss the first indictment based on this technical mistake, he made no effort to challenge the second indictment. Even though the white-only grand jury was illegally constituted, Turner filed no motion to dismiss this indictment. In fact, his motion to dismiss the first indictment was the only pleading he filed in the case.

On the same day, August 17, 1963, with Turner at their side, Pitts and Lee entered guilty pleas to these new indictments. Turner insisted that this was Pitts and Lee's sole idea, that they were resolved to do so, and that he had no obligation to advise them against taking such a drastic step.[9] Pitts and Lee, however, were terrified and were only doing what Turner and the police had forced them to agree to three days earlier.

As Turner had planned, this was an extraordinary "straight up" guilty plea that could lead to an immediate death sentence for Pitts and Lee. No plea deal of any kind had been reached in which the defendants would be sentenced to life imprisonment. In my entire legal career as a lawyer and as a judge, I have never heard of such a guilty plea in a capital case. It made no sense whatever. Those guilty pleas exposed the defendants to a death sentence and gained them nothing in return. All of this should have set off alarm bells that something terribly wrong was happening.

Nonetheless, Fitzpatrick accepted the guilty pleas and did not conduct an inquiry to determine whether they were freely and voluntarily entered. He did not ask Pitts and Lee whether anyone had threatened or forced them to plead guilty, whether any promises had been made to induce their pleas, or whether their pleas were the product of their own free will. Nor did the judge ask any questions to determine whether they understood the rights they were giving up by pleading guilty: their right to a jury trial on the issue of guilt or innocence, their right to cross-examine the witnesses against them, and their right to call witnesses and testify on their own behalf. These are routine questions that courts typically ask defendants before accepting guilty pleas in criminal cases, particularly capital cases. But no such questions were asked.

Instead, Fitzpatrick inquired only whether the defendants understood that they could be sentenced to death if they pled guilty and that a jury would be impaneled to hear this issue. Nothing more. This is the full extent of the court's plea inquiry:

> The Court. Is your name Freddie L. Pitts?
>
> Freddie L. Pitts. Yes, sir.
>
> The Court. Freddie, you are charged with two separate charges of murder in the first degree. Your attorney indicates you are ready to plead guilty to each of these indictments. You understand that if you plead guilty to either one or both of these indictments, you could be immediately sentenced to the electric chair?
>
> Freddie L. Pitts. Yes, sir.
>
> The Court. And you understand the Court will impanel a petit jury to determine if you should receive a recommendation of mercy? You understand that?
>
> Freddie L. Pitts. Yes, sir.
>
> The Court. Do you have anything to say at this time?
>
> Freddie L. Pitts. No, sir.
>
> The Court. Mr. Turner, do you have anything to say at this time?
>
> Mr. Turner. No, sir.[10]
>
> * * *
>
> The Court. Is your correct name Wilbert Lee?
>
> Wilbert Lee. Yes, sir.
>
> The Court. Have you also been known as Slingshot Lee?
>
> Wilbert Lee. Yes, sir.
>
> The Court. Wilbert, you have been indicted by the Grand Jury for murder in the first degree for the death of Grover Floyd, Jr., and another indictment for the death of Jesse L. Burkett. Your attorney states you desire to plead guilty to each of these indictments.

Are you aware that if you plead guilty to these indictments, or either of them, that you could immediately be sentenced to death in the electric chair?

Wilbert Lee. Yes, sir.

The Court. Do you understand that you would have a trial to determine only if you are entitled to mercy? Do you understand that?

Wilbert Lee. Yes, sir.

The Court. And that the Court could impanel a jury to determine if you are entitled to mercy and that would be only for that purpose?

Wilbert Lee. Yes, sir.

The Court. Do you have anything to say, Wilbert Lee?

Wilbert Lee. No, sir.

The Court. Do you have anything to say at this time, Mr. Turner?

Mr. Turner. No, sir.[11]

We will never know, but perhaps Fitzpatrick was reluctant to look too closely into whether these guilty pleas were voluntary. If he had done so, the harrowing facts of the brutal ordeal that Pitts and Lee had suffered that month might have been exposed and the state's entire case could have come apart. But that would have caused outrage among the local police and many in the white community. Perhaps it was best to leave the matter alone.

*   *   *

Under Florida law at that time, upon a plea of guilty in a capital case, the circuit court judge had the sole discretion to impose a sentence of death or life imprisonment. Accordingly, when Pitts and Lee pled guilty to the first-degree murders of Grover Floyd and Jesse Burkett, Fitzpatrick was the only person who had the power to determine whether to give these men the death penalty.

Although there was no legal authority for this procedure, Turner had asked Fitzpatrick in an informal conference to conduct a "mercy" trial for which a jury would be impaneled. The only purpose of such a trial was to determine whether the death penalty should be imposed on Pitts and Lee. Fitzpatrick had agreed, as he had always favored such a procedure in capital cases, and J. Frank Adams had no objection.

On August 28, 1963, an all-white jury was impaneled to determine whether to recommend mercy in this case, but no real case for mercy was ever presented. Instead, virtually all the evidence both the prosecutor and Turner presented called for the death penalty.

On the issue of mercy, Turner failed to show that Pitts had an exemplary record as a private in the United States Army. He could have called officers from the nearby army post where Pitts was based to vouch for Pitts's clean record. He could have introduced official records from the army to establish these facts. He also failed to show that Pitts had no prior criminal record, which he could have done by presenting official records from the FBI and other sources.

Friends and family of Pitts and Lee were also never called to testify to the defendants' good character. That included Ella Mae Lee, Lee's wife; Louise Brooks, Pitts's mother; and Pitts's fellow soldiers at the army post. All of these people were available and could have testified. They were in town or nearby. But Turner did no investigation in the community to bring these witnesses to court. Turner also failed to show that Pitts and Lee were totally cooperative with the police during the initial phases of the investigation and never made any attempt to flee the jurisdiction, although they had plenty of opportunity to do so.

At the August 1963 "mercy" trial, Willie Mae Lee was the first witness to testify. She was still in police custody and was brought over from her jail cell in Panama City, where she had been held for the previous three weeks. At the time, she no doubt feared that she might lose custody of her minor child if she deviated from the story the police had fed her. And there was also the fear that she might be charged with these murders or with perjury if she changed her testimony. To escape all of this, she knew what she had to do.

She accordingly repeated in dramatic detail her carefully rehearsed false confession that blamed Pitts and Lee for the murders. She would be released from jail later that day, but only after Pitts and Lee had been sentenced to death.

Her testimony, however, didn't fit the physical evidence in the case. She claimed that Pitts and Lee had marched Floyd and Burkett into the woods, leaving her behind near the alleged getaway car, and that she had heard two shots, had heard someone cry "Lord," and then had heard two more shots.[12] But the autopsy report filed in this case indicated that Floyd and Burkett were shot once each in the head. The two other shots Willie Mae Lee claimed she had heard were never accounted for.

She also claimed that when Pitts and Lee supposedly took the two attendants into the woods, Pitts carried a three-foot tire jack from the trunk of his car. This was the tire jack the state contended that Lee used to strike Floyd just before the shootings.[13] She also said that Pitts pistol-whipped

Floyd at the gas station.[14] But these statements were lies. The autopsy report indicates no exterior skull fractures or other injuries to Floyd's head other than the fatal bullet wound. And Gulf County Sheriff Byrd Parker's examination of the dead bodies at the murder scene found no injuries other than a single bullet wound in the head of each victim.[15] Moreover, the alleged tire jack and gun were never found despite extensive police efforts to find them.

The autopsy reports and Sheriff Parker's report of his examination of the bodies were never introduced in evidence to cast doubt on Willie Mae Lee's account. Also unmentioned was Willie Mae Lee's original statement to J. Frank Adams that blamed Lambson Smith for the murders. And most important, the jury was not informed that State Attorney J. Frank Adams suspected Willie Mae Lee of perjury.

Instead, everything came out nice and smooth without any distracting evidence that might contradict Willie Mae Lee's testimony. Turner's cross-examination of Willie Mae was short and reinforced what she had already said.

The remaining witnesses the state presented were equally incriminating and wrapped up the case. Sheriff Daffin testified that Pitts and Lee had confessed to the murders at the Bay County Jail in the presence of Fred Turner. Ludie Gaston, a local resident; Gulf County Sheriff Byrd Parker; Gulf County Deputy Sheriff Wayne White; and Dr. William Wagner further testified as to how the murdered gas station attendants were found dead in the woods, how the local police were called to the crime scene, how the bodies were transferred to a local funeral home, and how a physician pronounced the attendants dead and said that the deaths were caused by a single gunshot wound to each victim's head. Turner did not cross-examine any of these witnesses.[16]

Pitts and Lee were in court that day and listened carefully to Willie Mae Lee as she related her false story. They sat at counsel table with an attorney who was doing little or nothing to save them. They were terrified.

Fred Turner's advice to Pitts and Lee was simple: take the witness stand, repeat what Willie Mae Lee said, and beg for mercy. That was the only way, Turner said, he could save them from the electric chair.

Later, at the 1972 trial in Marianna, Pitts testified to precisely this account and the state called no witness to dispute it:

Q. Did you trust Mr. Turner?
A. Mr. Turner was like a friend to me and he was my last hope in a

situation I knew absolutely nothing about and I did place my complete faith and trust in him.

Q. Now he told you to take the witness stand and how did you know what to say?

A. Well, I had listened to Willie Mae Lee, there in the room with Sheriff Daffin and Mr. Turner present. I sit there in the courtroom and I sit here and listen to Willie Mae Lee testify.

Q. And what, if anything, did Mr. Turner tell you about Willie Mae Lee's testimony?

A. He told me that I was to take the stand and testify as to what Willie Mae Lee was saying was the truth.

Q. Had anyone else told you what the alleged facts were?

A. Sheriff Daffin through many hours of questioning, questions that would [say], "You took these men out, you killed them, you took them [to] this place, you took them [to] that place." This went on and on, I said, "all right, yes, I did it." I said this because I just got tired, I couldn't eat, my jaw was hurting me, I was tired, I was sleepy. They were questioning me all the time of the night and all the times of the day and I could only take so much.

Q. Freddie, did you have anything to do with this?

A. No, sir, I did not.

Q. Well, why did you take the witness stand and testify to a murder if you hadn't done it?

A. Mr. Turner had told me that this was the best way he could help me, and I thought with him being a lawyer that was what was supposed to be done, that he knew the best way to go about it and regardless of what was said or what was the outcome and he would come and get us out of it.

* * *

Q. Did Mr. Turner tell you that you were supposed to ask for mercy?

A. Yes, he told me that, but that was not all of what he said. He said to leave everything to him, to do what he wanted done and that he would help me.[17]

At the same 1972 trial in Marianna, Wilbert Lee gave similar testimony, which the state did not contradict:

Q. Well, during your conversation with [Turner], what did he tell you was the best thing to do in this case?

A. Well, he told me the best thing to do was for me to plea[d] guilty.

Q. Tell you anything about testifying in court?

A. Yes, sir.

Q. What did he tell you?

A. Well, when the time came for me to plead guilty I didn't know what to say. So I told him, "I don't know what to say." And he replied to me then, "Say, what Willie Mae is saying." ... He said, "After you say what Willie Mae is saying, at the end of it, tell the jury you were sorry that you committed this crime that you didn't mean to kill these men that you pray to the Lord every day to forgive you."

* * *

Q. And you say you got your facts from Willie Mae or did you get it anywhere else?

A. Well, during, from during the interrogation from Mr. Daffin and hearing these things day in and night in and out for hours and hours, well it's planted, let me tell you like this. It was run through me like a kid giving a speech. I didn't have no, I didn't know exactly what to say when I get there, see.

Q. Were you frightened when you got to court?

A. Well, of course, I was.

Q. You mentioned being physically mistreated by the police, did that have anything to do with your fear?

A. Yes, sir. It did.

Q. Tell the jury about that.

A. Well, by being in court and telling the same thing over and over again in front of the jury, well, I had to tell the same thing because the people that was surrounding me, I had to be in the[i]r custody. So, quite naturally, I wasn't going to change anything because my wife's life was threatened to shave the hair off her head and execute her and I was frightened and scared for my life as well. So, therefore, I didn't have no other choice but to say the whole thing over again which wasn't the truth, all of it was false.[18]

And so Pitts and Lee did what Turner told them to do in the August 1963 trial. They took the witness stand and in answer to Turner's prolonged questioning repeated in detail their false confessions to the police, tracking Willie Mae Lee's perjurious testimony.

Turner took twenty-one-and-a-half pages of trial transcript to walk Wilbert Lee through the events of the night in question, together with all the false things that both men had allegedly said and done, including the invented brutality that they supposedly visited upon Floyd. And Turner took another seven-and-a-half pages of trial transcript to do the same thing with Freddie Pitts. J. Frank Adams then cross-examined both Pitts and Lee about their confessions and took care to mention all the brutal and grue-some details of the two murders. This onslaught fully supported the state's case for imposing the death penalty.[19]

*   *   *

But there was a fatal flaw in the confessions Pitts and Lee made in court. Both defendants stated that Pitts had shot Floyd and Burkett at point-blank range while they were standing.[20] But according to Deputy James Graves's testimony at the March 1972 trial in Marianna, the two bodies were discov-ered stretched out full length on the ground in a more-or-less V position, which Graves visually demonstrated at trial.[21] Obviously, the bodies would never have landed on the ground in this neat, prearranged V position if they had been shot standing up. The killer had to have made Floyd and Burkett lie down on the ground in this V position before he shot them in rapid succession. Indeed, the Port St. Joe *Star* reported at the time of the ho-micides that both Floyd and Burkett had been forced to lie down or kneel on the ground before they were shot. This was an obvious conclusion from viewing the bodies at the time.[22]

Graves was never called as a witness and his findings concerning the po-sition of the bodies on the ground were not disclosed. Also not presented to the jury were the autopsy reports that showed that Floyd and Burkett were each shot once in the back of the head.[23] That report belied Lee's confession that Pitts had fired his gun four times at Floyd and Burkett at point-blank range as they stood directly in front of Pitts.[24]

Finally, Turner began presenting the defense case for mercy and it was pathetic. He left it up to Pitts and Lee to plead for themselves. Here is Wil-bert Lee's testimony:

Q. Wilbert, you know that the purpose of this jury is to determine whether or not they will recommend you to the mercy of the court?
A. Yes, sir.
Q. Do you want to give them any reason that they should do that for you?
A. Yes, sir.
Q. Then you may do that right now.
A. Jury mens, it wasn't—it wasn't my idea of killing these men. I was

only going to help this boy rob this station but as far as killing these men I didn't know it was going to happen and wasn't anything in my mind to kill those men. I am sorry the men lost their lives and I pray to the Lord each and every day to forgive me and spare me. Well, I didn't know this murder was going to happen and I don't believe I would have been there if I hadn't been drinking.[25]

Here is Freddie Pitts's testimony:

Q. Freddie, you know these twelve men here are here to see if there's to be a recommendation of mercy to the Court?
A. Yes, sir.
Q. Go ahead and tell them.
A. All I can say is I never been in any real trouble with the law and we was drinking there and just on the spur of the moment we thought about robbing the station. When I went there I didn't have any intention—I didn't have in my mind to kill these men but after we got them to this area I kind of got scared and when Slingshot hit them I just shot them. I don't know why. I had been drinking too much and it just got out of hand.[26]

I cringe whenever I read these abject pleas for mercy. And I grieve that these men had to grovel for their lives, that they were reduced to confessing to crimes they never committed, hoping against hope that somehow they would be spared.

At the conclusion of the testimony, both Fred Turner and J. Frank Adams made their final arguments to the jury. I have always been curious about what Turner could have possibly argued to the jury on the issue of mercy, given the mountain of evidence that he and the state had presented in favor of imposing the death penalty. Unfortunately, the court reporter did not record the final arguments, so there is no written record of what Turner said.

When I took Turner's deposition in February 1968, however, I asked what his strategy had been for convincing the jury to recommend mercy. Here is his reply:

Well, mercy is an ethereal quality. All our lives are built on quid pro quo. Mercy is not like that at all. I'm aware of the Merchant of Venice and Portia's statement in there about the quality of mercy, and all of the others, including the Sermon on the Mount. But we decided to put these men on, these *boys*, give them—give the jury some biographical history of their lives, and see if the jury would grant them mercy, because we were in a position, and I told them that mercy was something that you can't buy or barter, and they knew that, and they understood that, and I said, "Your appearance on the stand, if you go on the stand, will be most important."[27]

Not surprisingly, the jury was not persuaded by this hapless approach. After being instructed by the court on the law, the jury retired and within twenty minutes returned a verdict recommending that Pitts and Lee be sentenced to death.

Although he was not bound by this recommendation, Fitzpatrick imposed two death sentences on Pitts and Lee for the first-degree murders of Grover Floyd and Jesse Burkett. To a hushed and packed courtroom, he intoned the ritual of death:

You Freddie L. Pitts . . . You Wilbert Lee, alias Slingshot . . . it is the judgment of the Court and sentence of the law that you . . . be . . . delivered to the Superintendent of Florida State Prison at Raiford, Florida, to be kept by him safely until the Governor of the State of Florida shall issue his warrant commanding your execution and designating an execution date, and at the time so designated the person lawfully authorized to do so shall pass through your body a current of electricity of such intensity to cause your immediate death and the application of such current shall be continued until you are dead. And may God have mercy on your soul.[28]

The two condemned men stood before the court. They looked ashen and gaunt, like living corpses. Pitts had lost twenty-one pounds and Lee sixteen pounds during their nearly four weeks in jail.[29] Pitts's face was still swollen from the police beating he had received. But now their worst fears had come true.

Turner's assurance that all would be well if they confessed and begged for mercy had turned out to be a cruel hoax. And Turner was now through with the case. He was satisfied with the judgment and refused to institute any appeal. In his mind, justice had been done and that was the end of it. He packed up his papers, left the court, and literally abandoned his clients.

And so did everyone else in power that day—the judge, the prosecutor, the police. All satisfied that justice had been done. All blind to the fact that they had gotten it all wrong.

Lee was paralyzed with fear. Pitts collapsed into the arms of his mother, Louise Brooks, who was in the courtroom that day. She lived in Mobile, Alabama. Pitts sobbed over and over: "I didn't do it. I didn't do it."[30] The two defendants were then transferred directly from the courtroom by police car to death row at Florida State Prison in Raiford, Florida.

And on the same day that Pitts and Lee were sentenced to death, August 28, 1963, Dr. Martin Luther King Jr. was delivering his monumental "I Have a Dream" speech at the foot of the Lincoln Memorial. Speaking to the crowds gathered at the massive March on Washington, Dr. King issued a ringing cry for social justice for Black Americans, saying that he refused "to believe that the bank of justice is bankrupt."[31]

It is one of the enduring ironies of this case. As the crowd thrilled to Dr. King's soaring rhetoric in the nation's capital, a great injustice was coming to a climax in the Florida Panhandle—one that would take twelve long years to reverse.

10

The Appeal

From the moment they arrived on death row at Florida State Prison until their release from prison twelve years later, Pitts and Lee repeated over and over to anyone who would listen that they were innocent of the murders they had been convicted of.

I am well aware that many people convicted of crime and sent to prison claim they are innocent, that the vast majority of these claims are false, and that it is often difficult to discern which one of these claims have merit. Rarely, however, do prison inmates insist they are innocent with the intensity and consistency that Pitts and Lee did over such a long period of time. My colleague Maurice Rosen explained it best: "Most guys on Death Row say how they didn't get a fair trial. They talk about the legal technicalities they can employ to get out. But they never talk about guilt or innocence. The thing about Freddie Pitts . . . the thing was. He couldn't stop saying he was innocent."[1]

The same was true of Wilbert Lee. But claims of innocence were not uppermost in Lee's mind during his first days on death row. Judge Fitzpatrick had just sentenced him to die in the electric chair and had implored God to have mercy upon his soul. Any minute now, Lee thought, prison guards would come for him in his death row cell to carry out that sentence. They would drag him down the hallway, put him in the electric chair, and watch him die.

Turner had not advised his clients that none of that would be happening in the foreseeable future, that there would be an appeal in the case in which the conviction might be reversed, and that, in any event, the governor would not sign a death warrant for him until all his appeals had been exhausted, which was many years off. There would, in fact, be no immediate execution.

The prison guards on death row certainly knew all this. Executions were rare and most of the inmates on death row had been there for many years.

But they could see the fear on Lee's face and one of them decided to have some fun.

This is Lee's account of what happened:

The guard there, he say, "I want you to cut these two boys' hair, shave their head off, 'cause when they be executed we don't want it to smell bad, half scorching."

And they looked at me, see. And I was so scared to death, see. And the guy opened the door and he told the officer went away, and he said, "Get these guys a haircut 'fore they execute them. Don't want to smell their hair burning."

And he locked the door up and he hollered up to the third floor. I was on the second floor at that time. In the maximum security. They weren't putting the white and colored together.

So, after he locked the door, then he called this guy who cut hair. He said "Gena! Come down here." And some guy comes sliding down the pole like zoooooopeee, a fire house.

And he rides down and he jumps off and says, "Yes sir, boss man," and the officer says "Cut these guys hair off," and the guy had got the little tools. And the officer says, "Cut it all off" and he goes "eeeehh, eeeehh, eeh."

That's the way that went. He cut it all off. He skin it. And I thought, sure, any minute I would be executed. I was watching myself.

So the next morning the man opened the door. I want you understand this real good 'cause what I tell is the truth, see. Then the man opened the door and says, "Come on out."

I run from him and I wouldn't come out. Then he yelled for me to come out. I stuck my head out there and I was so scared. I thought I was going to be executed then, see. And they opened the door and I was shaking so bad.[2]

The prison guard, however, was there to take Lee to a nearby office in the prison building for a bureaucratic chore: to classify him as a prison inmate, not to execute him. Lee's hair had been shaved as a routine health measure that all inmates go through when admitted to Florida State Prison.

In the prison office, once Lee realized that it was all a cruel joke, that he had suffered the terror of death all through the previous night without cause, he began to calm down. But he was still shaking as the classification officer asked routine questions about Lee's identity, mail list, laundry, and the like.

Among other things, the officer inquired whether Lee had committed the murders for which he had been convicted. "Did you do this?" he asked. Here is Lee's account of what happened then:

> I told him no. I never committed no murder. Didn't know anything about it. And he said, "If you say that again God will strike you with lightning. He will strike you in that chair." And I say God won't do anything like that 'cause He knows I'm innocent.[3]

Similarly, in another interview, Freddie Pitts told his classification officer that he was innocent of the charged murders. But it was a quiet interview. Pitts was calm. He hadn't been told that they were going to execute him immediately.[4]

*   *   *

Shortly after arriving on death row, Pitts wrote to the FBI complaining about how he had been beaten by the police into confessing to murders that he had not committed. This was the first opportunity for Pitts to officially protest his mistreatment by the Gulf and Bay County police to outside authorities. It was the first of many statements that he would make in the years that followed to the effect that Deputy Sheriff George Kittrell had beaten him up during an all-night ride in a police car to find the bodies of the murdered gas station attendants and that Deputy Sheriff Wayne White was an accessory to this beating.

If what Pitts alleged was true, the actions of those two law enforcement officers were violations of federal civil rights laws.[5] Accordingly, the FBI was assigned to conduct an investigation—although, as it turned out, the investigation was perfunctory.

On October 24, 1963, two FBI agents assigned to the Jacksonville office, Clark L. Newton and John Page Jr., came to Florida State Prison, interviewed Pitts and Lee, and took statements from them that were typed up.

Here is the relevant part of Newton and Page's report of Pitts's FBI statement:

> Deputy Sheriff George Kittrell and Wayne White took me out in a squad car. Two white employees of Skipper's Mo-Jo station were missing after a robbery of the station during early morning hours of 8/1/63. Kittrell and White kept asking me where the bodies were and I kept telling them I didn't know. I was sitting on the right hand side in the back seat. Kittrell was sitting beside me. When I denied any

knowledge of the robbery or the bodies, Kittrell hit me on the head with a small blackjack. The blow knocked me out. When I regained consciousness they started to question me again.

Kittrell kept hitting me and the whole night became a blur. I remember being at Skipper's station and Skipper asking me "n——r, what did you do with those white boys?" Kittrell answered "He hasn't told us yet but he will before the night's over."[6]

Pitts also told the FBI agents that two army CID agents had seen him while he was in police custody. Pitts stated: "I told them I was innocent and they looked at the wounds I had received from the beating by Kittrell."[7] The FBI agents also interviewed Wilbert Lee, who corroborated Pitts's complaint.

Tullis D. Easterling, the FBI agent assigned to Panama City, then conducted a brief investigation. Easterling had close connections with the Bay County Sheriff's Office. He would later become the chief deputy sheriff in that office, and after Daffin died in 1971, he was elected sheriff of Bay County.[8]

Easterling briefly interviewed George Kittrell, Sheriff Daffin, and Fred Turner. All denied any knowledge that Pitts had been beaten. He also interviewed Sergeant Bruce Potts, who related his knowledge of the case.

The FBI investigation into Pitts's complaint was ultimately deemed inconclusive in the bureau's final report. Based on this finding, in December 1963, an attorney for the Civil Rights Division of the Justice Department closed out the case. No further action was taken.

If only the FBI had conducted a thorough investigation and dug a little deeper, if only Sergeant Potts's account of what happened had been taken seriously, if only the Justice Department had filed a civil rights complaint against George Kittrell and Wayne White, perhaps this tragic injustice might have been avoided and Pitts and Lee's convictions might have been overturned at the outset. But none of that happened.

The whole matter was treated as a routine prisoner complaint against local police, who denied the complaint. Brief interviews, conflicting accounts, inconclusive result, case closed.

*　*　*

At that time, however, Freddie Pitts's main concern was not the FBI. His top priority was to make certain an appeal was promptly filed and he was desperate for legal help to carry that out. Accordingly, within a week after his arrival at the prison, on September 5, 1963, Pitts began his appeal by preparing a notarized document, doubtless using other prison-written documents that he had access to and could copy as a model.[9] Pitts also wrote to Judge Fitzpatrick stating that he wanted to appeal his case but that his lawyer Fred Turner refused to do so.[10]

When Judge Fitzpatrick received this letter, he called Turner to his chambers and directed a reluctant Turner to file an appeal in the case. In his 1968 deposition, this is how Turner described what happened at that meeting:

> I was asked by Judge Fitzpatrick to come to Wewahitchka, which I did, and he told me to appeal. And I said "on what? They pled guilty. There was no recommendation of mercy. I have no grounds for appeal." He said, "appeal." I said "yes sir."[11]

Soon thereafter, Turner began an appeal for Pitts and Lee in the Florida Supreme Court but at an indifferent pace. Before long, he had missed the deadline for filing his appellate brief. His opposing counsel, Assistant Attorney General A. G. Spicola Jr., brought this matter to the court's attention and asked that Turner be ordered to comply with the appellate rules. Turner greatly resented this and wrote a bitter letter of complaint to Reeves Bowen, Spicola's superior in the Office of the Attorney General.[12]

Eventually, however, Turner filed his brief with the court. In that document, he made it clear that he had no desire to take this appeal, that he was only going through the motions, and that his clients were guilty. He even underlined the word "directed" to emphasize how reluctant he was to take this appeal:

> At the outset of this appeal, appellate counsel wishes the Court to know that he was *directed* by the Circuit Judge to institute and perfect this appeal. The undersigned could find no evidence that the defendants have been mistreated in any way at any state of these proceedings. Their pleas were freely and voluntarily entered.[13]

The brief itself was three pages long. It cited no legal authorities: no statutes, no constitutional provisions, no past court decisions. Truly extraordinary. By any standards, it was one of the worst appellate briefs in a capital case that one could possibly imagine.

The sole point raised on appeal was that Judge Fitzpatrick had erred in impaneling a jury to determine whether to recommend mercy, even though

Turner himself had asked the judge for such a trial, a fact that Turner's brief concealed from the court. Under Florida law, it is settled that on appeal a party is barred from claiming error for an action of the trial court where the party has asked the court for such action. It is called the Invited Error Rule.[14]

In later postconviction proceedings, Turner admitted in a deposition that there was no legal authority to support his argument and that his appeal, in effect, was frivolous:

Q. There are no legal authorities in your brief, are there?
A. I'm not sure. I think there was a case. Yes, I'm pretty sure there was at least one case, is there not?

* * *

Q. Let me give you a copy—what purports to be a copy [of] a brief with your name on it, and ask you whether or not that's the brief you filed in the Supreme Court?
A. That is no—
Q. There are no legal authorities cited on that?
A. No, no legal authorities cited. And it was on the sole question of whether or not he [the judge] erred in impaneling the jury.
Q. That was a frivolous point, wasn't it?
A. It was the only point I had.
Q. It was also frivolous, wasn't it?
A. It was not the—
Q. When you asked for it?
A. Just a moment. It was not frivolous. The court rendered a two and [a] half page decision, if you recall. You read the decision, I'm sure you have it.
Q. Well, you asked for this jury to be impaneled yourself, didn't you?
A. Exactly so, but you see—
A. Well, you are aware you cannot assign anything [as] error unless you preserve it in the lower court and object?
A. Exactly so.
Q. You didn't object to this, did you?
A. I did not. I requested it.
Q. How on earth can you assign it as error, then?
A. That was my question exactly to Judge Fitzpatrick, when he said, "Appeal." I said, "on what?" He said, "Appeal." I said, "Yes sir."

* * *

Q. In your career, have you ever written an appellate brief with no legal authorities in it, other than this one?
A. No.
Q. This is the first time you've written an appellate brief with no legal authorities in it?
A. That's correct.[15]

Instead of raising what was patently a frivolous point, Turner could have raised a point that had some real legal merit. He could have argued in his brief that Pitts and Lee's guilty pleas were improperly accepted by Judge Fitzpatrick because the judge never made any inquiry on the record to determine whether their pleas were freely and voluntarily entered.

The law is settled that a guilty plea in a criminal case must be shown to be freely and voluntarily entered. Otherwise, it cannot be accepted by the trial judge—particularly, as here, where a defendant may be sentenced to death. This legal principle requires the trial judge to conduct an inquiry of the defendant to determine whether the guilty plea is being freely and voluntarily entered. Because Pitts and Lee's guilty pleas were not shown on the record to be voluntary, their convictions should have been reversed and the case sent back to the trial court with directions to conduct a new trial.[16]

But Turner didn't raise this point. On the contrary, he was complicit with the police in obtaining Pitts and Lee's coerced guilty pleas. He even told the court that the guilty pleas were free and voluntary:

Q. Did either Mr. Pitts or Mr. Lee authorize you to state in the brief that quote: The undersigned could find no evidence that the defendants had been mistreated in any way at any stage of the proceedings. Their pleas were freely and voluntarily entered?
A. No, they did not authorize that statement.[17]

As a result, Pitts and Lee had no real advocate on appeal—any more than they had had a real advocate at trial. Indeed, it is surprising to me that the court didn't remove Turner as counsel on appeal and appoint another lawyer to represent Pitts and Lee or at least strike Turner's brief and order him to file a competent one.

* * *

While this appeal was pending and before the Florida Supreme Court rendered its decision, Pitts wrote a series of letters to the United States Army asking for legal help. Pitts was technically still a private in the army. In these letters, he said he was innocent and had been forced to plead guilty by the local police. The letters were referred to the army's Judge Advocate General's Office in New Orleans. First Lieutenant Jack M. Winick, a young lawyer, was assigned to the case.

On February 13, 1964, Winick telephoned Fred Turner to make an appointment to discuss the appeal. But Turner was unavailable. Winick spoke with the office secretary and left a message, requesting Turner to return the call. Turner never did.[18]

As a result, on February 17, 1964, Winick dropped by unannounced at Turner's office in Lynn Haven. A secretary there allowed Winick to read Turner's file on Pitts and Lee's case. The file was thin and included Turner's three-page appellate brief. What bothered him most was that Turner had pled Pitts guilty to a capital crime with no prior negotiated plea agreement wherein Pitts would avoid the death penalty and be sentenced to life imprisonment. In a detailed memorandum that he later wrote to his superiors, Winick wrote: "A plea of guilty is an extremely questionable plea to a charge of first degree murder."[19]

The next day, on February 18, 1964, Winick traveled to Florida State Prison, where he interviewed Pitts at length. After hearing the harrowing story of how Pitts had been treated by the police, Winick became greatly disturbed. He believed Freddie Pitts and resolved to do something about it.[20]

On March 16, 1964, Winick wrote a long memorandum to his superiors explaining the case in some detail, hoping that he might continue on the case so he could get some legal help for Pitts from the American Civil Liberties Union and maintain his correspondence with Pitts.[21] But the army refused on the ground that it had no jurisdiction in the matter and ordered Winick to remove himself from the case, which he did.[22]

But Winick never let go. After his discharge from the army, Winick returned to his home in Minneapolis, Minnesota, where he practiced law, and began a long correspondence with Pitts and others in which he sought legal help for Pitts. He visited Pitts and Lee in prison many times over the years and attended all of the important court hearings that followed in the case at his own expense. He was a modest man with a deep sense of justice based on his religious beliefs.

I got to know Jack Winick quite well after I entered the case in June 1965. I spoke with him many times at court hearings and elsewhere during my many years as defense counsel. Winick was always listed as one of the lawyers for Pitts and Lee in the pleadings we filed in the case. I liked and admired Winick for his steadfast loyalty to both these men. They considered Winick a dear friend, as indeed he was.

* * *

Meanwhile on May 29, 1964, the Florida Supreme Court issued its decision affirming Pitts and Lee's convictions. This result was not surprising, given Turner's virtual capitulation in the case.

The court was unaware that Turner had asked Judge Fitzpatrick to impanel the mercy trial jury that Turner was claiming on appeal was reversible error. In its opinion, the court did not recite this fact and expressed some uncertainty about why the judge proceeded as he did. Accordingly, the court did not discuss whether this issue had been properly preserved for appellate review as an invited error. Instead, the court decided Turner's claim on the merits and rejected it.

In its written decision, the court concluded that

(1)   it was error for Judge Fitzpatrick to have convened a jury to decide whether to recommend mercy in this case as there was no authority for such a procedure,

(2)   it would have been better procedure if the judge had rejected Pitts and Lee's guilty pleas and allowed the case to be tried on their pleas of not guilty, but

(3)   the error in convening the jury was harmless because the record showed that the judge made an independent decision to impose the death penalty aside from the jury's recommendation.

The court stated:

Under the law the responsibility for determining whether each defendant should atone for this double crime by forfeiting his life or spending the rest of his life in prison was strictly the judge's and there was no power vested in him to delegate that burden to the jury. It would have been more consonant with established legal procedure for him to have rejected the pleas, caused pleas of not guilty to be entered and proceeded to try fully the cases. It is indicated in the acts that refusal of a guilty plea may be proper as there is reference to what may be done "if" the court accepts pleas of guilty. But it does not follow that there was an actual delegation of responsibility by the judge or any attempt to shirk it. The record does not reveal why he pursued the course and we would only be guessing were we to undertake to explain it. The fact remains that after the testimony of the witnesses had been heard the judge decided independently, though his conclusion may have been strengthened by the verdicts, that no mercy should be shown, when he recited in his judgment, after referring to the verdicts, "and the Court having determined that you are not so entitled [to a recommendation of mercy] it is the judgment of the Court and sentence of the law that you" be executed.

* * *

The judgment is affirmed.[23]

Following this decision, Fred Turner filed no motion for rehearing, made no arrangements for another lawyer to take his place, and withdrew from the case. For his services as court-appointed counsel at trial and on appeal, Turner was awarded a total of $2,000 in attorney's fees—the statutory maximum.[24]

Fortunately for Pitts and Lee, Florida governor C. Farris Bryant did not sign a death warrant for them. In those days, the governor's office usually delayed issuing a death warrant in capital cases until all court proceedings in the case had been completed. The governor generally gave death row inmates ample time to acquire additional counsel after the Florida Supreme Court had affirmed their convictions so that new counsel could file additional legal proceedings in the courts.

The case remained in limbo for nearly a year while arrangements for substitute counsel were being made. Eventually, however, in the summer of 1965, the American Civil Liberties Union in Florida agreed to take the case and assigned one of its volunteer lawyers to represent Pitts and Lee, a representation that lasted for the next ten years.

But that is another story. The first major phase of this case had come to an end. The second phase was about to begin.

II

THE NEWLY DISCOVERED EVIDENCE (1965–1971)

11

Pitts and Lee Get a New Lawyer and the State's Case Begins to Collapse

Pitts and Lee were now on death row with no lawyer. In desperation, Pitts wrote a number of people, begging for legal help. One of those letters reached the American Civil Liberties Union (ACLU) in Miami, Florida. As in all his other letters at the time, Pitts asserted that he and Lee were innocent of the Floyd-Burkett murders and had been forced to plead guilty. Jack Winick wrote similar letters on Pitts and Lee's behalf.

At the time, the ACLU represented any indigent inmate on death row who asked for legal help because in its view, the death penalty constituted "cruel and unusual punishment" in violation of the Eighth Amendment to the US Constitution. A civil liberties issue is necessarily involved in any capital case, and the defense of civil liberties has long been the central mission of this historic organization.

So in the summer of 1965, the ACLU in Miami accepted the case of Pitts and Lee and assigned the matter to its legal panel, which consisted of a number of volunteer lawyers who worked pro bono. The panel was spearheaded by two prominent Miami lawyers, Irwin Block and Tobias Simon.

Block's initial reaction to the case was that Pitts and Lee didn't need a lawyer, at least not right then. Instead, they needed an investigator to look into their claims of innocence. Accordingly, the ACLU hired Charles Cook, a private detective, to go to Port St. Joe and investigate the case. Cook was an unfortunate choice. He had a Brooklyn accent and an abrasive manner. He spent a short time in the Port St. Joe area trying to dig into the case and got nowhere. No one in authority would talk to him. After a few days, Cook gave up and returned to Miami.[1] Soon thereafter, the ACLU assigned the Pitts-Lee case to me under the most fortuitous of circumstances. But first a little background.

*   *   *

In the summer of 1965, I was working as an assistant public defender with the Dade County Public Defender's Office in Miami. I had been hired in January of that year. It was a state office and my annual salary was $7,500, which in those days was a modest but livable income.

I was originally from Rock Island, Illinois, a midsize town on the Mississippi River about 250 miles north of St. Louis, Missouri. My wife Martha, a former schoolteacher, worked as a clerk at the University of Miami Library. She was originally from outside Birmingham, Alabama. We had a small apartment in the Miami area and managed nicely on our two incomes.

Miami at that time was considered a "northern city," not part of the Deep South. The greater Miami area was settled and later populated mostly by transplanted northerners. Miami Beach was thriving with a vibrant Jewish community. It was the golden era for the hotels there. Headliners like Frank Sinatra and Dean Martin regularly entertained the tourists. It was a vacation mecca. The total population of Dade County was more than 1 million, making it the largest county in the state. Like all large cities, Miami had its racial and ethnic problems, but it was in essence a northern city. It was said that the farther north from Miami you traveled, the further south you were.

I was 29 years old and filled with youthful idealism and energy that had yet to be tempered by much real-world experience. I had an unbounded optimism in the ultimate justice of our legal system and was swept away by the idealism of the 1960s. Progressive change was in the air, led by the great civil rights movement of the day, the soaring rhetoric of John F. Kennedy and Martin Luther King Jr., the legislative accomplishments of Lyndon Johnson, and the groundbreaking opinions of the US Supreme Court. It was an optimistic time.

Despite my young age, I was no novice to criminal law practice and was brimming with self-confidence. I had previously spent two years doing public defender work in Washington, DC, after graduating from Duke University Law School in June 1961. I worked in the E. Barrett Prettyman Legal Internship Program at Georgetown University Law Center (1961–1962), and at the Legal Aid Agency for the District of Columbia (now the Public Defender Service) (1962–1963). While working with both groups, I handled a wide variety of felony cases in the United States District Court for the District of Columbia. These cases involved charges such as murder, manslaughter, armed robbery, burglary, auto theft, and a host of other matters. I was in court frequently and tried twenty-five of these cases before a jury, winning most of them.

Based on this experience, I was hired in August 1963 as a criminal defense lawyer by the prominent Miami law firm of Nichols, Gaither, Beckham, Colson & Spence. I worked directly with founding partner Perry Nichols, who was a legend in the legal community. I helped Nichols try a highly publicized manslaughter case in West Palm Beach.

But I missed public defender work, my first love. So I returned to it a year later, when a position opened up at the Dade County Public Defender's Office. In response to the 1963 US Supreme Court decision in *Gideon v. Wainwright,*[2] which held that an indigent defendant charged with a felony was entitled to a court-appointed counsel, Florida immediately adopted a new statewide public defender system.

Public defender work was not just a job for me, it was a calling. I was dedicated to providing top-level legal services to people who were in terrible trouble with the law and had no lawyer to protect them. I considered it a public service, a contribution to the system of justice and a challenge to gain the confidence of my clients who were generally suspicious of public defenders. I longed to serve in a public defender office that equaled the legal talent and investigative power of the police and prosecutors who were arrayed against us. I fully intended to make a career out of public defender work.

At the time, the Dade County Public Defender's Office in Miami consisted of seven lawyers, an office manager, and two secretaries. We were located in a corner niche on the fifth floor of the Metro Justice Building, the local criminal court building, a modern twelve-story structure that was not luxurious but comfortable to work in. The much larger State Attorney's Office, which occupied an entire floor directly above us, had an impressive staff of lawyers, investigators, and secretaries.

I was assigned to handle all the appeals in the office with the aid of one secretary. My caseload hovered around seventy-five pending appeals, and keeping up with all the work was a daunting task. I was able to do my legal research across the street from my office in the law library of the Third District Court of Appeal of Florida, one of the three intermediate appeals courts in the state. This was the court before which I primarily practiced. The judges' law clerks also worked in the same library, and I soon became friendly with all of them.

Although I had only occasional success, I earned a good reputation before the District Court of Appeal. Several of the law clerks told me that the judges were impressed with my work, particularly Judge Charles Carroll, the chief judge. I was in court frequently making oral arguments.

Sometimes I had the whole court calendar for the morning, opposed by a succession of assistant attorney generals. And I was constantly filing briefs with the court, raising a variety of legal claims.

One of the judge's law clerks was quite helpful. He told me confidentially that the judges did not like my frequent reliance on US Supreme Court decisions. It was all right to cite these cases secondarily, he said, but I should place my main reliance on Florida Supreme Court and Florida District Court decisions. It was shrewd advice, and I soon followed it.

In those days, the US Supreme Court was extremely unpopular among many trial and appellate judges throughout Florida. This was less true in Miami, as the area was more liberal and centrist than the rest of the state. Nonetheless, with few exceptions, Florida judges across the state were judicial conservatives at odds with the Court's decisions, particularly in school desegregation and criminal cases. We public defenders faced an uphill battle in the Florida courts.

Despite these difficult times and the huge caseload we all had, the Dade County Public Defender's Office was exceptionally friendly and a joy to work in. Robert Koeppel, the elected public defender, was a charming, funny, and delightful man. The other six lawyers, the office manager, and the two secretaries were all cheerful, accommodating, and easy to work with.

Nonetheless, I greatly disapproved of one aspect of the office: it was a part-time office. Every lawyer was allowed to have a private civil law practice, and everyone did. These lawyers usually came to work only twice a week, on Tuesday and Thursday mornings, and tried their cases without a jury, spending about ten or fifteen minutes per case with everybody standing up as if it were a traffic matter. Defendants were almost always convicted and given a light sentence—no more than eighteen months imprisonment. Many were sentenced only to county jail time. I used to call these trials slow pleas of guilty.

In my opinion, no lawyer, no matter how talented, could handle the huge felony caseload we all had working on a part-time basis. Cases needed to be carefully prepared and tried with a jury by full-time lawyers, as had been my practice in Washington, DC. I was the only lawyer in the office who worked full time.

*   *   *

In those days, the public defender did not represent defendants charged with capital crimes. All of my appeals were from convictions for noncapital felonies. Because I wanted to broaden my experience by handling a capital crime appeal, I resolved to look outside the office for such a case. Fortunately, there was a way to do it. While I chose not to pursue a private civil law practice, I was allowed, under certain circumstances, to handle a pro bono criminal case, preferably an appeal outside Dade County.

Accordingly, in the summer of 1965, after getting the proper clearance, I volunteered my services for a pro bono capital crime appeal with the ACLU in Miami. The legal panel of this group assigned me to represent Freddie Pitts and Wilbert Lee. Maurice Rosen, the managing lawyer of the legal panel, delivered the file to my office and I started working on it. At that time, the Pitts and Lee case was not the high-profile affair that it would soon become. If it had been, I doubt I would have gotten it. It was just a routine matter that the ACLU was handling and entirely appropriate for a newcomer to the legal panel like me.

When Rosen gave me the Pitts and Lee file, he supplied some statistical research that the ACLU had done on the Gulf County Grand Jury that had indicted the clients I represented. This research showed that grand juries in Gulf County had been consistently all-white over a period of many years, despite the fact that 14.4 percent of registered voters in the county were Black men and women—all eligible for jury service yet somehow never called to serve on the grand jury.

Based on this research, I filed a postconviction motion with the Gulf County Circuit Court to vacate the convictions of Pitts and Lee. A motion to vacate asks the court to set aside a defendant's criminal conviction and order a new trial. The basis for my motion was the fact that Pitts and Lee had been indicted by a grand jury from which eligible Black voters had been systematically excluded in violation of the Fourteenth Amendment.

I communicated by letter with Pitts and Lee, sent them a copy of the motion, and kept them apprised about the progress of the appeal. I did not, however, interview them in prison at Raiford, Florida, which was hundreds of miles away in North Florida. I relied entirely on the appellate record for the facts of the case and did not look beyond it. Appeals are based on the written record at trial. Additional evidence and testimony from the defendant or other witnesses are not admissible in the appellate court. Appellate judges and lawyers therefore rely entirely on the appellate record for the facts of a given case. Only issues of law may be raised based on the facts as shown by that record, nothing else.

Shortly thereafter, a Gulf County circuit judge summarily denied my motion to vacate without conducting an evidentiary hearing as I had requested—a not unexpected result. I then took an appeal to the First District Court of Appeal in Tallahassee, where again I had little hope of success. I filed an extensive brief, and as expected, this intermediate appeals court affirmed the circuit court's decision without issuing a written opinion—a so-called PCA decision (per curiam affirmed).[3] Florida courts at that time were generally unfriendly to criminal defendants who raised federal constitutional claims.

I then petitioned the US Supreme Court for further review. I bypassed the Florida Supreme Court, as that court had no jurisdiction to review, as here, a PCA decision by an intermediate appeals court. My petition in the US Supreme Court was a long shot, as the Court granted very few of such petitions. I expected a denial and began making plans to file a federal habeas corpus petition in the lower federal courts. As expected, the US Supreme Court eventually denied my petition for review without issuing a written opinion.[4]

We turn now to what Curtis Adams was doing during this time. Before and while I was pursuing our motion to vacate Pitts and Lee's convictions, Adams was engaged in certain criminal activity that would lead to the collapse of the case against Pitts and Lee and to the defendants' eventual exoneration.

In August 1963, after Adams and Mary Jean Akins split up, Adams made his way to the Florida Keys, where he soon returned to his life of crime. On December 30, 1963, Adams and an accomplice, James Anderson, were arrested for armed robbery outside Marathon, Florida. Adams and Anderson had just held up a small loan company in Key West at gunpoint and were attempting to escape the area by car. US 1 is the only road to the mainland from Key West, and they were arrested at a police roadblock. On April 16, 1964, Adams was convicted and sentenced to twenty years in prison for this robbery.[5]

But Adams had no intention of serving this sentence. A few days later, he sent word that he wanted to talk to Lieutenant Terry Jones of the Key West Police Department. Jones was the investigating officer on Adams's Key West robbery. When Jones responded, Adams said that he had information about an armed robbery and homicide of two gas station attendants in Port St. Joe.[6] He wanted to be transferred to the jail in Port St. Joe and talk to Gulf County Sheriff Byrd Parker. Adams knew the Port St. Joe jail was rickety, and he had a plan to escape once he was transferred.[7]

Jones was skeptical but somewhat intrigued when he heard Adams describe the details of these murders, so he telephoned Gulf County Sheriff

Byrd Parker in Adams's presence, explained the situation, and handed the phone to Adams. Adams spoke to Parker for a short time, but Parker scoffed at the entire idea. He told Adams "he already had two n———s in Raiford waiting for the [electric] chair" for those murders.[8] Jones then got back on the phone and was told much the same thing and that Adams was a liar.[9] Jones seemed satisfied and dropped the matter.

But Adams was amazed. This was the first time he learned that two Black men had been convicted and sentenced to death for murders that he had committed. As Adams later told Warren Holmes, the Miami lie detector examiner who broke open the case:

Q. What were your thoughts when you knew that two [men] had been convicted of killing Burkett and Floyd when you knew that, in fact, you had done it?
A. I didn't know what to think when Mr. Parker told me they [Pitts and Lee] was convicted and waiting for the chair.
Q. Were you shocked?
A. Sure I was. I knowed that they had them, but I didn't know they convicted them and sent them to the chair, sentenced them to the chair.[10]

A week later, Adams soon hatched another plan to break free. On April 25, 1964, Adams and his accomplice, James Anderson, escaped from the Key West jail and once again tried to flee the area. But they were soon caught, and Adams was sentenced to ten years imprisonment for this escape, the sentence to run consecutively with his 20-year sentence for robbery, making a total of thirty years.[11]

A month later, Curtis Adams was transferred to Florida State Prison to serve his 30-year sentence. He had no contact with Pitts and Lee, who were held in an isolated part of the same prison on death row. Adams soon became acquainted with Jesse Pait, a wiry 42-year-old white inmate serving life imprisonment for first-degree murder. They had cells near each other across a corridor and used to gossip for hours to escape the boredom of prison life. They called it "celling."[12]

Time passed, and over a thirteen-week period in 1965, Adams began boasting that he had committed several murders for which he had never been caught. He explained in some detail how he had robbed and killed two gas station attendants in Port St. Joe and another gas station attendant in Fort Lauderdale. Pait returned the banter.[13]

This exchange of confidences among prison inmates was not surprising.

Murderers are respected and even feared in prison. Other inmates generally don't bother them. So the two men naturally gravitated toward each
other to share mutual experiences. They were both killers and had much in
common.

Jesse Pait was from Durham, North Carolina, and spoke with a nervous
southern drawl. During World War II, he had been a paratrooper for the
101st Airborne Division and was wounded in the D-Day invasion. But since
then, he had drifted into a life of crime.[14]

*　　*　　*

Seemingly unrelated to all this, something of significance was developing
in South Florida. On Sunday September 26, 1965, the *Miami Herald*, Miami's leading newspaper, ran a front-page story on the unsolved murder of
Floyd McFarland, the Fort Lauderdale gas station attendant whom Adams
had robbed and killed.[15] Accompanying that story on the front page was an
insert that offered a reward of $15,000 to anyone "furnishing information
resulting in the conviction of the person responsible for the death of Floyd
Earl McFarland."[16]

There was a reason for this reward. The *Miami Herald* had received
confidential information that Tal Buchanan, the elected sheriff in Dade
County, had accidentally killed McFarland in a hit-and-run traffic accident. The newspaper was investigating alleged wrongdoing by an important public official and the editor felt that the reward might help journalists
discover what happened. As it turned out, this confidential information
was entirely false; Buchanan had nothing to do with the McFarland murder. Five pathologists—including Joseph Davis, the Dade County medical
examiner—examined McFarland's body after it was exhumed and unani-
mously confirmed what the initial autopsy had found: Floyd McFarland
had died from two gunshots to the head, not in a traffic accident.[17]

Nonetheless, the *Herald*'s $15,000 reward helped solve the crime. While
in prison, Jesse Pait read about the reward in the *Miami Herald*, as he had
access to the major newspapers in the state. He remembered how Adams
had told him about the McFarland murder and decided to turn Adams in
for the money.[18] But he knew he had to be careful and remain anonymous.
If he did not, Adams would no doubt kill him.

On January 3, 1966, Pait wrote a carefully worded letter to Detective Edward Clode of the Broward County Sheriff's Office, who was working the
McFarland case.[19] In the letter, Pait said that he had sensitive information

that he could not then disclose and wanted to talk to Clode. After a further exchange of correspondence, Clode decided to respond.[20]

On March 7, 1966, Detective Clode and Deputy Sheriff Joseph Mazur traveled to Raiford and met Jesse Pait in the interview room at the east wing of Florida State Prison. They introduced themselves and displayed their police identification. Pait was extremely nervous and refused to speak in the presence of Mazur. Pait had written to Clode and would talk only to him. Mazur left the room, taking his audio recording device with him.[21] Pait had seen the device and wanted no tape recording of the interview. He asked if he could search Clode for any hidden listening devices. Clode agreed and the search revealed no such equipment. Even then, Pait was unwilling to talk. He said he feared for his life, and before he said anything he wanted to be transferred to another facility in the prison. He and Clode then verbally fenced for over an hour about that subject. Finally, Clode conferred with an assistant prison superintendent, who promised to arrange for such a transfer.

Given this assurance, Jesse Pait finally began with some hesitation: "Curtis Adams killed Floyd McFarland." He then explained in hushed detail everything Adams had told him about the murder. Clode took furious notes. He had been investigating the McFarland murder for over two years and thought that now he might have a lead that would break open the case. He did.

Pait would later reveal Adams's confession to the Port St. Joe murders to Broward police. He would do so soon, but not then. That confession carried no money; the McFarland confession did. But in writing this letter to Clode, Jesse Pait set in motion a series of events that would lead to the conviction of Curtis Adams for the murder of Floyd McFarland. It would also lead to the exoneration of Pitts and Lee for the Port St. Joe murders.

I have often reflected how serendipitous all of this was. If the *Miami Herald* had not put up the $15,000 reward based on totally mistaken information, Jesse Pait would have had no motive to turn Adams in to the Broward County Sheriff's Office, no one in authority would have known of Adams's confessions to the murders of McFarland or to the Floyd and Burkett murders, and Pitts and Lee would have remained on death row for crimes they did not commit. What set things in motion was a complete fluke—the *Miami Herald* reward based on misinformation. What a godsend for Pitts and Lee.

*   *   *

To check out Jesse Pait's story, Chief Detective Lawrence Lang of the Broward County Sheriff's Office tracked down Mary Jean Akins at her home in Winter Haven, Florida. Pait had said that Akins (known only as "Billie") was living with Adams when McFarland was murdered. Akins confirmed that this was true, although she had not seen Adams in two years. She had been pregnant by Adams when they had broken up in August 1963 and a lot had happened since then. She had given birth, her brutal husband had died, and she had remarried. She was now living in this small citrus town in Central Florida with her new husband and children. She said that she was happy for the first time in a long while.

Akins was still terrified of Curtis Adams and would never have turned him in because she was afraid that he would kill her. While Adams was in the Key West jail, she had even given him a metal file that he demanded so he could escape from that jail in order to keep him happy. But in the end, she was an honest person and felt that she had no alternative but to tell the police the truth when they sought her out. In a formal statement to Lang, Mary Jean related her knowledge of the McFarland murder, namely, that Adams had killed a gas station attendant in Fort Lauderdale. Her story checked out in part; the Broward County police confirmed through various sources that the two had been living together in Fort Lauderdale at the time of the McFarland murder.[22]

Broward County police thought that now it was time to confront Curtis Adams. On May 6, 1966, Lang questioned Curtis Adams in prison. But he got nowhere. Adams denied any knowledge of the murder of Floyd McFarland and demanded a lawyer. After that, Adams brooded for months. Why had the police come to see him? Who had tipped off the authorities? He soon became convinced that only Mary Jean Akins could have done this, not knowing that his "friend" Jesse Pait was the informer. And Broward police, who always protected Pait's identity, encouraged Adams to believe that. Adams was furious and slowly began to plan his revenge.[23]

Many months later, as the investigation continued on various fronts, Broward County police decided to zero in on Adams. They had him transferred from Raiford Prison to the Broward County Jail in Fort Lauderdale for questioning. Several days later, Chief Detective Lawrence Lang interrogated Adams again. And again Adams refused to talk and demanded a lawyer.

This time, the police honored the request. Broward Circuit Court judge Richard Saul appointed Charles Rich, a local criminal lawyer, to represent Adams. Rich interviewed Adams at the jail and gave the standard defense lawyer advice: don't talk to the police or anyone else about the case.[24] But Adams, now protected by a lawyer, had other ideas. With revenge apparently on his mind, Adams sent word from his jail cell that he wanted to make a statement concerning the McFarland murder. It would be his undoing.[25]

Lang, although wary, had Adams brought to the Detective Bureau at the Broward County Sheriff's Office. He also summoned Charles Rich. Despite Rich's advice, Adams told Lang that he would make a statement about the McFarland murder on one condition: he first wanted to go to Port St. Joe and confer with the state attorney, J. Frank Adams, who had been the local prosecutor in the Pitts and Lee case.

By then, Broward County police knew that Adams had been in Gulf County in July and August 1963 and were aware of the murders of Floyd and Burkett. They suspected Adams of committing this crime, which was extremely similar to the McFarland murder. In both cases, a gas station attendant had been robbed at gunpoint late at night, taken to a secluded rural area, and killed. This was a most unusual pattern for a gas station robbery/murder; typically in such cases, the victim was found killed at the station. And the two crimes had been committed only two weeks apart. It looked like the same person had committed both crimes.[26]

So on October 31, 1966, Broward County police chartered a private plane and flew Adams to the airport in Panama City. An impressive array of law enforcement officers came along, including Broward County sheriff Tom Walker; George Watts, an investigator for the Florida attorney general; and three Broward County police officers—Chief Detective Lawrence Lang, Deputy Sheriff George Sullivan, and Detective Elihu Phares. The police rented two cars to travel to Port St. Joe.[27]

Adams then told the police he needed to show them something to prove his good faith. Although skeptical, the police agreed. With Phares doing the driving, Adams directed everyone over a considerable distance to a particular spot in the woods in adjoining Gulf County. None of the Broward County officers had been to that location before.

Here is Phares's account of that trip in testimony he gave before the Gulf County Circuit Court in September 1968 at a hearing in Port St. Joe on our motion to set aside the defendants' convictions:

> When we arrived at Panama City, we rented two automobiles. I drove one of the rental automobiles in which Curtis Adams rode. We left Panama City airport and proceeded toward Port St. Joe. On the way

to Port St. Joe in the presence of Curtis Adams and Deputy Sullivan and Mr. George Watts was in the car, Curtis Adams said he wanted to display to us his sincerity in this trip because we questioned his sincerity. And he said that to show us his sincerity before we talked to Mr. [J. Frank] Adams there was something he wanted us to see.

Q. What happened?

A. I told him to give directions and he led me into the downtown area of Port St. Joe, pointed out the gas station where Burkett and Floyd were employed at the night of their disappearance.[28]

Q. Go ahead.

A. He led us north on Highway 71 in front of where this courthouse is located now, across a bridge which was unfamiliar to me, and on northward to an intersection on a highway, I believe if I recall it was Highway 387, directed us to turn right. I did, we went about a mile along this highway and he directed me to stop at a canal culvert that traversed this road on the far side of the canal. I did. I asked him what we were here for, and he said this is where the bodies of Floyd and Burkett were. This was where they were murdered, and [he said], "I will tell you who murdered them after I talk to J. Frank Adams."[29]

But there was more to come. This was only the general area where the murders had taken place. Adams then led Phares out of the rental car into the woods to the exact spot where Adams said the two men had been shot and killed. Phares continued:

Q. Did anything else occur at that place?

A. He led us out of the automobile down a dirt road for a distance of about—again I'm estimating—75 to 100 yards—and pointed back into the woods and said the bodies were under a tree.[30]

But was this really true? Was that the location where Floyd and Burkett had been shot and killed? Shortly thereafter, Phares found out. That day, he contacted Gulf County Deputy Sheriff Wayne White and asked White to show him the exact place in the countryside where the police had found the bodies of Floyd and Burkett in August 1963. White did so. And it was the same spot in the woods that Adams had led the Broward police to.[31]

In so doing, Curtis Adams had provided damning evidence against himself: he knew exactly where Floyd and Burkett had been murdered. Why would he do such a thing when he was under investigation only for the McFarland murder? It was extraordinary.

The next day, the meeting that Curtis Adams wanted with the local prosecutor took place. The Broward County police drove Adams to a restaurant facing the Gulf of Mexico outside Port St. Joe. At this prearranged location, J. Frank Adams, the Gulf County prosecutor, had a private conversation with Curtis Adams in a parked car in the restaurant's parking lot.

What would he tell J. Frank Adams? How could he explain away his knowledge of where Floyd and Burkett had been murdered? The Broward County police had no idea. It was here that Curtis Adams attempted his revenge. He told the prosecutor that he knew all about the murders of Floyd and Burkett, that he was an eyewitness, and that Mary Jean Akins had committed the murders. The prosecutor wasn't impressed. He listened in silence and left.

Everyone then returned to Fort Lauderdale, where the next day Curtis Adams tried to enact the second part of his revenge. He accused Mary Jean Akins of the McFarland murder, detailing how he had been an eyewitness to it all. Broward County State Attorney Quentin Long took a formal statement from Adams to that effect.[32]

Given these conflicting sworn statements about who had committed the McFarland murder, Long thought it best to charge both suspects and investigate further. On November 13, 1966, the Broward County grand jury indicted Curtis Adams and Mary Jean Akins for the first-degree murder of Floyd McFarland. To Akins's horror, she was arrested and taken to jail in Fort Lauderdale.[33]

Both Adams and Akins appeared in Broward County Circuit Court on October 30, 1966, for an arraignment. Adams, represented by Charles Rich, refused to plead and a plea of not guilty was entered for him. Akins was represented by Leonard Fleet, a prominent local attorney who would later become a Broward County circuit judge. Akins pled not guilty.[34]

Immediately thereafter, Adams and Akins faced each other for a brief encounter in a private interview room with their lawyers present. Still terrified of Adams, Akins asked in a quavering voice why Adams had blamed her for the Port St. Joe murders. Adams replied that he had done what he had to do. He had previously told her that he could buy his way out of prison camp and would come back and kill her. Holding back her tears, Mary Jean told Adams that she had never informed on him.[35]

Akins also told her lawyer that she hadn't killed anyone and was willing to take a lie detector test. At that point, Leonard Fleet made an offer on her behalf to Quentin Long, the prosecuting attorney. Fleet said that he would stipulate to the polygraph results as evidence in court. Long agreed, as the case against Mary Jean Akins looked shaky because it was based entirely on the word of a convicted felon.[36]

Long and Fleet selected Warren Holmes as the polygraph examiner in this case. It was an excellent choice. Holmes was a prominent criminologist, a self-employed lie detector examiner in Miami, and a former City of Miami homicide detective. He had extensive experience investigating murder cases and interrogating criminal suspects and witnesses. During his police career, Holmes obtained more than 500 murder confessions, five of which led to death sentences. He also was the past president of the Academy of Scientific Interrogation, a national organization of polygraph examiners.[37]

On December 15, 1966, after being briefed on the case, Holmes questioned Mary Jean Akins at the Broward County Jail and ran a polygraph test on her. She gave a detailed account of the events the day Floyd McFarland was murdered. Ultimately, Holmes concluded she was telling the truth. He immediately reported his results to Long and Fleet.[38]

After that, things happened rapidly. The next day, December 16, 1966, Adams came to court and pled guilty to the McFarland murder based on a negotiated plea that he would be sentenced to life imprisonment. With the advice of his counsel, Adams no doubt saw what was coming. Akins's testimony, supported by the stipulated results of her polygraph test, looked like powerful evidence against him. It was time to make a deal and avoid the death penalty.[39]

As an apparent part of the deal, Adams also testified in court that Akins had not been involved in the McFarland murder. The court then dismissed the indictment against Mary Jean Akins and she was released from jail. Greatly relieved, she went home to her husband and family in Winter Haven.[40] On March 9, 1967, Adams was sentenced to life imprisonment for the McFarland murder based on the plea deal that had been reached.[41]

Jesse Pait never collected the $15,000 reward from the *Miami Herald* for turning Adams in. But after Pait died in 1969, his heirs sued the *Miami Herald* for the reward and the case was settled for $7,000.[42] Ironically, Pait had been sentenced to life imprisonment for having murdered a *Miami Herald* employee.

*   *   *

Mary Jean Akins had also told Warren Holmes that Curtis Adams had committed the Port St. Joe murders. Holmes ran a polygraph test on her account of the events leading up to those murders and concluded she was telling the truth. Holmes had already been briefed that Pitts and Lee had been convicted of these murders and were on death row. He decided to investigate further.

Shortly thereafter, he learned that I was representing Pitts and Lee and telephoned me at my office. I was working on various appellate cases when the call came through. Holmes was a total stranger. I had never met him or heard of him. Holmes identified himself and asked if I represented two men who had been convicted of murders in Port St. Joe. I said I did.

He then announced in a commanding voice, "Well, they're innocent. I've got the man who committed those murders. Curtis Adams. He's in the Broward County Jail and I hope to question him and get a confession from him within the next few days." He then explained in detail the events surrounding his polygraph examination of Mary Jean Akins.

I was stunned. I knew innocent people were on occasion convicted and sentenced to prison. One of the reasons I was a public defender was to prevent that from happening. But here my clients had been sentenced to death, the ultimate penalty. At first, I could barely speak. I remember saying, "No. You're kidding. Is this really true?" But I soon recovered and listened in rapt attention to what Holmes was telling me. He spoke with absolute authority. When he was finished, I thanked Holmes for his efforts and asked him to keep me apprised about his further investigation.

Up to that time, I had thought Pitts and Lee were probably guilty of the murders of Floyd and Burkett based on the bare appellate record I had. They had, after all, confessed in court, and I had not looked beyond that. I thought that when a new trial was eventually achieved on our motion to vacate the convictions, Pitts and Lee's claims of innocence could then be addressed. That was my mindset.

But Holmes's phone call that day was an epiphany for me, my moment of truth, a bolt of lightning from out of the blue. I sat there at my desk in the public defender office completely flabbergasted. Someone else, a specific person, had apparently committed the crime for which my clients had been convicted and sentenced to death. The stakes could not have been any higher. I could not possibly let two innocent men die in the electric chair for a crime that someone else had committed. That other person had to be brought to justice, my clients had to be freed, and I had to make it happen.

I was filled with amazement and perhaps a little fear. The responsibility was enormous. My mind raced. I was no longer just a defense lawyer for Pitts and Lee. I was also, in effect, a prosecutor—I had to mount the case against the real murderer. And I kept thinking over and over that if everything panned out, an incredible amount of work lay ahead. New legal proceedings would have to be filed, new investigations launched, new legal research conducted. The whole case turned upside down in my mind. Soon I became immersed in the case of a lifetime.

12

Curtis Adams Confesses

While the McFarland investigation was ongoing, the Broward County Sheriff's Office began developing evidence that showed that Curtis Adams was guilty of the Floyd-Burkett murders in Port St. Joe, not Pitts and Lee. The two cases became almost intertwined. It began on October 7, 1966, when Jesse Pait told Broward police that Adams had confessed not only to the McFarland murder but also to the Floyd-Burkett murders in Port St. Joe. It was a turning point in the case and it came out of nowhere.

Broward County Chief Detective Lawrence Lang was in the process of taking a routine stenographer's statement from Jesse Pait concerning the McFarland murder when, almost offhandedly, he asked Pait if Curtis Adams had confessed to any other homicides besides the McFarland murder. The answer astonished Lang. Pait replied that Adams had said that he had killed two men somewhere on the west coast of Florida. The name he remembered was something like "Port St. George."

Pait then laid out in some detail the content of Adams's confession—that Adams had robbed a filling station in that area, that he had kidnapped the two station attendants, and that he had murdered the attendants in a wooded rural area many miles from the station. This was an almost exact replica of the McFarland murder that Lang was investigating.

Adams also told Pait that he had hidden in the station bathroom while an argument was going on between some Black people and the station attendants. Adams said that he had committed the robbery and murders after the Black people had left the station. On top of that, Pait related that two Black men who had been in the station that night had been convicted of this double murder and were awaiting execution on death row—a fact that Lang soon verified.

Pait specifically asked Adams whether his conscience didn't bother him that two men were on death row for murders he committed. Adams had no remorse. "The black sons of bitches ought not to have been there," he said.[1]

As it turned out, Pait's statement would prove to be consistent with a raft of other evidence in the case. And it would back up the statements of Pitts and Lee that when they left the Mo Jo station on the night in question, the attendants were alive and well and that Pitts and Lee had never returned to the station that night.

Given these details and the striking similarity with the McFarland murder, Lang took swift action to reopen the Floyd and Burkett murder case even though this crime had been committed outside his jurisdiction. Quentin Long, the Broward County state attorney, was at once informed of this important development. Long promptly telephoned J. Frank Adams, the Gulf County state attorney, to tell him of the breakthrough. Three days later, on October 10, 1966, Long wrote a follow-up letter to J. Frank Adams that detailed Curtis Adams's confession to Jesse Pait concerning the Port St. Joe murders and expressed a hope that the two men on death row would soon be cleared.[2] But J. Frank Adams wasn't interested. That case was closed, he said, and long forgotten. He didn't even remember the names of Pitts and Lee.[3]

Sadly, this stonewalling reaction to these disturbing events would characterize the attitude of the local power structure toward this case for the next nine years. As Chief Detective Lawrence Lang bluntly explained many years later, "The whole thing was just a red-necked mess, frankly. It was definitely racially motivated."[4]

*   *   *

The Broward County Sheriff detectives, however, were not deterred by the local prosecutor's dismissive attitude. They were determined to investigate further. A week later, on October 17, 1966, Detective Elihu Phares traveled to Port St. Joe. He was looking for the gun Adams had used in the McFarland murder. Simultaneously, Phares was investigating Adams's involvement in the Port St. Joe murders, because these murders, he said, "seemed to be a carbon copy of the homicide that I was presently investigating."[5]

He conducted a thorough check on Adams's activities in Gulf County, interviewed nineteen witnesses, and made some important findings. In particular, Detective Phares concluded that Curtis Adams and Mary Jean Akins had been living together as man and wife in the Port St. Joe area on July 31, 1963, and had suddenly left town the next morning, a few hours after Grover Floyd and Jesse Burkett were discovered missing from the Mo Jo station.[6]

Among other things, Phares discovered from the records of the St. Joseph Telephone and Telegraph Co. that Akins had abruptly quit her job as a telephone operator without giving a reason and had received her final payroll check dated July 31, 1963. He also learned from the records of Florida Power Corporation that the electric service at the upstairs apartment where Adams and Akins lived had been terminated as of August 1, 1963, "at the customer's request." Akins had said that she had done these things before leaving town with Adams on the morning of August 1, 1963.[7]

Phares also contacted Gulf County Deputy Sheriff Wayne White at White's office and had an extensive conversation with him about Curtis Adams. During that meeting, White made some revealing statements that I'm certain he never thought would be made public.

Here are the highlights of Phares's testimony at the February 1972 trial in Marianna concerning what White said during this meeting:

[White] told me that Curtis Adams was the prime suspect in the Burkett-Floyd homicide prior to the arrest of the other people that were subsequently convicted.

Q. How did he refer to the other people?

A. The two (n——s)

* * *

I asked him why Curtis Adams was a suspect in the Burkett-Floyd Homicide and he indicated that he [Adams] was the only man in Port St. Joe that he knew with a robbery background that he felt would be capable of this homicide.

He remembered [the case] very vividly and he related to us that the defendants [Pitts and Lee] were taken to court and removed to Raiford Penitentiary as expeditiously as possible due to the civil rights movement that was just beginning to get started in the Florida Panhandle area. There had been an incident in Pensacola, just prior to their arrest and due to the security circumstances in the county jail in Wewahitchka, that as soon as the court proceedings were over they were immediately removed to Raiford.[8]

Although Phares was a hardened police investigator and was no bleeding heart, he was greatly disturbed by the racially motivated way this investigation had been conducted and by how the local police had inexplicably ignored the prime suspect, Curtis Adams. But he kept these concerns to himself and returned to Fort Lauderdale. The following week, on October 31, 1963, Curtis Adams led Phares and Chief Detective Lang to the wooded area outside Port St. Joe where Grover Floyd and Jesse Burkett had been found murdered.

* * *

Two months later, the startling truth was revealed. On December 21, 1966, Warren Holmes left his office in Miami and drove to the Broward County Sheriff's Office in Fort Lauderdale with the sole intention of questioning Curtis Adams about the Port St. Joe murders, just as he had promised he would do in his telephone conversation with me. I was waiting in Miami to hear what he might learn.

After meeting with the Broward County Sheriff's Office and the Broward County state attorney, Holmes decided to seek formal court authorization for questioning Curtis Adams. This was an unprecedented move. To begin this process, Charles Rich, Adams's attorney, was summoned. Would he allow Adams to talk?

Rich, an experienced defense lawyer, was in a terrible dilemma. If he agreed to let Adams talk and Adams confessed to the Port St. Joe murders, Adams could be prosecuted for that crime as there is no statute of limitations for first-degree murder. On the other hand, Adams had just been sentenced to life imprisonment for the McFarland murder, and it was likely that in a later plea deal Adams would get a concurrent life sentence for the Port St. Joe murders because he would be seen as a hero for having cleared up a monumental miscarriage of justice.

Weighing these options, Rich agreed to let Adams talk. I'm not sure I would have done the same had I been Adams's attorney. Most defense lawyers would probably have told Adams to remain silent. But no doubt Rich was torn by the specter of two men going to the electric chair for a crime they didn't commit. No criminal defense lawyer should ever be placed in such an ethical bind and it is difficult to second-guess Rich's decision in this case.

With State Attorney Quentin Long's consent, Rich and Holmes went before Circuit Judge George Tedder in chambers and informed him of the extraordinary circumstances surrounding the case. Would the judge enter an order allowing Warren Holmes, as an agent of the Broward County Sheriff's Office, to question and administer a polygraph examination to Curtis Adams about the Port St. Joe murders? Tedder agreed and entered a court order to that effect.[9]

That evening Warren Holmes met Curtis Adams in an interview room at the Broward County Sheriff's Office. Charles Rich went with him and introduced Holmes to Adams. Then Rich left the room, having advised his client to talk. Polygraph examinations are typically conducted with only the operator and the subject present.

For the next twenty minutes, Holmes and Adams sat across the table from each other while Holmes calmly urged Adams to tell the truth about the murders of Floyd and Burkett. A polygraph machine encased in a metal suitcase sat on the floor next to the table along with a microphone and a reel-to-reel tape recorder.[10]

As he told me later, Holmes essentially appealed to Adams's ego. Adams—and no one else—knew exactly what had happened to Grover Floyd and Jesse Burkett that night. The police didn't really know; neither did the prosecutor, the court, or the jury. Adams alone knew the truth, and that put him in a superior position over everyone else. Holmes was in the truth business. He understood how it felt to know the truth, as Adams did. And Adams now had a chance to be a hero and tell the world what had really happened to Grover Floyd and Jesse Burkett that night. Eventually this strategy worked. Adams nodded, indicating that he would make a statement and was willing to take a polygraph test.[11]

I've never quite understood what went through Adams's mind when he agreed to do this. He had a sociopathic personality and was otherwise a pathological liar. But in the end, this was Adams's one opportunity in life to be the star attraction, the center of everyone's attention, the man in a high-profile murder case who could tell the world what had actually happened.

Upon hearing this, Holmes brought out his tape recorder and microphone, activated the equipment, and methodically began to question Curtis Adams. The taped interview that followed lasted ninety-eight minutes and filled sixty-seven stenographer's pages.[12] Holmes then ran a polygraph test on Adams and concluded he was telling the truth.

* * *

Here is Adams's account of how he robbed and murdered Grover Floyd and Jesse Burkett. It is powerful, detailed, and remorseless.

Q. Now, tell me everything that happened that you can recall from the moment you drove in that station, where you parked, and just go through the entire thing exactly the way it happened, recalling everything that you can about the robbery.

A. Well, I pulled in there between the station and the gas pumps and Jesse Burkett and Grover Floyd came out and asked what I wanted. I told them to fill it up with gas, and I looked around the station and seen there wasn't anyone else there and I come back out and about that time a car drove up. It had two colored boys and, if I'm not mistaken, three colored women in it. I didn't pay too much attention. I got in the station before anyone could see me. I got in the bathroom and latched the door from the inside.

While I was in there, I could hear some loud talking and arguing going on outside. I stayed in there while all that was going on. It quieted down. . . .

Sounded like an argument between them, between the fellows at the station and the women that drove up. . . . I couldn't understand what it was about. But he tried to get in the rest room there, someone did, and I had it locked from the inside.

* * *

Then after about five minutes, I reckon, I opened the door again and looked out and there was a truck up there with two 55-gallon drums on it and he was putting gas in them. I got back in the restroom and there was a little crack where you could see through the door and I could hear the truck when it pulled out.

I cracked the door and looked out and I thought that the colored guys and women had left, but it was around the side. I went back in the restroom and they started arguing and everything or something out there again and [they] tried to get back in the restroom, rattling on the door, and I stayed there until all the noise died down and everything.

Then I unlatched the door and tried to get back out and it was locked from the outside. I knocked on the door and one of them took the lock off it. They told me that the colored guys and the women that was out by the car had tried to use the rest room and they'd put a lock on it.

Q. Who told you that?

A. Jesse Burkett.[13]

Adams then recounted the actual robbery and murders:

So, we stood there and talked for just a minute or so to tell me that, and I pulled a gun out and throwed it on them and told them to put all his money in something. He took a box from under the counter or somewhere or other and took all the money out of the register and put in it, and I told him to take the gun that he had there and put it in the box too.

Q. What gun was that?

A. It's a gun that was there in the station. I knew it was there because I had seen it before. . . .

Q. What kind of gun was that they had at the station?

A. .38 to the best of my knowledge. . . . It was a revolver.

* * *

I told them to get all the money and put it in something, and he said, "Sure Boo," he said, "Skipper [the station owner] always told me if anybody come in here to rob us, not to resist, but to give it to them."

* * *

Q. All right. Then what did you tell these guys to do after they got all this stuff together?

A. Tell them to get in the car and told Jesse Burkett to get on the wheel and drive and Grover Floyd to get in the front seat beside him and I got in the back.

* * *

Q. All right. So then you put—you ordered Burkett to drive and get behind the wheel and you put Floyd to sit in the front seat and you got in the back seat?

A. Yes, sir.

Q. Now what gun were you holding on them?

A. The .25 Beretta automatic.

Q. And where was the box and the money that you—

A. It was in the back seat with me. Went toward Port St. Joe and turned off to the left, went toward Wewahitchka and we went to White City—that's seven miles from Port St. Joe—and we got on the other side of there.

And I unloaded my gun, put the clip in my pocket and put the gun back in my pocket and held the gun that was in [the] box [from the station] on them.

Q. Why did you unload your gun?

A. It was an automatic and sometimes automatics go off accidental and all. I didn't want to in the car if we hit a bump or anything. The revolver [from the station] was safer.

Q. What conversation were you having with these people on the way, on the road?

A. They was trying to get me to turn them loose. Said they wouldn't tell anybody that it was me, they'd say it was someone else they never saw before.

Q. Well, what did you tell them that you were going to do, as to where you were taking them and why you were taking them?

A. Told them I was taking them out in the woods and tie them up and leave them so I could get back to town and get Billie and the kids and get out of the state.

Q. All right. Then where did you have Burkett drive?

A. After we drive down the road a long ways—I can't say how far it was from Port St. Joe, I don't remember, but we went past Howard Creek Road and [we] pulled in on a dirt road and turned around and come back to Howard Creek Road and turned down it, then we went to what they call the St. Joe Paper Company ditch—canal, and pulled in at a gate of it.

Took them out of the car, walked them down, say between three and five hundred feet from the gate out in the bushes and made them lay down and shot them.

* * *

Q. Why did you pick this particular area to take them to?

A. It just popped in my mind as we was going out there.

Q. Had you been in that area before?

A. Yeah. I've been all over the place.

Q. Why?

A. I fished and hunted out there and been all over those woods. I know them all.

Q. Did you open the gate or how did you get through the gate?

A. The pipe going through the middle of the gate there, it was about two or maybe three foot at the most off of the ground, just bent over—stepped over it, went between it and top one. Two and half or three foot clearance between the pipe there.

Q. Did all of you go through the gate the same way?

A. Yes, sir.

Q. Who went through the gate first?

A. Grover Floyd went through first and Jesse Burkett went through second.

Q. And what did you do, leave the car parked right outside the gate?

A. Yes, sir.

Q. With the lights and motor running?

A. Motor was running and the lights was off.

Q. Did Burkett leave the keys in the car?

A. Yes, sir.

Q. How far did you walk them from the gate to the point where you shot them?

A. I'd say between three and five hundred feet. The best I can say. I didn't pay much attention.

Q. Was that a little dirt road that you walked them along?

A. Yes, sir. Walked them along it, they went over to a ditch, right on the other side of the ditch in the bushes next to a pine tree.

Adams then got to the grisly details of the murders:

Q. When you got to the pine tree, what did you tell these guys to do?

A. I told them to lay down.

Q. How did you tell them to lay down?

A. Grover Floyd, he laid down—you see, I had my back to the canal and I was facing the tree. He laid down to my right and Jesse Burkett laid to my left.

Q. And you had your back to the canal?

A. That's right. I was facing approximately north—not north, south. And Grover Floyd he laid down approximately west and Jesse Burkett about east.

Q. How close were they lying together?

A. Their feet was about three foot apart, I imagine something like that.

Q. Did you tie them up?

A. No sir.

Q. Who did you shoot first?

A. Grover Floyd.

Q. In what part of the body did you shoot him?

A. In the head.

Q. Do you recall exactly where you shot him [Floyd] in the head?

A. It was somewheres in the lower part of his head because it didn't kill him.

Q. Did he call out or something?

A. Yeah. He told me not to shoot him anymore, that I already hurt him and not shoot him anymore.

Q. Did Burkett say anything when he heard you shoot Floyd?

A. Jesse said, "What did you do? Did you shoot him?" Then I turned around and shot him.

Q. Where did you shoot him?

A. In the head.

Q. How many times did you shoot Burkett?

A. One time.

Q. Did you shoot Floyd again?

A. Turned around and shot him again.

Q. And where did you shoot him a second time?

A. I couldn't say, it was so dark and all but it was in the upper part of the head.

Q. Could you have missed him?

A. It's possible, yes, but I don't think so.

Q. But you did fire three shots.

A. Yes sir.[14]

This account is corroborated by the autopsy reports, which state that both Floyd and Burkett died as a result of a bullet wound to the back and side of the head "fired from a 38 caliber gun" that fatally penetrated the brain. These reports and the V position in which the bodies were later found on the ground by the police are consistent with Adams's statement that he shot both men in the back of the head in rapid succession after forcing them to lie on the ground, face down, in front of him. And he did so, he said, with a .38-caliber revolver he had stolen from the station. The second shot he fired at Floyd in the dark obviously missed its target, as there was only one bullet wound in Floyd's head.

But there was more. Adams then related how he killed Floyd McFarland in Fort Lauderdale. His description of the actual murder is harrowing:

I just pulled in there [to the Shamrock station] and told him [the attendant] to put some gas in the car, I don't remember how much or anything, walked over to the shed where the cigarette machine and the drink machine all was at. He put gas in there and he come over there.

And I put the gun on him and made him get in the front seat of the car and drive. Drove out of town approximately ten miles on 84, made him get out of the car and took him there in the woods and shot him.

* * *

Q. Was he standing or lying down when you shot him?

A. Standing.

Q. Where did you shoot him?

A. In the head.

Q. How many times did you shoot him?

A. Twice. He grabbed ahold of a tree—

Q. He grabbed a tree?

A. Yeah. The first time [he] didn't fall so I shot him again.

* * *

Q. Did he sink to his knees or did he fall all the way down?

A. No. He didn't fall until I shot him the second time.

Q. He was still standing holding the tree when you shot him the second time?

A. Yes.[15]

I will never forget the dramatic end to Adams's statement. In the space of seven pages of transcription, Holmes probed deeply into Adams's motivations and thinking:

Q. The fact that you killed three human beings, did that ever bother you?

A. Yes sir. It bothered me a lot for the first month on Grover Floyd and Jesse Burkett.

Q. Why did those two killings bother you the most?

A. One reason, Grover Floyd, he was a friend of mine, went out drinking with him and all, liked him and everything. And Jesse Burkett, he was a close friend of my father's. . . .

Q. What do you think now when you think about the fact that you killed three different people during the commission of an armed robbery?

A. I'd say it's hard to express just how I do feel. For sure, I don't feel proud of it or anything. But someone you don't know is not as bad as someone you know and liked and been close to.

Q. Well, when you were going to hold up this Mo Jo station and you knew you were going to have to kill two people that you knew, how were you able to get yourself mentally prepared to do this?

A. I don't know how to explain that. All I know, me or anyone else that does that there, there's something wrong with them somewhere. . . . There has to be something haywire some place.

Q. Well, do you figure it was maybe the way you were taught as a youngster?

A. No, sir. I had always been brung up to believe in the Bible and all. My mother, she was a Sunday school teacher and she always took me to church and taught me to respect others and what they had.

Q. Did you ever have a desire to kill people that you felt it would be fun to do this or that you would experience some kind of pleasure in doing it?

A. No, sir. Had never thought of it.

Q. What were your feelings when you killed these two men in Port St. Joe?

A. It was bad. I didn't sleep any that night. Didn't sleep any for several nights.

Q. Did you think about it all the time?

A. I did for the first month.

Q. And then what did you do, just put it out of your mind?

A. Started drinking more and more.

Q. Uh huh.

A. To where I drinked a fifth a day.

Q. Uh huh. Did you feel that you were going to be punished in some way for doing this?

A. I figured someday I would.

Q. And you believe in God?

A. Yes sir. I was always taught to believe in him.

Q. How is it that, if you believed in God and you knew it was against one of his commandments to kill somebody, that you went ahead and killed these people?

A. Well, sir. That's what I don't understand. That's the reason I say that anyone that does that, there's something wrong with them in some way. I'm not trying to say I'm crazy or was crazy at the time I done it, but there's something wrong with anyone that does that. There has to be. It's just not normal. There has to be something in a man's mind out of place at the time or something or other.

Q. Did you have any impulse to do this, some power that was driving you to do this even though you knew it was wrong?

A. No, sir. It wasn't easy to.

Q. But you needed the money?

A. I needed it but not that bad.

Q. Well, why, when you were thinking about committing this robbery just to get maybe a hundred dollars or less or maybe little more, would you make up your mind to kill two people just to do this?

A. Well, I can't blame anybody but myself for what I did. But a man do a lot of things sometimes to keep something he wants.

Q. And you felt that you were ready to do anything for this woman?

A. Not for the woman.

Q. For the children?

A. I wanted the children. I wanted them more than anything.

Q. Were the children very affectionate toward you, did they love you?

A. Yes, sir.

Q. That made you feel good?

A. Yes, sir. It did. . . .

Q. Well, now that you think back about all this, what are your thoughts now?

A. I don't know.

Q. Do you try to push all this out of your mind?

A. Have to. Can't think about it all the time.

Q. Yeah.

A. Just have to try pushing it further and further back.

Q. Uh huh. If you had your life to live over again, what changes would you make?

A. There are too many to even try to say in mine.

Q. Do you think you'd kill somebody again?

A. I know I wouldn't.

Q. Would you say that even though you haven't been in prison for these killings that you suffered knowing that you did them?

A. I know I have..

Q. What were your thoughts when you knew that two [people] had been convicted of killing Burkett and Floyd when you knew that, in fact, you had done it?

A. Well, I didn't know what to think when Mr. Parker told me they were convicted and waiting on the chair.

Q. Were you shocked?

A. Sure I was. I knowed they had them but I didn't know they was convicted and waiting for the chair.

Q. Well, did that bother you that two innocent people had been convicted for killings that you had done?

A. Sure it did.

Q. Did you ever wonder what it would be like to die in the electric chair for something you didn't do?

A. Well, sir, I never worried about dying because I knew everybody has got to die. They not going to prolong the time; they not going to rush it up. Everybody's days are numbered, so it don't matter what you do . . . you're not going to prolong it or you're not going to rush it. I'm not worried about that.

Q. Yes. But what did you think about this [man] dying in the electric chair for something he didn't do?

A. I don't want to see anybody die in the electric chair.

Q. Did you ever wonder about what must be running through his mind?

A. Yes, sir, I was wondering about that a lot.

Q. You know, he has a mother that writes him letters.

A. Well, sir, I never knew his name or anything until I read it in the paper down there in jail. I wouldn't know the man if he walked in the door right now. I know he's had a bad time up there.

Q. And his family too.

A. Yes.

Q. His mother worries every single day about her son. Did you wonder how the law could have made a mistake on this case?

A. Yeah. I wondered how they can take a man and punish him and all and make him confess to something that he didn't do, and people get up on the stand and swear lies on it, and convict him of something he didn't do.

Q. Uh huh.

A. And from what the state attorney told me in Port St. Joe and what I read in the paper and all, people had to get up and swear lies on account of the man, he's just as innocent as you are of it.

Q. Why, because you did it?

A. Yeah.

Q. That's right. You of all know the actual truth, right?

A. Yeah.

And then this confession came to a close with perhaps the most pertinent question of all:

Q. Well, that must be a strange feeling to know that you killed two people and yet two other people have been convicted for what you did.

A. Sure it is. It makes you wonder a lot of times, especially when you try to clear it up one time and you can't get anybody to listen to you.

Q. Uh huh.

A. They all think you're a damn idiot or something.

Q. Yeah.

A. They haven't got—I don't know how to put it, but they haven't got the guts or anything to admit that they have done something wrong and try to straighten it out.

Q. Uh huh.

A. And that's all they're doing up there, they just hate to admit that they are wrong and have got the two wrong men up there, and they're just not man enough to stand up and say it. They don't want—

Q. They'd rather leave two innocent people in prison than to admit that they were wrong?

A. Yeah.

There followed a brief pause in the taped interview until Holmes finally spoke in a hushed tone and Adams answered:

Q. It's an amazing life, isn't it?

A. Yes, sir. It sure is.[16]

Holmes then ran a polygraph test on Adams's statement and concluded that Adams was telling the truth.

The Broward County Sheriff's detectives were soon informed of this clinching development. And a month later, on January 17, 1967, Elihu Phares conducted a follow-up interview of Curtis Adams at the Broward County Detective Bureau in the presence of Adams's attorney, Charles Rich. In that session Adams orally repeated his confession to the Port St. Joe murders in some detail, an anticlimax to his blockbuster confession to Warren Holmes. And with that, the entire investigation of this case by the Broward County Sheriff's Office came to an end.[17]

When I finally found out about all this from Warren Holmes, I was elated. But it was one thing to amass evidence to clear Pitts and Lee and quite another to get that evidence admitted in court A long, drawn-out battle lay ahead of us to exonerate Pitts and Lee of the Floyd-Burkett murders.

13

The Struggle to Reopen the Case

After his session with Curtis Adams, Warren Holmes returned to Miami and immediately contacted *Miami Herald* reporter Gene Miller. Miller was a seasoned journalist and writer who had a keen interest in investigating wrongful criminal convictions. Holmes and Miller were friends and had worked together in the past on similar cases. Miller trusted Holmes implicitly and was eager to learn more.

Holmes also briefed both me and Maurice Rosen, the managing lawyer of the ACLU legal panel. Rosen promptly appeared in my office to offer his assistance, which proved invaluable. He took charge of any investigations we needed in the case. He also contacted people he knew at the NAACP Legal Defense Fund, Inc., and obtained financial assistance from them that covered much of the costs in the case. We were all enormously grateful to the staff of the "Inc. Fund," as it has long been called, for their steadfast support over the nine years we worked on the Pitts and Lee case.

Rosen was also needed for another important mission. Holmes wanted to take an immediate trip to North Florida to visit Pitts and Lee at Florida State Prison and run a polygraph test on them. But he needed an attorney for Pitts and Lee to get him into the prison as an investigator. Under prison rules, Holmes would not be allowed in there on his own. I was too engaged with court appearances in my other appellate work to make the trip, so Rosen agreed to go with Holmes.

On December 22, 1966, the day after Curtis Adams's confession, Holmes and Rosen flew to North Florida and visited Florida State Prison at Raiford. That evening, prison authorities admitted them into a small room reserved for attorney-client interviews. Pitts was brought into the room first. Lee remained in his cell. After making the appropriate introductions, Holmes interviewed Pitts at length, ran a polygraph test on him that showed that he was truthful, and tape-recorded the entire session, so we have a full transcript of what transpired.

When he was finished testing Pitts, Holmes announced:

All right. Now that I have concluded this test, I'm going to tell you something I didn't tell you before because I didn't want it to influence your behavior or demeanor in here today—and I didn't want it to cloud your thinking because a lot of the information that you gave us, I wanted you to dig back in your mind.

Last night I obtained a full confession from the man who actually killed these two people. And that's the truth.

Pitts sat in his chair in stunned silence. No one spoke a word for nearly two minutes. Pitts cupped his face in his hands and began to sob. Finally, when he managed to speak, tears were streaming down his face:

Pitts. Do you mean he actually told—
Holmes. Yeah.
Pitts. Still hasn't registered. I don't know what to say.
Holmes. Huh?
Pitts. I'm just thinking about it. I don't know what to say.
Holmes. Well, it's the truth and he went into this thing in detail and I tested him on it and it is a valid confession and I'm satisfied in testing you today that you're telling the truth, that you actually didn't have anything to do with this.
Pitts. After three years. What did—I mean, what.

Pitts continued sobbing as Holmes gave more background on the case and laid out what might lie ahead. But Pitts was still incredulous. And who could blame him? Abandoned on death row for three years, his cries of innocence ignored, and here comes this stranger out of nowhere to tell him the nightmare is over. It was a moment of overwhelming bewilderment for Pitts.

Pitts. It's just hearing it this way, I mean, and have some people to help me.
Holmes. It's a shock, huh?
Pitts. Right.
Holmes. This is almost as bad as when you got tied up in this thing, huh?
Pitts. I mean, after being on Death Row three years, boy, I mean, trying to convince people that you didn't, and then finally you hear the whole thing has come out. You're just wondering.

Holmes. You're hoping you're not dreaming, huh.

Pitts. You know I am.

Holmes. I want to assure you: you're not dreaming, I'm real, and Mr. Rosen, your attorney, is real, and this is the truth.

Pitts. If I'm dreaming, don't wake me up.

Holmes. Beg pardon.

Pitts. If I'm dreaming, don't wake me up.

Holmes. No, no, I wouldn't kid you about anything as serious as this. I know what it means to you. . . .

Well, in any event, we've got enough now, I'm satisfied, to get you out of here. It may take a little while, but it will happen. I don't want you to think we're going to walk you out of here tomorrow or next week or maybe even next month from now, but we've got sufficient evidence now and we'll have more when we're done.[1]

When the interview was over, Holmes asked Pitts not to say anything to Lee about the new evidence for now. Lee was then brought to the interview room and Pitts was returned to his cell.

Holmes conducted a thorough interview of Lee and then ran a polygraph test on him that showed that he was telling the truth. When it was over, Holmes told Lee the same thing he had told Pitts—that Curtis Adams had confessed, that Adams had committed the murders, and that Lee was innocent.

Lee broke down crying and was almost delirious. His deeply held religious beliefs came tumbling out. Just as Pitts had reacted, it felt so surreal to Lee. His response was so human.

I pray so . . . close to four years. I told Mr. . . . when he walked me to the door . . . but I was scared shaken, but I could barely talk to him when he came to the door. I told him "I didn't want to die for a crime I . . ."

I prayed, you know, I prayed to the Lord. "Lord," I said, "ever who commit this," I said, "bless him." Every night I prayed. . . .

I don't want nothing bad to happen. I just want my freedom. I didn't do it. I just want my freedom. I don't want nothing bad to happen to nobody.[2]

Holmes, a hardened homicide investigator, was deeply touched by Pitts's and Lee's reactions, but he told both men not to expect any quick results. It would take some time before they got their freedom. And with that, the meeting at Florida State Prison came to an end.

*   *   *

Three weeks later, on January 11, 1967, Holmes made another trip to North Florida, this time to Port St. Joe with Maurice Rosen, Gene Miller, and Broward County detective Elihu Phares. Holmes tracked down Willie Mae Lee, the frightened young Black woman the police had terrorized into becoming a witness against Pitts and Lee. She lived in a rented brick house in the Black section of Port St. Joe with her sister, Evelyn, and her brother-in-law, John Underwood.[3]

Holmes knocked on the front door of the house with Detective Phares. Miller and Rosen remained in their rental car on the street. When Willie Mae answered the door, Holmes made his introductions and explained why they were there. He wanted to know her version of what had happened the night of the murders. Upon hearing this and perhaps relieved by the police presence of Detective Phares, Willie Mae let them in the house and immediately burst into tears: "I've waited three years to tell the truth," she cried.

At that moment, John Underwood, her brother-in-law, marched into the room and shouted: "Get out! Leave! I want you to leave my house at once." Willie Mae protested, "It's all right. He's a police officer." Without saying a word, Holmes and Phares left the house and went back to their car. Willie Mae was still crying when Holmes and his colleagues drove off.

But soon the word spread. About two hours later, Gulf County Sheriff Byrd Parker pulled the group over in his police car on the public highway. He walked up to the car and demanded: "What are you doing intimidating a witness?" Rosen tried to identify himself as Pitts and Lee's lawyer. "What do they need a lawyer for?" Parker snapped. "They pleaded guilty didn't they?" Miller also tried to introduce himself, but Parker interrupted. "I don't want to see any of this in the newspaper, you hear. I ought to throw you all in jail for intimidating a witness."

Holmes had heard enough. He got out of the car, confronted the sheriff, and told him: "Now you listen to me. You're the one who belongs in jail." And he began to berate the sheriff for the way the police had beaten and intimidated Pitts and Lee and put them on death row for a crime they didn't commit. Parker was aghast. He staggered back to his police car and collapsed in the front seat. At 62 years old, he was the longest serving sheriff in Florida; he had been in office for thirty-two years. It is doubtful that anyone had ever talked to him that way before. To this day, I am astounded at Holmes's courage.

But that was the end of the encounter. Everyone drove off and went their separate ways. No arrests were made. No laws had been broken. After doing some more investigation in the area, this time without police interference, the group returned to Miami.

I have often reflected what would have happened on that trip if Willie Mae Lee had been allowed to talk to Holmes and Phares—if Robert Underwood hadn't thrown them out of the house. Maybe, just maybe, the state's case against Pitts and Lee would have collapsed, smoothing the way for a prompt release of Pitts and Lee from prison. After the case was over, Gene Miller and I talked about this possibility many times. Miller would often say, "The only thing left undone in the case is for Willie Mae to tell the truth."

My rational self, however, always prevailed in this speculation. Even if Willie Mae had fully repudiated her testimony that day, nothing would have prevented her from later renouncing that statement, which is exactly what she did several times in this case. The state attorney could always remind her that if she permanently changed her testimony, she could be prosecuted for perjury in a capital case and go to prison for a long time. That possibility always hung over her and kept her in line.

But what the encounter at the Underwood house that day did show was that Willie Mae Lee knew full well her testimony against Pitts and Lee was a total lie. Her anguished cry that day was a cry from the heart.

* * *

In January 1967 and the months that followed, I dove into the case. I began researching Florida law, planning what legal proceeding should be brought, poring over the evidence we had for use in court, and plotting out what additional evidence we needed. It was a long, drawn-out process, but I was charged with excitement.

One of the great things about being a lawyer is that you don't have to sit on the sidelines and watch bad things happen to other people. Most people have to do that. But a lawyer has access to the courts and can stand up and fight for what's right. "I will never reject from any consideration personal to myself the cause of the defenseless or the oppressed." That is part of the oath every lawyer must take when becoming a member of the Florida Bar. And this case was my challenge to try to live up to that portion of the oath.

But soon I descended into a thicket of legal problems. First I had to get Pitts and Lee a new trial and then I had to win an acquittal at the new trial. It was a two-step process. For the first step, I had to determine what proceeding should be filed and in what court to win a new trial and then plan out a strategy for prevailing in that proceeding. For the second step, I had to get all the newly discovered evidence on Curtis Adams admitted in court at the new trial and win an acquittal. Both proceedings involved tough legal problems and there were no easy answers that favored our side of the case.

Of course, all of this could have been avoided if the prosecutor and police in Gulf County had agreed to set aside Pitts and Lee's convictions, drop all charges, and release them from prison. That happens today with some frequency when newly discovered DNA evidence conclusively establishes that an imprisoned defendant is innocent. But there was no DNA evidence back then, and releases from prison based on claims of innocence were rare.

I knew that such a release could happen in this case based on the extraordinary new evidence we had, but I also knew that I couldn't count on it. I had to have a basic plan to win the case in the courts. My experience as a trial lawyer was that the best way to persuade the state to drop a prosecution was to prepare a winning defense case for court.

I eventually concluded that the only available legal avenue was to file a second motion to set aside Pitts and Lee's convictions before the circuit court in Gulf County. I wasn't happy with this decision because I didn't regard a court in Gulf County as a friendly forum. But my petition for review in the US Supreme Court from the denial of my first motion in Gulf County had been denied. And a federal court in North Florida had denied my earlier petition asking for a new trial (a habeas corpus action) on the ground that the case belonged in the Florida courts. There was no real choice; I had to file a second motion in Gulf County.

But the central legal problem in that proceeding was how to present our newly discovered evidence on Curtis Adams as a basis for getting Pitts and Lee a new trial. Florida law allowed only constitutional grounds as a basis for this motion—that is, the defendant had to show that his or her rights under the US or Florida Constitution had been violated. But was the fact that Pitts and Lee had been convicted of crimes they hadn't committed a violation of their constitutional rights? As strange as it may seem, I could find no Florida or federal decision that said so.

On the contrary, all of the cases said that once a defendant has been tried and convicted or has pled guilty to a criminal charge and has taken a direct appeal to the appellate courts and lost (as Pitts and Lee had done long before we got in the case), that conviction was final. The issue of guilt or innocence was determined then and could no longer be raised again. And there was some logic to this rule. Otherwise, if the issue of guilt or innocence could be raised at any time, there would never be an end to criminal trials. Convicted defendants could always say, "I've got new evidence, give me a new trial."

According to the case law, a convicted defendant was entitled to a new trial only under the most compelling circumstances. The defendant had to show that he or she was deprived not just of a constitutional right but of a fundamental right whose violation tainted the entire trial proceeding and led directly to the conviction, a formidable requirement that was rarely met. So I had a real problem. The prosecutors were bound to cite all of the Florida decisions mentioned above that went against us, and I had no case authority to the contrary.

But I did have a powerful argument, one that was difficult to answer. I could argue, and in fact did, that it defies logic and justice to say that a defendant must be put to death based on a capital crime conviction even though newly discovered evidence overwhelmingly shows that this crime was committed by someone else. At the very least, the defendant should be entitled to a new trial. To conclude otherwise, I urged, would be a travesty of justice and a denial of due process under the US and Florida Constitutions.

Besides, our new evidence was inherently reliable, had been uncovered by another police agency (the Broward County Sheriff's Office), and was fully corroborated by other independent evidence in the case. I plowed ahead, piecing together general statements from US Supreme Court decisions and Florida cases that might support our position.

In particular, I found an older line of Florida cases involving a postconviction motion to set aside a criminal conviction based on a pleading called a motion for a writ of error coram nobis. ("Coram nobis" means "the error before us.") These cases held that a criminal conviction could be set aside where newly discovered evidence established that the defendant was innocent of the crime for which he or she had been convicted. I argued that the law this older practice was based on should apply to the current rule of criminal procedure that we were relying on to obtain a new trial.

I also tried to develop facts that would support more traditional constitutional grounds for relief that the law *did* recognize for the motion I was filing: namely, that Pitts and Lee's guilty pleas were coerced, that their court-appointed lawyer was incompetent, and perhaps other grounds also.

Still, I needed to learn a lot more about this case. Although Holmes had briefed me on the interview he had had with Pitts and Lee, that wasn't enough. In my experience, I had found that judges and juries rarely credited the testimony of convicted defendants alone. I needed corroboration. I needed to know exactly what Deputy Sheriff Wayne White, Sheriff Daffin, Fred Turner, and others were going to testify to in court and build my case, in part, around their admissions. The best way to do this was to take their depositions.

But I could find no settled legal authority that would allow me to do this on the motion I was filing. According to some Florida cases, however, this motion was quasi-civil in nature. This meant, I argued, that the Florida Rules of Civil Procedure were applicable, which allowed parties to take depositions. Ultimately, the state agreed with this position, and I took numerous depositions in North Florida from a variety of people, including White, Daffin, and Turner.

I had another legal problem, one that in the end proved devastating. As incredible as this may sound, under the established rules of evidence, Curtis Adams's confession to the Port St. Joe and Fort Lauderdale murders were inadmissible in evidence. I could probably get this evidence in during our first step, the hearing on our motion to set aside the conviction. The rules of evidence are relaxed at such a hearing. But during our second step, the new trial, these rules were applicable and this evidence was inadmissible. It made no sense and was terribly unfair because the evidence was obviously relevant and credible, but that was the law.

I could find no decision in Florida that said that an out-of-court confession given by someone other than the criminal defendant was admissible at the defendant's trial. On the contrary, all the cases said that such a confession was as inadmissible as hearsay evidence. A hearsay statement is one that is made out of court—as Curtis Adams's confession was—and is introduced to prove that the statement is true. There are many exceptions to the rule that excludes hearsay evidence, but there wasn't one that would expressly allow Adams's confession to be admissible in evidence.[4]

We were, of course, allowed to call Adams as a witness at trial and have him confess to the murders of Floyd and Burkett on the witness stand. But Adams always refused to do this, saying "I will not sit in the hot seat [i.e., the electric chair] for these two boys." He did tell us, however, that he would confess in court if the state gave him immunity from prosecution for these murders, but the state steadfastly refused to do that. So in the end, all we had was Adams's confession.

In short, we had the justice of the case on our side, but the state had the settled law on their side. To win the case, we had to make new law, and that was the focus of most of my legal research and argument over the next nine years.

*   *   *

About this time, Gene Miller and Warren Holmes became interested in the legal aspects of the case and arranged a meeting with me. In the course of that meeting, they insisted that I include in the new motion to vacate the entire evidence we had that Curtis Adams was guilty of the charged murders and that Pitts and Lee were innocent. I disagreed. Besides being legally unnecessary, I explained, it was tactically unwise to allege everything we had in the motion, as it tipped off the state about how we were going to prove our case in court. But Miller and Holmes were adamant; they wanted everything in the motion. As a result, I almost resigned from the case.

Shortly after the meeting, I expressed my frustration with Maurice Rosen. Rosen was sympathetic and told me that I should have included him in the meeting. "You shouldn't face these guys alone," he said. "They can be overwhelming." That gave me some comfort, and with Rosen's support I cooled off. Miller and Holmes were good people, superb investigators, and invaluable assets. But winning cases in court was outside their expertise.

In the meantime, Miller and Holmes traveled to Tallahassee to try to interview Earl Faircloth, the Florida attorney general, about intervening in the case and agreeing to a new trial for Pitts and Lee. J. Frank Adams, the Gulf County prosecutor, had already told us that he was opposed to reopening the case and they were trying to go over his head. But Faircloth was unavailable. Instead they saw Reeves Bowen, the elderly, longtime head of the Appellate Division in the Office of the Attorney General. He was a former trial judge and a real gentleman of the old school.

Miller and Holmes outlined the new evidence in the case indicating that Curtis Adams had murdered Floyd and Burkett and that Pitts and Lee were innocent. Bowen insisted that Pitts and Lee's guilt or innocence was no longer an issue in the case, relying on a long line of Florida cases. "The issue," Bowen said, "was whether they received a fair trial."[5] I was well aware of these Florida cases; it was one of the major legal obstacles we faced.

But Miller and Holmes had no patience with such "legal technicalities." Holmes was particularly upset and said to Bowen, "You mean it doesn't make any difference if they are innocent men? You'd go ahead and electrocute them anyway if they received a fair trial?" That was exactly my argument, albeit with little legal authority. Bowen replied that he thought Pitts and Lee would be well represented in any future litigation in the case and the interview ended.[6]

Driven by the basic justice of our case, on December 8, 1967, I filed a twelve-page motion to set aside Pitts and Lee's convictions with the Gulf County Circuit Court. Several months later, I supplemented the motion with a two-page addition. The motion, as supplemented, recited the basic facts of the case and raised three basic constitutional grounds for relief:

1. Pitts and Lee were coerced into pleading guilty by the police and their court-appointed lawyer and were innocent of the crime for which they had been convicted, the crime having been committed by Curtis Adams;
2. Pitts and Lee were represented by an incompetent court-appointed lawyer who, in fact, helped convict them; and
3. The Gulf County state attorney suppressed evidence favorable to Pitts and Lee, namely Willie Mae Lee's statement blaming Lambson Smith for the charged murders.

Despite our earlier disagreement, Miller and Holmes were impressed with the motion even though it contained a shortened version of the facts. I was relieved. I was beginning to get to know these strong-minded men but resolved that I would never again allow them to be amateur lawyers. With that understood, we would eventually become good friends. Indeed, without them we would never have prevailed in the case.

14

Dueling Newspapers in Miami and Panama City

In early 1967, Gene Miller began preparations for a series of investigative articles on the Pitts and Lee case that he would write for the *Miami Herald*. He had access to what Warren Holmes had uncovered so far, but he wanted more. To assist Miller, the *Miami Herald* hired retired Miami police officer Willie Nicholson to investigate the case in Port St. Joe.

At the time Nicholson ("Big Nick") was one of the few Black officers that the City of Miami had ever hired. He was a big, heavyset, 40-year-old man who had recently been forced to take disability retirement after he had been shot in the stomach and groin during a high-speed police chase. He had worked for the City of Miami for sixteen years and was still recovering from his injury. Warren Holmes had known him well during Holmes's own career as a homicide detective for the same police department. It was tough for a Black officer to work for a predominately white police force, and Holmes liked and respected Nicholson.[1]

During his assignment for the *Miami Herald*, Nicholson spent a week investigating the case in Port St. Joe, locating and interviewing defense witnesses in the Black area of town. But when he tried to see Willie Mae Lee, Gulf County police picked her up and prevented him from interviewing her. This upset Nicholson. "Nobody fools with Willie Mae," he said, meaning no outsiders were allowed to talk to her. He returned home in an agitated state over this experience, which added to a continuing anxiety about his upcoming surgery. He turned over his findings to Miller, he was paid for his work, and his relationship with the *Miami Herald* came to an end.[2]

Gene Miller, in the meantime, decided to do some investigative work himself in the Florida Panhandle. He went to Blountstown, Florida, with my co-counsel, Maurice Rosen, and interviewed J. Frank Adams at the prosecutor's office. Miller also interviewed Sheriff Daffin in Panama City and Deputy Sheriff Wayne White in Port St. Joe. These public officials all claimed that Pitts and Lee were guilty and refused to reopen the case. Sheriff Daffin's comments were the most explosive: "I don't *think* they did it," he said. "I *know* they did it."[3]

Miller also tracked down Willie Mae Lee and interviewed her for about five minutes on the front lawn of her house without police interference. To Miller, she seemed almost suicidal: "If I die, you won't have any witnesses," she wailed. She was angry with Freddie Pitts and said she would testify against him again. Miller told her that he would be writing some newspaper articles about the case and asked if she would like copies. She said she would.[4]

Miller then returned to Miami and in February 1967 wrote two investigative articles about the case. The first article, which was front-page news in the Sunday paper for February 5, 1967, was two-and-a-quarter pages long. The headline read: "Two Face Death for Murders I Committed." The second article was also front-page news and filled another two-and-a-quarter pages. It appeared the next day with the headline "And May God Have Mercy on Your Soul."

Both articles laid out in exacting detail the complex facts of the case, complete with many photographs of the principal people involved and the crime scene in Port St. Joe. In particular, a photograph of Curtis Adams appeared on the front page of the first article with caption "I killed them," along with a photograph of Adams's former girlfriend, Mary Jean Akins, with a caption reading "I knew he did it."

In the Sunday edition, an insert on the front page introduced the two articles as follows:

Twice in the past year, individuals who had been wrongly convicted of murder have been freed through the efforts of Herald Staff Writer Gene Miller and lie-detector expert Warren Holmes. Recently they have been investigating another murder case. This article, the [first] of two, tells how two men confessed to a crime they didn't commit.

The articles that followed were riveting. Miller's sparse, Hemingway-like writing style was spellbinding. He wrote:

There is substantial reason to believe this new Adams confession is totally valid. For seven weeks, Warren D. Holmes, Miami polygraph-criminalist, and this newspaper reporter have subjected this confession to hard corroboration. Through Maurice Rosen, the appellate lawyer for the convicted men, the attorney general of Florida and police and prosecutor in Gulf County have been so informed. They are yet to act.

Miller then focused in detail on all the major aspects of the case. It was a comprehensive account of the case and a powerful brief for the innocence of Pitts and Lee and the guilt of Curtis Adams.[5]

There was also a prominent insert on the second page of the first article with a headline reading: "'Why This Injustice? Sloppy Police Work.'" In this insert, Miller quoted Warren Holmes's powerful overview of the case.

This is the third time that I have worked on a case where, in my opinion, someone was wrongly convicted of first degree murder.

The common denominator in all three cases was improper police interrogation and the acceptance of confessions not corroborated by physical evidence. We need police interrogation to combat crime but not at this price. . . .

I have administered polygraph examinations to the four principals involved in this case. The test results clearly indicate in my opinion that Curtis Adams is the true killer of Grover Floyd and Jesse Burkett in Port St. Joe and Floyd McFarland in Fort Lauderdale.

In the case of Pitts and Lee it is going to be hard to convince the authorities involved that there has been a miscarriage of justice.

I know from experience it is difficult not to personalize a murder investigation. To arrive at the absolute truth requires a degree of objectivity that tests the nature of man.[6]

When I read these articles back in February 1967, I remember thinking what a welcome surprise it was to have the press on my side. Media coverage of criminal cases was almost always adverse to the defense. Unfortunately, however, Miller's articles sparked a blistering counterattack from another newspaper in the Florida Panhandle—and an explosive incident.

*   *   *

While he was in the hospital awaiting surgery for his gunshot injuries, Willie Nicholson read Miller's coverage of the case in the *Miami Herald* and became greatly agitated. He was convinced that Pitts and Lee were innocent, that Willie Mae Lee was in some sort of danger, and that he had to act immediately.

He got dressed, left the hospital, and headed for the Florida Panhandle at night.[7] On the way, however, he tried to see Florida governor Claude Kirk in Tallahassee, supposedly to prevent a "riot." We are not sure what happened there, but afterward an aide to the governor called the mayor of Port St. Joe to alert him that Nicholson might be coming to town.

The next day, Nicholson went to the Port St. Joe police station and loudly proclaimed that 45,000 NAACP protesters would march on the town unless he got some cooperation. He was clutching his stomach and telling everyone he was sick. He demanded to see the Port St. Joe police chief, Buck Griffin, so that an interview with Willie Mae Lee could be arranged. Griffin telephoned the mayor, Frank Tate. Tate, in turn, went to see Willie Mae Lee, apparently to seal her off from Nicholson. Willie Mae claimed that Nicholson had telephoned her with unwelcome calls, something Nicholson denied.

J. Frank Adams got word of this dustup and went to Port St. Joe by car with Assistant State Attorney Paul Griffith. Griffith took a tape recorder with him to record whatever might happen with Nicholson that day. They picked up Police Chief Buck Griffin en route and began looking for Nicholson in town.

I've always considered this odd. Why was it necessary for the mayor of Port St. Joe, the prosecuting attorney for the entire five-county circuit, and the prosecutor's top assistant to spring into action and get involved in this matter at all? Why not let the local police handle the situation? Nicholson may have been acting irrationally, but he had done nothing illegal, nothing to propel the top public officials of the area to suddenly descend upon him with a tape recorder. In fact, Nicholson had gone to the police station in Port St. Joe to get permission to see Willie Mae Lee.

But all of this shows the temper of the times. Many white southerners were in a near-siege mentality because of the impact of the civil rights movement. Many whites thought that outside "agitators" were descending on the South to stir up local Black residents and cause trouble.[8] Willie Nicholson was believed to be an outside NAACP "agitator" and in the view of many, he had to be stopped at once.

As a consequence, J. Frank Adams, Paul Griffith, and the police chief went prowling around the town looking for Nicholson. They soon saw him leaving a local restaurant and confronted him. Adams was furious and wanted to know why Nicholson was in town "intimidating" a witness. At that point, the stories differ about what happened. But apparently Nicholson loudly denied the charge, demanded that the police chief tell Adams that he hadn't seen Willie Mae, and an exchange of some sort took place.

Adams then ordered the police chief to arrest Nicholson for public intoxication. Nicholson, who was not drunk, flew into a rage and went totally out of control. He drew his gun, grabbed the police chief, frisked him, slapped him hard twice, and shouted at him "Now goddamn it. You tell him the truth." Paul Griffith was still seated in their car and tried to activate his tape recorder. Nicholson saw the recorder, yanked Griffith out of the car, tearing Griffith's coat, and lined up all three men on the street—J. Frank Adams, Buck Griffin, and Paul Griffith—as if he were making an arrest.

A young boy saw what was happening and ran for help. According to Nicholson's statement, he fired one wild shot well over the boy's head. The three public officials, however, claimed that the shot was aimed in their direction. No one was hit. A Florida state trooper, Kenneth Murray, burst onto the scene, at which point Nicholson ran to Murray, crying "Take me. Take me."

Nicholson was arrested and charged with resisting arrest, aggravated assault, and aggravated assault with intent to commit murder. But everyone involved knew that Nicholson was mentally disturbed. He continued his out-of-control behavior in the local jail by manhandling several inmates.

The next day the court sent him to Florida State Hospital in nearby Chattahoochee for a psychiatric examination. The hospital filed a report that found Nicholson insane at the time of the crime. Based on this report, Nicholson was eventually committed to the hospital, although he was later discharged from custody and returned to Miami.[9]

*   *   *

The Nicholson incident made instant front-page news in the *News Herald* of Panama City, the major newspaper in the entire area. The newspaper's headline on February 10, 1967, announced: "Negro Charged In Spree To Undergo Mental Test." The opening paragraph of the adjoining article read:

> Willie Nicholson, who claims to be an official of the NAACP and a special investigator for the Miami Herald, was ordered to undergo psychiatric examination following a wild shooting spree in Port St. Joe Thursday afternoon which could have cost three area officials their lives.[10]

A photograph of State Attorney Frank Adams, Assistant State Attorney Paul Griffith, Police Chief Buck Griffin, Florida Highway Patrol Officer Kenneth Murray, and Deputy Sheriff Wayne White accompanied this article. The caption under the photograph claimed that Adams, Griffith, and Griffin "had narrowly escaped death." There was also a photo of an anguished Willie Nicholson being taken into custody by police with a caption that said that Nicholson had caused the police "plenty of trouble."

The thrust of the article was that the *Miami Herald* and the NAACP had sent Nicholson to Port St. Joe to stir up racial trouble and reopen the Pitts and Lee murder case even though the defendants were guilty. The article quoted the Port St. Joe police chief and Deputy Sheriff Wayne White as saying that Nicholson "was sent to Port St. Joe for the express purpose of deliberately provoking an incident."

But the article failed to report that the *Miami Herald*, in fact, had not sent Nicholson on this trip and had ended their relationship with him some time ago and that Nicholson was not an NAACP official. Mention of the NAACP was particularly incendiary to many white southerners at the time, who regarded the organization as a group of radicals.

But this article was mild compared to what followed two days later. On Sunday, February 12, 1967, the *News Herald* published a long article covering several pages entitled, "All Say Pitts, Lee Guilty," with a subheading that said "Blame Newspapers for Starting Furor." The article was written by staff writers Mike Darley and Guy Middleton.

The article attacked Gene Miller's coverage of the case but did not dispute any fact contained in this coverage. Instead, the article played into the us-against-them theme that was common among many white southerners at the time. According to this narrative, any factual exposé of the South's treatment of its Black citizens was an attack on the entire southern society and therefore should be rejected. The opening paragraphs announced:

> Two Florida newspapers have retried one of the Panhandle's most bizarre murder cases in their news pages, and in so doing have thrown the entire area into a furor.
>
> Serving as prosecutor, defense attorney, judge and jury, the newspapers have rejected the original verdict rendered by neighboring Gulf County's highest court of law.
>
> They find innocent two men who freely confessed to the crime and are now sweating out electrocution on death row at Raiford State Penitentiary—pending the outcome of appeals. . . .
>
> The newspapers have indicted a several-times convicted Port St. Joe felon, described by his own father as a pathological liar, as the real murderer.

In arriving at this summary judgment, the newspapers have impugned the integrity of the entire five-county Fourteenth Judicial Circuit and all its officers.

The two newspapers are The Miami Herald and its Northwest Florida satellite, The Tallahassee Democrat.

Spread out over several pages during a two-day period, the Miami newspaper depicted the people of this area in general as a bunch of red-necked half-wits straight out of an Erskine Caldwell novel. The Tallahassee paper later picked up the articles and serialized them.

Even the courts are held up to ridicule, and law enforcement officers are depicted as dim-witted clods with the inability to track an elephant across a snow bank.

Written in fiction style similar to that used by detective magazines, the articles have drawn criticism from officials and the public in general. . . .

Judge Warren L. Fitzpatrick, the senior jurist in the Fourteenth Circuit, refused even to discuss the claims of the two newspapers. He is the judge who pronounced sentence on the two men. Declared the jurist: "I would not give such trash credibility by commenting on it."

State Attorney J. Frank Adams of Blountstown expressed much the same views. He said: "There's not a word of truth in the whole mess. Better reading can be found in paperbook [sic] pulps."[11]

In all my dealings with the judges, lawyers, and police in this area, I never found anyone who had actually read any of Miller's articles in any detail. I doubt that Judge Fitzpatrick or J. Frank Adams ever did. They just stuck to the story that Pitts and Lee pled guilty and confessed in court and that there was no reason to look behind any of this.

The News Herald's article echoed this sentiment. The article quoted a number of people connected with the case who expressed the flat opinion that Pitts and Lee were guilty or that Curtis Adams was a liar and had nothing to do with the murders. Some said both of these things.[12] End of story. The full set of facts and questions involved in the case were discussed in detail in Miller's articles but were ignored in the News Herald article.

Most shocking to me, and probably the most persuasive for many white southerners in the area, were the opinions expressed by Fred Turner, Pitts and Lee's court-appointed defense lawyer in 1963–1964. Lawyers are ethically bound not to tell outsiders about confidential communications they have had with their clients unless the clients consent—much less tell lies to outsiders about these communications. The article continues:

"I feel they are guilty," said W. Fred Turner, who defended Pitts and Lee during the trial by jury to determine sentence for their confessed murders of Burkett and Floyd.

Turner, described by area lawmen and officials as one of the most able defense lawyers in Northwest Florida, said both Lee and Pitts had confessed to him in detail, and that these confessions "dovetailed" with each other and with the statements of the state's star witness Willie May [sic] Lee.[13]

When I took his deposition a year later, Turner flatly denied that he had been interviewed by any reporter from the *News Herald* for this article.[14] I suppose it was the only thing he could have said, as there is no way he could ever have justified the comments attributed to him in that article. Not surprisingly, Turner never demanded a retraction from the Panama City newspaper or filed suit against them for publishing this story about him.

Finally, attached to the *News Herald*'s article were two other photographs with captions. One was a photograph of Willie Nicholson making a telephone call while in police custody. The caption to the photograph inaccurately described him as an "official of the NAACP." The second photograph was a one of Curtis Adams's father with an overhead title reading "My Boy Didn't Do It." That caption promoted a totally bogus claim that Adams was not in Port St. Joe at the time of the murders.[15] This alleged alibi, however, never materialized and is not discussed in this article or in any other article published about the case. And no law enforcement officer has ever come forward with such proof.

Unfortunately, for the next five years the *News Herald* kept up its slanted news and editorial comment about this case and made it virtually impossible for Pitts and Lee to get a fair trial in this area. That paper's coverage and other telling factors constituted the basis for our continual motions for a change of venue so we could move the case out of the area and have it tried in a more neutral part of the state, such as Tampa, West Palm Beach, or Orlando. But that is another story. At the time, we only knew that we faced an uphill battle to win this case in Gulf County.

15

The Defense Prepares

In September 1968, a one-week hearing was held in this case before the circuit court in Port St. Joe on our defense motion that sought to set aside Pitts and Lee's convictions and order a new trial. But before that happened, some important events occurred.

In February 1967, shortly after Willie Nicholson was sent to the mental hospital in Chattahoochee, Warren Holmes and I decided to visit him there and to do whatever was necessary to get him back home. I also hoped to get some background on the case and to visit Pitts and Lee on death row at Raiford.

I telephoned my friend Virgil Mayo in Blountstown, Florida, to set up a meeting with him to discuss the case. Mayo was the elected public defender for the Fourteenth Judicial Circuit, which included Port St. Joe. I had first met Mayo at several statewide public defender conferences and we had become quite friendly.

I also telephoned the mental hospital and set up a meeting with Willie Nicholson's psychiatrist. Two days later, I flew to Tallahassee, rented a car, and drove to Blountstown, where I met Mayo at his office. We spoke at some length, and Mayo told me that the case was the talk of the entire area.

The following day, Mayo and I drove to the county seat at Wewahitchka, which was about twenty miles south of Blountstown. There I was introduced to George Core, clerk of the court, who showed me the court file on Pitts and Lee. In that file, I discovered two important documents: a Florida Sheriffs Bureau forensic report on the case and J. Frank Adams's motion asking that the 1963 grand jury testimony be typed up because he suspected a witness of perjury. The forensic report found no evidence linking Pitts and Lee to the murders of Floyd and Burkett.

As I learned later, the person J. Frank Adams suspected of perjury was his chief witness, Willie Mae Lee. Both discoveries would prove extremely useful.

The next morning, I left the area and drove to the Tallahassee airport to meet Warren Holmes, who had flown in from Miami. We drove to the mental hospital in Chattahoochee, which was about thirty-five miles west of Tallahassee near the Florida-Georgia border. We were scheduled to meet with Dr. Dunin, who we understood was Nicholson's psychiatrist.

When we arrived, things got a little confusing. We were met by Dr. Hanenson, the chief psychiatrist of the criminal ward and apparently Nicholson's primary doctor. He asked, "Where are the others?" I said I didn't know what he was talking about. Gradually, he told me that the state attorney was supposed to be there. I explained that I had no knowledge of this but the state attorney was welcome to join us, as I wanted to talk with him anyway. Apparently, someone at the hospital had notified the prosecutor of this meeting.

Eventually J. Frank Adams and his top assistant, Paul Griffith, arrived and introductions were made. We then went to Dr. Hanenson's office, where Holmes gave the doctor some background knowledge on Willie Nicholson. Holmes dictated his statement into a Dictaphone in the office and explained how he and Nicholson had previously served together as police officers for the City of Miami.

Later I was able to have a private conference with Adams and Griffith that lasted about half an hour. I had never met Adams before. He was very cordial, no doubt because he knew I was friends with Virgil Mayo. Griffith, however, was more distant and reserved. I apologized for Willie Nicholson's behavior in creating the huge disturbance in Port St. Joe and tried to assure them that he had acted on his own and was not working for either the *Miami Herald* or the defense team. They seemed to accept this explanation.

We then discussed the case of Pitts and Lee. When I asked, Adams acknowledged that he had a written statement by Willie Mae Lee blaming Lambson Smith for the murders of Floyd and Burkett. I asked for a copy, but he refused. I also said that I was greatly disturbed about the case and thought Pitts and Lee were innocent. He shook his head and emphatically said the two men were guilty and that Curtis Adams and Mary Jean Akins were both lying.

Then Adams told me that he was thinking about a grand jury investigation of Warren Holmes and Gene Miller for contempt of court and tampering with a witness. I was aghast and asked what evidence he had for such charges. He said that Willie Mae Lee had made the accusation. I replied that she was lying and that neither Holmes nor Miller had done anything improper. Adams had no answer to that, perhaps because he himself had suspected Willie Mae Lee of lying before the original grand jury back in 1963. At any rate, no such grand jury proceeding was ever held.

When the meeting ended, we shook hands and parted on cordial terms. I explained how I got involved in the case and gave him my card. Adams said I was welcome in his office at any time to discuss the case further and that I could use his telephone and library, although I couldn't look at his file. He was courtly in his manner, but less than forthcoming. There was no way in the world, I thought, that he would ever agree to a new trial for Pitts and Lee.

Then I joined Holmes, who was having a conference with Willie Nicholson in one of the mental wards at the hospital. Although Nicholson was quite agitated, he seemed to calm down when we assured him that we were there to help him and that nothing was likely to come of the charges against him.

The next morning Holmes and I drove to Raiford Prison, which is about 150 miles east of Tallahassee, where I met and talked to Pitts and Lee for the first time. I had never been to this prison. It was a dark and forbidding place, especially in the rain. The security was heavy and there were many iron gates to get through. We finally arrived at death row and were led into an interview room, where I met Pitts and Lee. We talked mainly about the contacts they had had with their court-appointed attorney, Fred Turner. Pitts gave me his huge file on the case, which included a number of army records and letters. My most dominant memory of these two men is how polite and courteous they both were.

One other incident is worth mentioning. I always shook hands with Pitts and Lee whenever I saw them. It was an automatic gesture for me whenever I met someone I hadn't seen in a while, and I never thought anything of it. Many years later, however, Lee told me that several of the prison guards were upset with me for doing this, as it indicated that I was treating them as equals. That incident always stuck in my mind as a sad indication of the era we were living in, that even this small act of courtesy was seen as somehow threatening and sinister. When the interview was over, Holmes and I returned to Miami.

* * *

Late in 1967, J. Frank Adams asked the Florida attorney general's office to represent the state at any hearings on our motion to vacate the defendants' conviction while he remained in the background. Earl Faircloth, the attorney general at the time, had ties to South Florida. I was surprised but delighted with this development, as I thought it brought a more independent perspective to the case. It gave me some hope that I might convince someone in that office that there was a reasonable doubt about Pitts and Lee's guilt or innocence, enough to give them a new trial. Although J. Frank Adams was adamant about opposing a new trial, the attorney general might see things differently.

S. R. "Speedy" DeWitt, an investigator with the attorney general's office, was soon assigned to the case and he came to Miami and looked me up. We had a long discussion, during which he impressed me with his openness and objectivity about the case. Ultimately, we agreed to exchange investigative information: he gave me his witness statements and I gave him mine. Although I didn't know it at the time, both Miller and Holmes thought this move was ill advised, that we were giving away more than we were getting. But as it turned out, this agreement proved to be crucial in our battle to get a new trial.

During one of my depositions in North Florida, DeWitt gave me a stenographer's written copy of the statement J. Frank Adams took from Willie Mae Lee blaming Freddie Pitts and Lambson Smith for the charged murders. I don't think we would have gotten it otherwise. Despite what he had earlier told me at the mental hospital in Chattahoochee, J. Frank Adams now claimed that the statement had been oral and that he had no such written statement in his file. But of course he did. And, as it turned out, it was the state's suppression of this evidence favorable to the defense that ultimately enabled us to obtain a new trial. It was a critical piece of evidence and it was DeWitt who gave it to me.

DeWitt, however, was less than candid about another important matter. On February 20, 1968, DeWitt and J. Frank Adams took a sworn written statement from Willie Mae Lee in Port St. Joe.[1] In this statement, she retracted her testimony against Pitts and Lee and said that she had no knowledge of the murders of Floyd and Burkett. Contrary to our agreement, however, DeWitt did not reveal this statement to me. This statement didn't surface until four years later, in 1972, during the new trial proceedings in the case.

The duplicity was astounding. At the time, we were litigating whether the state attorney had suppressed evidence of innocence back in 1963 by not disclosing Willie Mae Lee's statement blaming Pitts and Smith for these murders. Yet the state attorney was suppressing yet another statement by Willie Mae Lee that totally exonerated Pitts and Lee of these same murders.

When I eventually learned what Adams had secretly done, I was enraged at his cynical disregard of his legal duty to reveal to the defendant any evidence favorable to the defense. In the 1963 landmark decision in *Brady v. Maryland*,[2] the US Supreme Court had expressly imposed such a duty on the state. Yet in violation of that duty, Adams had suppressed one of the most vital pieces of evidence for the defense that one could imagine.

In the statement J. Frank Adams took from Willie Mae Lee in 1972, she flatly stated that she had no knowledge of the robbery of the Mo Jo Service Station and the murders of Grover Floyd and Jesse Burkett:

> Q. [DeWitt] Billie, is it your testimony under oath today that you were not present when Skipper's Mo Jo Service Station was robbed on August 1, 1963?
> A. [Willie Mae Lee] That's right.
> Q. At any time was Grover Floyd, Jr. and/or Jesse Burkett, the two men who were working at the service station, in an automobile in which you were riding?
> A. No.
> Q. Do you know of your own knowledge who, if anybody, killed these two men?
> A. No I don't.[3]

She then gave a four-and-a-half-page narrative account of her whereabouts on the night of the murders. It was substantially the same statement she had repeatedly told the police when she was first arrested—an account the police refused to believe. Although the statement meanders at times, she essentially said that she had joined Pitts, Lee, Dorothy Martin, and Ella Mae Lee at the Mo Jo station on the night in question, that they all went back to the party at Wilbert Lee's house, and that later she went off with Freddie Pitts in his car for the rest of the night. She was Pitts's alibi.

Willie Mae Lee had tried to explain all of this the year before, when Detective Elihu Phares and Warren Holmes had gone to her home in Port St. Joe and she had exclaimed, "I've waited three years to tell the truth." But now she had her chance. She could finally tell her story to State Attorney J. Frank Adams, someone she liked and trusted, and S. R. DeWitt, who represented the highest law enforcement agency in the state, confident that both men would protect her from any reprisals.

Ultimately, however, this statement would not stand. DeWitt and J. Frank Adams refused to believe her. Willie Mae Lee later reverted to her 1963 testimony, and that is the testimony she would repeat at the September 1968 hearing in Port St. Joe and later at the new trial in Marianna in 1972.

*   *   *

From the outset, both Gene Miller and Warren Holmes wanted a big-name criminal lawyer to take charge of the case. They thought, and I agreed, that we needed the power of a nationally known criminal lawyer to help carry this case to victory. Also, given the immense complexity of the case, I needed another experienced criminal lawyer to share the workload. Maurice Rosen, my current co-counsel, had taken himself out of the running for this role, given his limited experience as a criminal lawyer. He preferred to be a backup player and oversee some of the investigations in the case.

I therefore turned to Edward Bennett Williams, who was one of the most respected criminal lawyers in the country. He was the senior partner in the law firm of Williams & Connolly in Washington, DC, and had recently won an acquittal for Jimmy Hoffa, the former president of the Teamsters Union, on bribery charges. He also represented many prominent people who were under investigation by congressional committees.[4]

On February 16, 1967, I telephoned Williams and had a friendly conversation with him about the case. He seemed interested but wanted to know more. He asked me to write him a letter outlining the case in some detail. So the next day I wrote him a two-and-a-half-page letter reciting the basic facts of the case and asking if he would become the chief counsel for Pitts and Lee with me serving as his co-counsel.[5]

Several weeks later, I heard from Williams's office that Williams wanted to discuss the case further with us. So I flew to Washington, DC, with Warren Holmes and Gene Miller and we saw Williams in his office. We each explained the case in some detail. Williams was courteous, listened intently, and asked occasional questions. But I could tell from his manner that he was less than enthusiastic. At the end of the meeting, he said that he would "help" us without stating what that help might consist of. He said he'd be in touch with us later and the meeting ended.

Miller and Holmes were much encouraged and thought that Williams had joined the defense team. I was skeptical, however, because I didn't think Williams had committed himself to much—only that he would "help" us, whatever that meant. Still, I was willing to wait and see what might develop.

*   *   *

For the next year and a half, I plowed ahead with the case, taking depositions from numerous witnesses in North Florida, filing pleadings, writing memos, researching the law, and developing a coherent defense for court.

I also got to know Gene Miller and Warren Holmes better. Early on, I had asked Holmes if he would investigate a minor matter in the case. Holmes declined and said to check with Gene. I felt odd doing this, but I turned to Miller with the same request and he readily agreed. It was the first time that I had ever asked a news reporter to take on a task in one of my cases.

But I soon became comfortable with this arrangement. I found Miller to be a relentless investigator who was obsessed with detail. He was friendly with everyone but never took no for an answer. He almost always tracked down what I was seeking, plus what he wanted as a journalist. In fact, that was Miller's trademark. He overwhelmed his readers over the next eight-and-a-half years with a thicket of facts in the many lengthy investigative articles he wrote on the case for the *Miami Herald*.

Indeed, throughout the entire case, Miller regarded every member of the defense team, including me, as a potential news source. He relished talking to us so he could learn more about the progress of the case, just as he kept in constant touch with many other important figures in the case. In doing all this, Miller in effect became an adjunct to the defense team, although he never acted under our direction. On the contrary, he was a fiercely independent reporter and maintained that role throughout the case. He was convinced that Pitts and Lee were innocent and was always eager to uncover evidence for his readers that showed just that. As it happened, that fit perfectly into what we also wanted as defense counsel.

Miller would often telephone me two or three times a week, wanting to know what was happening or might happen in the case, suggesting things he could do that would help us and help him as a reporter. In his conversations with me, I had full confidence that he would never quote me in the newspaper without my consent. And whatever I suggested that he investigate would often lead him to other people and important information that he would later report to me and to his readers. He was a master at networking.

In this happy association, I learned what a superb news reporter Gene Miller was and how dedicated he was to rectifying miscarriages of justice. Indeed, in 1967 Miller had won a Pulitzer Prize for his exemplary news reporting. In a series of investigative news articles he wrote for the *Miami Herald*, he had helped exonerate Mary Katherine Hampton, an 18-year-old girl of minimal intelligence who had pled guilty to murders she did not commit in Louisiana. Miller did the same journalist work that helped exonerate a US airman, Joseph Shea, who had been wrongly convicted of murder in Dade County, Florida.[6]

Ultimately, Gene Miller—with Warren Holmes's help—located, interviewed, and kept tabs on all the defense witnesses in the Pitts-Lee case, including Mary Jean Akins, Broward County Deputy Sheriff Elihu Phares, and the army CID investigators, Bruce Potts and Donald Hoag. Miller also tracked down the critical army CID reports that Potts and Hoag filed in August 1963. But of utmost importance, Miller kept the case in the public eye by writing a continuous stream of news articles on the case for the next eight-and-a-half years, for which he would win another Pulitzer Prize. Indeed, Miller's name became almost synonymous with the case in the Florida Panhandle, drawing the extreme ire of the political and legal establishment in the Fourteenth Judicial Circuit of Florida.

Throughout, Miller had little use for all the "boring" legal obstacles that stood in our way. He, like Holmes, regarded such "technicalities" as a nuisance that had little justification—a legal thicket that had to be cut down to free Pitts and Lee. I admired Miller's pursuit of justice at all costs, but I was also a lawyer with enormous respect for the law and the courts.

In Robert Bolt's play *A Man For All Seasons,* Thomas More, the lord chancellor of England, has a telling speech that I have always admired. More rejects his son-in-law's demand "to cut down every law in England" to get to the Devil so that a "dangerous" man, an enemy to More, could be arrested. And More replies:

> Oh, and when the last law was down, and the Devil turned round on you—where would you hide, Roper, the laws all being flat? This country's planted thick with laws from coast to coast—Man's laws, not God's—and if you cut them down, and you're just the man to do it—d'you really think you could stand upright in the winds that would blow then? Yes, I'd give the Devil benefit of law, for my own safety's sake.[7]

That speech always stuck in my mind whenever I heard Miller or Holmes express their exasperation with the law and the glacial progress the case was taking in the courts. With all its merits and shortcomings, I've always believed that our Constitution, our law, and our courts are what hold this diverse country together.

Indeed, as defense lawyers, we were convinced throughout that despite the adverse Florida law and our tough grind in the Florida courts, we would eventually win this case in the US Supreme Court. At the time, the Court was led by Chief Justice Earl Warren. In my view, that Court was one of the greatest courts in our history. Its members include such giants as Justices Hugo Black, William Douglas, Felix Frankfurter, William Brennan, Thurgood Marshall, and John Harlan. It was our beacon of hope as we battled in the Florida courts.

*　*　*

In the late spring of 1968, as the scheduled hearing in Port St. Joe was drawing near, I gave up on Edward Bennett Williams. We had not heard from him for nearly a year, and his silence meant only one thing. He was not going to take over this case. Williams, citing a conflicting trial date, would eventually send an able young lawyer in his law firm, Michael Tigar, to attend the Port St. Joe hearing and briefly advise us.

So I reached out for help to an able and experienced criminal lawyer in Miami, Irwin Block. I thought Block was just as good as and perhaps better than Williams. He accepted immediately. I knew Block slightly and admired his trial skills in court. I had also heard him lecture at local legal seminars and thought he was excellent. Block, in fact, was a member of the legal panel of the local ACLU and was already somewhat familiar with the Pitts and Lee case.

Gene Miller was in complete agreement with this choice and later wrote that Block was "a remarkable attorney," "cautious, methodical, precise, and a prophet of doom he usually averted."[8] Originally from Brooklyn, he had served in the United States Marines in the late 1940s and had later graduated from the University of Miami School of Law. He was the chief of the Capital Crimes Division of the Dade County State Attorney's Office for four years, during which he was in charge of every capital murder prosecution in Dade County. He entered private practice thereafter with the law firm of Fine, Jacobson & Block, handling a wide variety of criminal and civil cases. Richard E. Gerstein, the elected state attorney, often said that of the 500 attorneys who had passed through the Dade County State Attorney's Office, "Irwin Block was the one attorney I most wanted back."[9]

Block immersed himself in the case. He studied all the pleadings and memos I had filed and read all the depositions I had taken. We had numerous conferences, planned strategy, divided up the legal work, issued witness subpoenas, prepared pleadings and memos, plotted out examinations and cross-examinations, and thoroughly prepared over the summer for the Port St. Joe court hearing in September 1968.

Over the next eight years, we were colleagues and eventually became good friends. We worked well together and respected each other's talents. But most important, we both had what this case absolutely demanded—a deeply held commitment to civil rights and a fierce determination to get justice for Pitts and Lee, no matter what the odds against them were.

Block put in thousands of hours on the case, which cost him and his law firm an untold amount of attorney's fees that he could have otherwise earned in other paying cases. I always admired him for that sacrifice. I put in thousands of hours too, but I was on a state salary; Block wasn't.

He was also about ten years my senior and had eighteen years of legal experience compared to my seven years of practice.[10] So there was no question that this tall, friendly but imposing figure would be the chief counsel in the case and that I would be his co-counsel. We were now ready for the circuit court hearing in Port St. Joe.

16

The Port St. Joe Hearing Begins

From September 23 through September 27, 1968, a hearing was held before the circuit court for the Fourteenth Judicial Circuit in Port St. Joe on our motion to set aside Pitts and Lee's convictions and order a new trial. Thirty witnesses testified during that tumultuous week, and almost daily something happened—both in and out of court—that I marveled at or had never before experienced. The media coverage was pervasive; reporters were in attendance from the *Miami Herald,* the *News Herald* of Panama City, and the *Star* (a local paper). Spectators jammed the courtroom every day, and it was the talk of the entire area.[1]

The chief justice of the Florida Supreme Court had appointed Circuit Judge Charles Holley of Clearwater to preside at this hearing. Because of the notoriety of the case and possible conflicts of interest, all the judges in the Fourteenth Judicial Circuit had recused themselves from the case and had asked the Supreme Court to appoint a judge from outside the circuit.

Judge Holley was quite prominent in the state. Before becoming a judge, he had been the Republican nominee for governor of Florida in 1964. His campaign had presented him as someone who was to the political right of Barry Goldwater, the highly conservative GOP nominee for president that year. Holley lost the governor's election in a landslide to Democrat Haydon Burns, the mayor of Jacksonville. But Burns was followed several years later by Republican Claude R. Kirk Jr., who appointed Holley to the circuit court in Clearwater.

Neither Block nor I had ever appeared before Holley and were wary of him because of his conservative background. Still, he also had a reputation for being a maverick and was perhaps, we thought, capable of ruling against expectations. He was independent enough to be a Republican in a state that was dominated at that time by the Democratic Party, and he didn't seem to be connected with the good old boy political network in North Florida. We thought we had a chance with him.

At the time of the hearing, the county seat for Gulf County had just been moved from Wewahitchka to Port St. Joe. The hearing took place on the second floor of a beautiful, brand-new courthouse located on a large tract of land near the outskirts of Port St. Joe. A newly constructed building that housed the sheriff's office and jail was situated next to the courthouse and a large parking area adjoined these buildings.

The courtroom was modern. Gone were the spittoons and overhead fans that had long adorned southern courtrooms. The judge's bench, the jury box, and counsel tables were enclosed inside a railing that opened in the middle with small swinging doors. There was also a large seating area containing long benches for spectators. It was a typical American courtroom.

All of these new facilities were air conditioned, except for the jail cells where Pitts and Lee were held for this weeklong hearing, which was probably a deliberate decision not to "coddle" the prisoners. Deputy Sheriff Wayne White had put both men in maximum-security cells with no windows because, he said, he feared someone might try to shoot them with a high-powered rifle.[2] The temperatures in these cells went to 100 degrees during the day, and, as a result, Pitts and Lee perspired so heavily at times that they had to remove their clothes. But they were apparently allowed to shower each day, because they always came to court looking refreshed.[3]

Irwin Block and I were the chief lawyers representing Pitts and Lee. Also serving as defense counsel were Maurice Rosen and Pitts's former army lawyer, Jack Winick. Rosen continued his work of overseeing our outside investigations; he directed the logistics of getting our witnesses to court. Winick, who had left the army some time before, did any backup legal work we needed. At his own expense, he volunteered his legal services at this hearing and all other important hearings in the case. Of all the lawyers in the case, I think Pitts and Lee felt closest to Winick in gratitude for his steadfast loyalty. Mike Tigar, the young lawyer from Edward Bennett Williams's office, also made a brief appearance and consulted with us concerning the case. He sat at defense counsel table for two days, following which he concluded that the case was in good hands and returned to Washington, DC.[4]

Two veteran lawyers in the appellate section of the Florida attorney general's office, George Georgieff and Ray Markey, represented the state. I knew and had faced both lawyers in the past in the many appeals I had argued in the Florida courts, although at the time of this hearing I was no longer doing appeals and was trying cases in the felony trial division. State Attorney J. Frank Adams also appeared for the state in a backup capacity, along with his assistant Paul Griffith.

Georgieff, the lead counsel for the state, was the most colorful of the prosecution team. He was aggressive and supremely confident and had a quick mind. He often elicited shocked reactions from the occasional blunt pronouncements that he relished making. Ray Markey was not nearly as colorful but nonetheless had a feisty manner. He, too, was aggressive and confident when he got going, often pounding away in arguments before the court.

What I particularly remember about both these men is how disdainful they were of the federal courts. Georgieff once told me that Black criminal defendants always won their cases in the US Supreme Court once the case was accepted for review. He thought it futile to argue for the state when that happened and said if there was any way he could transfer the case to a younger and less-experienced lawyer in the office, he would do so. I was appalled at that comment, as it accused the court of being racially biased, which was a totally baseless charge.

Nonetheless, both Georgieff and Markey were honorable men whose word I trusted. Indeed, throughout the hearing, Georgieff seemed intent on getting to the truth of the matter rather than winning at any cost. Prior to the hearing, I had hoped that Georgieff and Markey might bring an independent perspective to the case that would lead them to agree to a new trial. But I soon realized that they intended to oppose our motion for a new trial at every turn.

* * *

The courtroom was jam-packed with spectators on the first day of the hearing. I estimated that about 300 people watched the proceedings throughout the week. Most were white, although a few scattered Black people attended who chose to sit together. Whites and Blacks, however, were not officially segregated, as some southern courtrooms had been not so long ago. Although everybody seemed quiet and respectful, we always sensed an air of possible violence against us. We were outsiders defending men convicted of murdering local residents. We never felt comfortable.

Holley opened the court proceedings by identifying what he understood were the four grounds we were urging as grounds for setting aside Pitts and Lee's convictions and ordering a new trial. As the judge stated and the defense counsel agreed, those grounds were: innocence, suppression of evidence favorable to the defense, coerced confessions, and incompetent court-appointed counsel. In the motion I had filed in December 1967, those were the grounds I had alleged, and they were the contested issues at this hearing.[5]

At the outset, Holley ordered that all witnesses in the case were to remain outside the courtroom until called to testify and were not to discuss the case with anyone except the lawyers.[6] This order, often referred to as the "rule on sequestration of witnesses," is a routine directive in court hearings and trials. The order is designed to make certain that witnesses do not tailor their testimony by listening to the testimony of other witnesses. As is sometimes done, however, Holley made an exception for the parties' investigators S. R. DeWitt and Warren Holmes—and for Gene Miller as a member of the press and for J. Frank Adams as one of the lawyers for the state.

As a result, Gene Miller was able to remain in the courtroom and see and talk to Pitts and Lee for the first time. Until then, he had been prohibited by prison and jail regulations from seeing them in custody.[7] It was an emotional meeting, one of many Pitts and Lee would have with Miller in other courtrooms in the years to come.

Because he felt he was too close to the case to objectively observe the proceedings, Miller did not cover the hearing for the *Miami Herald*. His colleagues Bill Mansfield and Jim Minter were assigned this task. Miller had already written a number of comprehensive articles on the case. In addition to his two lengthy articles in February 1967, Miller continued to publish additional stories on various aspects of the case,[8] including two overviews that the *Herald* published on the eve of the Port St. Joe hearing.[9]

* * *

After the sequestration rule was invoked, Holley was handed a note from the sheriff's office. The note stated: "Willie Mae threatened by someone. She scared to death. Sheriff ready to swear to this if requested."[10] Willie Mae Lee (the state's alleged "eyewitness") was at that time in jail, having been brought there at the direction of Deputy Sheriff Wayne White.[11]

Holley decided to look into the matter and ordered that she be brought to the courtroom. Willie Mae Lee soon appeared. She was sworn in, and, after some probing by the court, testified that the previous night an un-named person had come to her house. She continued:

> This boy told me, say if I go to Court—he didn't threaten me, he told me that he overheard somebody say that if I go to Court that there was going to be a black mob at me.
> * * *
> I don't know him, but he know my name and he came to our house last night. He asked my brother could he talk to me, and my brother in law told him no.
> The Court. Are you afraid?
> Miss Lee. Yes, sir. Anybody would be scared, I guess.
> The Court. Are you afraid?
> Miss Lee. Yes, sir.
> The Court. You afraid of testifying? You afraid somebody's going to do something to you?
> Miss Lee. I don't know whether they going to do something or not. I just hope they don't.
> The Court. What do you want us to do about it?
> Miss Lee. (No response)
> The Court. Nothing? If you want us to do something we'll do it.
> Miss Lee. I don't know. I don't want to get killed. That's for sure.
> The Court. More people get killed by automobiles than anything else. That what we're talking about?
> Miss Lee. I don't know.
> The Court. All right. You want the Sheriff to hold you in custody?
> Miss Lee. What you mean, how—
> The Court. You want him to hold you over in the jail so nobody can get to you?
> Miss Lee. I just left the jail.
> The Court. Is he holding you over there now? Is he letting you stay at the jail?
> Miss Lee. Yes, sir.
> The Court. Do you want him to let you stay there overnight so no-body can get to you?
> Miss Lee. If I got to—yes.
> The Court. What do you want, Willie Mae?
> Miss Lee. Yes, sir, I rather stay in jail than for someone to kill me.

The Court. All right, the witness will be held in protective custody until further order of the court. Take her out, please.[12]

Willie Mae Lee was then removed from the court and locked up in a jail cell until she was called as a witness. Once again she was under the control of the police and knew full well what would happen to her if she displeased the authorities. The state didn't want to hear that she had no knowledge of these murders. She had to tell the story the state wanted to hear and she was in a place that would greatly encourage her to do so.

Tellingly, Willie Mae Lee was never offered the option of receiving police protection while she remained at her home in Port St. Joe. That would have been a routine choice, I would have thought, for most other people in the community, particularly for white people. Instead, she had to "consent" to jail if she wanted protection. The police didn't even try to investigate and arrest the person who was threatening her. What for? They had her where they wanted her—in jail and frightened.

*   *   *

Block and I put on an array of witnesses that first day in court, and it all went as expected. On our claims of innocence and coerced confessions, we called the following people:

- The two army CID officers, Sergeants Bruce Potts and Donald Hoag, who testified to their investigation of this case. They concluded that there had been insufficient evidence to charge Pitts and Lee with the murders of Floyd and Burkett.[13] They also related how the Bay County police had refused to give them permission to see Pitts for an entire week, that when they did get to see him, he was all beaten up, and that they took a written statement from him repudiating his prior confession to the police.[14]
- Wilbert Lee's wife, Ella Mae Lee, who had been jailed and questioned by the police for several weeks without a formal charge, testified that she had seen Pitts in jail and that he was all beaten up.[15] Wilbert Lee would later testify that the police had threatened to execute Ella Mae Lee, who was still in jail, if he didn't confess—and, in fact, he did confess after receiving physical blows to the head from one of the officers.[16]
- Thomasina Stallworth, Pitts's former girlfriend, who was also jailed

and questioned by the police for several weeks without a formal charge, testified to Pitts's beaten-up condition when she saw him in jail.[17]

- Henry Hogue, the elderly Black gentleman who gave Pitts and Willie Mae Lee a shove when their car stalled on the night in question, gave similar testimony that he had seen Pitts's beaten-up condition when he was picked up by the police and saw Pitts in jail.[18]
- Dr. C. W. Ketchum, the pathologist who did the autopsy in this case, identified the autopsy report that he filed.[19] Later we showed that the findings in this report contradicted Pitts and Lee's confessions and Willie Mae Lee's statement.

But the most important witness we called that day, the central witness who helped us win a new trial, was the state attorney, J. Frank Adams. His testimony fully supported our claim that the state had suppressed evidence of innocence, namely, a statement by Willie Mae Lee naming Lambson Smith as one of the killers of Floyd and Burkett. Holley ultimately accepted this claim and the Florida Supreme Court upheld it.

Here is Adams's testimony:

Q. [By Mr. Hubbart]. Mr. Adams, let me show you what's been marked as Plaintiff's Exhibit 5 for Identification and ask whether or not this was the statement which you took from Willie Mae Lee during the course of the investigation of this case in which Willie Mae Lee blamed Lambson Smith and Freddie Pitts for the murders of Grover Floyd and Jesse Burkett?

A. [Examining]. It appears to be, yes, a copy of it.

Q. Do you have the original in your file?

A. I'm not sure whether I do or not. I have several witness statements in there, but I'm not sure that I have that one.

Q. You took the statement yourself, did you not?

A. I believe I did. Yes—'by Mr. Adams.'

* * *

Q. All right. Did you have this statement in your file, reduced to writing, in August 1963?

A. Yes, sir.

Q. Now during your discussions with Fred Turner in August 1963, subsequent to his appointment to represent the Petitioners in this case did you ever give Mr. Turner a copy of this statement?

A. I don't recall that I did.

Q. Did you ever disclose to Mr. Turner of the existence of this statement?

A. I don't recall that I did. I discussed it with him several times, the facts, some of the facts, and I won't say that it wasn't mentioned or it was. I'm not sure, just offhand conversation between he and I, but as far as giving him any official notice of this, that, or the other I don't recall that I did.[20]

Later, Judge Holley admitted in evidence Willie Mae Lee's statement to J. Frank Adams blaming Freddie Pitts and Lambson Smith for the charged murders.[21]

I also elicited from Mr. Adams an admission that he suspected Willie Mae Lee of committing perjury before the grand jury when she blamed Pitts and Lee for the charged murders. Mr. Adams had conducted the grand jury hearing himself and wanted her testimony typed up for a later possible perjury prosecution. This testimony also supported our claim of innocence.[22]

When I returned to the defense table after this colloquy to confer with co-counsel, Mike Tigar whispered to me, "Home run!"

*   *   *

While all went well in court that day, things happened out of court that reminded us of the precarious position we were all in.

It began during a break in the hearing that day. Pitts told us that he had left some papers in the jail cell adjoining the courtroom and needed to see them. Jack Winick volunteered to get the papers. As Winick left the courtroom and approached the cell area, he overheard one of the sheriff's deputies talking to a fellow officer. "Goddamn Jew lawyers from Miami," the deputy said, "coming up here and making all this trouble." As it happened, all of the defense lawyers in the case were Jewish except for me. Winick ignored the comment, retrieved the papers, and returned to the courtroom. He was uneasy about this encounter but not surprised.[23]

A more threatening incident occurred after court was adjourned for the day. We defense lawyers had packed up our files and were on the way to our car in the parking lot. I was with Block and Rosen. As we approached the car, Rosen happened to see several sharp one-and-a-half-inch spikes hidden under the two front tires. They would have punctured the tires if we had driven off without noticing them.[24] But almost immediately, we all thought of something more ominous. Because I had no children at the time and Block and Rosen did, I was elected to look under the car hood for a possible bomb. I did so without hesitation and luckily discovered no explosive device.

About that time, Judge Holley appeared in the parking lot looking for his car. We called him over so he could see the spikes under our tires. He didn't seem too concerned and later referred to the incident as a "malicious prank."[25] After removing the spikes, we drove to our motel for the night with great relief. That night we planned our strategy as usual for the next day's court proceedings.

Imprisoned 12 Years, 48 Days

Pitts, Lee Walk as Free Men

'We'll Keep
Our Plans
To Ourselves'

By GENE MILLER

Arrival at Miami Airport: For Pitts, Left, and Lee, No Bus Was Fast Enough

Freddie Pitts and Wilbert Lee at the Miami International Airport, September 19, 1975, being greeted by a crowd of well-wishers after they were released from prison earlier that day. The photo appears on the front page of the *Miami Herald* with an accompanying article by Gene Miller. Courtesy of Albert Coya, *Miami Herald*.

Mo Jo Gas Station outside Port St. Joe, Florida, where service station attendants Grover Floyd and Jesse Burkett were robbed and kidnapped on the night of July 31, 1963. Courtesy of Warren Holmes.

Hand-painted "White Ladies Only" sign at the entrance to the women's restroom at the Mo Jo gas station. Site of an argument in which the service station attendants, Grover Floyd and Jesse Burkett, barred Dorothy Martin, a Black woman, from using the facilities on the night of July 31, 1963. Courtesy of Warren Holmes.

Telephone booth at the Mo Jo gas station where Wilbert Lee made a phone call on the night of July 31, 1963. Courtesy of Warren Holmes.

Freddie Pitts, 25, and Wilbert Lee, 33, leave the courtroom at the Pinellas County courthouse, April 30, 1969, in Clearwater after Circuit Judge Charles Holley dismissed murder convictions against the two men. Courtesy of AP Images.

Freddie Pitts and Wilbert Lee leaving Gulf County Jail, Port St. Joe. 1971. Courtesy of State Archives of Florida, Florida Memory.

Reubin Askew, governor of Florida from 1971 to 1977. After an eighteen-month investigation, Askew led the effort to pardon Freddie Pitts and Wilbert Lee on the ground of innocence. The pardon became effective on September 19, 1975. Courtesy of State Archives of Florida, Florida Memory.

Robert Shevin, Florida attorney general from 1971 to 1977. Shevin's confession of error in the Pitts-Lee case before the Florida Supreme Court led to a new trial. Shevin also voted to pardon Freddie Pitts and Wilbert Lee on the ground of innocence. Courtesy of State Archives of Florida, Florida Memory.

Circuit Judge Charles Holley of Clearwater, Florida. Holley granted Freddie Pitts and Wilbert Lee a new trial on April 28, 1969. Courtesy of State Archives of Florida, Florida Memory.

George Core, clerk of the Circuit Court for the Fourteenth Judicial Circuit of Florida. Core testified that no Black person had ever served on the Gulf County grand jury during the period 1948–1963. He later amended his testimony to say that one Black person had so served. Courtesy of Phillip Hubbart.

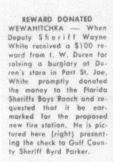

REWARD DONATED
WEWAHITCHKA — When Deputy Sheriff Wayne White received a $100 reward from I. W. Duren for solving a burglary at Duren's store in Port St. Joe, White promptly donated the money to the Florida Sheriffs Boys Ranch and requested that it be earmarked for the proposed new fire station. He is pictured here (right) presenting the check to Gulf County Sheriff Byrd Parker.

Gulf County Sheriff Byrd Parker (*left*) and Gulf County Deputy Sheriff Wayne White (*right*). White was one of the two major investigators in the Pitts-Lee case. Parker did some investigative work in the early stages of the case. Courtesy of *The Sheriff's Star* magazine.

Gene Miller, Pulitzer Prize–winning journalist with the *Miami Herald*. Miller's pervasive coverage of the Pitts-Lee case 1967–1975 and his book *Invitation to a Lynching* led directly to the pardon of Pitts and Lee on the ground of innocence. Miller earned a Pulitzer Prize for his news coverage of the case—the second in his career. Courtesy of Caroline Hecht-Miller.

Miami private polygraph examiner Warren Holmes. On December 21, 1966, Holmes obtained a detailed tape-recorded statement from Curtis Adams in which Adams confessed to the Port St. Joe murders of Grover Floyd and Jesse Burkett and to the Fort Lauderdale murder of Floyd McFarland. Courtesy of Warren Holmes.

Freddie Pitts and Wilbert Lee with their defense team, circa early 1980s, after they were pardoned and released from prison. *From left to right*: Freddie Pitts, Gene Miller, Wilbert Lee, Irwin Block, Phillip Hubbart, Maurice Rosen, and Warren Holmes. Courtesy of Tim Chapman, *Miami Herald*.

Doris Block, wife of Irwin Block. On March 17, 1972, when Pitts and Lee were sentenced to death, Block came out of the audience, ran into the well of the court, and shouted at the judge, D. R. Smith, and the prosecutor, Leo Jones, "I hope you have this on your conscience until the day you die." Courtesy of Phillip Hubbart.

Freddie Pitts and Wilbert Lee after their second murder trial, 1972. Courtesy of State Archives of Florida, Florida Memory.

Jesse Pait, fellow inmate with Curtis Adams at Florida State Prison. Informed on Adams to the Broward County Sheriff's Office to obtain a $15,000 cash reward from the *Miami Herald*. Pait said that Adams confessed to him that he (Adams) committed the Floyd McFarland murder in Fort Lauderdale, and the Floyd-Burkett murders in Port St. Joe. Courtesy of Warren Holmes.

Curtis Adams testifying before the Florida House Select Committee in Tallahassee, Florida, on September 27, 1979, regarding a proposed bill to award Freddie Pitts and Wilbert Lee compensation for their twelve years of wrongful imprisonment. Freddie Pitts (*left*) and Wilbert Lee (*right*) sit behind Adams. Courtesy of State Archives of Florida, Florida Memory.

Mary Jean Akins, former girlfriend of Curtis Adams. Akins testified that Adams confessed to her that he committed the murders of Floyd and Burkett in Port St. Joe on the night of the murders and again in more detail the following night. Courtesy of Warren Holmes.

The Gulf County Circuit Courtroom in Wewahitchka, Florida, where Freddie Pitts and Wilbert Lee were tried and sentenced to death on August 28, 1963. Courtesy of Ted Hubbart.

Gulf County Circuit Courtroom in Port St. Joe, Florida. On September 23–27, 1968, an evidentiary hearing was held in this courtroom on the defendants' motion to vacate their murder convictions and order a new trial. Courtesy of Ted Hubbart.

Jackson County Circuit Courthouse. On February 21–March 8, 1972, Freddie Pitts and Wilbert Lee were retried and sentenced to death in this courthouse. Courtesy of Ted Hubbart.

Pitts and Lee's defense lawyers going to court for a hearing in Clearwater, Florida, on April 28, 1969. *Left to right*: Maurice Rosen, Phillip Hubbart, and Irwin Block. Courtesy of the *Miami Herald*.

Phillip Hubbart and Irwin Block, defense lawyers for Freddie Pitts and Wilbert Lee, arriving for court at the new trial in Marianna, Florida, circa March 1972. Courtesy of Jim Birmingham, *Miami Herald*.

Wilbert Lee and Phillip Hubbart in Lee's home in Miami circa the early 2000s, many decades after Pitts and Lee had been released from prison. Courtesy of Phillip Hubbart.

17

The Port St. Joe Hearing Continues

If the first day of the Port St. Joe hearing was relatively quiet despite some disconcerting incidents, the second day was explosive, filled with dramatic and extraordinary events.

Our opening witness was Bay County Sheriff M. J. "Doc" Daffin, the chief police investigator in the case. It was the last time Daffin would ever testify in court concerning this matter, as he died in 1971. We called him as an adverse witness—that is, a witness opposed to our interest in the case—which allowed us to cross-examine him. Irwin Block did the questioning.

I had previously taken Daffin's deposition and knew what a dominating personality he had. He was a political power in the Florida Panhandle and had been for nearly twenty years. But on that day in court, Daffin was a different person. He cowered under Block's withering inquiry. Block's manner was polite, but he asked pointed, rapid-fire questions that left little room for evasion.

Block began with a barrage of questions. He got Daffin to admit that Fred Turner had been in the police interrogation room when Pitts and Lee had confessed.[1] This testimony supported our claim that Turner was incompetent as Pitts and Lee's lawyer because he participated with the police in obtaining confessions from his own clients. This testimony also supported our claim that Pitts and Lee's ensuing pleas of guilty and confessions in court were involuntary because they were extracted from them by their incompetent court-appointed lawyer.

Block then cut down Daffin's standing as a law enforcement officer, demonstrating that he was simply a politician.

Q. Now Sheriff, your job is an elected office.
A. That's correct.
Q. All right. You didn't start as a deputy in that office and work your way up, did you?

A. No, sir.

Q. And before being elected sheriff you had no law enforcement experience, did you?

A. Well, not exactly, no sir.

Q. And you never graduated from any police academy.

A. No, sir.

Q. And you never attended any training courses put on by Northwestern University on police science.

A. No.

Q. And you never attended any police training courses put on by any university, did you?

A. No, sir.

Q. And you never attended any FBI police training courses did you?

A. No, sir.[2]

Block then exposed the runaround technique that Daffin used on the two army CID officers, Bruce Potts and Donald Hoag, when they tried to see Pitts in the Bay County Jail. Block showed it was all a ruse to hold Pitts incommunicado until Daffin got the confession he wanted.[3]

Block then reached the high point of his inquiry in an exchange that was stunning to watch:

Q. Fine. Sheriff, you've got a big department down there, don't you?

A. Well, I wouldn't say a big department. I've got, I expect, the largest department besides Pensacola in this section.

Q. And you can't watch the prisoners, can you?

A. Yes, sir, I keep pretty well tabs on them.

Q. Isn't that the jailer's job?

A. I've got jailers there, yes sir, but after all, it's all my job. I'm responsible for everything that goes on there.

Block paused, looked Daffin straight in the eye, and spoke in a tone of voice that echoed throughout the courtroom:

Q. You certainly are, aren't you.

A. Yes.[4]

Daffin almost whispered that last answer and slowly sank into the witness chair. The spectators that packed the courtroom sat in transfixed silence.

Block then proceeded to ask a line of questions that used Daffin's Bay County–Gulf County runaround technique with the army CID officers as a sword against him. Block established that Daffin had paid no attention to Freddie Pitts's physical condition at the Bay County Jail because Pitts had been beaten up by police in Gulf County—and, by Daffin's own admission, he had no control over what happened in Gulf County.

> Q. And you had no authority to tell Gulf County how to treat [their] prisoners, did you?
> A. No, I have nothing to do with Gulf County.
> Q. So, if a prisoner was brought over from Gulf County involving some incident that occurred in Gulf County, you'd have nothing to do with it, would you?
> A. No.
> Q. So if Freddie Pitts was beat up in Gulf County that would be out of your jurisdiction.
> A. Out of my jurisdiction.
> Q. And if Sheriff Parker of Gulf County sent over a prisoner whose face was swollen just to leave him with you for custody, that would be out of your jurisdiction to look into it, wouldn't it?
> A. No, sir, if one came in there and needed attention of a doctor or something it would be my—and he's in the Bay County Jail, it would be my place to call a doctor.
> Q. But if he didn't need the attention of a doctor, you wouldn't pay any attention to it, would you?
> A. Not necessarily, no.
> Q. And isn't it true that you have no recollection today of what Freddie Pitts's physical condition was when he was interviewed by Sergeants Hoag and Potts of the CID?
> A. I didn't pay any attention to anything, if there was anything there.
> Q. Then your answer is, you have no recollection.
> A. No, sir, I have no recollection.
> Q. Sheriff, you never ordered Wayne White and Kittrell to drive Pitts around Port St. Joe, did you?
> A. No, sir.
> Q. So if they did that that would be without your knowledge.
> A. That's right.[5]

Block's next line of questions centered on Willie Mae Lee. He showed that Daffin had unlawfully jailed her for nearly a month, had subjected her to prolonged interrogation, had accused her of lying when she wouldn't confess, and had finally gotten the statement he wanted. This was the statement that we claimed he fed to her that falsely blamed Pitts and Lee for the charged murders.

Q. You remember Willie Mae Lee, don't you?
A. Yes.
Q. How long was she kept in custody?
A. My records would show that.
Q. Does 25 days sound about correct?
A. Now, I wouldn't say. My records would show it.
Q. Sheriff, wasn't she kept in jail from the time she was picked up until after the mercy trial was over?
A. Yes, sir.
Q. You didn't place any charges against her, did you?
A. No, sir. Now Gulf County might have placed a charge, but Bay County didn't.
Q. Do you know of any law that permits you to keep anybody in jail for 25 days without a charge?
A. Not unless it's a material witness.
Q. Did you get any court order declaring anybody a material witness?
A. (Indicating in the negative)
Q. Other than if you had a [c]ourt order as a material witness, do you know of any law in this [s]tate that permits you to keep a witness in jail for 25 days without a charge?
A. No, sir.
Q. Now during those 25 days, Willie Mae was questioned, wasn't she?
A. Yes, sir.
Q. You questioned her?
A. Yes, sir.
Q. Chief Barron questioned her?
* * *
A. Yes, sir.
* * *
Q. (Mr. Block continuing) When you first talked to Willie Mae, didn't she deny knowing anything about this?
A. Yes.
Q. And the second time you spoke to her, she said she didn't know anything about this?
A. I don't recall which time now that she did say it and which time she didn't, and all I know is she eventually said she did.

Q. After how many days in jail?

A. I couldn't say that, I couldn't recall.

Q. Would your best approximation be more than 5?

A. I wouldn't say.

Q. You wouldn't say it wasn't more than 5, would you?

A. I wouldn't say it wasn't more than 5 and I wouldn't say it was 5.

Q. And you don't know how long she was interrogated in your jail.

A. No.

Q. And she was questioned days?

A. Questioned what?

Q. During the daytime.

A. Yes, sir.

Q. And she was questioned during the night?

A. She was, yes, sir.

* * *

Q. You remember when you first questioned Willie Mae and she denied knowing anything about this and you told her she was lying?

A. I remember telling her that she was not telling me the truth. I don't know as I said lying.

Q. You wouldn't *deny* that you said she was lying, would you?

A. I could have.

Q. Thank you. And do you know how long it was before she changed her story.

A. No, sir. I don't recall.[6]

Block concluded his cross-examination with a line of questions centered on Daffin's weeklong, day-and-night interrogation of Pitts and Lee and Lee's wife, Ella Mae. Block showed that these people had been treated as if they had no rights and that the confessions Daffin had extracted from them were false and involuntary.[7]

When it was all over, when Block had finished his questioning and sat down at counsel table, there was a hushed silence in the courtroom. It was obvious that everyone had just witnessed a masterpiece of a cross-examination.

* * *

Our next witness was Wilbert Lee, who gave testimony in support of our claims of innocence, coerced confessions, and incompetent court-appointed counsel. He was an important witness, but there were no surprises.

All went exactly as planned. Lee listened to every question asked and was never argumentative or evasive. His alibi was straightforward. He explained his whereabouts on the night in question and told how he had fully cooperated with the authorities, how the police had questioned him day and night, how the police had beaten him and threatened to execute his wife unless he confessed, how his court-appointed lawyer had actively participated with the police to convict him, and how he had been home in bed with his wife at the time of the charged murders.[8]

On the final day of the hearing, Judge Holley called Lee back to the witness stand for additional questions. The judge wanted to know why Lee had pled guilty. Lee's answers, as always, were polite and candid:

> The Court. All right. I want you to tell me as best you can why you at that time pled guilty. I don't remember whether you said that you did it or Mr. Turner did it, but either way, why?
> A. Well, I plead [sic] guilty, Your Honor, through advice of my attorney. He said that was the best way out, was to plead guilty.
> The Court. All right. Well, let me ask you this now: Did the fact that you had been hit in the head with a blackjack and that they had threatened your wife back 10 days before, did that have anything to do with your pleading guilty at that time?
> A. Well, only way I can answer this, Your Honor, the best way I know how, is through taking advice from Mr. Turner, because I did not know.
> The Court. Yeah, I understand that, but were you in any fear at the time you were pleading? That's what I'm trying to find out.
> A. Well—
> The Court. I know you were afraid of going to the electric chair, people always are, but that's not what I am asking about. Were you in any fear of any of the officers or anyone else at the time from the standpoint of their interfering with your wife? I know she was still being held at that time.
> A. Yes. Well, I feel sure I was, sir. I will have to answer that yes, I was, sir.[9]

* * *

But the most explosive witness we called that day was Curtis Adams, the man who murdered Grover Floyd and Jesse Burkett. Like Daffin, we called Adams as an adverse witness, which allowed us to cross-examine him.[10] He was also a problematic witness, a killer, and a sociopath serving life imprisonment. We had no idea what he would say in court.

We had his tape-recorded statement to Warren Holmes in which he confessed in detail to the murders of Floyd and Burkett and his oral confession to Sergeant Elihu Phares of the Broward County Sheriff's Office. But he had told us many times that he was not going to "sit in the hot seat" (i.e., the electric chair) for Pitts and Lee by confessing to those murders in court. Indeed, at Raiford Prison, a week before the hearing, he had told Warren Holmes that he might repudiate his confession when he came to court. According to Holmes's later testimony, "I told [Adams] to let his conscience be his guide, and he told me he didn't have a conscience."[11]

Our strategy with Adams was twofold. First, if he elected to take the Fifth Amendment and refused to testify—which he might do—we planned to ask the court to grant him immunity for the murders of Floyd and Burkett so he could confess to these crimes without fear of criminal prosecution. I had filed a motion to that effect. Unfortunately, I could find little legal support for the motion and relied entirely on the court's inherent power to see that justice was done.

On the other hand, if Adams chose not to take the Fifth Amendment and testified that he had not committed the murders—which we thought he probably would do—we planned to impeach (i.e., discredit) him with his taped confession to Warren Holmes and his oral confession to Detective Elihu Phares. Block and I decided to let me cross-examine Adams, as I was best prepared to argue the legal issues that might arise with this witness, having written all the motions, pleadings, and legal memos in the case. Beyond that, we agreed that the best approach with Adams was to quietly extract admissions from him, which was something I was reasonably good at. And if things got tough, we thought I could face him down.

Adams, however, had another idea. He was shrewd. When he appeared in court pursuant to our subpoena, he refused to testify unless he was represented by counsel of his own choice. Adams named two Port St. Joe lawyers he wanted. Judge Holley agreed and appointed Cecil Costin Jr., who had been practicing in Gulf County for twenty years. Costin conferred with Adams during a brief recess. Adams then returned to the courtroom, was sworn in, and took the witness stand. Wiry and muscular, dressed in baggy prison clothes, he sat there stone-faced with sunken, menacing eyes, ready to do combat. Costin stood next to him as his lawyer.[12]

I was able, as planned, to extract a number of incriminating admissions from Adams. He admitted that he had been living with his former girlfriend, Mary Jean Akins, in Port St. Joe in the month of July 1963. He admitted that he had been at the Mo Jo station on the night Grover Floyd and Jesse Burkett were robbed, kidnapped, and murdered. He admitted that he had driven Mary Jean Akins's 1960 white Ford to the Mo Jo station and that he owned a .25-caliber Beretta automatic pistol. He admitted that he had seen the two gas station attendants, Grover Floyd and Jesse Burkett, at the station that night and that he had gone into the station bathroom and locked it from the inside.

He further admitted that he had left Port St. Joe the morning right after the murders, together with Mary Jean Akins and her children. He admitted that several months later in the spring of 1964, he had told Lieutenant Terry Jones of the Key West Police Department that he "knew something" about the murders of Floyd and Burkett and that he had repeated this statement to Gulf County Sheriff Byrd Parker in a telephone call that followed. And he admitted that two years later, in December 1966, he had confessed to these murders to Warren Holmes and that a few days later, he had confessed again to Sergeant Elihu Phares of the Broward County Sheriff's Office.[13]

Adams, however, repudiated these confessions in court and denied murdering Floyd and Burkett. Instead, he blamed Freddie Pitts for these crimes. He once had blamed Mary Jean Akins for these murders when Broward County police had questioned him two years earlier. Now it was Pitts's turn.

Adams claimed that while he was in the Mo Jo bathroom, he had heard voices outside saying "don't anybody move or I'll shoot," that he had cracked open the bathroom door and had seen a group of "colored people" in the area, and that two "colored men" were in the process of "walking off" with the two attendants. He identified Pitts as one of the men who drove off with the attendants.[14]

But there was a fatal flaw in this story. Adams testified that he hadn't called the police to report the crime that he claimed he had just witnessed. He gave no explanation for this behavior. Instead, he said, he had left the station, notified no one in authority, and had left town soon thereafter, completely oblivious to what had happened to Floyd and Burkett, who were, in fact, his good friends. Obviously, Adams had "witnessed" no such crime. The story was a total lie.[15]

The state, however, was delighted with this turn of events. In fact, they knew exactly what was coming, as Adams had told them what he was going to say in court. Ray Markey, in particular, could hardly contain himself. He erupted with glee when Adams was in the process of making his so-called identification. Here is George Georgieff's examination of Adams:

Q. On the night you said you were at the Mo Jo Service Station look-
ing out the bathroom door, you said you saw the two men walking
away with the two attendants of the service station, is that correct?
A. Yes, sir.
Q. Do you see those two men in this room?
A. I can recognize one, but I couldn't recognize both of them.
Q. Which one do you recognize?
A. Recognize the one on this side.
The Court. Which person are you referring to?
Mr. Markey. Petitioner Pitts, I believe.
The Court. Be quiet, Mr. Markey

Georgieff then walked over to the defense table until he was directly in
back of us.

Mr. Georgieff. When I walk back there, will you tell me where to stop
when I get to the right one?
The Witness. Yes, sir. . . . Right there. . . .
The Court. Let the record reflect the witness was identifying Pitts.[16]

Freddie Pitts sat at counsel table, put his face in his hands, and whispered
"God, God, I can't believe it."
But it was all a charade, and I don't think anyone in court that day, including the state, believed this bizarre account. I certainly made no effort
to conceal my disbelief. I even lost my temper with Adams on occasion and
had to apologize to the court.
Here are a few of the exchanges I had with Adams:

Q. [Mr. Hubbart continuing]. Now, state whether or not you ever
told [Broward County Sergeant] Elihu Phares, on January 17, 1967, at
the Broward County Jail that you committed the murders of Grover
Floyd and Jesse Burkett?
A. Against my wishes, yes.
Q. Against your wishes! Well, what happened?
A. I was doped, threatened, hung up on the bars and beat and full of
liquor.
Q. Oh, well who did all this to you?
A. Sergeant Eugene Sullivan, the head jailer of Broward County Jail,
had 16 Negroes to put me in a cell and threaten, hang me on the bars,
and beat me with a sheet wrapped up, in my kidneys.
Q. Well, did you have to go to the hospital after all that?!

A. You're trying to be a comedian now, aren't you.

Q. Did you have to go to the hospital!

A. You think I could go to the hospital after all that?

The Court. Mr. Adams, did you go to the hospital?

A. No, sir.

Q. Did you make any complaint to anybody about this?

A. Who was I going to complain to? Sergeant Sullivan?

The Court. We'll accept that as a no answer, counsel.

* * *

Q. [Mr. Hubbart continuing] State whether or not you confessed to the murders of Grover Floyd and Jesse Burkett to Mr. Warren Holmes in the Broward County Jail, Fort Lauderdale, Florida, on December 21st, 1966.

A. Because I was forced into it.

Q. You did confess to it, didn't you?

A. I was forced into it and doped up.

Q. This is—this was a doping up by what, the Sheriff down there?

A. Not the Sheriff, the head jailer.

Q. The head jailer.

* * *

Q. You went in that bathroom and you stayed there for 40 minutes, didn't you.

A. No.

Q. You heard an argument, didn't you, over the use of a "white only" bathroom, didn't you?

A. Wasn't no argument what—

Q. That's why you locked the door, isn't that right?!

Mr. Costin. I object to him badgering the witness.

The Court. When I start talking, everybody else keep quiet.

Mr. Hubbart. My apologies to the Court. I raised my voice and I'm sorry.

The Court. Not only that counsel, proceed.

* * *

Q. Did you see any women there?

A. Two of them was women.

Q. And they were having an argument, weren't they, over the use of the bathroom.

A. It was a long argument, if they was, them in the car and the others in the station.

Q. Well, you heard it, didn't you?

A. Wasn't no argument.

Q. Weren't they having words?

A. Sure it was words when they told them "Don't nobody move or I'll shoot you."

Q. They were having words about the bathroom, weren't they?

A. No, nothing said about the bathroom.

The Court. Mr. Hubbart.

Mr. Hubbart. Yes, sir.

The Court. You're badgering the witness.

Mr. Hubbart. My apologies.[17]

I momentarily lost my cool with this despicable killer. But I think I got the message across to the judge that we on the defense side were convinced that Curtis Adams had murdered Grover Floyd and Jesse Burkett. We weren't just going through the motions.

In any event, we got what we wanted from Adams and we were now prepared to impeach him with his tape-recorded confession to Warren Holmes and his oral confession to Sergeant Elihu Phares. But that would have to wait until the next day. Judge Holley was through taking testimony for now.

* * *

But before adjourning court, the judge had two announcements to make. We were astounded when we heard the first announcement. It concerned Willie Mae Lee. In laying out what he wanted, Holley showed, I think, the maverick streak in him:

> I'm calling [Willie Mae Lee] as a witness. Now that's the reason I wanted to bring it up now, to put you on notice. I suspected that either or both of you might be hesitant to call this individual.
>
> Now, secondly, I'm going to request that the State arrange—see if they can arrange for a competent psychiatrist in this area to appear before the Court at the time of the interrogation of Willie Mae Lee for the purpose of seeing whether he can, under hypnosis, regress her to the night of July 31, August 1, 1963.[18]

We couldn't believe what we were hearing. The judge apparently wanted to hear hypnotized testimony from Willie Mae Lee in open court. But that was unheard of. There was no provision in Florida law or anywhere else for such an oddball procedure. Besides, we knew of no scientific findings that showed that hypnosis prompted anyone to tell the truth.

Nonetheless, we were in a difficult position to object. We too were seeking to introduce unprecedented evidence—Curtis Adams's confessions—and we were also urging innocence as a new ground for setting aside a criminal conviction. So we held our fire.

Instead, we convinced the judge to put off Willie Mae Lee's hypnotized testimony for a few days. This would give both sides time to prepare for this witness and allow the state to obtain the psychiatrist the judge wanted. Also, the state announced that they had a licensed hypnotist from Orlando who had already examined Willie Mae Lee and was coming to court the next day. Judge Holley was delighted and wanted the hypnotist to be in court when Willie Mae Lee testified, presumably to put her in a trance on the witness stand.

Although our minds were still reeling, we were relieved when Holley moved on to his second announcement. Mindful of the menacing spikes that had been placed under our car tires the previous day, he told the lawyers to be seated. He then delivered a stern warning to the spectators who were standing room only in the packed courtroom:

The Court. Ladies and Gentlemen, I know there's been considerable interest in Gulf County for five years relating to this case. Now, I think it's obvious to all of you present—if it isn't obvious to you I want to tell you, it is obvious to me—that all the persons who are involved on this side of this rail are trying the best they can to do their job and do them well, whether they happen to be representing the State or whether they happen to be representing the Petitioners, who are the Defendants as it were.

And it doesn't make any difference to me who you may have sympathy with, whether you have sympathy for Pitts and Lee or whether you may have sympathy for Burkett or Floyd, if any matter comes to my attention where any of you are doing anything you shouldn't be doing to affect the procedure in this Court, I'm going [to] do everything I can do to see to it that you're prosecuted to the fullest extent of the law.

And if you're prosecuted, you might remember this, that I've been assigned to handle this case all the way through and I'll handle your case if you're prosecuted for interfering with this case, and my theory on sentencing is that I give the maximum possible sentence unless somebody shows me a good reason not to do so.

Now, I don't want anybody interfering with these lawyers. Is that clear? I trust it is.[19]

We greatly appreciated Holley's concern for our safety and we could scarcely have asked for a more comprehensive warning. All the spectators listened to the judge in silence, transfixed by his every word. Holley then adjourned court for the day and we returned to our motel, somewhat exhausted, and planned our strategy for the next day.

18

The Defense Rests

On the third day of the Port St. Joe hearing, the courtroom was once again filled with spectators, every seat taken and people standing near the back of the courtroom. We were apprehensive, as always, about this mostly white audience from the local area and sensed their silent hostility. We called six witnesses that day and concluded the presentation of our case.

Irwin Block opened the day's proceedings:

> If it please the Court, at this time we respectfully move that the State be required to produce any tapes or statements that it may have of the [witness] Willie Mae Lee.[1]

As grounds for the motion, Block noted that we had "just received word" that Willie Mae Lee may have recently made some statements to the state's representatives in New York City. State Attorney J. Frank Adams and the attorney general's investigator S. R. DeWitt confirmed this to be true and agreed to produce these statements for the defense.

Judge Holley ratified this agreement. He ordered that these statements be turned over to the defense as requested and any other statements this witness may have given to the state.

> The Court. All right, this will, of course, come within the scope of my prior order, I believe. You have no objection to furnishing these as soon as he [a New York emissary] arrives.
> Mr. DeWitt. That's my understanding, Your Honor, so I don't violate anything the Court has said. That concerns the tapes that were taken in New York.
> The Court. Well, actually, my prior order was everything you have be made available.[2]

Block wasn't satisfied with getting just the New York statements. He wanted *all* of Willie Mae Lee's statements, as his motion had requested.

So he pressed the state to produce some recent statements we just heard about that were taken in Orlando. And once again, the state agreed to this request.[3]

As previously noted, however, the state also had in their files a sworn statement that Willie Mae Lee had given in February 1968 to J. Frank Adams and S. R. DeWitt. In this statement, Willie Mae Lee had provided a complete alibi for Freddie Pitts and said she had no knowledge of the Floyd-Burkett murders. Yet in defiance of the court's agreed order, J. Frank Adams and DeWitt did not reveal this statement to the defense or to the court. They suppressed it.

*   *   *

As our opening witness, we called Warren Holmes. He gave the necessary foundation testimony to introduce in evidence the tape-recorded statement he took of Curtis Adams in December 1966 in which Adams had confessed to the Port St. Joe murders.[4] Judge Holley then admitted Adams's taped-recorded confession in evidence and the entire one-and-a-half-hour statement was played in open court.[5] The courtroom was dead silent. No one stirred or walked out. The details in the statement were particularly striking, as were Adams's dark motivations and the horror he said he had felt in killing Floyd and Burkett.

Then George Georgieff proceeded to cross-examine Holmes, and I was astonished at his line of questioning. Georgieff violated a bedrock rule in the trial lawyer's technique handbook, a professional insider's principle that both prosecutors and defense lawyers routinely follow: never ask a question of an adverse witness in a critical area unless you know what the answer is or has to be. If you ask wide-open questions, you run the risk of getting an unfavorable answer that could weaken or destroy your case.

Heedless of this basic maxim, Georgieff asked for Holmes's expert opinion concerning Curtis Adams's veracity, having no idea what Holmes might say. And Holmes unloaded on him. Although this testimony would be inadmissible at trial, it was admissible at this postconviction hearing where the rules of evidence are relaxed.

Here is Georgieff's wide-open line of questions.

Q. After you took your statement from Curtis Adams, tell us whether you believed what he told you.
A. I did believe him, with the exception of one thing.
Q. What was that?

A. I felt he was exaggerating the involvement of Mary Akins. I didn't feel she was guilty to the degree he portrayed her.

* * *

Q. You watched him [Curtis Adams] on the witness stand under oath.

A. (Indicating in the affirmative). [Adams had denied killing Floyd and Burkett].

Q. Did you believe the testimony he gave then?

A. No.

Q. Why not, Mr. Holmes?

A. Because I know from my own experience in testing over a thousand people accused of murder that he is the actual killer in this case.[6]

Despite these disastrous answers for the state, I had to admire Georgieff's pursuit of the truth. He sought to lay out all the facts of the case for Judge Holley, often heedless of where that might lead, risking results that might damage the state's case, and I had to respect that.

But Georgieff was not through with his style of inquiry. He asked for Holmes's expert opinion of a state witness, Cleve Backster, a controversial polygraph examiner from New York City. At the state's request, Backster had previously tested Curtis Adams's former girlfriend, Mary Jean Akins, and had concluded that she was untruthful.

What follows is Georgieff's interrogation of Warren Holmes and Holmes's reluctant but emphatic response. This colloquy, in my view, virtually destroyed the state's position that Backster was a competent polygraph examiner:

Q. Do you know Cleve [Backster]?

A. Yes.

Q. What do you think of him as a polygraph man?

A. I'm not allowed to make any statement regarding a man in my profession by the Code of Ethics of the American Polygraph Association. However, if I am directed to do so by the judge, I will comment on it.

Mr. Georgieff. May we ask for such instructions, your Honor.

The Court. Answer the question.

A. I think any man that says he talks to shrimp and plants is nuts.

Q. Now may I have a responsive answer.

A. I think he is a disgrace to the polygraph profession.

Q. Would it be fair to say that you do not think him to be a competent polygraph examiner?

A. Yes.[7]

Cleve Backster was indeed a bizarre figure. He was well known for his strange experiments in which he connected polygraph electrodes to plants, tomatoes, eggs, and dried blood and then tested the "reaction" of these items as he physically harmed them (i.e., cutting a leaf off a plant) or when he verbally threatened harm to these items or when he placed shrimp in boiling water that was electrically connected to the plants. Backster once tested a plant for the New York City police as a possible "eyewitness" to a murder by monitoring the plant's "reaction" when various suspects were paraded past the plant. His findings, to say the least, are controversial and have never been accepted by the scientific community. Botanists, in particular, have rejected his results because of his failure to conduct controlled experiments that could be replicated by others.[8]

I never understood why the state would hire such an odd lie detector examiner at such a distant location as New York City when there were plenty of competent, mainline polygraph examiners in Florida. Perhaps they were trying to match the national prominence of Warren Holmes—the former president of the American Polygraph Association—with a well-known polygraph examiner of their own. If so, they failed miserably. Backster was nationally well known because he was an eccentric, especially within his own profession.

Holmes also testified that he had taken a detailed statement from Mary Jean Akins during his investigation for the Broward County Sheriff's Office in December 1966. He had run a polygraph test on Akins and concluded that she was telling the truth, contrary to Backster's dubious results.[9]

*   *   *

Our next witness was Mary Jean Akins, who testified to what she had told the Broward County Sheriff's Office and Warren Holmes back in 1966. She related how Curtis Adams had confessed to her that he had murdered the filling station attendants in Port St. Joe and Fort Lauderdale. Her testimony included detailed information about the circumstances that led to those confessions.[10]

She also testified to a critical series of intimidating confrontations with J. Frank Adams and S. R. DeWitt in which these officials tried to get her to retract her prior testimony against Curtis Adams. The first encounter took place on February 16, 1968, at the sheriff's office in Bartow, Florida, several months before the Port St. Joe hearing. Akins had been brought from her home in nearby Auburndale to be questioned. In the three-hour interrogation that followed, Akins related in detail her knowledge of the case. J.

Frank Adams had granted her immunity from prosecution and invited her to change her statement, which she refused to do. DeWitt filed a report at the time stating that "the writer and Mr. [J. Frank] Adams were of the opinion that Mrs. Smith [Akins's new married name] was telling the truth and Willie Mae Lee was not."[11]

But they couldn't leave things at that. They had to break her down somehow. So without notifying me or Irwin Block, they took Akins by commercial airline to New York City, ostensibly with her "consent," to be polygraphed by Cleve Backster. Backster tested Akins on February 26, 1968, and accused her of lying. Afterward, DeWitt was particularly brutal. He told her that the only thing she had said to Backster that was true was her name and address, everything else was a lie. He also told her that she could be prosecuted for perjury if she persisted in her statement. All of this weighed heavily upon her, but she adhered to her prior testimony.[12]

Ten days later, on March 6, 1968, they delivered the telling blow. Adams and DeWitt again interrogated Akins at the sheriff's office in Bartow—this time in the dead of night between midnight and 1:00 a.m. She was awakened at her home in Auburndale at about 10:00 p.m. after she had gone to bed and transported to Bartow to be questioned. Once again she was accused of lying when she related her knowledge of the case. Finally, she could take no more. They broke her down, and she retracted some of the details in her statement—although she still insisted that Curtis Adams had confessed to her that he had murdered Floyd and Burkett.

Akins stated that "he [Curtis Adams] just told me that he had killed them [Floyd and Burkett]," that "the only details that he went into was that he took them out on the road between Port St. Joe and Wewahitchka and took them off on a side road down there and killed them," that "he was in the [station] bathroom when the two Negroes were there. And then he robbed the station," but she retracted all the details about the circumstances surrounding Curtis Adams's confessions that she had previously given.[13] When she was no longer in those intimidating interrogations, however, Akins soon returned to her original statement accusing Curtis Adams of the murders of Floyd and Burkett in great detail.

Here is Mary Jean Akins's testimony at the Port St. Joe hearing about the state's attempt to get her to retract her statement. I did the questioning:

Q. Did you ever change your statement in any way?
A. Yes, I did.
Q. Would you tell us about that.

A. In February Mr. Speedy DeWitt and Mr. J. Frank Adams came to Bartow and took a statement from me and they asked if I would be willing to go to New York to take a polygraph test.

Q. In the statement what did you say?

A. The same as I've told here, to the best of my knowledge. And I told them yes, that if it was all right with my lawyer that I would go. So they called—I called Mr. Fleet and Mr. Adams talked to him and they agreed for me to go to New York. And I don't remember the exact time that we left, but Mr. DeWitt came to the house one afternoon before we left and spent the night in Orlando and the next morning we caught a plane out of Orlando to New York. And when we got there we ate and we didn't take the polygraph test until the next day.

Q. Who conducted the polygraph test?

A. Mr. Cleve Backster.

Q. Tell us what happened when you were tested by Mr. Backster.

A. Well, he took—the first test was on this case and what Curtis had told me, and when he got through he went out of the room and Speedy DeWitt came back in and they said I had lied.[14]

Georgieff then cross-examined Akins with an open-ended line of questioning that broke all the rules of trial technique and undermined the state's position that Akins was lying. He nonetheless got to the truth of the matter:

Q. Mrs. Smith, as a matter of fact, when you went to New York with these people that you've just testified about[,] were you mistreated?

A. Physically, no.

Q. Mentally?

A. Well, the fact that I was sick at the time, I was pregnant, first time I had ever flown, and I sat there waiting while they polygraphed this colored girl for several hours. I hadn't eaten and I was very upset.

* * *

Q. Did you tell Mr. DeWitt and/or J. Frank Adams that what you had told Warren Holmes and what you had told Speedy DeWitt before was not true?

A. Yes, I did.

Q. Then did you then give a different version?

A. Yes, I think I did.

Q. Which time was it that it was the truth?

A. First time, the original statement is the truth.

Q. Were you under oath both times?

A. Yes.

Q. Why did you change your statement?

A. Because I—seemed like I had taken all of it I could.

Q. All of what, ma'am?

A. Of the questions. I was sick. The night that I made the statement I was gotten out of bed around 10:00 o'clock and it was well after midnight before they come to make the—for me to make the statement.

Q. Get your lawyer's permission to give that statement?

A. No, I didn't.

Q. You didn't call him.

A. No, he told me don't make a statement, but I was so upset about it, my husband was there and he was upset, and that made me more upset than what I was, and I would have done just about anything to have got rid of it and get out of it.

Q. So you wound up telling a different story.

A. Yes, I did.[15]

When I first learned what J. Frank Adams had done to Mary Jean Akins, I was enraged at his arrogant abuse of power. To begin with, he had no trouble granting Akins immunity from prosecution to persuade her to change her statement and help his case. Yet he steadfastly refused our request to grant Curtis Adams immunity from prosecution for the murders of Floyd and Burkett. This prevented us from calling Curtis Adams as a witness in court to testify that he had committed those murders—something he had told us he would do, but only if he were granted immunity. As a prosecutor, J. Frank Adams had a sworn duty to see that justice was done, not a duty to convict.

But something else enraged me. Adams had the statutory power to take sworn testimony from witnesses at his discretion, and he used this considerable power to intimidate and break down Mary Jean Akins. We couldn't touch Adams's witness, Willie Mae Lee, without risking Adams's wrath, but he could do what he wanted with our witness, Mary Jean Akins.

After Akins had testified on our behalf at the Port St. Joe hearing, Adams confronted her in the courtroom hallway, took her into his adjoining office, and demanded angrily, "Who is paying you?"—a not-too-subtle threat to prosecute her for perjury.[16] Once again he flagrantly misused the powers of his office. After that, I lost whatever confidence I ever had in Adams's capacity to pursue the truth wherever it might lead. He was, in my view, blinded by this case and incapable of seeing the horrific injustice that had been inflicted on Pitts and Lee.

We never gave any thought to complaining to Judge Holley about Adams's conduct. It would have been futile. As a visiting judge from Clearwater, Holley would have had little stomach for sanctioning the local elected prosecutor who was a political powerhouse in the circuit. It was all we could do to hold our own in the hostile atmosphere we were in.

*   *   *

There was a moment during the day when we finally found something to laugh about, something that relieved the tension of the hearing. Holley had taken a brief recess and was off the bench. Miller and Holmes were seated in the first row of spectators. They leaned over the court railing to talk to us lawyers who were seated at the defense counsel's table.

Tell the judge this, tell the judge that, they both told us—this is important. They went on and on. They meant well, but once again, they were trying to be amateur lawyers and, unfortunately, had nothing to say that was of any use in court.

When they were through, Irwin Block spoke. "I tell you what," he said. "When the judge comes back, you tell him that."

"We can't do that," they said.

"Why not?"

"We're not lawyers."

Block grinned and looked straight at them: "That's right."

It was an inside joke and probably not funny to anyone else. But to all of us, it was a lighthearted message to Miller and Holmes that they had stepped outside their area of expertise.

With that, Miller and Holmes smiled broadly, slowly sat back in their seats, and we all had a good laugh—Miller and Holmes included. I remember thinking at the time, thank heaven I had Block to deal with these two strong-minded men in such a humorous way. We were all friends, but the lines of authority had to be clear. Friendly suggestions and ideas were always welcome, but not orders. Miller and Holmes never again told us what to do in court.

*   *   *

One of the most important witnesses we called that day was Freddie Pitts. Like Wilbert Lee, Pitts gave extensive testimony in support of our claims of innocence, coerced confessions, and incompetent court-appointed counsel. I did the questioning and there were no surprises. Pitts testified exactly as expected.[17]

Pitts was intelligent and had a facility with the language that exceeded his eighth-grade education. But in 1963, he, like Wilbert Lee, had been isolated and overwhelmed by the authorities in charge of this case and had been brutally beaten and terrorized by the police. Back then, as a 19-year-old Black teenager, he had only a limited understanding of the law and was in no position to insist on his legal rights without incurring the wrath of the local white power structure that lined up against him. The trial judge, W. L. Fitzpatrick, had said that Turner was the best criminal lawyer in the circuit, and Pitts had trusted Turner to somehow make this entire nightmare go away.

This is how Pitts tried to explain to Holley why he followed Turner's advice and pled guilty:

The Court. Let me ask you this: By the time you got around to appearing at—where you said the indictment was read to you, where you pled guilty—Do you remember?
A. Yes, sir.
The Court. By the time you got around to that, you knew that you had a choice of either life imprisonment or the electric chair, didn't you?
A. Yes, sir, I did.
The Court. Why did you plead guilty?
A. Because it was agreed to with Mr. Turner that I would plead guilty.
The Court. Why would you agree to something that you were going to go to jail for life or go to the electric chair?
A. I didn't know what else to do, your Honor.
The Court. You could say not guilty.
A. Mr. Turner had told me the best thing was to plead guilty.
The Court. To agree to go to the electric chair or to go to prison for life.
A. I guess so.
The Court. And this was the best thing to do.
A. He said in the interest of the case it was the best thing. I didn't know the circumstances under which I was pleading. I mean I wasn't

familiar with what was happening. I didn't even know what was going on.[18]

Pitts testified that during a police interrogation session in which Turner participated, Turner had announced that he would have to withdraw from the case if Pitts didn't confess and plead guilty. In this exchange, I did the questioning:

Q. And what, if anything, did Turner say to you?
A. After a while Mr. Turner said, "Well, Willie Mae telling her story, Wilbert has confessed to it, and unless you confess I'm going to have to tell the judge there's a conflict in your story and I can't handle your case."[19]

Small wonder that Pitts capitulated. Everyone, including his own lawyer, was arrayed against him.

*   *   *

We next called Fred Turner to the witness stand and Irwin Block cross-examined him as an adverse witness. Turner had never seen Block before, and we felt he might be rattled by Block's stern manner. We were right. Block—tall and intimidating, wearing a dark suit and a wry smile—proceeded to train his eyes on Turner and grill him with rapid-fire questions. Turner, an otherwise crafty country lawyer, wilted in the process.

Block showed that Turner, in fact, had participated with the police to extract a confession from Pitts and Lee, his own clients, which confession was then introduced in evidence against them at the August 1963 mercy trial. Although Turner had interviewed Pitts and Lee, he had never investigated their defenses. Instead, several days later, he had rushed the case to a swift resolution. With no prior plea negotiation agreement, he had pled Pitts and Lee guilty to first-degree murder, following which they were sentenced to death.[20]

But this is the most important testimony that Block elicited from Turner:

Q. All right. May I ask you this, Mr. Turner: Did you at any time before the plea of guilty see the written statement of Willie Mae Lee accusing Lambson Smith instead of Wilbert Lee of this crime?
A. No I don't recall ever seeing any statement of her accusing Lambson Smith of this crime.[21]

J. Frank Adams had previously testified that he had kept this statement in his file and had never given it to Turner. Without dispute, the state had suppressed evidence of innocence, and this suppression is what ultimately won us a new trial as later determined by the Florida Supreme Court.

One other important matter should be mentioned. Turner claimed that Pitts and Lee had insisted on pleading guilty "straight up" to this capital crime with no plea agreement in which they would be sentenced to life imprisonment; that he had had nothing to do with Pitts and Lee's alleged decision; and that he had made no effort to talk them out of it. On its face, this statement that two young men who had little or no experience with the law, in full possession of their faculties, would push aside their lawyer and, on their own initiative, plead guilty to a capital crime and fling themselves on the mercy of the court with no prior plea agreement, knowing full well that they could be sentenced to death was preposterous.

In our twenty-five years of combined experience with criminal cases, neither Irwin Block nor I had ever known or heard of a defendant who engaged in such suicidal conduct, particularly where, as here, the defendants were Black, were charged with murdering two white men, and were appearing before an all-white southern court in the midst of the civil rights crisis in the 1960s.

All parties agreed, however, that Turner had tape-recorded his conversations with Pitts and Lee. So these tapes would definitely determine who was telling the truth concerning this issue. Was it Pitts and Lee who said they had told Turner they were not guilty? Or was it Turner, who said that Pitts and Lee had told him that they were guilty?

This is Block's incisive questioning of Turner on this subject:

Q. May I have those tapes.
A. I do not have them, Mr. Block.
Q. May I have a transcript of them.
A. I don't have a transcript of them, Mr. Block.
Q. Who has the tapes?
A. The tapes were sent to the Adjutant General's Office, Fort Rucker, Alabama.
Q. May I see your letter of enclosure.
A. I do not have a letter of enclosure, Mr. Block.
Q. May I have the name of the man you sent them to.

A. Well, I can identify him only this way: After the convictions I got a call from Fort Rucker, the Adjutant's General's Off[ice] and—

Q. Your Honor, may I—

A. I do not know his name, Mr. Block.

Q. So you just put the tapes in an envelope and sent them off.

A. My secretary did.

Q. No letter of enclosure.

A. No letter of enclosure.[22]

Gene Miller contacted the Office of the Adjutant General at Fort Rucker, Alabama, and conducted a thorough investigation of who might have received the tapes that Turner had allegedly sent. Miller talked to dozens of people in that office who searched their records. No one at Fort Rucker had ever heard of Fred Turner. Nor had anyone there ever received such a tape recording.[23] Clearly, these tapes had been suppressed for fear of what they might reveal.

* * *

Our final witness was Detective Elihu Phares of the Broward County Sheriff's Office.[24] We reserved the best for last so as to end our case on a high note, and Phares did not disappoint.

He was a strong and self-assured witness. He had complete command of the facts concerning his investigation of both the murder of Floyd McFarland in Fort Lauderdale and the murders of Floyd and Burkett in Port St. Joe. His professionalism gave a solid police context to this case, as he showed that Curtis Adams was, indeed, the man who had murdered Grover Floyd and Jesse Burkett.

Phares further testified to the remarkable similarity between the McFarland murder and the Floyd and Burkett murders. He had never before investigated a gas station holdup murder where the attendant had been kidnapped and murdered at some distance away from the station rather than simply murdered at the site of the station. Both the Fort Lauderdale and the Port St. Joe murders had been committed in virtually the same way.

Judge Holley was convinced and admitted this testimony as "similar crimes" evidence. It tended to show that this was Curtis Adams's modus operandi in holdup murders of this nature, and the proof that Adams had committed the McFarland murder tended to show he had also committed the murders of Floyd and Burkett.[25]

Phares also testified that Curtis Adams had given him a detailed oral confession to the Floyd-Burkett murders and had led him to the exact spot where the bodies of Floyd and Burkett had been found by the local police in Gulf County.[26] On cross-examination, George Georgieff zeroed in on Phares's comparison of the McFarland murder and the Floyd and Burkett murders. He asked:

> Q. What makes you think that there was a remarkable similarity between what happened to McFarland and what he [Curtis Adams] told you happened to these two [Floyd & Burkett] at his hands?

It was a convoluted question, but Phares's answer was comprehensive and devastating to the state's contrary position:

> Both of them were gas station attendants at an all-night gas station on the outskirts of town, they were working the night shift when they are missing, they were both found—all three of them found shot in the head, all three of them had their personal effects removed from them, all three of them were found near a canal bank off a main highway, a distance of eight to ten miles from the scene of the abduction and robbery.[27]

Phares agreed that when taken individually, none of these factors were unusual. But when taken all together, "it becomes a unique situation." Stated differently, this was Curtis Adams's signature method of committing gas station holdup murders. With that, we rested our case and court was adjourned.

But another startling event soon followed. Once again J. Frank Adams felt free to throw his weight around and abuse the power of his office. He confronted Phares in the courtroom hallway and threated to have him arrested for larceny based on an incident that had happened two years before.

Phares had met with Gulf County Deputy Sheriff Wayne White in Port St. Joe in the fall of 1966 to discuss the murders of Floyd and Burkett. In that meeting, White had given his file on the case to Phares to review. During the course of this review, Phares had used a nearby Xerox machine to copy a portion of the file he was interested in, thinking he had White's consent to do so. The file was later returned to White, who was busy with other matters at the time.[28]

The detective's so-called larceny was the photocopying. But nothing had been stolen and no charges were ever filed. Phares had just copied what he had been allowed to see. I had long before revealed this Xeroxing to Adams, otherwise he probably would never have known of it. It was much ado about nothing, and Phares was unfazed.

On the whole, we were satisfied that things were going well, relieved that the strain of presenting our basic case was at last over. We returned to our motel feeling exhausted but upbeat. Our task now was to prepare for the state's rebuttal against us. That case would unfold over the next two days.

19

The Port St. Joe Hearing Concludes

The fourth and fifth days of the Port St. Joe hearing were momentous. The morning session of the fourth day was particularly explosive. The courtroom was again packed with mostly white spectators eager to hear the expected hypnotized "testimony" of Willie Mae Lee. What ensued was a spectacle like no other.

Judge Holley orchestrated everything. He called Willie Mae Lee as a court witness, who was transported from her jail cell to the courtroom. As expected, she returned to her grand jury and trial testimony, falsely accusing Pitts and Lee of the Floyd-Burkett murders. Forgotten was her sworn statement six months before to J. Frank Adams and S. R. "Speedy" DeWitt retracting that testimony, evidence the state had brazenly suppressed.

Holley then arranged for Willie Mae Lee to be hypnotized on the witness stand and "regressed" to the night of July 31, 1963. Joe McCawley, a trained hypnotist from Orlando, conducted the session. He had been enlisted by the state to conduct two prior hypnosis sessions with Willie Mae Lee. At Holley's request, he had been brought from Orlando to conduct a similar session in open court.

McCawley presented himself as an "ethical hypnotist" and did his work, he said, with psychiatrists, medical doctors, and their patients. He was tall and dapper, wearing a dark suit and a polka-dotted tie. He held an occupational license for his work. No examination was required to obtain that license, only a $35 fee.[1]

I objected to the entire proceedings and asked the court to bar Willie Mae Lee from testifying as a witness, whether in or out of hypnosis.

> Your Honor, at this time we would move that the witness Willie Mae Lee not be permitted to testify in this case on the ground that the State has already subjected this witness to . . . two separate hypnotic sessions with . . . Joe B. McCawley. . . . We've been supplied with two transcripts of the hypnotic sessions.
> * * *

We strongly object to having this witness be permitted to testify in this case, because the State has in effect brainwashed this particular witness, gone through a long hypnotic session trying to take her back in a post-hypnotic suggestion and go through all this, and I suggest have implanted in her mind, from reading this transcript, implanted in her mind, the story which the State wants her to say at trial.

And as a result of tampering with this witness's mind, taking her through these hypnotic sessions and so on, we believe it would be a violation of due process under the Fourteenth Amendment, denial of a fair trial to these two Petitioners, for the Court to call this witness.[2]

I had other constitutional objections as well, including a denial of the defendants' right to cross-examine the witnesses against them that was guaranteed by the Sixth Amendment. Holley took the matter under advisement but eventually overruled these objections and allowed Willie Mae Lee to testify both in and out of hypnosis.

The hypnosis session began when Willie Mae Lee, at McCawley's direction, began staring at the eagle on top of the American flag that stood near her. "Now, if you'll just watch the little eagle up there," McCawley intoned. "Let your body relax and just easily listen to me. Just watch the top of the flag there, the eagle on top, and easily listen and just gradually let your body begin to relax." Willie Mae Lee complied. And McCawley slowly began to count backward from twenty and gradually brought Willie Mae Lee into an apparent trance. Her eyes closed and her body became limp.[3]

McCawley then sought to slowly bring Willie Mae Lee back to the night of July 31, 1963, to allegedly relive the events of that evening. But he didn't ask her to give a narrative account. Instead, he asked a series of questions covering thirty-four pages of transcript and she replied with fragmented, nonnarrative answers, often giving one-word or one-sentence responses.[4]

All of this was unprecedented. To my knowledge, this is the only time in the legal history of Florida that a person was placed under hypnosis on the witness stand to give "testimony" in court. Gene Miller discovered only one other such incident in the history of the country.[5]

McCawley finally got to the critical part of the evening in question, and Willie Mae Lee started sobbing and crying. It was great theater. Gene Miller later called it "Show Biz Justice."[6]

Here is McCawley's questioning of Willie Mae Lee. He called her by her nickname "Billie Mae:"

Q. Tell me what's happening, Billie Mae?

A. He got mans in car.

Q. Got who in car?

A. That fat man and that old man.

Q. Who's got them in the car?

A. Say for them to get in. Me in back seat.

Q. Who's in the car, Billie Mae?

A. Man.

Q. What man?

A. Me—Wilbert, and Mr. Burkett and Floyd. No.

At that point, Willie Mae Lee began giving unintelligible answers and McCawley instructed her to speak up. But she continued giving fragmented answers to numerous questions, including: "Don't beg that n——. Don't beg that n——." She started crying, appeared in an extreme emotional state, and began screaming: "Don't do it. Don't do it. Let me go. Let me go. Oh no! Oh no! Don't!" "Shut up your goddamn mouth." She said she was talking to "Freddie."

She continued crying and moaning, often speaking in fragments:

A. Lord have mercy, don't do it, don't kill men! Don't carry men down there! (unintelligible words) Oh, dear God! I'm sorry I ran away. So scared. So scared. (unintelligible words).

Q. All right, Willie Mae, I want you to sit up now. Come, sit up. It's all right. You can sit up. Come on, you can sit up now. That's it, just like this. Now tell me what's happening. Exactly what's happening.

A. (moaning)

Q. What is it?

A. I'm running.

Q. Hum?

A. I'm running.

Q. You're running? Where are you running?

A. Down the side of the road.

Q. Running down the side of the road.

A. Coming back, nowhere to go. "Freddie what you did (unintelligible words) What you did! What you did! What you did!"[7]

Irwin Block and I watched this spectacle in utter disbelief. The entire session was pointless. As McCawley himself had admitted in his earlier testimony in court, "A person's hypnotic behavior is really determined by his nonhypnotic behavior. If he would normally lie out of hypnosis, he can also lie in hypnosis."[8] So why go through the charade? Willie Mae Lee was lying both in and out of the staged performance that day. Putting her in a trance did not give her any extra credibility.

When McCawley was through, Judge Holley allowed us to ask nonleading questions of Willie Mae Lee. But we weren't permitted to ask the questions ourselves. We had to submit our questions to McCawley for him to ask the witness. We declined. We objected to the entire hypnosis session.

*   *   *

Holley had earlier expressed a desire to have psychiatrists examine Willie Mae Lee to determine if she was a fit subject for a hypnosis session and to advise the judge on the nature of the session. He asked the state and later the defense to make the necessary arrangements to bring in whatever doctors we chose.

We complied and brought in Dr. Michael Gilbert, a practicing psychiatrist from Miami with an extensive background in and experience with hypnosis. The state complied by producing Dr. Israel Hanenson from the state mental hospital in Chattahoochee, who had no such background and who was the same doctor Holmes and I had encountered when we had visited the mental hospital a year and a half before to talk to Willie Nicholson.

Both doctors examined Willie Mae Lee and found her to be competent to testify and a fit subject for a hypnosis session. They also attended Willie Mae Lee's hypnosis session in court. After this session, both doctors testified about what they observed.

Gilbert testified first and expressed some doubt about how deep in a trance Willie Mae Lee had been during the session. He also explained the nature of the hypnotic state and agreed with McCawley that a person who would lie while they were not under hypnosis would continue to lie when placed in a hypnotic trance.

Irwin Block did the questioning:

Q. Doctor, can you lie in a hypnotic state?
A. Yes, a person can lie in a hypnotic state. Can result from several different ways. . . . A person during a hypnotic state will not do anything more than he is accustomed to doing, that is, which his personality will permit him to do. For example, you can't get a person to commit a murder in a hypnotic state if he never would have committed a murder when he is conscious. Similarly, if a person is a habitual

or pathological liar, just simply an extension of his basic personality, he will lie.

What hypnosis does is selectively remove the conscious inhibitions of behavior so that by putting the inhibitory cells to sleep, so to speak, of the brain, then material which has been actively repressed comes forth because the inhibitors have been inhibited.

* * *

Now if a person is a habitual liar, there is no inhibition to lie and he just lies all along.

And this is another reason why hypnosis—another fact is if a person has talked himself into believing something to be so, repeated it enough so that he consciously believes it to be so, then under hypnosis he still believes it so.[9]

Hanenson then testified and did not disagree with Gilbert. Judge Holley asked a pertinent question:

The Court. What experience, Doctor, have you had with hypnosis in your work?

The Witness. Well, to be frank, none. To compare myself with the illustrious colleague, Dr. Michael Gilbert, I would classify him as a giant and I am a plain Lilliput.

The thing is, we state psychiatrist[s]—without disrespect to Dr. Gilbert—we can't go into any fancy psychiatry. We would have to be very rich. The state man works. So I regret in a way I don't do it, but I know a little bit of it. I don't have time to read that stuff, you know, however, because I'm too busy to go to one Circuit Court to the other.[10]

We did not cross-examine Hanenson. It was obvious he was unqualified to evaluate Willie Mae Lee's hypnosis session in court.

* * *

For the balance of the fourth day and into the fifth day of the hearing, the state presented seven witnesses from the local legal and law enforcement community, all of whom knew each other well, some for many years. These witnesses testified that Pitts and Lee had freely confessed their guilt and had eagerly wanted to plead guilty and throw themselves on the mercy of the court and that the police had never mistreated them.

This was the testimony of their own lawyer, Fred Turner, and nearly everyone followed in lockstep. They were, in my view, banding together and defending their community against "outside agitators" like Gene Miller, the *Miami Herald,* and the ACLU defense lawyers from Miami, who in their view were "stirring up trouble" and "defaming" the people of Gulf County. It was literally a case of us against them.

We cross-examined each of these witnesses, discovered discrepancies in their accounts, and showed how absurd their stories were—that two young Black men in August 1963 at the height of the civil rights movement in the South would go on a suicide mission, that they couldn't wait to confess to murdering two white men and jump in the electric chair. The testimony was utterly fantastic.

These witnesses also turned a blind eye to the obvious beating Freddie Pitts had suffered when Deputy Sheriff George Kittrell had battered him to a pulp with blackjack blows to the head during an all-night ride in a police car. I can't say I was surprised at this testimony, but I was dismayed.

Marion Knight, a former state senator and local lawyer, really laid it on thick. He testified that he had spoken to Pitts and Lee in the courtroom during a recess in a hearing in the circuit court and that both men had told him how eager they were to plead guilty. One defendant, he said, stated: "We ain't been talked into nothing, we ain't been beat into nothing. We told it like it was. And we are going to do it again." According to Knight, the other defendant had said, "I told the truth about it and the sooner it's over with the better I'll like it." According to Knight, their attorney Fred Turner had also said that "they had confessed to everybody that would let them" and that "he couldn't stop them."[11]

David Gaskin, the defendants' court-appointed attorney at the first appearance hearing, testified that Pitts and Lee had shown no signs of physical beating when he had talked to them, that he had asked both men whether they had been mistreated by the police, that both men had denied any such mistreatment, and that it had been "necessary" for him to advise them to plead not guilty.[12] Sam Husband, the nonlawyer county judge who had presided at the first appearance hearing, also testified that he had seen nothing unusual about either Pitts or Lee in court and in particular had noticed no facial bruises on either man.[13] Circuit Judge W. L. Fitzpatrick, the trial judge, testified that Pitts and Lee had assured him that they had not been mistreated by the police during a private conference he had had with both men in the judge's chambers, although the judge vacillated about when that had happened and whether anyone else was present.[14]

Deputy Sheriff Wayne White testified that he had never witnessed any physical beating of Freddie Pitts by Deputy Sheriff George Kittrell. As for the bandage Kittrell had on his hand after this beating, that injury had supposedly happened when White had slammed a police car door on Kittrell's hand.[15] Robert Sidwell, the owner of the local radio station and a volunteer deputy sheriff, echoed the same story. He testified that he had transported Pitts and Lee from the Port St. Joe Jail to the Bay County Jail in Panama City and had noticed no signs of a physical beating in either defendant.[16] Joe Townsend, the Florida Sheriffs Bureau official who had participated with the local police in innumerable coercive interrogations and lie detector tests, denied that he had ever mistreated Pitts or Lee.[17]

Tellingly, however, Deputy Sheriff George Kittrell was never called as a witness to deny that he had brutally beaten Freddie Pitts. He sat alone in the courtroom hallway while everyone else testified. People barely talked to him. Not even the state had the nerve to put on the witness stand the man who had unmercifully beaten up Freddie Pitts.

Only George Core, the clerk of the circuit court, did not join the local chorus. Although Pitts and Lee did not recall this event, Core testified that during a recess in a court hearing, one of the defendants, he couldn't remember which one, had made a vague comment about how he, the defendant, "couldn't believe we did this." Core testified "I placed no significance on the statement whatever at the time." When pressed, however, Core did say "it was my thinking" that "they meant they were guilty" but conceded that he had no way of knowing that as the comment was never explained. We contended that the remark, if made, was simply a sigh of regret that they "couldn't believe" they had confessed and pled guilty—nothing more. In any event, the testimony added little or nothing to the state's case.[18]

The only witness the state called who was not from the local community or otherwise associated with the police backfired on the state. Army Captain Thomas Arata, Pitts's commanding officer, testified that when he had seen Freddie Pitts in custody at the Bay County Jail, Pitts had looked "very tired" and had complained that the police had beaten him. Arata had run his hand over Pitts's head and had felt "several bumps" there. Arata wouldn't "speculate" about how Pitts had gotten those injuries, but he did say that "it had to have been something that hit him on the head." Captain Arata likened it to the injuries he had once received when he had been hit in the head with a baseball bat or when his little boy had injured his head falling down a flight of stairs. This testimony confirmed the testimony of army CID investigators Bruce Potts and Donald Hoag.[19]

* * *

At last, the weeklong hearing came to an end. There was some additional testimony in rebuttal, but it was all brief and mostly covered minor matters. Judge Holley then methodically went through all the official court documents that had been filed in the case and took judicial notice of them.[20] He had previously announced on the first day of the hearing that he was *not* taking judicial notice of the depositions that had been taken and filed in the case.[21]

Holley also announced that he would be visiting several scenes in the county, including the Mo Jo gas station, to better understand the testimony.[22] He then ordered that a transcript of the entire hearing be prepared for his review and directed the state and the defense to file briefs containing our final arguments.[23]

After that, the judge took a brief recess, had the courtroom cleared of spectators, and conducted a hearing devoted to the security concerns in the case. We recounted the menacing incident that had occurred the first day of the hearing when spikes had been placed under the tires of our car in the court parking lot. Wayne White explained why it was necessary to place Pitts and Lee in a security cell with no windows for their own safety.[24]

The chief custodian recounted how he had spoken with a spectator in front of the court building the day before and that person had said that he had heard that the judge's life had been threatened if a new trial were not granted. A Port St. Joe police officer said that he had also talked to one of the spectators, who had said that he didn't think justice would be done, that "all the attorneys was just lying," and "the courthouse should be burned down on all of them."[25] Everyone laughed at that remark, but it was a nervous laugh because we all knew the potential danger that hovered over this hearing. Indeed, although it was not mentioned at the hearing, Judge Holley had ordered that one white male spectator be searched for a weapon when the man looked particularly agitated during one of the hearings.[26]

But the highlight of this closed session came when Frank Pate, the mayor of Port St. Joe, pleaded with the judge not to rule just then on our motion to vacate and order a new trial. Racial tensions were running high in the community, he said, and a cooling-off period was needed.

What follows is Frank Pate's statement. Judge Holley did the questioning.

The Court. I want you to tell these folks exactly what you told me. Mr. Pate is the mayor of Port St. Joe.

Mr. Pate. I talked to you Wednesday afternoon, I believe, at four o'clock.

The Court. That's right.

Mr. Pate. I came out to see him with regard to the people in this city. It seemed that the feelings were running very high here on both sides, both races, and I talked to him in the light of hoping that he would not render a decision today, if the court ended today.

In other words, I was hoping that he would allow a cooling-off period and time for him to study the evidence that was presented on both cases for the benefit of the people in our city.

* * *

I have a business. I have people from both sides coming in, for and against, and both races, and they're all my friends. I work with them and you just hear people talking, you know. And as you can tell very well that there is great interest by the courtroom being full, in the halls and in the parking lots.[27]

We all knew what the mayor meant: there was a possibility of racial violence if the court ruled immediately. In particular, he confirmed what we had long believed to be true, namely that the local white community was bitterly opposed to any effort to reopen the Pitts-Lee case and that we were in some physical danger.

Judge Holley, however, took great pains to assure everyone that all security matters had been handled, that the hearing had gone well without serious incident, and that he would not issue a final ruling for some time. He thanked everyone for their participation and court was adjourned. The Port St. Joe hearing was over, it seemed. But not quite.

As the defense team packed up our files and left the courthouse, Gene Miller went ahead of everyone else with Warren Holmes while the rest of us lagged behind. Miller, ever in good physical shape, carried a 50-pound cardboard filing cabinet on his right shoulder as he walked down the front steps of the courthouse. Then, out of nowhere, a young, muscular, red-headed white man charged Miller from the front and punched him in the mouth. With his file cabinet flying, Miller dropped to the pavement with the man on top of him throwing more punches. Holmes, a lit cigar clenched in his teeth, grabbed the man by the neck, put a hammer lock on the attacker, and pulled the man off Miller.[28]

Fortunately, the assailant was not armed—although he might have been had he not been searched and watched earlier by court security personnel.

He was the same man Judge Holley had ordered to be searched because of his agitated conduct in court. He was Bobby Burkett, the nephew of Jesse Burkett.[29]

It was not surprising that Burkett chose Miller to physically attack. Miller's comprehensive articles on the case for the *Miami Herald* had brought great attention, much of it unfavorable, to the local community. The white citizens in the area regarded Miller and the *Miami Herald* as the "chief villains" who were responsible for the reopening of the Pitts-Lee case.

After Burkett was subdued, we defense lawyers caught up with Miller and learned what had happened. Burkett was turned over to the police. Miller, who was shaken but not seriously hurt, signed an assault complaint with the police but never pursued it. For our own safety, the entire defense team received a police escort out of Port St. Joe to the county line. We were relieved that we had escaped the area without being seriously injured or worse.

20

The Ruling and the Appeal

It was seven months before Judge Holley made his ruling on our motion to vacate Pitts and Lee's convictions—the long "cooling-off" period that Mayor Frank Pate had pleaded for in open court. A complicated series of appeals and other occurrences followed this ruling that strung out the case for another two years.

On April 28, 1969, everyone on both sides of the case was summoned to Holley's courtroom in the circuit court in Clearwater, located on the west coast of Florida near Tampa. The hearing that followed was typical of the drama we had all gone through in Port St. Joe.[1]

At the outset, Terry Furnell, a young criminal lawyer practicing in Clearwater, stepped forward in a hushed courtroom and asked to be heard on a motion he had filed. He represented Curtis Adams in other proceedings that sought to set aside Adams's conviction for the Floyd McFarland murder in Fort Lauderdale.

The motion asked the court to enter an order directing J. Frank Adams to enter into a contract that would grant Curtis Adams immunity from prosecution for the Floyd-Burkett murders and for perjury that Adams had committed in his testimony at the Port St. Joe hearing. The motion, which Adams had signed, contained the following significant admissions:

1. Curtis Adams, Jr., is possessed of information which will demonstrate conclusively the innocence of Freddie Lee Pitts and Wilbert Lee of the offenses for which they have been convicted and sentenced in the above-styled cause.
2. Such evidence is prejudicial to and incriminating of the said Curtis Adams, Jr., as to the homicides attributed to Freddie Lee Pitts and Wilbert Lee.
3. That if immunity from prosecution as above requested is *not* granted to Curtis Adams, Jr., he will thereby be precluded from testifying in order to protect himself from prosecution, which may

result in the wrongful execution or continued wrongful confine-
ment of two innocent individuals.

4. That if immunity from prosecution as above requested is granted
to Curtis Adams, Jr., he will testify truthfully in all matters material
in the above-styled case and will thereby conclusively establish the
innocence of Freddie Lee Pitts and Wilbert Lee.[2]

This motion, particularly the last paragraph, was a complete repudiation
of Curtis Adams's perjurious testimony in the case, which had blamed Freddie Pitts for the Floyd-Burkett murders. Adams was now saying through his
counsel that Pitts and Lee were innocent of these murders; that *he*, in fact,
had committed those criminal homicides; and that if given immunity from
prosecution, he would so testify.

This motion may have been the clincher for Judge Holley, although no
one will ever know. The judge never ruled on the motion, but he certainly
considered it a part of the case. By signing the motion, Curtis Adams had,
in effect, made an incriminating statement that indirectly implicated himself in the Floyd-Burkett murders.

The basic question Judge Holley had to answer based on the evidence
before him was whether Pitts and Lee or Curtis Adams had murdered Grover Floyd and Jesse Burkett. After hearing argument from both sides, Holley took a brief recess. He soon returned to the courtroom and announced
his decision by reading his written order.

After rejecting several preliminary grounds for relief, the judge came
to the four central grounds we had raised for setting aside the defendants'
convictions. We all held our breath as the judge plodded through his legal
analysis:

It is the opinion and holding of this court that the rule of law originally enunciated by the State of Florida in Nichels vs. State [citation
omitted] and Chambers et al. vs. State [citation omitted] is applicable to the other grounds raised in the motions. It is the opinion of
this court that each of these four grounds would have been proper
grounds for consideration under a writ of error coram nobis.[3]

My heart pounded as I listened. The judge was accepting one of the arguments I had made in the brief we had filed with the court.

It is the opinion and holding of this court that the quantum of proof
required as to these grounds is that sufficient to raise a reasonable
doubt as to the validity of the prior proceedings.

Upon this predicate of law this court finds for Pitts and Lee on the issue of knowingly or negligently withholding evidence by the state—and innocence.[4]

Upon hearing these words, I felt a jolt of adrenaline. Freddie Pitts grabbed my arm and openly wept as we sat together at counsel table. Wilbert Lee, seated nearby, shivered with joy. Irwin Block and Maurice Rosen broke out in big smiles.

But Judge Holley continued:

This court finds *against* Pitts and Lee on the issues of incompetent counsel and coerced confessions. With respect to the coerced confessions finding, this court however does find that on the legal predicate above stated the guilty pleas *may* have been the result of fear.[5]

When I heard this, my feeling of elation subsided somewhat and my thoughts began to race. To me, the evidence on those rejected grounds was overwhelming. And if the guilty pleas may have been the result of fear, why weren't their confessions the result of that same fear? Still, a win was a win, and I was willing to accept it any way the judge wanted to manage it.

Holley concluded his order by reading the magic words that we had long wanted to hear:

It is therefore ordered and adjudged that *the judgments of guilt* of Freddie Lee Pitts and Wilbert [Slingshot] Lee entered by the Circuit Court of the Fourteenth Judicial Circuit in and for Gulf County, Florida, August 17, 1963, are set aside, vacated and declared naught.

It is further ordered and adjudged that *the death sentences* imposed on the defendants, Freddie Lee Pitts and Wilbert [Slingshot] Lee by the Honorable W. L. Fitzpatrick, circuit judge, August 28, 1963, are set aside, vacated and declared naught.

Done and ordered in open court in Clearwater, Pinellas County, Florida, this 29th day of April, 1969.

Charles Holley (s)

Circuit Judge[6]

In a newspaper interview several years later, Holley revealed his underlying thinking about the case:

I think they [Pitts and Lee] will ultimately be turned loose because in my opinion Adams's testimony should go in [evidence], and if that testimony goes in, no jury will convict them. If you combine that with three statements Willie Mae Lee has made, the case gets to the point of utter confusion. The state has an obligation to prove guilt beyond a reasonable doubt. And I do not believe that 12 people can sit and listen to all the evidence, and say there is no doubt.[7]

Under Holley's order, however, only the judgments of conviction and death sentences entered were set aside. The August 1963 indictments charging Pitts and Lee with first-degree murder still stood. We faced a new trial based on those indictments. Beyond that, the state had a right to appeal Holley's order within thirty days of the entry of that order. We left that courtroom jubilant but wary about what the next step in the case might be. Would it be a new trial or would the state appeal this order?

It was front-page news in the *Miami Herald* that we had won a new trial in the case. I was teaching a class in criminal law at the University of Miami as an adjunct professor. When I showed up at the law school to teach the next class, my students gave me a standing ovation. I savored the moment, but unfortunately this victory was short lived.[8]

*　　*　　*

At first, it looked like the state wouldn't appeal the order. George Georgieff immediately announced that no appeal would be taken. Shortly thereafter, Earl Faircloth, the Florida attorney general, agreed, stating, "The court has ruled and I am satisfied with the decision. I do not feel an appeal is warranted or desirable."[9]

But J. Frank Adams had other ideas. He had stalked out of the courtroom with Sheriff "Doc" Daffin upon hearing Judge Holley's order, obviously unhappy with the result. And on May 30, 1969, the last day for doing so, Leo Jones, Adams's first assistant, filed a notice of appeal on behalf of the state with the circuit court in Port St. Joe and later followed it with additional pleadings. The appeal was to the First District Court of Appeal in Tallahassee, one of the intermediate appellate courts in Florida. Generally speaking, however, only the Florida attorney general could prosecute the appeal any further, and Faircloth came under tremendous political pressure to join the appeal.

The *News Herald* in Panama City led the charge, condemning Judge Holley for his decision and Earl Faircloth for refusing to appeal it. At the time, Faircloth was preparing to run for governor of Florida the following year. On June 11, 1969, the *News Herald* opened fire with an editorial, the first of many. "Northwest Florida residents," the paper declared, "were stunned" at Judge Holley's order and "were even more shocked" by Faircloth's refusal to appeal this decision.

Attorney General Faircloth apparently concurs with Judge Holley since he says he has no intention of filing an appeal. Why? Only Mr. Faircloth can answer this question and so far he has not come up with one. The people of Florida are entitled to an answer and we challenge Mr. Faircloth in his role as the state's chief prosecutor to come up with one.

The paper then attacked the *Miami Herald*'s coverage of the case:

The chain of events preceding Holley's bombshell decision started with a series of highly sensational articles in Florida's largest newspaper, the *Miami Herald*. Residents of this sector were depicted as a bunch of red-necked, illiterate, bloodthirsty, idiotic clods.

On the other hand, the murderers were depicted as innocent creatures of nature who were beaten, coerced and convicted under kangaroo court conditions. Nothing could be further from the truth. The newspaper, which joined hands with the NAACP and the Civil Liberties Union, based its clamor for a new trial on the words of a convicted professional felon who "confessed" to the Port St. Joe crimes. He later recanted his "confession."

The *News Herald* ignored Adams's motion for immunity which, in effect, constituted a return to his confession to the Floyd-Burkett murders. The paper then tore into both Faircloth and Holley:

In his unsuccessful bid last year for the Democratic nomination for the United States Senate, Mr. Faircloth ran on a law and order platform. He is now an announced candidate for governor in 1970. Since he lost out in the Senate race, perhaps Mr. Faircloth has changed his campaign strategy. *What sayeth ye, Mr. Faircloth?*

The defendants have more than had their day in court and now the people of Florida demand theirs. The defendants have stalled off paying their debt to society for six long years and the people also must be given due consideration.

Judge Holley ran for governor several years ago and reports are making the rounds that he will be a candidate for Florida Supreme Court justice in 1970.

We recommend to the voters that they carefully examine the names of FAIRCLOTH and HOLLEY if they appear on the ballot next year.[10]

Ten days later, the *News Herald* "commended" Leo Jones, Adams's principal assistant, for announcing his intention to appeal, calling him "a real champion of law-and-order" and remarking that "our judiciary system needs more men of your caliber."

At first, Earl Faircloth, who had political ties to South Florida, resisted this public pressure and sent a letter to the editor of the *News Herald* defending his position. He argued that there was substantial evidence to support Holley's decision, which, in fact, was true.[11] But thereafter, the public pressure proved too great. Faircloth soon entered the case and took charge of the appeal. He was running for governor and needed the support of the Florida Panhandle.

*   *   *

George Georgieff was assigned to represent the state on appeal. He argued in his brief that the guilty pleas that Pitts and Lee had entered were voluntary and that that meant that all grounds to set aside their convictions had no force and effect, including our claim of innocence.

I filed an extensive 50-page brief together with Barry Semet, an outstanding appellate lawyer with Irwin Block's law firm. We argued that there was substantial competent evidence to support Judge Holley's findings in our favor. We also assigned as error Judge Holley's findings that rejected our grounds of incompetent counsel and involuntary confession and asserted that the order should be affirmed based on these grounds as well. We also objected to the testimony Willie Mae Lee had given under hypnosis.

On April 20, 1970, about a year after the notice of appeal had been filed, an oral argument was held before the First District Court of Appeal in Tallahassee. The court consisted of three appellate judges: Judges John Rawls, Dewey Johnson, and Sam Spector. The argument did not go well for us.

Rawls, in particular, was openly skeptical that a duly entered criminal conviction could be reopened years later based on newly discovered evidence of innocence. He said if that were the law, no one could be constitutionally convicted and the gates of Raiford Prison would be thrown wide open. J. Frank Adams attended the argument and smiled broadly at Rawls's questions.[12]

Barry Semet and I argued for the defense. We left the courtroom in a pessimistic mood. George Georgieff, who had argued for the state, was his usual expansive self. He approached me in the hallway outside the courtroom.

"Well, Phil," he said, "I climbed into the tank for you today," meaning he had pulled his punches in his oral argument. "Bullshit, George," I replied and walked away. He had done no such thing.

By then, I had resigned my position as an assistant public defender in Dade County in November 1969 and was now appearing for Pitts and Lee as a private lawyer. My boss, Robert Koeppel, had stepped down as the public defender of Dade County, and I had announced my candidacy as a Democrat to replace him in the next election. Public defenders in Florida are elected on a partisan basis. I won the Democratic primary and several months later, in November 1970, I defeated the interim-appointed public defender, Hughlan Long, in the general election and became the elected public defender of Dade County. I held that position for six years, from 1971 to 1977.

Meanwhile, in 1962, in *Baker v. Carr*, the US Supreme Court had ordered the fair apportionment of the rural-dominated state legislatures, including Florida.[13] Subsequently, the 1970 election ushered in "the golden age of Florida politics." Outstanding public servants like Robert Shevin, Dick Pettigrew, Louis de la Parte, Sandy D'Alemberte, Marshall Harris, Kenneth Myers, and Murray Dubbin emerged to occupy powerful positions in the Florida Cabinet and in the state legislature. But the crown jewel in this golden era was state senator Reubin Askew. He won the Democratic primary for governor against Earl Faircloth and other challengers and later defeated the incumbent Republican governor, Claude R. Kirk Jr., in the 1970 general election.[14]

A political moderate from Pensacola in the Florida Panhandle, Askew accomplished many lasting government reforms during his two terms as governor. As it turned out, he became one of the real heroes in the Pitts-Lee case. Askew later appointed me, in my capacity as the public defender of Dade County, to continue my representation of Pitts and Lee outside my circuit to the conclusion of the case.

On December 3, 1970, a month after the November elections, the First District Court of Appeal issued its opinion, authored by Judge Rawls. To our great disappointment, the court reversed Holley's order. But fortunately, it also certified the case to the Florida Supreme Court for a final decision on the ground that the case involved "a question of great public interest."[15]

Regarding the central ground of innocence that Holley had relied on to set aside Pitts and Lee's convictions, the district court ruled:

> We find that the trial court erred in finding for the appellees on the issue of innocence. By this decision we are not holding that the appellees are required on collateral attack to prove beyond a reasonable doubt that a third party committed the crime, but we are holding that a movant who has pleaded guilty, declining to resist the State's charge of guilt or proof thereof, must establish on collateral attack as least some clear showing by competent substantial evidence there was a significant insufficiency in the State's evidence so as to warrant a new trial.[16]

But contrary to this ruling, at the five-day hearing in Port St. Joe, we had shown plenty of evidence that Curtis Adams had murdered Grover Floyd and Jesse Burkett and that Pitts and Lee were innocent of this crime. Unfortunately, the court gave little or no weight to this evidence and basically accepted the state's contrary version of the facts. In so doing, the district court committed reversible error.

It is a well-established principle of Florida law that when an appellate court reviews a trial court order after an evidentiary hearing, it must resolve all conflicts in the evidence and all reasonable inferences from the evidence in favor of the prevailing party—in this case the defendants, not the state. The only question on appeal was whether there was substantial, competent evidence to support the trial court's ruling, and there was an abundance of such evidence in this case.[17]

George Georgieff later told my colleague, Maurice Rosen, that the district court's opinion was so extreme that it was embarrassing.[18] The court simply cherry-picked the testimony it liked, ignored or discounted the testimony it didn't like, and retried the case on appeal. These were totally improper actions for an appellate court.

Compounding the error, the court relied in part on the depositions filed in the case when it recited its distorted version of the facts.[19] But the depositions were never part of the appellate record in the case. Indeed, at the very outset of the hearing, Judge Holley had expressly stated that he was *not* taking judicial notice of the depositions in deciding this case.[20] But the district court ignored this ruling and relied on the depositions when it retried the case on appeal.

However, we welcomed one aspect of the district court's opinion. Although the court stated that it had "grave concerns" about whether innocence could ever be used to attack a criminal conviction on a postconviction motion to vacate, it nonetheless decided to recognize the ground in this case, given "the gravity of the claim" and the "favorable decision" of the trial court on this claim.[21] It was precious little. But at least the court had recognized that innocence could be a ground for setting aside a criminal conviction—something I had found little legal support for when I first entered the case. Beyond that, the opinion was bleak for us, as the court could find nothing in the record that even remotely pointed toward Pitts and Lee's innocence, despite the mountain of evidence we had presented to establish this position.

Strikingly, although the court even expressed its sympathy for the "pressures" Willie Mae Lee claimed she had endured to get her to change her testimony, it refused to even acknowledge the possibility that there might be a miscarriage of justice in this case, as Judge Holley had found, and to face up to the horrific suffering Pitts and Lee had undergone as a result.[22] The court's sympathies were for the false accuser and not for the victims of this appalling injustice.

Early on in his opinion, Rawls sounded a most disquieting note. He wrote, "On December 19, 1967, Pitts and Lee filed the instant motion to vacate represented by three attorneys from New York City, one from Washington, D.C., and four from Miami."[23] What did the residency of the defense counsel have to do with this case, except to let everyone know that we were not from the South.? In my view, that was a coded message that we were among the "outside agitators" the Deep South despised at the time and were not to be trusted. No mention was ever made about where the prosecutors lived; we defense lawyers were singled out for a reason. Judge Rawls had previously served in the Florida State Senate and was a staunch segregationist during his service, a bitter opponent of public school integration.

Rawls further rejected our claim that the state had suppressed evidence of innocence:

> There is no showing of prejudice here nor is there any showing that under the circumstances here related this is the type of evidence which is required to be revealed prior to trial rather than at trial, assuming it could be classified as "favorable" to the defendants. Since the defendants chose to plead guilty and went to trial on the issue of punishment only, and since their testimony corroborated that of the State, the evidence here was clearly immaterial to the issue tried.

The trial judge erred in finding for the [defendants] on the issue of suppressing evidence.[24]

The reasoning here is convoluted and unpersuasive. There was no dispute about the fact that the state attorney himself, J. Frank Adams, had suppressed evidence of innocence; namely, a written sworn statement from Willie Mae Lee in which she blamed Lambson Smith and Freddie Pitts for the Floyd-Burkett murders. This statement exonerated Wilbert Lee entirely and constituted devastating impeachment evidence for Freddie Pitts. Their ensuing guilty pleas, which were entirely coerced, were entered without knowledge of this exonerating evidence, thereby further tainting their involuntary pleas of guilty. Based on the US Supreme Court decision of *Brady v. Maryland,* this constitutional error invalidated Pitts and Lee's convictions.[25]

The rest of the district court's opinion was a lengthy discussion that rejected our assignments of error. Although we strongly disagreed with this analysis, it is unnecessary to get into these matters in view of what ultimately happened when the case reached the Florida Supreme Court.

Gene Miller was particularly incensed with the First District Court's opinion. In an unusual opinion piece for the *Miami Herald,* Miller wrote a comprehensive two-and-a-quarter-page analysis of the court's opinion that demonstrated how badly it had distorted the facts of this case. The article was featured on the front page of the Viewpoint Section in the Sunday edition.

At the outset of his analysis, Miller announced:

A North Florida court opinion which reinstates death sentences in the Pitts-Lee case is filled with gross factual errors and questionable legal reasoning.

This is my opinion. I realize this is an unusual statement to make about an appellate court decision. I do not make it lightly. I believe the court is wrong. . . .

In my view, the court misstated facts, garbled events, recited half-truths without clarification, repeatedly glossed over contradictions from the witness stand, and concentrated solely on reversing a lower court that set aside the convictions.[26]

We on the defense counsel team were in total agreement. This opinion piece earned Miller the ire of the political and legal establishment of the Fourteenth Judicial Circuit in the Florida Panhandle. Judge John Rawls, the author of the district court's opinion, was from Marianna, Florida, the small town in which the Pitts-Lee case would eventually be retried. To many in that area, Gene Miller and the *Miami Herald* were the real villains in this entire affair.

* * *

In the general election of 1970, Robert Shevin, an able state senator from Miami, was elected as the attorney general of Florida. Earl Faircloth had stepped down from that office to run for governor, a race he lost in that election to Reubin Askew.

Shortly after the election, the defense team—Irwin Block, Gene Miller, Warren Holmes, and I—met with Shevin. We asked Shevin to look into the Pitts-Lee case once he was sworn in as attorney general. He agreed to do so. Shevin was familiar with the case from the newspaper articles published in the *Miami Herald* and the *News Herald*. By 1970, the *Miami Herald* had published over 130 columns devoted to the case, most of them written by Gene Miller.[27] When he took office, Shevin examined the state's file and discussed the case at length with George Georgieff and Ray Markey. Both Georgieff and Markey expressed the view that Pitts and Lee would probably prevail in the federal courts based on the issue of suppression of evidence favorable to the defendants.[28]

Shevin mulled over the case for about three months. He was enormously popular throughout the state, having won his race for attorney general in a landslide. He had a bright political career ahead of him, possibly as a future governor or a US senator. The safest political move for him was to let the appellate process play out in the courts, as his predecessor Earl Faircloth had done. Shevin could have announced that the courts, including the federal courts, should make the final decision on all the legal issues involved in the case, not the attorney general.

But Robert Shevin was a man of honor and courage—one of the real heroes in this case, along with Governor Askew. Shevin no doubt entertained serious doubts about Pitts and Lee's guilt or innocence and about the fairness of their original trial.

On April 15, 1971, only three months into his term of office, Shevin made a decision that risked his entire political career. He filed a pleading entitled "Motion in Confession of Error," which incorporated a memorandum of law, with the Florida Supreme Court.[29] This pleading and the accompanying memorandum conceded that Pitts and Lee were entitled to a new trial based on the ground that the state had suppressed evidence of innocence—namely Willie Mae Lee's written statement to State Attorney J. Frank Adams blaming Lambson Smith and Freddie Pitts for the Floyd-Burkett murders. Georgieff and Markey also signed this confession of error.

Relying on the controlling case of *Brady v. Maryland* and several other similar cases, Shevin argued that the state's suppression of Willie Mae Lee's statement about Lambson Smith had deprived Pitts and Lee of a fair trial. He concluded, "Your respondent is compelled, in light of the decisions discussed herein, and the corresponding duty to see that justice is done, to respectfully suggest that the petitioners be awarded a new trial."[30]

In so doing, Robert Shevin, as attorney general, acted in the highest traditions of the legal profession as stated under former Canon 5 of the Florida Code of Ethics Governing Attorneys:

> The primary duty of a lawyer engaged in public prosecution is not to convict, but to see that justice is done. The suppression of facts or the secreting of witnesses capable of establishing the innocence of the accused is highly reprehensible.[31]

This ethical obligation was later restated in the revised Florida Code of Professional Responsibility, which took effect on October 1, 1970:

> A public prosecutor or other government lawyer in criminal litigation shall make timely disclosure to counsel for the defendant . . . of the existence of evidence known to the prosecutor or other government lawyer, that tends to negate the guilt of the accused.[32]

However, the Florida Supreme Court was under no obligation to accept Shevin's confession of error. The Court could have rejected this confession of error, directed Shevin to file a brief on the merits, and affirmed the district court's decision. But the Florida Supreme Court chose not to do so. Instead, on April 21, 1971, it accepted the attorney general's position and reversed the district court's decision:

> By "motion in confession in error," the Attorney General has requested that the above cause be returned to the trial court for the purpose of a new trial. Under such circumstances, it is not necessary for this Court to pass upon the question certified to us.
>
> The opinion of the District Court of Appeal is vacated without any determination on the questions of law discussed therein.
>
> The cause is remanded to the District Court of Appeal for further

remand to the trial court with instructions to vacate the judgment and sentence and the plea of guilty so that the Defendants may be rearraigned and the cause set for trial.[33]

The case then went back to the District Court of Appeal, which followed the Supreme Court's mandate and ordered a new trial in the case.[34]

On April 28, 1971, shortly after the Supreme Court's ruling, the *News Herald* published a vitriolic editorial condemning Shevin for confessing error in the case. The editorial denounced Shevin for having "made a mockery of justice and destroyed any public confidence in government," for "taking the law into his own hands," and for "sett[ing] himself up as judge and jury." And it continued with more ad hominem attacks:

Well, Mr. Shevin, we don't need your breed in a position of vast importance in Florida government. We'd be better off without any laws period if you intend to dispense justice in the manner you exemplified in the Pitts-Lee case.

We submit, Mr. Attorney General, that you were playing politics when you filed your unprecedented petition April 15, which, in effect, sold the people of Florida down the river. . . .

The Miami Herald got involved in this case in 1967 when Curtis Adams, a Port St. Joe felon with a long criminal record, "confessed" to the Burkett-Floyd murders at Raiford. He made his confession to a private polygraph expert who has been associated with the newspaper in several investigations.

Following a long series of sensational newspaper articles, Pitts and Lee were granted a hearing before a Pinellas County Circuit judge in Port St. Joe. The American Civil Liberties Union and the National Association for the Advancement of Colored People by this time had become allied with the newspaper. Pitts and Lee were represented by a battery of glib-tongued, silk-suited ACLU lawyers.

My eyes lit up when I first read that portion of the editorial, as it was nothing more than a personal attack on the defense legal team as a group of "outside agitators" allied with the ACLU that the white South so despised at the time. Incidentally, I have never owned a silk suit in my life.

The editorial continued with venom and a disregard of known facts that is hard to comprehend, except that it reflected the distorted views of many white people in the South during the civil rights era of the 1960s and 1970s:

Pitts and Lee have been portrayed as two helpless blacks grabbed by Negro-baiting Northwest Florida lawmen and beaten into confessions.

Yes, the Pitts-Lee case has been made into a race issue and it is for that very reason that they will be free men in a few months. We are convinced that Pitts and Lee are being granted a new trial only because they are black and their case was made a cause celeb by the big city newspaper. Were Pitts and Lee white men we don't believe they ever would have commanded any public attention, much less a new trial from the Attorney General.

Every dirty trick in the book has been used in the long campaign to set Pitts and Lee free. A private investigator who said he was in the employ of the NAACP on February 9, 1967, attempted to kill State Attorney J. Frank Adams of Blountstown, Assistant State Attorney Paul Griffith of Marianna and Port St. Joe Police Chief Buck Griffin.[35]

Great effort also has been made to get the state's star witness to change the testimony she gave at the Pitts-Lee trial eight years ago. They include bribery attempts. What do you say about this, Mr. Attorney General?[36]

Mr. Shevin has stated that he asked the Supreme Court to give Pitts and Lee a new trial "in the interest of justice."

Well, Mr. Shevin, what about the injustices that have been done in the all-out effort to obtain a new trial for these men?

How about some justice, Mr. Shevin, for Jesse Burkett and Grover Floyd, Jr.? And, how about the widow and four young children Burkett left, are you interested in justice for them, Mr. Shevin?

The editorial finally ended with this demand:

In the interest of justice, Mr. Shevin, we suggest you resign the post of Attorney General.[37]

Several days later, on May 9, 1971, the Sunday edition of the *News Herald* ran another editorial that again attacked Shevin for taking "law into his own hands" and for "impugn[ing] the integrity of the [First] District Court of Appeal, if not the entire judiciary in Florida." The editorial demanded that the Gulf County Grand Jury be convened to address a long series of loaded questions that cast doubt on the integrity of the attorney general's decision to confess error in the case.[38] No such grand jury, however, was ever convened, as these "questions" were nothing more than veiled political attacks.

What concerned me the most about all these inflammatory editorials and the slanted news coverage was that it made it virtually impossible for Pitts and Lee to get a fair trial in this area. The *News Herald* was the leading newspaper in the circuit and was widely read in both Port St. Joe and Marianna, Florida. The paper's us-against-them editorials and news coverage and its unrelenting attacks on the *Miami Herald*, the attorney general, the defendants, and the defense team poisoned the potential jury pool available in the area. Indeed, their coverage fanned the flames of racial hatred and division that was convulsing the country at the time.

In this entire ordeal, however, I was never discouraged and neither was anyone else on the defense team. On the contrary, the implacable opposition we faced in the Florida Panhandle only encouraged us to battle on. We were all having the time of our lives fighting for justice, battling for what we knew was right, and that spirit never left us. And so the stage was now set for the tumultuous retrial of the case that would take place, over our protest, in Port St. Joe and Marianna, Florida.

III

THE NEW TRIAL AND ITS
AFTERMATH (1971–1975)

21

Phase I of the Pretrial Proceedings

In June 1971, the case was in the circuit court in Port St. Joe for a new trial with Circuit Judge Robert McCrary presiding. As was true of the post-conviction proceedings, however, no judge from the Fourteenth Judicial Circuit presided permanently on this case. This was ostensibly because the state could call one of the judges of that circuit, W. L. Fitzpatrick, as a witness in our case, thereby making it inappropriate for any colleague of that judge to hear the case. As a consequence, various judges from outside the circuit were assigned to hear different phases of the case.

* * *

We were fearful about returning to Port St. Joe and retrying the case in that circuit, as we had zero confidence that we could get a fair trial there and were also concerned for our own safety. So we decided on a two-step legal strategy.

First, we filed a petition for a writ of prohibition with the First District Court of Appeal asking that the arraignment of the case be removed from Port St. Joe to another location within the Fourteenth Judicial Circuit where the defendants and their lawyers would be physically safe. Second, at the arraignment, we planned to enter pleas of not guilty and file a motion to remove the entire case to a more neutral location in the state for trial, such as Tampa or West Palm Beach.

In our prohibition petition, we asked that the site of arraignment be moved because the defendants and the defense lawyers would be "in actual physical danger if the arraignment is held as scheduled in Port St. Joe, Florida, July 7, 1971." To support this request, we relied on the disturbing events that had happened during our last appearance in Port St. Joe at the September 1968 postconviction hearing, culminating with the mayor's request for a cooling-off period, and Bobby Burkett's physical attack against Gene Miller on the courthouse steps.

An oral argument before a three-judge panel of the First District Court of Appeal in Tallahassee was held on this petition. It is the custom for lawyers to identify themselves and the party they represent at the outset of an oral argument before an appellate court. That requirement, however, was generally relaxed in Florida for public defenders and assistant attorneys general who appear regularly before the same court because they are so well known to the judges that no introduction is deemed necessary.

I had gotten out of the habit of making such a formal introduction, given my heavy public defender appellate caseload. So when I rose to argue our petition before the First District Court, I followed my usual practice. I just launched into my argument, failing to realize that this was only my second argument before the First District and that most of these judges would not know who I was.

But instead of politely asking me to identify myself, Judge John T. Wigginton, one of the appellate judges on the panel, boomed out in a hostile voice that could have been heard in the court hallway: "WHO ARE YOU???"—reminding me of the scene from Alice in Wonderland in which the smoking caterpillar demanded the same of Alice. I immediately apologized, identified myself, and continued with my argument.

The judge, however, was entirely unconvinced and said our showing of probable violence was pure speculation. He did concede, however, that there was a *possibility* that we might be in some danger. "It may be," he said, "that you are right, that the minute you get out of the car, someone will shoot and kill you." I immediately shot back, "I'd rather not take that chance." Given even the outside possibility of such violence, one would have thought that the venue of the arraignment should be changed as a precautionary measure. But the judge wasn't persuaded.

When the argument concluded, I had no doubt that we had lost. As I left the courtroom, I was greeted in the hallway by a friendly assistant public defender from Tallahassee who had witnessed the argument. He shook my hand vigorously and said, with some irony, "Welcome to North Florida."

Shortly thereafter, on July 6, 1971, the First District Court of Appeal entered an order denying our petition,[1] as expected. On July 13, 1971, the court issued an opinion authored by Judge Wigginton. "We have reviewed the record before us," the judge wrote, "but fail to find any allegation or proof of any overt act committed by anyone which constituted a threat to the lives and safety of either the petitioners or their attorneys."[2]

As he had in the oral argument, however, the judge conceded that an atmosphere of potential violence surrounded this case. He noted that

Attorney General Robert Shevin had stirred up such animosity in the community when he agreed to a new trial that "the existence of such feeling might render it unhealthy for him to personally appear in Gulf County any time within the near future."[3] That animosity, I thought, spilled over to everyone on the defense side of the case.

But the judge was clear. We were in no personal danger; there was nothing to be concerned about. In this connection, I was reminded of what the novelist Somerset Maugham once wrote: "Nothing is easier than to bear other people's calamities with fortitude."[4]

*   *   *

Meanwhile, Leo Jones, the assistant state attorney assigned to prosecute this case, was busy inflaming the community against Pitts and Lee. He was furious about the fact that we had gotten a new trial and made it known publicly. Indeed, throughout his appearance in this case, he reflected the attitude of his boss, J. Frank Adams, that Pitts and Lee were guilty and that the effort to upset these convictions was an outrage instigated by nefarious outside forces.

In May 1971, Jones addressed the Rotary Club in Port St. Joe, where he scoffed at the idea that the state had suppressed Willie Mae Lee's statement blaming Lambson Smith for the Floyd-Burkett murders—the legal basis on which the Florida Supreme Court had ordered a new trial. Jones claimed that Willie Mae Lee had admitted all along that she had blamed Lambson Smith for the murders. He asserted that she had made that admission in open court at the time of the August 1963 trial and that her admission was "part of the transcript" of that trial. This claim was totally false. The transcript contains no such testimony.[5]

Jones said: "If I sound indignant, it's because I am indignant—that a circus can be made of justice in Florida such as it was in the Manson, Chicago Seven and Speck trials. Now the people of Gulf County are bound for the darnedest draw on their tax money that they had ever seen."[6] He continued: "This case had been through many courts of the judicial system, this State, the Supreme Court of Florida, two or three times, the Supreme of the U.S., two or three times," and "it [is] a tragic situation this county should now have to bear the expense of a re-trial in view of the fact every court in Florida had ruled for Florida and the Attorney General six or eight weeks after taking office could cancel the whole thing out."[7]

Attorney General Robert Shevin soon reacted to Jones's false claims and to demands for his resignation: "I suffered these vitriolic comments because

I chose to do what, in my conscience, was the only thing to do. . . . Now I understand that the prosecutor and his assistant are saying that defense counsel did, in fact, have knowledge of the statements supposedly withheld. If this is true, of course, defense counsel W. Fred Turner is guilty of perjury."[8]

In May 1971, Leo Jones went on national television in a CBS program dealing with the case of Pitts and Lee that aired throughout the circuit. In that program, he dismissed Mary Jean Akins's statement blaming Curtis Adams for the Floyd-Burkett murders and asserted that Akins "came into open court and repudiated that confession in each and every detail."[9] This claim was totally false. At no time has Mary Jean Akins ever repudiated her basic statement, either in or out of court, that Curtis Adams confessed to her that he murdered Floyd and Burkett.[10]

But Leo Jones's distorted public statements, the vitriolic editorials in the *News Herald,* and slanted news coverage meant that the people of North Florida never got a clear picture of the newly discovered evidence indicating that Curtis Adams was guilty of the Floyd-Burkett murders and that police had beaten Pitts and Lee's confessions out of them. Instead, the public was fed a false narrative that it was all the doing of nefarious "outside agitators" seeking to upend the southern way of life and that the new trial ordered was an outrage and a waste of taxpayer money. For that reason, a fair trial anywhere in the Fourteenth Judicial Circuit was virtually impossible.

*   *   *

On July 7, 1971, the arraignment took place in Port St. Joe behind locked courtroom doors. Five armed guards were present. To our great relief, the hearing took place without incident. We entered pleas of not guilty and were granted time to file motions.

Although Judge Robert McCrary presided at the arraignment, he had no wish to remain on the case. A few days before the arraignment, Judge McCrary had sent a letter to Chief Justice B. K. Roberts of the Florida Supreme Court requesting that Circuit Judge John Crews from Gainesville be appointed to handle the case. Judge McCrary had already contacted Judge Crews, who had said that he was willing to serve. On July 22, 1971, Roberts appointed Crews "to hear, conduct, try and determine the cause or causes . . . and to dispose of all matters."[11]

Judge Crews was an excellent choice. He had served in the Florida legislature for fourteen years representing Baker County in the Florida

Panhandle. In 1958, during that service, he had opposed a racist-inspired bill to close the public schools rather than integrate them as required by the federal courts. That courageous act had almost ended his public career; he was reelected by a margin of only ten votes. Later he moved to Gainesville, home of the University of Florida. He became a circuit judge from that area in 1966 and earned a sterling reputation for being fair, smart, and independent.[12]

One of our main missions in the pretrial phase of the case was to change the venue of the case from the Fourteenth Judicial Circuit to a more neutral part of the state. In support of our motion to change this venue, we sent an investigator to Port St. Joe to obtain statements from local residents on whether they thought Pitts and Lee were guilty. We chose David Helman for that task, a savvy and experienced private investigator from Miami.

In less than a week, Helman interviewed approximately 300 persons in Gulf County. As a precautionary measure, Helman wired both his car and his briefcase for sound. He obtained twenty-three affidavits from local residents expressing the opinion that Pitts and Lee were guilty. Fifty more individuals expressed the same view but wouldn't sign affidavits. Helman didn't count the people who refused to talk to him. He encountered only one man who expressed some doubts on the issue of guilt or innocence. One resident, Mixon Layton, expressed a typical opinion: "Everyone knows they're guilty." Another put it bluntly, "Those [B]lack sonsabitches ought to be hanged. They're causing so much trouble here."[13]

During his survey, Helman ran into several police officers. One was an off-duty Florida highway patrolman who advised Helman to be careful. "You might get yourself hurt," he said. Later, Gulf County Deputy Sheriff H. O. Glass pulled Helman over in Wewahitchka, the county seat, and took him to Port St. Joe for questioning. "You're agitating these people," Sheriff Byrd Parker told Helman, "and we don't need any agitators in town." Helman was not charged with any crime, but he was given some "friendly" advice to stop talking to local people about the case. Deputy Sheriff H. T. "Sonny" Dean put it bluntly: "You can get yourself shot that way." Helman got the message and left the area without finishing his assignment.[14]

On August 27–28, 1971, a hearing was held in Port St. Joe with Judge Crews presiding. Three of our pretrial motions were heard: a motion for change of venue, a motion to suppress Pitts and Lee's confessions, and a motion to dismiss the August 1963 indictments. Extensive testimony was taken and physical exhibits were introduced on each of these motions. It was at this hearing that we became impressed with Judge Crews.

Leo Jones represented the state and made a number of unfounded arguments that Judge Crews rejected. In opposing our motion for change of venue, Jones claimed that we were attacking "the populos [sic]" of Gulf County, "saying that the people in that county . . . [are] so inflamed from top to bottom that nowhere in that county can you find twelve jurors that will try the case." He claimed, with no citation of authority, that this was the test as to whether the venue should be changed. The judge reminded Jones that, on the contrary, the test for a change of venue is whether the defendant has a "reasonable apprehension" of prejudice against him or her in the community, not whether it was theoretically possible to find twelve people who claimed to be unbiased if one looked long enough to find them.[15]

Jones also protested to no avail when we called him as a witness to attest to the inflammatory speech he had given to the Rotary Club in Port St. Joe. His feeble defense for this improper address was "if I didn't have a feeling about this case . . . I wouldn't be prosecuting it so."[16] Jones was certainly entitled to have a "feeling" about the case, but he had no right to broadcast it with inflammatory rhetoric to the public with twisted lies and prevent the defendants from getting a fair trial.

When we proved on our motion to dismiss the August 1963 indictment that no Black registered voter had ever served on the Gulf County Grand Jury during the period 1948 to 1963 even though 14 percent of the jury pool of the county were eligible Black registered voters,[17] Jones at first made no real effort to defend the indefensible. Instead, he argued that Crews could not entertain the motion because "we are only here on a new trial," nothing else.[18]

Jones was wrong. It is the established practice that when an appellate court reverses a final judgment in a criminal or civil case and orders a new trial, the case is returned to its original status with directions to follow the law announced in the appellate court's opinion. Pretrial motions may be entertained and ruled on as a routine matter. Judge Crews overruled Jones's objection and ultimately entered an order stating that "it would be a strange, if not harsh rule of law, if a defendant whose retrial has been mandated were precluded for raising for the first time before trial, constitutional issues."[19]

Later Jones tried to belittle our position by arguing that we were asking the court "to declare there must be fifteen or twenty percent . . . of the black voters on the [grand] jury," as if this were a legislative reapportionment case.[20] Judge Crews immediately rejected this characterization of my argument. On the contrary, I based my argument on the law of probabilities:

Mr. Core testified he has been the Clerk of Court since 1948. He knows many people and in his memory no black has ever served on the Grand Jury in the history of this county, in his memory. It seems to me the probability of that happening by chance is rather remote.[21]

Obviously, someone in authority was deliberately keeping eligible Black voters from serving on the Gulf County Grand Jury for a period of fifteen years (1948–1963). None of this could have happened if the grand jury had been selected randomly, as the law requires.

We also submitted testimony from the clerk of court, George Core, and the county supervisor of elections, Mrs. Parker, that established a pattern of extreme underrepresentation of Black voters on the jury rolls from which the eighteen grand jurors were drawn, in contrast to white voters who were placed on the same rolls for the years 1958–1964.[22] Someone was obviously tampering with these voter lists to keep Black voters from being placed on the grand jury rolls. None of that could have happened randomly.

At the conclusion of the hearings, Crews took our motions under advisement, indicating that he would rule later on each motion. He then addressed the packed audience in the courtroom with a gracious and stirring speech:

> Alright. Now ladies and gentlemen, the court is getting ready to recess. Before I do I want to express my appreciation to counsel for the State of Florida and counsel for the defendants for their very able representation of their respective clients and for the benefit they have been to the court and in the matter the court has under consideration. You have observed a part of what goes on in nearly every criminal case.
>
> * * *
>
> You have observed members of a very learned educational profession who have donated their services to represent one or two accused of crime. You have seen the people of the State of Florida ably represented by a fine and diligent counsel. I hope you have observed the judge of the trial court who seeks to be enlightened and to hopefully make a judgment based on the law and the facts that the court has before him.
>
> As we consider our own individual liberties and our rights and privileges, though there are defects in our judicial system, never can we be completely satisfied because we must strive to make it better,

[y]et let us appreciate that in this country one can and one will have the right to a fair hearing and of a fair and impartial trial.[23]

On September 15, 1971, nearly three weeks later, Judge Crews demonstrated his judicial courage by granting our motion to dismiss the indictment. In a seven-page scholarly order, the judge concluded that "it is the duty of this court to dismiss the indictments against the defendants, rendered by the grand jury in 1963 because there was a systematic exclusion of Negroes from the jury lists contrary to the defendants' Constitutional rights." The state was then given sufficient time to reindict the defendants "with a lawfully constituted grand jury."[24]

I can't begin to express my satisfaction about prevailing on this motion. The systematic exclusion of eligible Black voters in Gulf County from serving on the Gulf County Grand Jury was the basis of my original motion to vacate Pitts and Lee's conviction filed in 1965. Now we had a judicial ruling that we were right. And this ruling contradicted Leo Jones's inflammatory claims before the Port St. Joe Rotary Club that our attack on those convictions was frivolous.

*　　*　　*

On October 20, 1971, the Gulf County Grand Jury reindicted Pitts and Lee for the first-degree murders of Grover Floyd and Jesse Burkett. An arraignment on the new indictment was held on October 26, 1971, but to our surprise, Judge Crews did not preside. Instead, Judge Robert McCrary decided to take the case back and preside from that point forward. He had apparently been getting pressure from many people in the area to handle the case himself. No doubt many in the county wanted Judge Crews removed from the case. His order dismissing the 1963 grand jury indictment based on racial discrimination grounds had likely not gone down well with many white people in the area.

We objected to this procedure on the ground that the Florida Supreme Court had appointed Judge Crews to try this case and that Judge McCrary had recused himself because his colleague, Judge Fitzpatrick, might be a witness in the case. McCrary overruled our objection, stating that the reason for his recusal centered on "scheduling conflicts," which he said had since cleared up. But that didn't explain how he could take the case back after the Florida Supreme Court had ordered Crews to hear the matter.

As a result, we filed a petition for a writ of prohibition with the Florida Supreme Court, arguing that McCrary had lost jurisdiction to try this case. Years later, we learned that Crews had been disturbed by our petition. Crews apparently thought we had put him in an awkward position inasmuch as he had previously ruled in our favor on the motion to dismiss. I never understood this. As a legal matter, McCrary had no jurisdiction to hear this case; we were simply seeking to enforce the Florida Supreme Court's order. It was a matter of law and in no way reflected on Judge Crews or anyone else. But Crews saw it differently.

To our great disappointment, on November 3, 1971, Crews asked the chief justice to relieve him of his duties in this case, citing his heavy caseload in Gainesville. The chief justice granted this request and removed the judge from the case. As a result, we lost our best chance to get this case moved to the central part of the state, where we might get a fair trial.

The chief justice, however, did not return the case to McCrary. Instead, he appointed Circuit Judge David R. Smith of Ocala, Florida, to preside in the case, and Judge Smith handled the matter to its conclusion at the trial level. He was 58 years old, a somewhat overweight, easygoing southerner with a florid face. He had tragically lost one of his arms in a grist mill when he was growing up in Ocala.

On November 18, 1971, Judge Smith conducted his first hearing at the courthouse in Port St. Joe to rule on our various pretrial motions. At the outset of the hearing, he announced:

> Gentlemen, I believe we are here to hear certain motions filed on behalf of the defendants' attorneys. I don't know exactly how you would like to proceed or in what order you would like to take up these motions. I have reviewed these motions and I'm inclined to grant the motion for change of venue. I wondered if you would want to argue that, gentlemen.[25]

My heart leaped up at this announcement. Irwin Block stated that we had no argument to make in view of the court's tentative ruling. Leo Jones, representing the state, was caught by surprise and asked the judge for the basis of his ruling. The judge replied:

> Because I think this case has gotten too much publicity in a small county. Most of the people of the county would be familiar with the case and would probably have formed or expressed an opinion in regard to the guilt or innocence of these defendants.[26]

Judge Smith further stated that he had based his ruling on reading our motion for change of venue, which had attached the voluminous vitriolic editorials in the *News Herald* and the slanted news articles on the case that had flooded the Fourteenth Judicial Circuit, including Gulf County. The judge declined to review the testimony Judge Crews had received on our motion, deeming the news coverage enough to change the venue. After hearing additional argument from Jones, Judge Smith announced his final ruling: "The motion to change venue is granted."[27] We could barely contain ourselves. For the first time in this long struggle, we thought we were on a road to victory.

And the good news continued. Judge Smith took testimony on our motion to dismiss the recent October 1971 grand jury indictment, which showed that one of grand jurors had a felony conviction, thereby invalidating the indictment.[28] The judge also heard various other pretrial discovery motions involving depositions and generally gave rulings that were favorable to the defense.

But when we rested our case on all our motions for the day, the judge took a brief recess and conferred with counsel off the record in his chambers.[29] Our hopes and expectations were dashed at this conference. To the delight of the state, Smith announced that he was moving the case to Marianna, Florida, a tiny town of 6,741 located in Jackson County, approximately seventy miles north of Port St. Joe within the same judicial circuit where the case was also extremely well known.[30]

The *News Herald*'s slanted news coverage and inflammatory editorials on this case had wide circulation throughout the entire circuit, including Marianna and all of Jackson County. According to James Smith, the assistant circulation manager of the *News Herald* in 1971, the newspaper had a daily circulation of 19,554 subscribers and a Sunday circulation of 22,523 subscribers.[31] Their wholly owned subsidiary, the *Jackson County Floridan*, reprinted many of the *News Herald*'s articles and editorials, and that coverage circulated throughout Jackson County. Beyond that, as the jury selection process would later demonstrate, the Pitts-Lee case was the talk of the entire county. It made no sense to move the case to that location.

I was particularly stunned at Smith's reason for selecting Marianna. He said he didn't want to inconvenience the witnesses from Gulf County, so he had selected nearby Marianna so they wouldn't have to travel far. But witness inconvenience pales in significance compared to the defendants'

Sixth Amendment right to a fair trial before an impartial jury. Judge Smith granted our motion to protect that right but moved the case to a town where that right could not possibly be honored.

When we left the judge's chambers, Gulf County Sheriff Byrd Parker asked a deputy who had been present during the conference where the case was going. When the deputy replied it was Marianna, Parker was pleased. "Good," he said.[32] Parker knew full well that his case was safe in Marianna, as safe as it had been in Port St. Joe. We would have to file another motion for a change venue from Marianna, which we knew would be denied. Our entire effort to move this case to the central part of the state had accomplished nothing.

If only Crews had remained on the case, I thought. If only we had a judge who understood the applicable law and had the courage to follow it, we might have gotten a neutral venue to try the case in a place where we had a chance of winning an acquittal. But it was not meant to be. In a way, we were living out a Shakespearean tragedy. Like *King Lear,* the case as it unfolded was full of false dawns.

On December 15, 1971, Smith conducted his last hearing in Port St. Joe. He heard argument from both sides and granted our motion to dismiss the October 1971 grand jury indictment on the ground that one of the grand jurors had a prior felony conviction. He then gave the state sufficient time to present its case to the Jackson County Grand Jury for a reindictment that was certain to follow.[33] Like it or not, we would have to try this case in Marianna, where we had virtually no chance of prevailing.

22

Phase II of the Pretrial Proceedings

Throughout our experience in Marianna in January to March of 1972, Irwin Block and I concentrated largely on making a record for appeal. That is, we sought to raise federal constitutional issues in the circuit court that we thought would be winning points for appeal. We hadn't given up hope that we might, against all odds, win an acquittal or at least a hung jury, and we worked furiously to prepare our case for trial. But we were not naive. We knew that a conviction before an all-white jury in Marianna was a virtual certainty, and we set about to lay the groundwork for a reversal on appeal.

Also, Irwin Block and I were "in the zone," something every trial lawyer is well aware of when trying a criminal or civil case. We knew what we had to do to advance our case and were oblivious to anything unrelated to that goal. We were like foot soldiers battling in the trenches, knowing that in spite of everything, justice would somehow prevail.

To that end, during the course of the pretrial and trial proceedings, we raised a variety of constitutional and legal issues. Our primary points, however, were these, all based on the Sixth and Fourteenth Amendments to the US Constitution:

- The grand jury that indicted the defendants was chosen from a panel from which eligible Black voters had been systematically excluded.
- The defendants' confessions to the police and in court were the product of violence, fear, and coercion and were inadmissible in evidence.
- The defendants' motion to change the venue of the cause from Jackson County to a more neutral part of the state was required due to excessive and inflammatory pretrial publicity.
- The defense evidence that Curtis Adams murdered Grover Floyd and Jesse Burkett was admissible at trial.
- The prosecuting attorney used his peremptory jury challenges to

systematically exclude all Black potential jurors from serving on the trial jury.

- The prosecuting attorney gave an inflammatory final argument to the jury appealing to sectional and racial prejudice.

We anticipated adverse rulings from Judge Smith on all of these federal constitutional issues, and, as it turned out, that is exactly what happened. Indeed, these six points would later become the basis for reversing Pitts and Lee's ensuing convictions when we filed our petition for certiorari review before the US Supreme Court.

*　*　*

On January 3, 1972, the Jackson County Grand Jury convened in Marianna with Judge Smith presiding. My co-counsel, Maurice Rosen, and Irwin Block's law partner, Ted Kline, were present in Marianna at the time of the grand jury session. They offered to present testimony that Curtis Adams had committed the Floyd-Burkett murders. Warren Holmes was present with his taped confession from Curtis Adams. Also, Mary Jean Akins and Army CID investigator Bruce Potts were on call. But the state declined to present such evidence, claiming the grand jury did not want to hear evidence of innocence. The ensuing result was not unexpected. The all-white Jackson County Grand Jury reindicted Pitts and Lee on the original first-degree murder charges, and on January 4, 1972, these indictments were officially filed with the court.

During this court session, Judge Smith revealed his folksy manner to the eighteen members of the grand jury. He explained how he had lost his arm in a tragic accident as a child and told his favorite story. He said one morning he was stopped for speeding in a school zone on his way to court. The law enforcement officer who pulled him over approached the car, but didn't recognize the judge. When asked where he was going in such a hurry, the judge said he was on his way to circuit court. "What judge you got to go before?" the officer wanted to know. "Judge Smith, the one-armed judge from Ocala," the judge responded. "If you got to go before that one-arm judge from Ocala," the officer replied, "you are in enough trouble. Drive on."[1]

I suppose this lighthearted story was harmless enough, but I was always suspicious of judges with a folksy manner who joke about how tough they are on criminal defendants. There are exceptions, of course. But I often thought they used a down-to-earth persona to excuse their bias against criminal defendants. And the longer I saw Judge Smith in action, the more my preconceived notions about him were reinforced. Although he was generally easygoing, he was also part of the good-old-boys network in North Florida, totally unlike the more reserved and knowledgeable Judge Crews. This case demanded a judge who was sensitive to the federal constitutional issues involved and who was willing, if required by law, to make unpopular rulings. Smith was not that kind of judge.

At any rate, I was convinced that the Jackson County Grand Jury, like the Gulf County Grand Jury, was drawn from a venire in which eligible Black voters had been systematically excluded in violation of the US Constitution. But I needed proof. So in early January, I traveled to Marianna and spent a week in the office of the circuit court clerk and in the office of the supervisor of elections, going over the voting rolls and grand jury venires in Jackson County for the past decade.

Both offices could not have been more accommodating. Indeed, I later wrote a follow-up letter to Alyne Pittman, the Jackson County supervisor of elections, that she and Mrs. Bell, a clerk in the same office, "will always stand out in my mind as [some] of the nicest people I had the pleasure to meet in Marianna."[2] What I discovered, however, was a clear pattern of racial discrimination against Black voters eligible for jury service.

Based on this examination, I prepared a chart that showed the number of qualified white and Black voters in Jackson County compared to the number of white and Black voters who were actually placed on the grand jury rolls. Although Black voters constituted 20 to 23 percent of the qualified voters in Jackson County for the years 1963–1971, a consistently lower percentage of Black voters actually made the jury rolls. Here are those percentages:

- January 1964—5.61 percent
- January 1965—8.28 percent
- January 1966—10.56 percent
- January 1967—5.85 percent
- November 1967—20.39 percent
- January 1969—9.75 percent
- March 1970—7.23 percent
- December 1970—2.78 percent
- December 1971—13.67 percent

In the four predominately Black voting precincts in Jackson County, white voters consistently outnumbered Black voters on the grand jury rolls from 1963 to 1971. And, strikingly, no voter, Black or white, from the following Black precincts ever made the grand jury venire in the following years. They were totally ignored.

- January 1969—Precinct 32
- December 1970—Precincts 2, 13, 30, and 32
- January 1971—Precincts 13 and 30[3]

Someone obviously was handpicking jurors from the voting lists to exclude eligible Black voters. Those juries could not have been selected randomly, as the law required.

Based on this evidence, I filed a motion to dismiss the January 1972 grand jury indictment against the defendants and stated:

> The Defendants have been indicted by a grand jury from which qualified Negro voters in Jackson County have been systematically excluded by the State in violation of the Equal Protection Clause of the Fourteenth Amendment to the United States Constitution and the Constitution of the State of Florida.[4]

On January 21, 1972, Judge Smith heard argument from both sides on this motion. At that time, I introduced the statistics chart I had prepared in evidence. The law on this issue was plain. "In an unbroken line of cases stretching back almost eighty years," Justice Hugo Black wrote for the US Supreme Court, "this Court has held that a criminal defendant is denied equal protection of the laws guaranteed by the Fourteenth Amendment if he is indicted by a grand jury . . . from which the members of his race have been excluded because of his race."[5]

Leo Jones, however, dismissed our statistical chart as meaningless. "You can do everything you want to do with statistics," he said. "Right on down the line you can take these figures and do anything you want with them."[6] Judge Smith was equally unimpressed. He denied the motion to dismiss and said, "I don't think there's been a systematical exclusion of Negroes from this jury, which composed the grand jury."[7]

But neither Jones nor Smith could give any logical explanation for how eligible Black voters were so consistently underrepresented on the Jackson County Grand Jury rolls (and in some cases totally ignored) for nearly a decade unless someone had tampered with them. Still, we had properly preserved our first point for appeal.

* * *

We next filed a motion to suppress the confessions Pitts and Lee had given on the ground that they were involuntarily obtained. The motion alleged that their confessions to the police "were the product of coercion, terror, threats of physical beating, and physical beating . . . in violation of the defendants' constitutional rights guaranteed by the Due Process Clause of the Fourteenth Amendment to the United States Supreme Constitution, and the Constitution of the State of Florida." The motion further alleged that the confessions the defendants had given in court during the mercy trial constituted "the fruit of the illegally obtained police confessions." We relied on the fruit of the poisonous tree doctrine that required the exclusion of any evidence that was the product of prior illegal police activity.[8]

On January 21, 1972, a hearing was held before Judge Smith on this motion. The parties agreed that the testimony Judge Crews had previously taken on this motion, together with the testimony Judge Holley had taken on our motion to vacate, would be the evidence submitted on this motion.

At the outset, Judge Smith announced that he had read the motion, had reviewed the testimony, and had reached a tentative decision. He stated:

> I have a feeling actually that the invalid confessions are inadmissible. . . . [The defendants] were held in jail about a week incommunicado, maybe in the meantime they were appointed an attorney who had not actually, actively representing [sic] them. They were questioned in the absence of their attorney after that. . . . I'm of the opinion and I don't mind hearing argument, I'm of the opinion those confessions were inadmissible.

I breathed a momentary sigh of relief: the police confessions were being held involuntary and inadmissible. But it was just another false dawn.

Smith then ruled, to the delight of the state, that the confessions made in court at the mercy trial hearing were "freely and voluntarily given" and were admissible in evidence. The judge stated:

> I don't believe that those statements made at the [m]ercy [h]earing were the fruit of the poisonous tree. . . . I have given this, I have lay awake at night thinking about this and I want to be fair to everybody in this case and whether or not a later confession is the fruit of the poisonous tree depends on the circumstances, and I feel that the circumstances in this case eliminate the doctrine of the fruit of the poisonous tree.[9]

But what Smith refused to acknowledge was that Pitts and Lee had been subjected to a reign of terror from the time they were arrested to the time they were sentenced to death, a process that had happened at the breakneck speed of less than four weeks. There was no sudden break in this terror when they got to court. The terror continued throughout. Indeed, Judge Fitzpatrick, the trial judge, testified that Pitts and Lee were so frightened that they looked like corpses whenever they appeared in court. Even their own court-appointed lawyer, Fred Turner, had helped the police extract guilty pleas and confessions out of them. As a result, all the confessions Pitts and Lee had been forced to make during this short period—both out of court and in court—should have been suppressed as involuntary.

Smith, however, turned a blind eye to all of this. He ruled that Pitts and Lee "had a competent lawyer" in Fred Turner, that they "had been advised of their constitutional rights," that they made so-called admissions to other people in court, and that sufficient time had elapsed between the coerced police confessions and the confessions in court.[10] But all of that was pure fiction that had no basis in truth, just excuses to cover up one of the worst injustices in Florida history.

I argued strenuously and at great length that Judge Smith should reconsider his tentative ruling, but to no avail. I argued, and the judge agreed, that the state had the burden of proof on our motion to suppress, that they had to show by "at least a preponderance of the evidence" that Pitts and Lee's statements had been voluntary.[11] But I could not persuade the judge that the state had woefully failed to meet its burden, even though the judge had ruled that the defendants' prior statements to the police had been involuntary. Still, we had properly preserved our second point for appeal.

*   *   *

Our final pretrial motion was a motion to change the venue of the case from Jackson County, in many ways our most important motion. The motion, which relied "on the due-process requirements of the United States Constitution," alleged as grounds that "[a] fair and impartial trial cannot be had in Jackson County, or, in any of the surrounding counties in North Florida"[12] and requested that the case be transferred "to a county outside of North Florida wherein [the defendants] may obtain a fair and impartial trial."[13]

Attached to the motion was a series of newspaper articles and editorials from the News Herald and the Jackson County Floridan that had been published in the period 1967 to 1972. These articles and editorials had pervaded the entire circuit, including Jackson County, during those years and were strongly prejudiced against Pitts and Lee. They continually proclaimed that the defendants were guilty of the Floyd-Burkett murders. They carried articles that quoted statements by police, court officials, the trial judge, and Fred Turner that Pitts and Lee were guilty as charged. Our motion alleged that "excessive, prejudicial, pre-trial, news publicity, has created a huge wave of public passion so prejudicing these defendants that no jury voir dire examination could cure, regardless of the statements of prospective jurors."[14]

On January 21, 1972, Smith heard the motion in court. We knew we had no chance to win this motion, but we nonetheless presented a number of witnesses in order to properly preserve the record for appeal. We led with three prominent white members of the Jackson County community.

Roy Beall, the chair of the Jackson County School Board, testified that racial tensions in the county were already at a fever pitch, that the Pitts-Lee case had increased those tensions, and that he had recently announced that view on a local radio broadcast.[15] William Reddoch, a longtime merchant in Jackson County, testified about the racial tension in Jackson County which, he said, the Pitts-Lee case had exacerbated.[16] Robert Childs, the superintendent of schools in Jackson County, testified that the Pitts-Lee case was the talk of Jackson County.[17]

Reverend Alonzo Parker, who had been pastor of St. Luke's Baptist Church in Marianna for nearly twenty-five years and was one of the leaders in the local Black community, testified that he had lived in Jackson County since 1921 and flatly stated that "from past history and from the publicity and everything, I don't think [Pitts and Lee] could get a fair trial in Jackson County."[18] He described the history of lynching in Jackson County which, he said, further aggravated the situation.[19]

We presented two more witnesses from the Black community in Marianna, Aaron Marks and Gye Long, who also testified that Pitts and Lee could not get a fair trial in Jackson County.[20] We closed the hearing by submitting approximately 600 affidavits, signed mainly by Black residents of Jackson County, stating that the case had received pervasive adverse media publicity in the county and was widely discussed among residents of the county, that an atmosphere of passion and prejudice existed against Pitts and Lee, and that they could not get a fair trial in Jackson County.[21] Some of these affidavits were, unfortunately, not notarized properly and were therefore presented as unsworn statements. The state offered no witnesses in opposition to our motion and presented no counter-affidavits or statements.

Judge Smith, as expected, was unimpressed with our evidence. He stated:

> I want to say with reference to your argument. I don't think in a county the size of Jackson that this case has too much legal interest. I think many people would not read these articles with all due respect to the newspapers. . . .
>
> I'm going to deny your motion for change of venue because of that because I don't think it has the local color and interest to prejudice the entire county by this.[22]

The judge, however, was unable to point to any evidence adduced in court to support his opinion. Nobody testified to that effect. No affidavits or witness statements were presented to that effect. It was nothing more than a hunch that would soon be exploded by over two weeks of jury selection and by other matters. Beyond that, Smith was not from Jackson County and, so far as I could determine, had no personal knowledge of the area.

After making this explicit ruling, however, Smith quickly caught himself and said that he would technically reserve ruling on the motion until trial.[23] But, in fact, the judge had made up his mind, and his ultimate ruling was never in doubt.

When we left court that day, Irwin Block and I were emotionally drained. We traveled by car to Tallahassee for a flight back to Miami and compared notes on how things had gone. Irwin was blunt. He thought Smith was a disaster, someone who was fully connected with the North Florida power structure and was incapable of making the kinds of unpopular decisions this case demanded. I agreed entirely. Smith's rulings were consistently in favor of the state on every critical issue. We had expected these rulings, but we couldn't help feeling dismayed at the direction the case was taking despite our best efforts.

* * *

One bright spot for the defense, however, finally appeared. Due to Gene Miller's tireless investigation, we finally got our hands on Willie Mae Lee's February 1968 sworn statement to State Attorney J. Frank Adams and Attorney General Investigator S. R. "Speedy" DeWitt in which she retracted her prior testimony and exonerated Pitts and Lee of the Floyd-Burkett murders.

On December 16, 1971, Miller flew to Tallahassee and was allowed by Attorney General Robert Shevin to look through the state's file in his office. Armed with a tape recorder, Miller dictated everything of interest that he found in the file. While reading a report by S. R. DeWitt, Miller was astounded when he found this gem:

> The writer [S. R. DeWitt] and J. Frank Adams questioned Willie Mae Lee in Port St. Joe on February 20, 1968 . . . at which time she changed her story and said that none of her previous testimony was true, that Pitts and Lee did not kill Burkett and Floyd, and she wasn't along, and had no personal knowledge of it.[24]

Heretofore, Miller and the defense team had no knowledge of such a statement. The state had suppressed it.

Miller surmised that DeWitt must have tape-recorded Willie Mae Lee's retraction because DeWitt made it a practice to tape all of his witness statements. But the attorney general's file contained no tapes. The tape had to be in the files of J. Frank Adams, Leo Jones, Wayne White, or S. R. DeWitt. The trick would be to obtain that tape before it somehow disappeared. Miller had asked Shevin to keep this revelation confidential and Shevin had done so. Miller had then informed the defense team of what he had found.

On January 21, 1972, Irwin Block filed "A Motion to Compel the Disclosure of All Evidence Favorable to the Defense'" based on the authority of *Brady v. Maryland*.[25] In this motion, Block asked for any and all statements made by Willie Mae Lee to the state that exonerated Pitts and Lee of the Floyd-Burkett murders. Judge Smith heard and granted this motion. The stage was set for a dramatic court session.

On January 31, 1972, Assistant State Attorney Leo Jones and I met in the Fourteenth Judicial Circuit's courtroom in Panama City and methodically went through the attorney general's file on the case. A court stenographer recorded the entire proceeding. Gene Miller was also in the courtroom covering this event for the *Miami Herald*. When I came to the critical portion of DeWitt's report that Willie Mae Lee had retracted her prior testimony and exonerated Pitts and Lee, I read that recitation into the record and demanded Willie Mae Lee's retraction statement.

As planned, Miller immediately left the courtroom and telephoned Irwin Block, who was waiting for Miller's call. Block then telephoned DeWitt and got him to admit that Willie Mae Lee's retraction statement had been taped. But DeWitt said that he didn't have the tape and that if Wayne White or Leo Jones didn't have it, then George Georgieff had it in Tallahassee. Suspecting the runaround, the following exchange occurred:

Block. You didn't destroy those tapes, did you?
DeWitt. Hey, I don't do things like that. I don't destroy anything, you know that.

Back in Panama City, Leo Jones told me he didn't know anything about such a tape. But under the court order, he was required to produce it to us if the state had it in its files. On February 4, 1972, J. Frank Adams finally produced the tape for us during a deposition of S. R. DeWitt. Irwin Block then had the tape transcribed by a stenographer for our use at trial.

This retraction statement became the centerpiece of our attack against Willie Mae Lee's incriminating testimony at trial. Once again we were indebted to Gene Miller for his brilliant journalistic work in discovering this invaluable evidence that the state had suppressed.

*　　*　　*

While all this was going on, about four weeks before the trial began, our worst fears were realized. On January 26, 1972,[26] the Ku Klux Klan conducted a nighttime motorcade rally through the Black residential area of Marianna and then hung an effigy of a Black man with an attached sign reading "A dead f——ing n——r by the KKK."

We brought this matter to Judge Smith's attention on February 21, 1972, just before jury selection began. As we methodically presented three Black residents who had witnessed this terrifying spectacle, the courtroom was in a deadly hush that crackled with tension. It was one of the few times in the entire case that Judge Smith became visibly upset, his easygoing manner no longer on display. This was not the benign county that Judge Smith had posited as a basis for denying our motion for change of venue.

Tony Gilbert, the owner of a local gas station, opened with a stark recitation of the event. I did the questioning:

Q. Last month, Mr. Gilbert, did anything happen in the black section of Marianna last month that you observed that night?
A. Yes, sir. Coming through there with crosses on it. . . . I was between my business and the funeral home . . . on Orange Street, I was standing there on the way to my car. I heard a rumbling like an airplane. I looked and there were a bunch of cars and I seen the cross on top. I sat there.

Q. You saw a cross?

A. Yes, on top of that. The first thing all lite [*sic*] up.

Q. All lite up?

A. All lite up, from the cross and I stood there by the road until they passed on.

Q. How many cars were there?

A. When they started slowing down I counted twenty five and thirty. . . .

Q. You described the cross. Was that on one of the cars?

A. On top, right on top of the car.

Q. On the lead car?

A. Yes, sir it was headed, it was—yes, sir, it was the lead car cause it was—there was another truck behind it had a flag.

Q. What kind of flag?

A. Confederate. . . .

Q. You say this cross was lite up?

A. Lite up just like a Christmas tree.

Q. Had lights on it?

A. White lights.

Q. Was this motorcade going slow or fast?

A. Between twenty-five and thirty miles. . . .

Q. You said you stood there and watched?

A. Yes, I stood there by the road and watched everyone to pass. I was scared to move until the last one passed.[27]

James Rhynes, another Black resident, gave similar testimony concerning the KKK motorcade rally, which he said had taken place in the evening around 10:30 or 11:00 p.m.[28] Raymond Prather, a wood-pulp worker, testified to the same effect. He also testified to the remnants of a Black effigy that the KKK had hung on an overpass to the entrance of the Black residential area of Marianna:

Q. Early that morning just about sun up that same day, did you see anything else happening, did you see anything?

A. When I was on my way to work, I went to the station to pick up a battery.

Q. The sun was just coming up?

A. Just before sun-up. I looked aside of the street just as you—just as I passed the underpass and I thought I saw a dead man. . . . I thought it was a man, when I jumped out of my truck and looked it wasn't a

man. I kicked it to see if it was going to go off and I picked it up and
[put it] in my car.

Q. What was it?

A. It was a dummy.

Q. Did you see any signs?

A. There was writing on the front.

Q. What did the writing say?

A. The writing said, "a dead f——ing n——ger by the K.K.K."

Q. You saw this beside the road near the underpass.

A. Yes.[29]

That completed our testimony concerning this alarming incident. The state called no witnesses and presented no evidence.

I then gave a brief argument in support of our motion for change of venue. This time, however, Smith no longer looked upon us with his usual friendly countenance. Instead, he stared at me, visibly upset, or so it seemed to me, that we should even bring up such an explosive matter. When I was through, the judge tersely announced: "I'm going to still reserve my ruling on your motion for change of venue."[30]

But what more was needed, I thought, to persuade any reasonable mind that this case did not belong in Marianna?

23

Phase I of Jury Selection

The jury selection in Marianna began on February 21, 1972, and continued for twelve days. By that time, I had been elected the public defender for the Eleventh Judicial Circuit in November 1970, and Governor Askew had appointed me to continue with my representation of Pitts and Lee. Three months later, from May 23 to 27, 1972, one of the controversial Quincy Five defendants was brought to trial in Tallahassee (see chapter 3). The civil rights era with all its upheavals was still raging.

At the start of each day of trial in the Pitts-Lee case, I renewed our motion for change of venue and filed with the court additional newspaper articles from the *Jackson County Floridan* that stated over and again that Pitts and Lee were guilty of the Floyd-Burkett murders, that they had confessed to these crimes, and that they had been tried and sentenced to death. I argued that the pervasive and inflammatory press coverage of the case over the previous six years in the circuit made it impossible for Pitts and Lee to get a fair trial in Jackson County. Judge Smith, however, was unimpressed with this argument. He stated:

> I'm going to reserve ruling on the motion for change of venue. . . . I don't think this case has any particular local interest to the citizens of Jackson County and I don't think these newspaper articles are read too much by the citizens of Jackson County and maybe the headlines are but nothing more than that.[1]

In other words, the judge was of the view that the citizens of Jackson County didn't keep up on the news, that they wouldn't know much about the biggest criminal case to hit the county in decades, and that if we found twelve jurors who were that oblivious to the world around them, Pitts and Lee would get a fair trial.

The jury selection began and the case was tried in a courtroom on the second floor of a modern courthouse that had been built in 1963. Just inside the front door of the courthouse, however, was an ugly reminder of something that had not changed in the area for over a century. It was a Civil War display case commemorating a brief skirmish in Marianna between Union and Confederate forces in 1865. Tellingly, the Union forces were referred to as "the enemy."[2] For some people in Marianna, it was obvious that the Civil War was still being fought.

The prosecuting attorney, Leo Jones, and his colleague, Paul Griffith, sat at the counsel table nearest the jury box in the courtroom. Some distance away, to Jones's left, was a second counsel table where Irwin Block and I sat with our clients. Both counsel tables faced the judge, who was seated on an elevated bench facing the spectator section. Several clerks and a bailiff were seated just below the judge. The witness box was located to the left of the judge, between him and the jury box. The spectator section consisted of long and shiny parallel pews with an aisle in the middle leading from the courtroom entrance door directly to the well of the court, which was enclosed with a railing and two small swinging gates.

Once again Gene Miller watched the entire proceedings from the spectator section, but he did not cover the case for the *Miami Herald*. He didn't feel that he was objective enough for the task. His colleague, Rob Elder, performed that assignment. Indeed, on the eve of the trial, Miller had published an unusual opinion piece on the front page of the Viewpoint Section of the Sunday edition to the *Miami Herald* in which he expressed his firm belief that Pitts and Lee were "innocent" and that they were "the victims of a gross miscarriage of justice."[3] Miller continued to write a great number of news articles for the *Miami Herald* that kept the case in the public eye.[4]

Maurice Rosen, the third lawyer in the case, did not participate in the trial but remained nearby to perform the vital task of coordinating the appearance of defense witnesses in court. Warren Holmes was one of those witnesses who remained on call outside the courtroom, along with other defense witnesses.

Even though Judge Smith claimed that the case had no local interest, the spectator section was almost always packed to capacity—particularly after the jury had been selected and the trial proper had begun. Also, the judge took no chances when it came to courtroom security. Five highway patrol troopers and two Jackson County deputy sheriffs guarded the courtroom for the entire trial. Two of the troopers, dressed in civilian clothes, stood at attention and were stationed at each end of the judge's bench, surveying the spectators and guarding the judge. Another trooper in civilian clothes stationed himself in the audience, and two uniformed troopers sat in chairs just outside the courtroom. Finally, two uniformed deputy sheriffs sat behind the defense counsel table guarding us against any possible attack. All of these officers were armed. At night, armed troopers also guarded the judge's motel room.[5]

Shortly before all of this began, I had asked my friend and colleague Virgil Mayo, the public defender for the Fourteenth Judicial Circuit, if he or one of his assistants could sit with us at counsel table and help us select the jury. But Mayo declined. He said: "I can't, Phil. I've got to live here after you go home."[6] Mayo was an elected official and could never have gotten reelected in that circuit if he had been seen supporting us in any way. We were that unpopular in the circuit. In fact, we could find no lawyer in the entire area who would act as our local counsel and assist us in court. We had to face the jury venire alone as "outsiders" from Miami up against Leo Jones, the wily local prosecutor who was a longtime resident of that circuit.

I have a vivid memory of being visited briefly by a friend from Miami during the jury selection process while the court was in brief recess. Herb Klein, who decades later would become my law partner, was working at the time in Tallahassee as counsel for the Florida Board of Business Regulation. He had traveled to Marianna to cheer us up. It was a welcome sight. In a crowded courtroom, he surprised Irwin Block and me as he approached us at counsel table. We shook hands and Herb said with a big smile: "I thought you'd just like to see a friendly face." We certainly did.

Pitts and Lee had been transferred out of death row at Raiford and were being held in the local jail run by the Jackson County Sheriff's Office about a block away from the courthouse. They were both glad to be off death row for a time and to be held instead in the less confining local jail facilities. Freddie Pitts, wearing knit pants and a white shirt with an open collar, sat stoically next to Irwin Block at counsel table. Wilbert Lee, wearing a red pullover shirt and striped gray pants, sat next to me at counsel table and at times slowly shook his head as the case unfolded in court.[7] Although pessimistic that they would ever get a fair trial in Marianna, both men kept up a brave front.

Strange as this may seem, Pitts and Lee also became friendly with the personnel of the Jackson County Sheriff's Office. One incident in particular stands out. In the early morning hours of February 25, 1972, during the jury selection process, three prisoners at the local jail used a smuggled hacksaw blade to saw through the bars of the cell they were being held in and fled the area. Pitts and Lee occupied a cell that was connected to this cell with an open doorway but made no effort to escape. "I didn't commit no crime," Lee later said. "I didn't have no reason to run."[8]

The sheriff and his deputies, including the jailor Jack Hansford, were impressed. Hansford said that Pitts and Lee could have escaped then if they had wanted to. But he said they had been model prisoners ever since they had been transferred to the jail two months before the jailbreak. "They've been as nice as they can be," Sheriff Barkley Gause said. "We haven't had an ounce of trouble out of them."[9] This was all the more surprising because twenty years earlier Sheriff Gause had been involved in a notorious case in Marianna in which he and other officers had extracted a coerced confession from a Black man named Cellos Harrison who thereafter was wrongfully convicted of murdering a white filling station attendant and was eventually lynched.[10]

As the Pitts-Lee case progressed, it was a common sight to see two of Sheriff Gause's deputies on the public street escorting Pitts and Lee back and forth between the jail and the courthouse, the deputies in front chatting with one another while their handcuffed prisoners strolled behind them without a single incident. "Desperados and killers," Irwin Block would say in his usual sardonic manner. It was the one bright spot in our entire ordeal in Marianna: oddly enough, the Jackson County Sheriff's Office was sympathetic to us.

Irwin Block and I stayed and ate our meals at a local Holiday Inn in Marianna for the duration of the four-week trial. Irwin's wife, Doris, and my wife, Martha, eventually joined us after the jury was selected. It was there that Irwin and I planned out our strategy every night and conducted a postmortem about what had happened in court that day.

*　　*　　*

The jury selection process was long and arduous. Most juries in routine criminal cases are picked in one or two days. But this jury selection lasted twelve business days, from February 21 to March 8, 1972. An astounding 226 prospective jurors were examined individually in open court. The jurors were kept in a separate room in the courthouse and were called to the jury box in the courtroom one by one, where they were questioned—first by Judge Smith, and then in order by Leo Jones, me, and Irwin Block. I represented Wilbert Lee and Block represented Freddie Pitts. If the juror was not excused after this examination, they were sent to another jury room to stay until a final decision was made about which jurors would sit on the twelve-person jury. At the end of each day, the jurors were allowed to go home for the night.

Judge Smith had previously prequalified the prospective jurors regarding the citizenship and residency requirements for jury service. He had also entertained any excuses prospective jurors might have given for not serving, granting some excuses and denying others. He had also warned the jury venire that the case could last a week to ten days. Actually, the trial lasted four weeks.

At the outset, our strategy was to ask each white juror about certain racial issues inherent in the case in order to challenge any juror who we thought might be racist or believed in white supremacy. Smith, however, precluded us from probing into these sensitive areas. During my inquiry of the first prospective juror, Hoyt Roberts, the following transpired:

Q. Do you have any feelings one way or the other generally speaking as to whether or not members of the white race are superior to those of the black race?
A. I could not—
The Court. I don't see that's a fair question of this juror at all. . . .
Q. Mr. Roberts, do you approve of integrated school systems or do you feel we should return to the dual system?
The Court. Now that's not a fair question at all in this case. It doesn't have a thing in the world to do with this case.[11]

But on the contrary, it had everything to do with the case. We represented two Black men charged with murdering two white men at a time of racial crisis in the South generally and in Jackson County in particular. We were entitled to know whether a white juror in any way held prejudiced or bigoted racial views and those questions were designed to reveal just that. But Smith ruled that we were precluded from pursuing these two lines of inquiry with any other juror.[12]

Block and I then fell back on a different line of questioning. We asked the white jurors whether they were familiar with some or all of the inflammatory media coverage that had flooded the circuit from 1966 to 1972 or had otherwise heard about the case through conversations in the community. If so, we tried to get them to admit either that they had a firm opinion about the case that they could not set aside or that they knew so much about the case that they could not render a verdict based solely on the evidence presented in court. Some jurors would admit to this, others wouldn't.

With Black potential jurors, our strategy was different. We inquired generally about their background and whether they could be fair and impartial and tried to block Leo Jones's consistent effort to excuse them. We were striving to get a racially integrated jury, an unrealistic hope, as it turned out.

Both the state and the defense had an unlimited number of challenges for cause, in which a prospective juror could be excused if there was any reasonable doubt about whether that juror could be fair and decide the case based solely on the evidence presented in court. Judge Smith had the final decision about whether the challenge had merit. Also, each side had forty peremptory challenges apiece, which meant we both could excuse a given prospective juror without having to give a reason. Sixty-four, or about one-third of the 226 prospective jurors examined were excused for cause because of their stated opposition to capital punishment. Most of these (forty-two) were Black prospective jurors. Eleven others were excused for cause based on other reasons.

Of the remaining 151 jurors, virtually everyone said they were familiar with the case from the news publicity and general conversation in the community. Seventy-four, or almost half of those prospective jurors, were excused for cause because they admitted they had fixed opinions about the case or were otherwise extremely familiar with the facts. Many of these individuals stated that they could not give the defendants the benefit of the presumption of innocence, as Florida law requires, and thought that Pitts and Lee were guilty. These statements proved that Judge Smith's view that this case had little or no local interest in Jackson County was naive.

*   *   *

Here are a few examples that are representative of statements many of the white prospective jurors made in open court. All of those individuals were excused for cause or excused by the defense using a preemptory challenge. Their sworn responses show how pervasive this notorious case was in Jackson County and why the case should never had been tried there.

George Bennett, the second prospective juror called, was typical of the white jurors examined. He was employed as the superintendent of a local scrap metal business. He said, as did virtually all jurors, that he had heard the names of Pitts and Lee before coming to court, that he had read about the case in the local newspaper.

Q. Can you tell us what you remember [about what] you have read?

A. If I remember right, it started with these boys admitted one time they were guilty, did they not?

Q. I'm just asking you what you read.

A. Then turning the thing around and went to trial and that's been five years ago, I don't know how or why they ended up. They had plead [sic] guilty one time and they had a retrial and here we are with another. That's about all I know.

Q. Do you remember reading something in the paper about how they admitted they were guilty?

A. Yes. . . .

Q. Don't you think that will prejudice you against these defendants?

A. Well, it should, it should anybody as far as that is concerned, if anybody is truthful as to what they say. . . .

Q. Have you ever heard anyone else express any opinion in your presence about this case?

A. I have heard them talking a lot of angles to this case.

Q. You have heard a number of people discussing this case?

A. Sure, you would.[13]

He added that the recent Ku Klux Klan rally in Marianna was well known throughout the community:

Q. Mr. Bennett, do you have any knowledge about a motorcade that went through the black section of Marianna last month?

A. Well, if you didn't, you would have to be deaf, I reckon, that was the main topic for many days.[14]

Hoyt E. Roberts, a retired Air Force veteran and the first prospective juror called, was candid about his sympathy with the Ku Klux Klan.

Q. Do you sympathize in any of the Klan's activities?

A. I don't know whether I do or not, somethings they do is good and some things they do is bad. . . .

Some things they do as making a man take care of his family, I go along with that, but taking a man out and whipping him like he is a dog, I don't go for that.[15]

Otis Pittman, another prospective juror, made a typical comment about how well known this case was in the area. He was employed as a parts man for Buford Equipment Co. just outside Marianna:

Q. Have you heard anyone talking about this case, say in the last several weeks in Marianna?
A. Yes, sir. You hear talk of it most everywhere you go.[16]

Martha Lewis, another juror and housewife, agreed:

Q. Have you ever heard the names "Pitts and Lee" before you came to court today?
A. Yes, sir, they have been very familiar to everyone in this area, I think, if you read the newspaper or listen to the radio.
* * *
Q. All right. Have you talked to anybody about the case before you came to court?
A. Yes, everybody talks about it.[17]

And in these conversations, many prospective jurors heard people express the opinion that Pitts and Lee were guilty and that it was a waste of taxpayer money to retry the case. Thomas Pumphrey, a social studies teacher, stated:

Q. Now in the general conversation that [you] mentioned, has anybody expressed any opinions in your presence as to whether or not these defendants were guilty or not?
A. Yes, sir, I have heard opinions about that.
Q. And those opinions you have heard were that they were guilty, is that right?
A. That seemed to be the intimation, yes sir.[18]

Charles Benefield, a dredge operator:

Q. And this case has been a topic of pretty much general conversation in Jackson County, hasn't it?
A. It has. . . .
Q. And many people have expressed opinions that they're guilty, haven't they?
A. Well, they didn't say it that way. . . . Most of the conversation is that's just a waste of people's time and taxpayer's money, that's the topic of it.[19]

Hubert Hales, a line foreman for the Florida Public Utility Company, said:

Q. Now, have you heard people talking about this case prior to coming to court?

A. Why sure, I hear my employees talking about it on the job quite a bit.

Q. It's been a general topic of conversation?

A. Well, some, quite a bit.

Q. And the people on the job have expressed the opinion that they think the defendants are guilty?

A. Why some of them does.

Q. Did anybody express the opinion that they think they are innocent?

A. I can't say I really heard it, anybody say they thought they were innocent.[20]

Juror after juror repeated the same thing: they detailed how widely this case was known throughout Jackson County.[21]

Finally, Judge Smith elicited these statements from William Baxter, a local resident, which illustrate perfectly why this case did not belong in Jackson County:

Q. If accepted upon this jury can you lay aside anything you have read or heard or discussed and decide this case solely upon the facts you hear from the witness stand and from the law as charged to you by the Court? Can you do that?

A. I don't think everything could be laid aside, no, sir.

Q. You think you would have to consider some of the stuff you have read or heard?

A. Well, not one hundred percent, but it would be in my mind, that's something you can't get rid of, it's past.[22]

Exactly right. But Judge Smith was unpersuaded. In spite of all the evidence to the contrary, he was resolved to try this case in Jackson County.

24

Phase II of Jury Selection

During the twelve days of jury selection, Leo Jones asked few questions of most of the white potential jurors and with few exceptions found them acceptable to serve on the jury. But when it came to the Black potential jurors, his strategy was totally different. He always cross-examined them at length and tried to get them excused for cause. When that tactic failed, he invariably exercised a peremptory challenge and struck the Black juror from the panel.

Jones exercised a peremptory challenge on every one of the fourteen Black jurors who survived a challenge for cause. Both the Florida Supreme Court and the US Supreme Court have since condemned this practice as a violation of the defendant's right to a fair and impartial jury trial guaranteed by the Florida Constitution and the US Constitution.[1] Indeed, this would be one of our major points for appeal.

All of the Black jurors Jones excluded said that they could presume the defendants innocent, that they would require the state to prove the defendants' guilt beyond a reasonable doubt, that they could render a guilty verdict and impose the death penalty if the evidence warranted it, and that they would try this matter solely on the evidence presented in court. They were perfectly qualified to try this case. Yet Leo Jones excused them all.

Mamie Lawrence, an elderly Black woman with a grown daughter who had been a widow for six years, made it clear that she knew nothing of the facts of the case, that she thought it was wrong to murder, and that if the defendants had committed murder she would have no trouble convicting them and sentencing them to death. Judge Smith was charmed by this juror and said:

I think the juror has pretty well qualified herself. She said if they're guilty they ought to be punished and if they are not they ought to be turned loose, is that correct?
The Juror. Yes sir.[2]

Even Leo Jones was impressed. "That's a right good statement," he said.[3] Yet Jones excused Mrs. Lawrence.

Other Black jurors said much the same thing. Robert Robinson, a farm worker, said he had learned this was a murder case only when the deputy sheriff served him with a jury summons.[4] Jeffro Nix, a lumber company worker, said he first found out about the case when he showed up for jury duty.[5] Mike Stephens, a cleaning company worker, said he knew that two men were charged with murder but nothing beyond that.[6] Nonetheless, Leo Jones excused them all.

On the other hand, Jones had no trouble accepting white jurors who said much the same thing as these four Black jurors. Billie Beck, the man who served as the jury foreman in this case, and William Tyus, who also served on the jury, said that they knew little or nothing about the facts of this case and would try the matter solely on the evidence presented in court.[7] Jones accepted these two white jurors, yet struck the four Black jurors who said virtually the same thing.

Jones continued this same pattern of racial discrimination with the remaining Black jurors. He got visibly upset and cross-examined at length any Black prospective juror if either the juror or the juror's spouse had dared sign an affidavit stating that Pitts and Lee could not get a fair trial in Jackson County in support of our motion for change of venue—something every citizen had a legal right to do.

Cora Beecham, a teacher's aide in a public school; George Myrick, a school custodian; and Benjamin Pete, a food service instructor at the local state institution for imprisoned juveniles,[8] said they had signed such an affidavit. Both Reverend Andrew Hodges, a Baptist minister, and Lillian Ward, a school teacher, said their spouses had signed such an affidavit.[9] But these episodes had nothing to do with Jones's decision to strike these jurors. He excused them because they were Black.

This was made plain during the examination of Benjamin Pete. This potential juror had signed such an affidavit but disavowed it in court, stating emphatically that Pitts and Lee could get a fair trial in Jackson County.[10] When Judge Smith asked him "You're sorry you actually signed [the affidavit]?" Mr. Pete replied, "Well, I certainly am."[11] Leo Jones fully accepted this disavowal and said "First, let me thank you for being candid and extremely honest."[12] Nevertheless, Jones excused Mr. Pete.

Jones also excused two Black jurors who expressed some sensitivity concerning the death penalty. Equilla Edwards, whose husband was a retired veteran, said she could vote to sentence someone to death if the circumstances warranted it but added she would "feel bad" if she had to do it.[13] And Ceophas McGriff, a teacher's aide, said he would "rather not" impose the death penalty but would if he had to.[14] Judge Smith agreed and said, "I think most of us would rather not [impose the death penalty]."[15] Jones no doubt wanted jurors who had no qualms about this issue, but that was not the main reason he excused them. He excused them because they were Black. The fact that they also had some sensitivity on the issue of capital punishment just reinforced that decision.

At times, Leo Jones was abusive with Black potential jurors. Rhoda Porter is a prime example. She was a mother of six whose husband worked as a cable splicer for the local telephone company. Mrs. Porter said that she remembered hearing the names of the defendants years ago on the radio and that she knew they had previously gone to trial but didn't know what they were charged with.[16]

Leo Jones grilled Mrs. Porter with rapid-fire questions as if she was a hostile witness rather than a prospective juror, for over twenty-five pages of trial transcript.[17]

Here is a sample of his abusive questions:

Q. Why is it when I just ask you, to give an honest opinion, why is it not knowing whether it was stealing a shirt or alleged of murder, you would have remembered this particular case went on trial and yet didn't know what it was for?

A. I was in my husband's car and we were going on a trip at that particular time. I was listening to it.

Q. Why would you remember their names and nothing more?

A. I don't know why I just remembered their names. I remember two last names. I don't know the first names. I remember last names and they were going to trial.

Q. You remember that for all these years yet in your conscious or subconscious mind you have no recollection as to what they were charged with?

Mr. Hubbart. I'm going to object to it as repetitious.

The Court. I think it's repetitious, you have gone far enough.

Mr. Jones. I have copied Mr. Hubbart's questions and asking it identical.

Mr. Hubbart. I don't ask them twice.

Mr. Jones. No. Six times.

Mr. Hubbart. I object, I'm sure Mr. Jones didn't mean that.

The Court. Objection sustained.[18]

When Leo Jones ended his inquiry and I had just begun to question Mrs. Porter, Jones interrupted and excused her.

Charles Vann, another potential Black juror, suffered the same type of abusive questioning by Jones. Mr. Vann, a self-employed funeral director in Marianna, said he first learned about the case from conversations when it was moved to Marianna but knew nothing else about the facts.[19] Leo Jones grilled Mr. Vann about an incident in which a Black minister came to his funeral parlor and asked the juror to notarize affidavits stating that Pitts and Lee could not get a fair trial in Jackson County:

> Q. When Reverend Gooden came from Tallahassee, he had to say something to you as [to] what these petitions were about and what had happened and why he was getting up these petitions. Now what did you learn from him about what this thing was, what started it all, and why he was getting up petitions?
> A. We didn't discuss at the time he was there at the place of business.
> Q. If I walked up to—
> Mr. Block. The juror is entitled to answer the question.
> The Court. Let him answer.
> A. He came to the place of business. . . . I told him I was tied up and asked him what he wanted. He asked me would I notarize papers concerning Pitts and Lee and I said "No." I wasn't notarizing unless a person signed them in my presence. He said "Okay" and he left. I haven't seen him anymore. He didn't discuss anything about the case at that time.
> Mr. Jones. He had to tell you something.
> Mr. Hubbart. I object to counsel arguing, this juror has answered the question. This is argument, Your Honor—
> Mr. Jones. He had to—
> Mr. Hubbart. I have an objection. I wish you'd stop questioning the juror. I object, he's arguing with this juror.
> The Court. I think the juror, I think the objection should be sustained.
> Mr. Jones. We'll excuse the juror.[20]

And so Leo Jones got exactly what he wanted. No registered Black voter in Jackson County would ever be allowed serve on this jury.

I had never before encountered a prosecutor like Leo Jones who used his peremptory challenges in such a racially biased manner and who at times was so disrespectful to Black potential jurors. I was used to trying cases before racially integrated juries in Miami and Washington, DC, against able but tolerant prosecutors with whom I was usually quite friendly. But Leo Jones was different. He was tough and difficult to get along with. He was also an extremely persuasive lawyer before the courts and juries of the Florida Panhandle, although he might not have done so well if the case had been moved to Tampa or West Palm Beach.

* * *

On March 8, 1972, the last day of jury selection, the courtroom erupted with an explosive issue. Irwin Block notified the court that the defense had received "confidential information" from an informant that the Ku Klux Klan had plans to kill Pitts and Lee if they were found not guilty. That plot, Block said, involved R. E. McCurley, a high-ranking member of the KKK in Panama City. Block had sent investigators to locate McCurley and serve him with a witness subpoena and McCurley, responding to that subpoena, appeared in court. McCurley had a sticker on the car he drove to the courthouse that day reading: "United Klans of America."[21] Block asked that the Klansman be called as a "court witness" so that both sides could cross-examine him concerning this alleged plot.[22]

Both Leo Jones and Judge Smith were outraged at this suggestion. The mere mention of the KKK sent both the prosecutor and the judge into a near frenzy.

Jones led the charge:

> If the court please, this appears to be highly irregular when an officer of this court makes an announcement that a witness that he has subpoenaed is a member of such and such an organization and therefore he wishes the court to take responsibility to call anybody. It appears to me it would be just as preposterous for the State to stand up here and represent to you that I have a member of the Nazi party or anything else and that therefore I want you to call so and so. The fact that there may be a Klan in West Florida, there may be a Nazi party, there may be an American Civil Liberty Union leader, N.A.A.C.P. leader has nothing at all to do with this case. I don't see the relevancy, I don't see the materiality, or anything else to do with this case.[23]

But this information had everything to do with this case because it dealt with a serious security issue that the court had an obligation to look into in order to protect the safety of our clients, particularly since the KKK had already announced its presence in Jackson County with its terrifying motorcade through the Black section of town.

As Jones spoke, however, Judge Smith's face grew red and I could tell he was beside himself with anger. He interrupted Jones with an outburst of his own:

> The Court. Now, I want to make this comment. And I want it to be understood, I haven't seen any Klan activity in this county with reference to this case. I don't anticipate any and I don't like for it to be stirred and I'm not accusing you of stirring it up but to summons a Klan member from another county to this county to testify in this case is absolutely ridiculous to me.
>
> Mr. Block. Your Honor please—
>
> The Court. And until I see that there is some evidence of some Klan activity, I wouldn't begin to hear any testimony from this man.
>
> Mr. Block. Your Honor please—
>
> The Court. You summons him here, I didn't and you are the one who brought the subject up, I didn't. And the State didn't and the public didn't. And I just don't believe that and until I do I'm not going to have any part of it. This case has been going on for two and a half weeks. I haven't seen any public interest in this county in this case at all. And I don't believe there is any public interest in this case in this county.
>
> Mr. Block. I would have no objection if your Honor would take this testimony in executive session.
>
> The Court. No sir, I'm not going to take any testimony, no sir, I'm not going to mess up a trial of this case with such foolishness at this time without any evidence of anything taking place.[24]

Over our objections, Smith refused to look into this serious security issue and turned a blind eye to the KKK's obvious activity in this case. He also refused to recognize the widespread public interest in this case throughout Jackson County.

*　*　*

On March 8, 1972, after twelve days of jury selection, we used the last of our allotted forty peremptory challenges and were forced, over our objection, to accept an all-white jury consisting of ten men and two women.

Although all these jurors were polite to us, I always felt a certain tension when addressing them. Irwin Block and I were complete strangers from the big city in the eyes of these jurors, who lived in small towns and in rural areas. These jurors seemed much more comfortable with Leo Jones, an assistant state attorney from their community who spoke with the idioms and drawl of North Florida. In short, we were the Yankees in this court drama and Leo Jones was one of their own.

All of the jurors who sat on this case gave the correct answers to the questions asked of them in order to serve on the jury. They told Judge Smith that they would follow the judge's instructions on the law, that they would presume the defendants innocent and require the state to prove their guilt beyond a reasonable doubt, that they would base their verdict solely on the evidence in court, and that they would disregard anything they might have read or heard about the case before coming to court.

But it was humanly impossible for anyone to do all of this, given the avalanche of pretrial publicity adverse to Pitts and Lee and the widespread conversations about the case in Jackson County. Eleven of the twelve jurors who were finally selected to try this case said they had heard the names Pitts and Lee before coming to court and were otherwise familiar with the case. A prime example is Jim Sims, a postal worker. He said he had read about the case in the *Jackson County Floridan*.[25] He knew that the defendants had been tried and sentenced to death.[26] He knew that service station attendants had been murdered, that they had been shot, and that the murders had taken place in Port St. Joe.[27] He said that he had heard people discussing the case at times, that he heard some people express the opinions that the defendants were guilty, that they had had a fair trial the first time, and that there was no need to retry the case.[28]

Another example is James A. Zeigler, a federal revenue agent. He said he had read about the case in the *Jackson County Floridan*. He knew the case had been tried before in Gulf County, that the defendants had been convicted, that the murders had taken place in the Port St. Joe area at a location just south of Wewahitchka, and that the victims had been shot and killed. He also said he knew some key witnesses in this case. He knew Deputy Sheriff Wayne White, the officer who saw George Kittrell beat up Freddie Pitts. And he was "well acquainted" with Fred Turner, the defendants' lawyer who had helped the police get confessions out of Pitts and Lee.[29]

Juror after juror acknowledged their familiarity with this case. Agnes Schack, a nurse who taught at the local community college, said she had read "one or two articles" about the case in the *Jackson County Floridan* and had engaged in "general conversation" about the case with people in the community. She had heard people express opinions about the guilt or innocence of the defendants.[30]

George Williams, a boiler operator at the state mental hospital; William Tyus, a farmer who worked nights as a plumber's helper at the same hospital; James Fears, the manager of a local grocery store; Richard Tidwell, who worked for the West Florida Equipment Co.; and Florence M. Jordan, a mother of three who helped her husband run a local grocery store all said that they had heard about the case to a greater or lesser extent from the local newspaper or in conversations in the community or both.[31]

Two jurors, Harry Jeter and Tommy Whidden, require special mention. Mr. Jeter was a plumber at the state mental hospital and Mr. Whidden was the manager of a local peanut plant. Like the other jurors, they had been exposed to all the prejudicial media publicity and conversations in the community about the case. But in retrospect, they were the two members of the jury who I think were open to a not-guilty verdict. I say that because three-and-a-half years later, in September 1975, when Governor Askew was considering pardoning Pitts and Lee on grounds of innocence, both jurors expressed their support for the pardon and said they were not "upset" with the prospect.

As the *Florida Times-Union* in Jacksonville reported on September 13, 1975, Harry Jeter said the pardon was "definitely the right thing if the governor has evidence we didn't have at the trial" and "that if the governor has evidence that we the jury didn't have, then good for them." He was referring to our defense evidence that Curtis Adams had murdered Grover Floyd and Jesse Burkett, not Pitts and Lee—evidence that Judge Smith had ruled inadmissible at trial. Tommy Whidden agreed. He stated that he was glad Pitts and Lee "are getting a chance to be free if they are innocent." As he put it, the governor "had the evidence we didn't."[32]

Only Billie Beck, an electrician who turned out to be the jury foreman, said he had never heard the names Pitts and Lee before coming to court and knew nothing of the case. He was quite assertive and well spoken, a natural, I think, to be selected as the jury foreman. He also volunteered that he was against interracial marriage.[33]

The only person who served on the jury who we thought was openly hostile to us was A. J. Holley, a 71-year-old retiree from the hardware business. He was one of the last jurors called for examination and had a menacing look on his face as he approached the jury box. Irwin Block leaned over at the time and whispered his concern to me at counsel table.

When I asked Mr. Holley whether he had heard the names Pitts and Lee prior to coming to court, he growled, "Anyone living in this area, I don't think could have helped from hearing the names." He admitted he had "glanced at headlines" in the newspaper about the case but added with contempt, "I don't read that trash, period!" He said that he knew the case had been tried before; that he had known Sheriff "Doc" Daffin, who had gotten confessions from Pitts and Lee, for twenty-five years; and that he also had known the prosecutor J. Frank Adams for about the same length of time, stating "he's a friend." He accused Irwin Block of "continually" asking "superfluous" questions. And he also said to Block, "There is no need of repeating that, sir, you have heard what I have said already."[34]

I moved the court to challenge the juror for cause on various grounds, noting that "the demeanor" of the juror was "antagonistic" toward the defense. This motion was denied.[35] At that point, we had exhausted our allotted forty peremptory challenges and could not excuse the juror using such a challenge. I asked the judge to grant us an additional peremptory challenge so that we could excuse this juror, but this request was also denied.[36]

*   *   *

I then announced to the court that we did not accept the jury and proceeded to make a number of lengthy motions outside the presence of the jury that took up fourteen pages of trial transcript.[37] As I plowed through this procedure, the judge's face once again turned red, although he retained his composure and let me continue.[38]

I later learned that in the midst of my argument, Gene Miller, who was in the spectator section of the courtroom, leaned over and whispered to his colleague Rob Elder, who was covering the case for the *Miami Herald,* that I was really talking to US Supreme Court Justice Thurgood Marshall, not Judge Smith. Elder whispered back that I might have to.[39] They were both so right. I was laying the basis for an eventual appeal to the US Supreme Court.

I renewed our motion for change of venue, moved the court to excuse all twelve jurors for cause, asked the court to grant us twelve additional peremptory challenges so that we could excuse the entire jury, and moved the court to strike all twelve jurors from the panel. With each motion, I argued that to impanel that jury to try that case would violate the defendants' right to a fair and impartial jury guaranteed by the Sixth and Fourteenth Amendments to the US Constitution.

I had taken careful notes and compiled statistics on the 226 potential jurors who were questioned during the jury selection, and this information became a major part of my argument. Among other things, I argued that "the jury panel has been so saturated with prejudicial news publicity, featuring the defendants' confessions, guilty pleas, convictions and death sentences that the defendants cannot get a fair and impartial trial by jury on the issue of guilt or innocence or on the issue of mercy, guaranteed by the Sixth Amendment and Due Process Clause of the Fourteenth Amendment to the United States Constitution."[40]

I particularly noted that the prosecuting attorney had used his peremptory challenges to systematically exclude all fourteen Black jurors who had survived a challenge for cause. I read into the record the names of the fourteen Black prospective jurors the state had excused and argued that the defendants were being deprived of their constitutional right to a fair and impartial jury trial.[41] Judge Smith became somewhat agitated at that point but did not interrupt me.

When I was finished, Leo Jones had no reply. He made no effort to defend his blatant race-based use of peremptory challenges. Nor did Judge Smith dispute or comment on anything I had said on this issue. Instead, the judge made the following terse ruling:

The motions are denied and including the motion for change of venue. I interpret the law to state that if you can secure a fair and impartial jury, that they're not entitled to a change of venue and I believe we have selected a fair and impartial jury that will give the defendants a fair and impartial trial. That's all they are entitled to. So the motion for change of venue is denied and all the other motions are denied.[42]

The twelve-member all-white jury was then sworn in by the clerk, after which Judge Smith instructed the jurors that during the trial they were not to discuss the case with anyone, that they were not to discuss this case among themselves until they received the case for their consideration, and that they were not to read or listen to anything in the media concerning this case.

With the consent of both the state and the defense, Smith sequestered the jury. He instructed the jury that they would be kept together for the balance of the trial and would stay overnight at the local Holiday Inn, the same motel Irwin Block and our wives were staying at. He then permitted the jury to go home that day to get their affairs in order and directed them to return to court the next day with bags packed, ready to hear the case and be kept together, warning them that they would be barred from any outside forms of communication until the trial was over. The jury then left the courtroom.

The rest of the day was short and anticlimactic. Nine prospective jurors were then called in an effort to select one or two alternate jurors with each side having four peremptory challenges. Seven of the jurors were excused for cause, either because they couldn't presume the defendants were innocent or because they were opposed to capital punishment. We excused the remaining two jurors with peremptory challenges.[43] Smith then announced: "Gentlemen, that exhausts the jury venire. . . . We'll have to try this case with twelve jurors. . . . If one of the jurors gets sick, we'll have to recess until he gets well."[44]

Court was then adjourned. The stage was now set for one of the most dramatic trials in Florida history.

25

The State's Case

As I sat at counsel table on the first day of trial testimony on March 9, 1972, I could feel my heart beating faster than usual. I also felt some slight perspiration on my forehead, although the court was air conditioned. I had eaten a light breakfast, unlike the usual huge breakfast I was used to. I was nervous and anxious to get started. Irwin Block and our clients, Freddie Pitts and Wilbert Lee, sat at counsel table alongside me. We hardly spoke a word. This was the moment we had fought for six years to get to and we were ready for trial.

A short distance to our right was Assistant State Attorney Leo Jones with his assistant, Paul Griffith. They were seated, grim-faced, at a counsel table nearest the jury box. The spectator section was filled to capacity, standing room only, Blacks mostly seated on one side of the courtroom and whites mostly on the other side. I heard some murmuring from the spectators behind me, but I barely noticed them. I was focused on the elevated judge's bench in front of me. It was empty. We all awaited Judge Smith's entrance.

Promptly at 9:00 a.m., Judge Smith entered the courtroom dressed in his traditional court robes. The bailiff announced: "All rise." Everyone in the courtroom rose, all talking ceased, and we all waited until Judge Smith was seated. After we had sat down, Smith addressed us. "Good morning," he said. "Good morning," we all replied. "All right, Mr. Clerk, I expect you better call the roll of the jury."[1]

The bailiff promptly walked to the adjoining jury room and led the twelve jurors into the courtroom. As he did so, we defense lawyers and the prosecutors rose again until the jurors were seated. The clerk, who was stationed at a long table below the judge's bench, stood up and read off the names of the jurors who would try this case. The jurors announced "here" when their names were called: ten men and two women, all white, no alternate jurors.

Smith then gave a standard instruction to the jury, outlining what the procedure in this case would be:

> The Court. Ladies and gentlemen, you have been selected and sworn as [jurors] to try this case of the State of Florida against Freddie Lee Pitts and Wilbert Lee wherein, as you have been told, this is a criminal case and they're charged with the alleged commission of first degree murder. It is your solemn responsibility to determine the guilt or innocence of the defendants and . . . your verdict must be based *solely* on the evidence presented to you in this trial and the law on which the court instructs you at the close of this trial.[2]

I had heard this standard instruction many times in my legal career, but this case was different. These jurors, I thought, could not possibly base their verdict *solely* on the evidence presented in court. I knew that once the jury heard testimony in court that confirmed what they already had heard from the media and elsewhere, this case was over. Still, we hoped that maybe, just maybe, one or more of these jurors would listen to us, vote not guilty, and hang the jury. But an acquittal in Marianna was out of the question.

Smith continued:

> Before proceeding further, it is necessary that you understand how a trial is conducted. First, the attorneys will have an opportunity to make opening statements to you. The opening statements are not evidence. They are to be considered only as a guide so you may better understand and evaluate the evidence as it comes to you.[3]

As a matter of strategy, I have always considered the opening statement to be a critical stage in the trial of any criminal case. Opinions differ, but I have long believed that the jury's first impression of the case, the one they get from opening statements, heavily influences how they ultimately decide the case. As a result, I had prepared a detailed opening statement of what the evidence would show in this case. So had Irwin Block.

The judge continued:

> Following the opening statements, witnesses will be called to testify. They will be placed under oath, then examined and cross-examined by the attorneys. Documents and other tangible exhibits may also be produced as evidence.[4]

Here, of course, was the essence of the case. The state would go first and present its case. When the state rested, we would present our witnesses.

Irwin Block and I had plotted our basic approach in the case, how we would cross-examine each of the state's witnesses, and who would present our defense witnesses.

Smith continued:

When the evidence is completed, the attorneys will argue the merits of the case. What the attorneys say is not evidence. Their arguments are persuasive only and their arguments may be accepted or rejected in whole and [in] part as you see fit. These arguments are given for the purpose of assisting you in evaluating the evidence and arriving at the correct conclusions in this case.[5]

I had always loved closing argument. I considered myself an excellent public speaker and felt at home pleading my case before a jury. But I was in alien territory and had a formidable task ahead of me.

Smith concluded his instructions:

Following the arguments of counsel, the Court will instruct you on the law applicable to the case. And after the instructions are given, you will retire to consider your verdict.[6]

After issuing some additional instructions about avoiding all contact with any media coverage of the case, Smith turned to the packed spectators in the courtroom and gave this warning:

Now I want to say to you spectators that during the course of this trial: you are welcome to remain in the courtroom. You are not to show any reaction to any comment made, any questions asked or any answers given. You are to watch this case solemnly and without expression, and if you do not abide by this instruction, you will be removed from the courtroom.[7]

As it turned out, all of the spectators followed this instruction and re-mained silent for the rest of the trial—that is, until the very end.

Leo Jones then rose from his seat at counsel table, stood in front of the jury, and gave the state's opening statement. After some preliminary com-ments, Jones, in his best southern drawl, detailed in essence the state's dis-torted theory of the case. There were no surprises in this recitation, as it essentially tracked Willie Mae Lee's perjured testimony and recited Pitts and Lee's false and involuntary confessions.

I was, however, struck by one aspect of his statement. Jones played down the racial argument at the Mo Jo station between Dorothy Martin and the two white gas station attendants in which Martin was barred from using the white-only ladies' restroom.

This argument was what Deputy Sheriff Wayne White saw as the motive for the murders he was investigating; namely, that this was a Black-on-white revenge murder for this racial slight. And it was the basis for the police roundup of all the Black people who had been at the station that night and all the Black people who had been at Wilbert Lee's party that night. It was also the reason the police had not arrested any of the white people who had been at the station that evening.

But in Jones's telling, this racial incident was of no moment. "There was some joshing there. One of the women in the party wanted to use the bathroom. . . . There was something about using the bathroom and there was no colored bathroom there, so there was some discussion about there being a bathroom or not being a bathroom."[8]

There was a reason for burying this crucial incident. The racial motive reflected badly on the police. It showed how racist their investigation was, something the two army CID investigators Bruce Potts and Donald Hoag would testify to at this trial. And it was an otherwise incendiary reason for murder that might stir up racial tensions during the trial in Jackson County when tensions were running high as it was. Best to bury it.

A much safer motive for the robbery-murder was the old-fashioned one: money. According to Jones, even though Pitts had just cashed his army check, he somehow wanted cash from the station "to take a girl to New Orleans." Jones said that Pitts "was from New Orleans and he had a little girl apparently that he wanted to take to New Orleans."[9] Pitts, however, was from Mobile, Alabama, not New Orleans, and the motive Jones had spun for the murders was pure fiction.

Irwin Block and I then made our opening statements: Irwin on behalf of Freddie Pitts and me on behalf of Wilbert Lee. We went into detail about what our clients were doing the night of the murders, how they were innocent of the Floyd-Burkett murders, and how their confessions were involuntary and false.

We also laid out all the evidence we had that Curtis Adams had murdered Grover Floyd and Jesse Burkett. We knew we would have a difficult time convincing Judge Smith to admit this evidence, but, as a matter of strategy, we decided we had nothing to lose by detailing it all. Ordinarily, it is a cardinal rule that in an opening statement a trial lawyer should never promise to produce evidence that never materializes at trial, as that undermines the lawyer's credibility before the jury. But this case was different.

We felt that we were so far behind that we had nothing to lose. Even if we failed to get this evidence in, the jurors would at least know what we had. And maybe that would help, even though our opening statements were not considered evidence.

After the opening statements, Smith entertained an unusual request. The jurors asked the judge whether they could vote in the upcoming Democratic presidential primary the following Tuesday, March 14, 1972. Smith said that they could and when the time came, a bailiff would escort the jurors to the polls. Court was then adjourned for the day and the jurors were driven to the Holiday Inn to get settled for their stay there during the trial.

That year a number of candidates were running for president, including segregationist Alabama governor George Wallace and US senator George McGovern, the eventual Democratic nominee. Wallace was riding the white backlash of the times, fanning the fires of racial discord and resentment against so-called liberal elites in Washington, DC, a strain in our politics that unfortunately remains with us today.

In advance of the primary, the jurors on their own initiative conducted an informal straw poll among themselves about their preference for president. The results of this poll were leaked to the press on March 13th: 11–1 for Wallace.[10] We never did find out what candidate the holdout juror voted for. Probably not the eventual nominee, George McGovern, who was an unabashed liberal, but maybe someone more moderate like US senator Henry "Scoop" Jackson, who opposed court-ordered school busing to achieve racial integration in the schools. Wallace later won the Florida primary, but Jackson finished third. At the time, we thought that this lone dissenter in the straw poll might be our only hope to win a not-guilty vote and hang the jury.

*   *   *

The time finally arrived for Leo Jones to call witnesses and outline the state's case, which, as it turned out, was simple and straightforward. It would take only a day and a half of court time. Considering the complexity of this case, Block and I were amazed. But Jones knew his jury. He knew that he didn't have to present much to get a conviction.

First, Jones called a number of witnesses who established that Grover Floyd and Jesse Burkett had been robbed, kidnapped, and murdered, including the circumstances surrounding those murders and the initial investigation. This evidence was undisputed.

Second, Jones introduced three oral confessions that purported to link Pitts and Lee to these murders: namely, Willie Mae Lee's incriminating statement in court as a live witness, and Pitts and Lee's August 1963 confessions in court. The state's case rose or fell on the credibility of these three confessions.

Leo Jones presented no murder weapon, no proceeds of the robbery, no fingerprints, no autopsy findings, no tire tracks from the murder scene that had been compared to the tires on Pitts's car, no dirt from the defendants' clothing that had been compared to the soil at the murder scene, no tire jack that had allegedly been used to hit Grover Floyd, no physical evidence of any kind. In fact, the Florida Sheriffs Bureau had been called in during the investigation of the case but had found no forensic evidence linking Pitts and Lee to this crime.

There were no surprises in the first part of the state's case, but one significant incident is worth mentioning. It's a detail that has always troubled me. Richard Skipper, the owner of the Mo Jo station, testified that on the evening before the murders, July 31, 1963, Freddie Pitts had come to the Mo Jo station on two occasions and had spoken to Skipper. The first time, Skipper had cashed an army check for Pitts; the second time, Skipper had replaced a water hose in Pitts's car.[11] On the morning after the murders, August 1, 1963, at around 7:00 a.m., Pitts returned to the Mo Jo station, had another conversation with Skipper, and may also have bought some gas for his car.[12] Skipper testified that on all of these visits, Pitts had been polite.[13]

I ask you: would this polite young man in the US Army, who had just had his army check cashed by Skipper at the Mo Jo station turn around and just a few hours later go back to the station and rob, kidnap, and murder Skipper's two attendants? And then, just several hours later the next morning, would this same man return to the Mo Jo station to gas up his car and have another chat with Skipper? It really makes no sense.

I also ask: doesn't this robbery-kidnap-murder scenario seem totally out of character for Pitts? He had no criminal record. And what was the purpose of his supposed crime? Money to take his girlfriend to New Orleans, as Leo Jones claimed? Pitts already had money. He had a steady job in the army and Skipper had just cashed his army check.

* * *

For the second part of the state's case, the alleged connection of Pitts and Lee to the charged crimes, Jones presented Willie Mae Lee's live testimony blaming Pitts and Lee for the charged murders (but also, in effect, incriminating herself in these crimes) and Pitts and Lee's August 1963 trial confessions in court.

Jones presented no corroboration to support any of these three confessions, no forensic evidence of any kind. On the contrary, those confessions were the product of a reign of terror that the authorities subjected these three Black people to throughout the month of August 1963, and all were false and involuntary.[14]

Willie Mae Lee, however, was presented as the jewel in the state's case. She took the witness stand and defiantly repeated her previous trial testimony. It was quite a performance, and I feared that the jury would believe her in spite of everything we could throw at her.

But what about the two contradictory statements that Willie Mae Lee had made under oath to State Attorney J. Frank Adams? In her 1963 statement, she had blamed Lambson Smith, an army private stationed outside Port St. Joe, for the Floyd-Burkett murders and exonerated Wilbert Lee. And in her 1968 statement she had retracted all her past testimony blaming Pitts and Lee for the charged crime and had said she knew nothing about the case.

Here is the explanation Willie Mae Lee gave for telling her first story blaming Lambson Smith for the charged murders. Leo Jones did the questioning:

> Q. Well, did you later then, right there at the first tell them who did it?
> A. No, not at first, I didn't tell them who did it. They questioned me some more, then I told them that, see Mr. Daffin and them questioned me, Mr. [J. Frank] Adams came and he questioned me, and when they carry me back to my cell, see, I went back there with Wilbert's wife Ella Mae Lee, and she started crying, talking to me and I was scared and I was sleepy. I wanted to be left alone where I could rest. . . . I told them, well, I said, the first thing in my mind. [Ella Mae Lee] told me, what she told me to say I said; she told me to tell them that it was Smitty and Freddie and that's what I said.[15]

But this testimony made no sense. It only shows the terror that both Willie Mae Lee and Ella Mae Lee were under at the time. Ella Mae Lee was in no position to tell anyone what to do; she was a fellow prisoner. In fact, both of these women were in jail for nearly a month, were questioned constantly, were never charged with any crime, and were not released from police custody until Pitts and Lee had been sentenced to death.

But what about the major contradiction to Willie Mae Lee's trial testimony—her February 1968 sworn statement to the state attorney that all her past sworn statements blaming Pitts and Lee were false? Shouldn't that statement alone totally discredit her trial testimony?

Again, this was not a problem for the state. Here is Willie Mae Lee's explanation at trial for telling her retraction story. Leo Jones did the questioning.

> Q. All right. Tell the jury why you told Mr. Adams and Mr. DeWitt that?
> A. I told them that because it seemed nobody believed me, part of them don't believe me now and this white man had said he did it and that man right there sent me a picture of the electric chair.

She pointed at Gene Miller, who was seated in the spectator section of the courtroom. Leo Jones hurriedly walked across the courtroom facing the audience and asked:

> Q. Which man are you pointing to?
> A. Gene Miller.
> Q. This man here? (indicating)
> Q. Yes sir.[16]

That, of course, explained it all for the state. Gene Miller and the *Miami Herald* were to blame. And it fed nicely into the narrative that the *News Herald* had been proclaiming for the prior six years in its editorials—that nefarious forces led by the *Miami Herald,* and in particular Gene Miller, were behind the dastardly effort to upset Pitts and Lee's convictions. Miller was the perfect target.

On January 12, 1967, five years before this trial, Gene Miller had spoken to Willie Mae Lee on the front lawn of her home in Port St. Joe as part of his investigation of this case as a journalist. With her permission, Miller had sent Willie Mae Lee a copy of one his news stories on the case in the *Miami Herald* on August 21, 1967. Miller's cover letter to her was written on *Miami Herald* stationery. The tone of the letter was entirely courteous:

> Dear Willie Mae Lee,
> As I promised when I talked to you last January, I would mail you copies of the news stories I wrote on the Pitts-Lee case. Enclosed is one.
>
> You have never fully understood, I suspect, why Pitts blamed you when he first confessed.

This story should give you a good idea. He was beaten so badly he said anything the police wanted him to.

I believe you also gave the testimony you did because of police pressure. You will read in the story how the other women were also forced to tell lies.

If you should ever like to talk about this case, you should telephone collect a Negro lawyer in Panama City, Theodore R Bowers. His office is 1018 North Cove Boulevard. His telephone number is 785-0241 or 763-1564.

I am positive that the truth about this case is soon going to come out.

Sincerely,
Gene Miller[17]

On page 25A of the February 6, 1967, article, which Miller had written and enclosed in this letter, there appeared a number of photos, including a photo of the electric chair indicating the fate that Pitts and Lee faced. After that, Miller had no further contact with Willie Mae Lee.

Obviously, this photo had nothing to do with Willie Mae Lee's retraction statement. But her explosive testimony that day had a huge impact, I think, on the jurors. They all glared at Miller when Willie Mae Lee pointed him out in the audience. We objected to this testimony and moved for a mistrial. The motion was denied. At our request, Judge Smith then instructed the jury to disregard the reference to Gene Miller and the electric chair.[18] But the damage had been done. No doubt to the delight of the state, this "stricken" testimony explained it all. In fact, I couldn't help thinking at the time that Leo Jones had orchestrated this entire charade. How better to get around this damning retraction statement?

Besides all of these extraordinary shifts in stories, what is also striking about Willie Mae Lee's trial testimony was her inability to give a coherent account of the exact events of the charged crimes. Leo Jones had to lead her through the critical events of that evening. His examination of her covered twelve pages of trial testimony. Her responses were often reluctant, jumbled, confused, and she made one- or two-sentence replies.[19]

We objected, to no avail, to Jones's leading questions, but Judge Smith overruled our objections, stating, "Well, I think he's going to have to lead the witness a little bit but make your questions as direct as possible."[20] But why was it necessary to lead Willie Mae Lee? She was an intelligent witness and was fully capable of telling her story. Unless, of course, she was also a reluctant witness who knew full well that she was spinning a fictional account and had to be coaxed into it.

Willie Mae Lee said over and over: "I don't know what all did happen"; "I can't remember everything happen like it was yesterday"; "I don't know what happened really, I just can't remember"; "I can't remember all the words for word what was said, I just can't"; "I told you what I remember."[21] Nonetheless, Leo Jones was able to lead Willie Mae Lee into dramatic flourishes in which she blamed Pitts and Lee for the charged murders.

The state had this witness exactly where they wanted her. In October 1971, a few months before this trial, Deputy Sheriff Wayne White, one of the chief police investigators in this case, had traveled to upstate New York, arranged to get Willie Mae Lee out of jail on a minor charge in that area, and brought her back to Port St. Joe. She had thereafter stayed in White's home and was working, of all things, as a maid for Wayne White's wife at the time of the trial, making $6.00 a day for her work.[22]

Once again, Willie Mae Lee was under the physical control of the police, who were closely watching her to make sure she would stick to her latest statement blaming Pitts and Lee for the Floyd-Burkett murders. And she was being paid off in the process for her favorable testimony. As I look back on it now, the brazenness of the state's conduct is almost beyond belief.

I was disheartened by all of this. I sat at counsel table furiously taking notes on Willie Mae Lee's testimony with the sinking feeling that she was going over well with the jury. She was telling them what many had already heard about the case from the media coverage and conversations in the community, and nothing we could say or do was likely to shake their belief.

Irwin Block conducted a searing cross-examination of Willie Mae Lee and exposed many material inconsistencies in the myriad stories she had previously told about the case. She could never tell her story straight about whether Pitts did or did not pistol-whip Grover Floyd during the robbery[23] or whether she went in Pitts's car to a place called Kenny's Quarters before or after the murders[24] or whether she was in the back or front seat of Pitts's car on the way to the murders[25] or whether she ever heard three to four gunshots or no gunshots at all fired at Floyd or Burkett.[26]

My cross-examination of Willie Mae Lee was short and explosive. I was always sympathetic with her because of the ordeal the police had put her through. At the same time, I was exasperated with her vitriolic attacks on anyone who would challenge her story.

I tried to impeach her trial testimony with the information in the deposition she had given on February 2, 1968, in which she stated:

Q. You didn't kill these two men, did you?

A. No, sir.

Q. You're completely innocent of these murders, aren't you?

A. Yes.

Q. You're not involved in them at all, were you?

A. No sir, I didn't know nothing about this.[27]

At trial, as I cross-examined her, Willie Mae Lee accused me of threatening her with jail. I did the questioning.

Q. Do you remember me asking, taking your deposition in Panama City, in—on February 2, 1968, in which I was present, Mr. Rosen was present, do you remember that?

A. Yes, I remember that.

Q. Mr. Adams was present, State Attorney of this circuit, remember that?

A. That was the time you left a subpoena and them as going to put me in jail because you left the subpoena with my brother-in-law, I didn't have to go.[28]

After I heard that answer I lost my temper, which I shouldn't have done. But she really got to me with all her lying. I exploded, which I'm sure shocked everyone:

You're lying. Willie Mae, now you know that's a lie.

Mr. Jones. Now he just called the witness a liar.

The Court. Gentlemen, you—yes, you are.

Mr. Hubbart. I certainly am.

The Court. It's improper.

Mr. Jones. Wait a minute.

Mr. Hubbart. I'm not going to stand by and see a witness call me a liar.

The Court. She didn't call you a liar, you called her one.

Mr. Hubbart. She said that I threatened her.[29]

There was a pause and everyone looked at Willie Mae Lee. She then stammered:

The Witness. I didn't tell you.

Mr. Hubbart. You tell me what you accused me of.

The Witness. I won't answer a question you ask me, you can lock me up judge.[30]

I saw no point in pursuing the subject, as it was obvious I had made no such threat. I moved on to impeaching her with her deposition testimony and to her retraction statement to the state attorney.

Here is her explanation for why she retracted all her testimony against Pitts and Lee in her sworn statement to J. Frank Adams and S. R. DeWitt in February 1968.

> Yes, I recall them and the reason why I said it because Mr. DeWitt had went down south and came back and said this man had killed them and I had been telling them for years and years that who did it and when this man said he did it, and he know he was lying when he said he did it, didn't nobody want to believe me because I'm black, cause my own people my black people really.[31]

At least this time she didn't blame Gene Miller. She just rambled on, portraying herself as a victim.

Finally, I ended my cross-examination on a softer note in which Willie Mae Lee seemed to agree—at least it seemed to me—that she really knew nothing about this case. I may have caught her, I think, in a moment of truth.

> Q. You really don't know anything about this case, do you, Miss Lee?
> A. Well, that's for me to know and for you to find out, cause don't but three people really know what happened, that's me, Freddie and Wilbert, you were probably in Miami trying to hurt somebody's feelings.
> Q. You find all this trouble for nothing, haven't you?
> The Court. I think that's an unnecessary question.
> Mr. Hubbart. You just want people to leave you alone, don't you, isn't that right?
> A. That's right.
> Mr. Hubbart. No further questions.[32]

In the end, she was right. Willie Mae Lee, Freddie Pitts, and Wilbert Lee all knew what happened that night—they all knew they knew nothing of the Floyd-Burkett murders.

*   *   *

Leo Jones ended his case on a high note for the state. Over our objections, he introduced the confessions that Pitts and Lee had made at the August 28, 1963, trial. I renewed our motion to suppress these confessions and the motion was again denied.[33] Mrs. Betty Owens, the court reporter at the 1963 trial, was called to the witness stand, and she read the in-court confessions of Pitts and Lee for the jury.[34] The denial of our motion to suppress these confessions would be one of our major points for appeal.

Besides being involuntary as the product of a reign of terror, those confessions were also entirely false—pure "gibberish," as Warren Holmes would call them. They were uncorroborated by any physical evidence in the case and were contradicted by other physical evidence. Nonetheless, I am certain that those confessions had a devastating impact on the jury.

After Mrs. Owens had completed her testimony and stepped down from the witness stand, Leo Jones announced before the jury: "If the Court please, the state now rests its case."[35] It was Friday, March 10, 1972, around noon. We had not anticipated that the state's case would conclude so soon and we had no defense witnesses available to testify that day. So Judge Smith excused the jury to return to their rooms at the Holiday Inn for the weekend.

> Ladies and Gentlemen, this case has moved along a little faster than the attorneys anticipated . . . so I'm going to shortly recess until Monday at nine o'clock. I know it's going to be a long weekend for you at that motel. I hope that you are as comfortable as you possibly can be and that you have somebody in your group that's a good entertainer. You are excused until Monday morning at nine o'clock and you may retire from the courtroom at this time. Thank you very much.[36]

Everything that happened after the jury left the courtroom was anticlimactic. I made a routine motion for a mistrial and a motion for judgment of acquittal based on various legal grounds. These motions were denied. Court was then adjourned and we retired to our rooms at the Holiday Inn. We avoided all contact with the twelve jurors who were staying at the same motel in a secluded area. And we used the weekend to relax and to plan our strategy for presenting our defense case in court the following Monday morning.

26

The Defense Case

On Monday, March 13, 1972, at 9:00 a.m., Irwin Block and I walked into the Marianna courtroom eager to present our defense case. We had planned the sequence we would use to call our witnesses, and our colleague, Maurice Rosen, had made the travel arrangements so the witnesses would appear when we needed them. We sat down at counsel table with our clients, unpacked our briefcases, and briefly conferred with one another.

Our adversaries, Leo Jones, and his assistant, Paul Griffith, were seated at their counsel table, no doubt pleased at the way the case had gone so far for the state. As usual, the spectator section was packed, every seat taken.

Judge Smith soon entered the courtroom with his black robes flowing, and everyone in the courtroom stood until the judge was seated. "Good morning," the judge said. "Good morning," all the lawyers replied.[1]

Irwin Block then spoke:

> If the Court please, for the purpose of the record, I will be presenting the defense on behalf of the defendant Freddie Pitts, all witnesses in evidence will be on behalf of the defendant Freddie Lee Pitts. Can we have as a standard understanding, it's not necessary for me to make the same announcement? Each time I call a witness to introduce?
> The Court. That'll be all right.[2]

Although all our witnesses would benefit both Pitts and Lee, by technically calling them only on behalf of the defendant Pitts, we gained a procedural advantage that I will explain in the next chapter. I was permitted to question each witness after Block had completed his examination but would not be formally calling any witness other than my client, Wilbert Lee. I would also not be formally offering any physical exhibits in evidence, leaving that duty to Irwin Block.

Over the next two days of trial proceedings, three basic lines of defense were presented to the jury:

- First, we attempted to show that Curtis Adams had murdered Grover Floyd and Jesse Burkett and that he also committed a remarkably similar gas station holdup, kidnapping, and murder in Fort Lauderdale, sixteen days after the murders of Floyd-Burkett murders.
- Second, we attempted to establish that Pitts and Lee were far removed from the place and time of the Floyd-Burkett murders and had no knowledge of those crimes.
- Third, we attempted to show that Pitts and Lee's confessions to the police and in court, like Willie Mae Lee's confessions, were the product of a reign of terror that Pitts and Lee had been subjected to during the month of August 1963 and that all of those confessions were involuntary and false.

Our first defense, however, was by far our most important one—that Curtis Adams was the real murderer in this case. We had a great deal of evidence establishing Adams's guilt, as outlined in chapter 13. I sat at counsel table nervous about this prospect, hoping against hope that we could persuade Judge Smith to let this evidence in, although I knew it was going to be an uphill struggle.

As I held my breath, Irwin Block called Warren Holmes to the witness stand to introduce our most persuasive piece of evidence: the dramatic tape-recorded confession to the Floyd-Burkett murders that Curtis Adams had made to Holmes in December 1966 at the Broward County Jail. I was convinced that if the jury could hear that one-and-a-half-hour confession, we had a fighting chance of hanging the jury. We had to get that tape in evidence.

But, as expected, Leo Jones asked that the jury be excused and objected to the introduction of that confession. He argued that the confession was "an out of court statement, not subject to cross-examination" and was "inadmissible under the hearsay rule and many other rules."[3] I then responded with a lengthy legal argument and submitted a written memorandum of law to Judge Smith in support of our position.

Our basic argument was that although the taped confession was a hearsay statement, it was admissible as a legal exception to the rule barring hearsay evidence: namely, the declaration against interest exception. Under this exception, if a person who is not a party to the case—such as Curtis Adams in this instance—has made an out-of-court statement against his or her own interest, the declaration is admissible in evidence. The theory underlying this exception is that ordinarily people don't made statements against their own interest unless they are true. The cases in Florida, however, had applied this exception only to declarations against the declarant's proprietary or financial interest.[4]

I argued that the exception should be extended to include a declaration against a person's penal interest, such as Adams's confession to first-degree murder. I cited a number of decisions by courts that had reached this result in California, New York, Hawaii, Idaho, New Jersey, Arizona, Maryland, Virginia, Missouri, Illinois, Texas, South Carolina, and Minnesota and urged Judge Smith to follow those cases.[5]

Leo Jones summarily dismissed this argument. He said that Adams's taped confession was *not* a declaration against interest because it "was not an admission against these defendants' interest, penal, pecuniary or otherwise" and therefore had to be "thrown out the window."[6] But Jones misunderstood this exception. A declaration against interest is by definition a declaration against the *declarant's* interest, not the criminal defendant's interest.

Judge Smith was not impressed. He ruled: "I don't think your tape is admissible as direct evidence, now you can put Curtis Adams on the stand and ask him about the tape and what he says and so forth, but I think you're going to have to put Curtis Adams on the stand."[7] He added, "I don't think the fact that [the taped confession] was made at the direction of a circuit judge has anything to do with it. I'm going to rule the tape inadmissible at the present time."[8]

My heart sank when I heard this ruling. If we couldn't get that tape in evidence, the most compelling evidence we had, I knew we weren't going to get in any other of our Curtis Adams evidence. But Block plowed ahead anyway, hoping we could get the judge to change his mind.

Block called Curtis Adams as the next defense witness and asked the court to treat Adams as a court witness so both sides could cross-examine him. Judge Smith agreed. Terry Furnell, Adams's lawyer, then stepped forward to be heard on a motion he had filed. The jury was excused for a legal argument. Furnell then presented his motion requesting that Adams be granted immunity regarding the Floyd-Burkett murders so that he could testify that he alone had committed those murders. Although the state steadfastly maintained throughout this case that it had no intention of ever prosecuting Curtis Adams for the murders, Leo Jones took the position that the state would not grant Adams immunity for these murders. Given that refusal, Judge Smith denied Adams's motion for immunity.[9]

But Block had one last gambit to play. The jury was returned to the courtroom and Curtis Adams took the witness stand. In a moment of high drama, Irwin Block asked Curtis Adams twenty-two questions concerning Adams's involvement in the Floyd-Burkett murders in Port St. Joe and the Floyd McFarland murder in Fort Lauderdale. In response to each question, Adams took the Fifth Amendment. Here is a portion of this line of questioning:

Q. Mr. Adams, did you rob and kill Jessie [*sic*] Burkett and Grover Floyd, Jr.?
A. I refuse to answer the question on the grounds that it might tend to incriminate me.

* * *

Q. Did you during the early morning or late night hours of August 16, 1963, rob and kill Floyd McFarlin [*sic*] in Broward County, Florida?
A. I refuse to answer the question on the grounds that it might tend to incriminate me.

* * *

Q. Did you, sir, while in Broward County, Florida, give a tape recorded statement with reference to the murder of Jessie [*sic*] Burkett and Grover Floyd, Jr. to Warren Holmes?
A. I refuse to answer the question on the grounds that it might tend to incriminate me.[10]

The jury was then excused, and the one-and-a-half-hour tape-recording of Curtis Adams's confession to Warren Holmes was played in open court for the judge to hear. The entire courtroom was transfixed at Adams's ghastly descriptions of the murders he had committed (see chapter 13).[11]
At the conclusion of the tape, Block asked:

Mr. Adams, is that your voice?
The Witness. I refuse to answer the question on the grounds that it might tend to incriminate me.[12]

With all of this as a backdrop, Block made one last plea to admit Curtis Adams's taped confession. On this last-ditch argument, I thought, rested the admissibility of all our Curtis Adams evidence. The usually stoic Irwin Block became emotional and gave it everything he had.

May it please Your Honor, the court has had an opportunity to hear this tape, and [I] bring to the Court's attention that Mr. Jones said that as an objection to the introduction of it, that the witness is available, the witness could be called. In truth and in fact the witness is not available: the witness has refused to testify.

Block's voice then quavered:

Your Honor has heard the tape, has heard the demeanor, has heard the voice, in the interest of fairness and justice, if I have to, I will beg—to please have this tape introduced.[13]

Judge Smith seemed moved by this sincere plea, asked Block a few questions, and then said that he would adjourn for lunch and think the matter over.

But when court was reconvened after lunch, Judge Smith stuck to his earlier ruling:

The Court. You know during the lunch hour I meditated about the admissibility of that statement and at present I'm going to hold it inadmissible because I think in the first place the state was barred from any cross-examination with reference to that statement at all, and . . . at the present time I'm going to hold it inadmissible.[14]

All was lost. There was no point in continuing to argue the point. Judge Smith didn't understand our argument. The judge was content to bar the tape from evidence simply because it was hearsay—that is, the state had had no opportunity to cross-examine it—and that, in the judge's mind, ended the matter. He saw no need to consider any exceptions to the hearsay rule, such as the one we were relying on, the declaration of interest exception. In his mind, apparently, there were no exceptions.

It was here that I yearned to have Judge Crews back as our trial judge instead of Judge Smith. Judge Crews understood the law of evidence. He would have understood our argument. I'm not sure he would have agreed with our position, but he would have given it a fair hearing.

Judge Smith's ruling held firm on this issue for the balance of the trial. Smith ruled virtually all of our evidence tending to show that Curtis Adams had murdered Grover Floyd and Jesse Burkett inadmissible as hearsay or as otherwise irrelevant. Three major items of evidence were excluded.

First, Warren Holmes was not permitted to testify to the circumstances leading up to his interrogation of Curtis Adams at the Broward County Jail or to the taking of Adams's tape-recorded confession, as outlined in chapter

13. We made a proffer of what that testimony would be, including the taped confessions, but Judge Smith denied the proffer.[15]

Second, Mary Jean Akins was not permitted to testify that Curtis Adams had confessed to her that he had committed the murders of Floyd, Burkett, and Floyd McFarland, together with the circumstances leading up to these murders. We made a proffer of what her testimony would be, but Judge Smith denied the proffer.[16]

Third, Detective Elihu Phares of the Broward County Sheriff's Office was not permitted to testify that he had taken an oral statement from Curtis Adams in which Adams confessed to the Floyd-Burkett murders and the murder of McFarland. We made a proffer of what this testimony would be and Judge Smith denied the proffer.[17]

All these proffers were made to preserve the record for appeal. To further preserve this record, I objected to the denial of all these proffers based on the following federal constitutional grounds:

> We submit that the denial of this proffer, as well as all the other evidence Mr. Block has proffered, constitutes a denial of due process of law guaranteed by . . . the Due Process Clause of the Fourteenth Amendment to the United States Constitution, in that it denies these defendants . . . their right to a fair and impartial trial by jury, as guaranteed by the Sixth Amendment, as well as the Due Process Clause of the Fourteenth Amendment to the United States Constitution, and furthermore that it denies to these defendants the right to compulsory process of witnesses guaranteed by the Sixth Amendment and the Due Process Clause of the Fourteenth Amendment.[18]

We were further prohibited from proving that Curtis Adams had committed a robbery, kidnap, and murder of Floyd McFarland in Fort Lauderdale sixteen days after the Floyd-Burkett murders. This crime was remarkably similar in modus operandi to the robbery, kidnap, and murder of Grover Floyd and Jesse Burkett and was admissible under the similar crimes rule in Florida.[19] We made a proffer of the evidence we had about this crime and Judge Smith denied the proffer.[20] I objected to the court's ruling on the same constitutional grounds I had raised about the denial of all our other evidentiary proffers regarding Curtis Adams.[21]

In the midst of this debacle, however, there were a few bright spots. We were able to get in a few hints that Curtis Adams was the real murderer in this case.

First, Curtis Adams had taken the Fifth Amendment twenty-two times before the jury about questions relating to his involvement in the Floyd-Burkett murders and the murder of Floyd McFarland. Technically, this was not evidence, but it did tend to put Adams in a bad light. Maybe that would help.

Second, we were able to get in evidence Curtis Adams's motion for immunity, which stated that if given immunity, Adams would provide testimony exonerating Pitts and Lee of the Floyd-Burkett murders. Adams had signed the motion himself and had admitted before the jury that this was his signature.[22] Again, this was no substitute for Adams's confessions, but at least it was something.

Third, Detective Elihu Phares was able to testify that he had transported Curtis Adams to Gulf County, Florida, and that Adams had led him to the exact spot in the county where the bodies of Floyd and Burkett had been discovered murdered. Phares also testified that Deputy Sheriff Wayne White had told Phares that initially Curtis Adams had been a prime suspect in the Floyd-Burkett murders because Adams was the only man in Port St. Joe with a robbery record who was capable of committing these murders.[23] This was excellent corroborating evidence to Adams's many confessions, but it was no substitute for the confessions themselves.

*　　*　　*

For our second line of defense, we presented alibi testimony on behalf of Pitts and Lee that they were elsewhere at the time and place of the Floyd-Burkett murders. Pitts testified in detail that he was in the company of Willie Mae Lee in a lover's tryst at the time of the murders.[24] Wilbert Lee testified that he was home in bed with his wife, Ella Mae Lee, at the time of the murders.[25] Ella Mae Lee gave similar alibi testimony.[26]

Leo Jones's cross-examination of Ella Mae Lee was particularly memorable. Jones attempted to impeach her with a written statement that Ella Mae Lee had given to the police in August 1963 after a week of questioning in jail. In this statement, she had retracted her earlier statement that Wilbert Lee was home in bed with her at the time of the crime. She testified at trial, however, that this statement was a lie, that the only reason she gave it was "because I was tired and I knew that was the only way they would leave me alone."[27] Wilbert Lee, she testified, had been home in bed with her at the time of murders.[28]

But Leo Jones persisted. He kept asking Ella Mae Lee over and over whether she remembered specific questions and answers in her police statement. And Ella Mae Lee consistently replied that she couldn't remember but that if she had given the answers Jones was reading, those answers were lies.

She testified: "I can't remember."[29] "I don't remember making it."[30] "If I said it, it was a lie."[31] "Look here. Wilbert did not leave the house, he came back together but he didn't leave the house."[32] "That's a lie, because Wilbert was home. I know . . . where he was, I'm not crazy. I know when somebody is home or not."[33]

Then, in an exchange I will always remember, the following transpired:

Q. All right. Now, were you asked this question and did you give this answer: "How long was Freddie Pitts, Wilbert Lee, your husband, Wilbert Lee, gone after they left the house." And didn't you give this answer: "When I really woke up I saw Wilbert standing in the house and it was eight thirty or nine o'clock that morning."
A. That's a lie, when I woke up how am I sending him [Wilbert] after sausages if I'm just waking up, I know when he is there, I woke him up to go get [the sausages].
Q. Now, did the Sheriff ask you that question and did you give that answer?
A. I don't know, they asked me so many questions, I can't recall, that's been nine years ago. How can I think of a lie that long [ago].[34]

If ever a witness was telling the truth, it was Ella Mae Lee. If ever a witness was mistreated by the police, it was Ella Mae Lee. She was arrested, she was never charged with a crime, she was questioned for a week, and she was held in jail for nearly a month without a court order until Pitts and Lee were sentenced to death. She was treated as if she had no rights at all. But she was a stellar alibi witness for Wilbert Lee.

*   *   *

Regarding the third line of our defense, namely, that Pitts and Lee's confessions were involuntary and false, our evidence, in my view, was overwhelming.

Both Pitts and Lee testified in detail about their three-week ordeal with the police and their court-appointed lawyer, Fred Turner, in August 1963. They told how Pitts had been viciously beaten by Bay County Deputy Sheriff George Kittrell; how the police had told Lee that his wife, who was in police custody, would be executed if he didn't confess; how Turner had cooperated with the police in getting Pitts and Lee to confess and plead guilty.[35]

As corroborating witnesses to the beating Pitts had received, Block called army CID investigators Donald Hoag and Bruce Potts,[36] Dorothy Martin,[37] Henry Hogue,[38] and Ella Mae Lee,[39] all of whom had seen Pitts in police custody and testified to Pitts's beaten-up condition.

Leo Jones ignored the entire ordeal that the police and other authorities had put Pitts and Lee through in August 1963. All he wanted to talk about was Pitts and Lee's confessions in court on August 28, 1963, as if the terror had magically ended there when their own lawyer, acting like a prosecutor, had put them on the witness stand with directions to confess.

In particular, Jones challenged Wilbert Lee's testimony about why he had been forced to give his courtroom confession. Lee may have looked like easy pickings, a witness who could be easily intimidated, but Jones soon learned that Wilbert Lee was not a man to be trifled with.

Here is Jones's cross-examination of Wilbert Lee:

Q. If you remember hearing your statement read right here in the court the other day that you gave in Wewahitchka on August 28, 1963, you remember hearing it read?
A. Yes, sir.
Q. Was it in open court like it is now?
A. Yes, sir.
Q. Was there spectators in the room?
A. Yes, sir.
Q. Was Mr. Turner sitting at a table with you?
A. Yes, sir.
Q. Was there a circuit judge sitting up there on the bench?
A. Correct, sir.
Q. And didn't you tell the same story that was read from that witness stand the other day?
A. Yes, sir.

Jones then launched into a loud and sarcastic line of questions. In response, Wilbert Lee almost came off the witness stand with fire and fury.

Q. And it's your testimony that you were able to memorize it so well from what Doc Daffin and these people told you that you were able to testify to it exactly like Willie Mae told it here the other day?

A. As I stated before, it was given to me just like giving a kid a speech—you hear it every day, hour after hour and hour after hour and all through the night. They changed shifts on me running the same thing and if they tell it so many times and telling me I'm supposed to say it, that "if you don't, we are going to shave the hair off your wife's head."

Mr. Jones, if you had been in my position, you'd had to get up there and said the same thing in front of the jury to save your wife's life and your own self too.

Q. So you told the jury that you had helped, that you had helped robbed and murdered two men to keep your wife's head from being shaved?

A. From being electrocuted, and I was told by the law enforcement and Mr. Daffin and the rest of them around there.

Q. Are you swearing to this jury that you thought in your own mind that M. J. "Doc" Daffin was going to electrocute your wife? . . .

A. I don't know which one of those men would have done it. I don't know who would have done it, but it was told to me and I'd been slapped up side of my head and around like that—let me tell you something, if you were in my position and you'd had to live with these people, Mr. Jones, you'd saved your life and your wife's life, if you had been in my position. . . . But it was all false and untrue.[40]

I sat at counsel table in absolute awe at how well this polite young man had stood up for his rights and defended himself that day. It was one of the most thrilling moments of the entire case.

After two days of defense testimony and after various written statements had been received in evidence, Irwin Block and I formally rested our case.[41] In rebuttal, Leo Jones placed in evidence Ella Mae Lee's police statement and then rested his case.[42] Jones called no witnesses in rebuttal. After Judge Smith denied certain routine defense motions, court was adjourned for the day. The trial was rapidly moving to a conclusion.

27

The Final Arguments

On March 15, 1972, the Pitts-Lee jury trial in Marianna finally came to an end. That morning at 8:30, Judge Smith held a brief conference in his chambers with counsel from both sides, during which he went over the instructions on the law that he was going to give to the jury. It was a routine proceeding and nothing of any great moment occurred. Both sides had an opportunity to offer proposed jury instructions and object, if necessary, to any of the judge's proposed instructions.

When the conference ended, we all reassembled in the courtroom and the jury was summoned for the final arguments of counsel. The courtroom was filled to capacity with spectators. The place fairly bulged with people, both seated and standing.

Under Florida law at that time, a criminal defendant who offered no evidence other than his own testimony was entitled to the last argument before the jury.[1] In representing Wilbert Lee, I had offered no evidence other than Lee's own testimony and therefore I had the legal right to the last argument before the jury. Irwin Block, who represented Freddie Pitts, had formally called all our witnesses and offered all our physical exhibits solely on behalf of Pitts. Irwin and I had planned it that way, although in the end, having the final say before the jury in this case meant very little. Nonetheless, the order of final arguments as directed by Judge Smith was Hubbart—Jones—Block—Jones—Hubbart.

As I got into my opening argument, which lasted about thirty minutes, I could tell I was not making much headway with any of the jurors. I saw no smiles from anyone, no nods of the head in agreement, no rapt attention, only polite but blank stares. I found myself referring too much to my notes and that added to my discomfort. As a consequence, the argument was not one of my best in terms of delivery. Substantively, however, I thought the argument was well organized, comprehensive, and worthy of serious consideration.

After some introductory remarks, I began with a bedrock principle of American jurisprudence. I said that the judge would instruct the jury that the defendants under the law are presumed innocent of the charges against them, that they enter the courtroom clothed with the presumption of innocence, and that this presumption abides and continues with the defendants throughout the trial—unless and until the state overcomes that presumption and establishes beyond and to the exclusion of every reasonable doubt and to a moral certainty that these defendants, and no one else, committed the charged crimes.[2]

I continued:

> Now with that in mind, ladies and gentlemen, let's make a systematic analysis of the case for the prosecution and let's see whether or not the prosecution has established beyond and to the exclusion of a reasonable doubt and to a moral certainty that these defendants and no one else committed this crime—because I submit they have not.
>
> I think you will agree with me, after hearing the testimony in this case, that the case for the prosecution rises or falls on the testimony of first, Willie Mae Lee, and secondly, the statements of the defendants in court.[3]

The state had presented nothing else. No physical or forensic evidence linking the defendants to the Floyd-Burkett murders was ever introduced, despite determined efforts by the police to find such evidence.

> Ladies and gentlemen, with two sheriff's offices, separate sheriff's offices, investigating this case, literally around the clock, with all kinds of deputies involved, with the Florida Sheriffs Bureau involved, Mr. James Halligan and Mr. James Kelly . . . making crime scene searches and fingerprints, et cetera. With all the extensive investigation, there isn't the first piece of physical evidence presented to you that these defendants committed this crime.[4]

I then listed the forensic evidence that was lacking in this case.

- No murder weapon
- No proceeds of the robbery of the Mo Jo station
- No tire jack allegedly used to "flam" the deceased Grover Floyd

- No fingerprints of the deceased, Floyd or Burkett, in Pitts's car, the car the state claimed the defendants used to take the deceased to the murder scene in the country
- No fingerprints of the defendants on the cash register of the Mo Jo station where money and a gun was stolen from the register
- No tire tracks at the murder scene matching the tires on the defendant Pitts's car
- No clothing of the defendants [which the police seized] with blood on it or otherwise linking the defendants to the murder scene.

I then turned my attention to the two items of evidence the state did present to the jury—Pitts and Lee's statements in court and Willie Mae Lee's statements. I reviewed the testimony in the case establishing that the defendants' statements were the product of the relentless intimidation that the police and their own lawyer, Fred Turner, had put Pitts and Lee through in August 1963 and emphasized that those statements were entirely coerced, false, and unworthy of belief.[5]

I turned to Freddie Pitts's testimony, detailing how he was brutally beaten with a blackjack by Bay County Deputy Sheriff George Kittrell during an all-night ride in a police car on August 2, 1963, in a futile effort to find the bodies of Floyd and Burkett. Gulf County Deputy Sheriff Wayne White had driven the police car during this ride and Kittrell had repeatedly beaten Pitts in the back seat as Pitts went in and out of consciousness and lost track of time.[6]

I then referred to the testimony of the many witnesses who had seen Pitts in police custody during this time, all of whom said that Pitts had been badly beaten. These witnesses included the two independent army CID investigators, Bruce Potts and Donald Hoag; Dorothy Martin, Ella Mae Lee's sister; and Henry Hogue, the elderly gentleman who gave Freddie Pitts and Willie Mae Lee a push at Kenny's Quarters.[7]

I then emphasized that the state had not contradicted any of this evidence:

Where is George Kittrell? They could have called George Kittrell to the stand to deny this if it was not true. They had a right at the end of our case to present rebuttal testimony. They haven't called George Kittrell to the stand, because he beat Freddie Pitts, and you know it.

They could have called Wayne White back. He was driving that car, and he [Jones] hasn't given you any police officer [to testify] that they didn't mistreat this man, [because] they did.[8]

I next discussed the testimony of the second defendant, Wilbert Lee, and explained that he, too, had been mistreated by the police.

> The Defendant Lee took the stand and testified that they kept him up all night on August the sixth questioning him from three o'clock in the afternoon until eight o'clock the next morning, sixteen straight hours. . . . . They bring down Ella Mae Lee his wife . . . who they have held in custody for an entire month. She starts crying, hysterically, and one can imagine the emotions going through that room. "Take her out of the room," they said. And they tell him, "We're going to shave the hair off your wife and electrocute her."
>
> And [the state] did not [offer] the first piece of police testimony to deny it because it is true, Ladies and Gentlemen.[9]

But the terror did not end with the confessions to the police. It continued with the court appointment of Fred Turner, who was supposed to represent the defendants but instead acted like a prosecutor. According to Pitts and Lee's testimony, Turner cooperated with the police in their investigation. He urged them to repeat their confessions to the police, which they did. And when they got to court, he told them to take the witness stand and repeat those confessions once again, which they did. He told them that this was the only way he could save their lives. I continued:

> They don't have a friend in the world. They haven't got any money or influence, nothing. Do you think for one minute that if these people had had the money or influence or power they'd be in death row for the last six and [a] half years? Of course not. They didn't have anybody but Fred Turner. Fred Turner sold them down the river.
>
> Did the State, when they had an opportunity, call Fred Turner to the stand to present any testimony that that's not true? They didn't present Fred Turner and you know why, because these men are telling the truth.
>
> * * *
>
> So Ladies and Gentlemen, it's uncontradicted before you that these defendants were physically mistreated by the police and that Fred Turner participated in selling these defendants down the river and you don't have the first piece of evidence to contradict it, either from Fred Turner, or Wayne White or from George Kittrell.[10]

My argument was solid, but unfortunately it was not registering with this jury. No one was hanging on my every word. Undaunted, I argued that

the known physical evidence in the case contradicted the defendants' statements in material respects and that rendered the statements entirely false. I
noted three glaring contradictions:

First, both statements say that Lee struck Grover Floyd, presumably in
the head, with a tire jack. Yet the autopsy reports, which we introduced in
evidence, showed no skull injuries to Floyd.[11]

Second, both statements say that Pitts shot Floyd and Burkett at point-
blank range. Lee's statement adds that Pitts fired four shots. Yet the autopsy
reports show only *one* bullet wound to the head of each victim.[12]

Third, both statements say that Pitts shot both Floyd and Burkett while
the victims were standing erect. Yet Gulf County Deputy Sheriff James
Graves testified that he found the dead bodies in a wooded area, stretched
out head to head in a V position.[13] I argued that "the chances were one in a
million" that both bodies could have landed on the ground together in such
a neat position.[14]

I then turned my attention to the remaining item of the state's case, the
many statements of Willie Mae Lee:

> In February of 1968, the cold hard facts remain, which try as they
> may, the State can never erase. Willie Mae Lee came before the State
> Attorney, not a defense lawyer, not a defense investigator, not a de-
> fense investigation, came before the State Attorney of this Circuit,
> Mr. J. Frank Adams. . . . [She was] placed under oath by Mr. Adams,
> and questioned by Mr. S.R. DeWitt, an investigator for the Attorney
> General's Office. She wasn't being harassed by anyone, nobody was
> bothering her.[15]

I then quoted at length from Willie Mae Lee's sworn statement in which
she repudiated all her past testimony and statements about Pitts and
Lee and said that she had no knowledge of the murders of Floyd and Burkett.[16] I also relied on three other statements by this witness: (1) Willie Mae
Lee's anguished statement to Warren Holmes in January 1967 at Ms. Lee's
home that "I've been waiting three years to tell the truth about this case;"[17]
(2) Willie Mae Lee's deposition testimony in February 1968 in which she
stated that she was totally innocent of the murders of Floyd and Burkett
and that she "didn't know nothing" about the case;[18] and (3) Willie Mae
Lee's statement under oath to State Attorney J. Frank Adams in August
1963 that Lambson Smith, not Wilbert Lee, was one of the two murderers
in this case.[19]

I asked the jury: "Would you make a decision in your own life, much less the life of someone else, on the word of that witness. Think about that. You have the [lives] of two men in your hands."[20] But no one on the jury seemed much interested.

I covered many other aspects of this case, including Wilbert Lee's alibi that he was home in bed with his wife at the time of the murders and Pitts and Lee's complete cooperation with the police in the few days before they were arrested. I tried to argue that Curtis Adams was the real murderer in this case, but because of Judge Smith's rulings I was deprived of all the major evidence we had to prove it. All I had were bits and pieces: Adams's signed motion for immunity, Adams's refusal to testify by taking the Fifth Amendment before the jury (which really wasn't evidence), Wayne White's admission that initially Adams was the "prime suspect" in the case, and Adams's ability to lead Broward County police to the exact spot in the woods where the bodies of Floyd and Burkett had been found. I ended by asking the jury for a verdict of not guilty.[21]

* * *

The court took a ten-minute recess, then Leo Jones stood before the jury and delivered his opening argument. Unlike the indifferent response I had gotten, the jury listened in rapt attention to Jones's argument. After a few introductory remarks, Jones came right to the point. He made an unabashed us-against-them argument that blatantly appealed to white southern prejudice against outsiders like me and Irwin Block. The argument could not have been more inflammatory and would constitute one of our major points for appeal.

This is what Jones argued:

Let me tell you this. I'm proud also to stand before a jury and defend what seems to be the course nowadays in America and that's to defend our system of justice.

I think counsel made me more proud to stand before you as a State Attorney and attempt to defend our system which every day in the world is being torn down or attempted to be torn down. As you've heard today.

The argument here which you have heard today sums up in about three words or four, it sums up, really isn't what he's saying—*that the Panhandle is bad.*

Mr. Block. Your Honor, that is objected to, we never said that. That's totally improper.

Mr. Hubbart. I move for a mistrial.
The Court. Motion for mistrial denied.

Jones continued unabated with this line of argument over our continuous objections. These objections and motions were legally required in order to preserve for appeal our point that Jones was committing reversible error with his inflammatory final argument. The jurors, however, were giving Jones their undivided attention.

That all the police, now just follow me and see if this isn't the sum and substance of their argument, all the police are bad.

Recall the opening statement that was made last Wednesday or Thursday. Recall the statement that you just heard and really analyze and what I'm saying is not fair then you think about it. All the police are bad, isn't this what [the CID officers] said, the biggest thing they had to say about Mr. White was the language he used.

Then kind of by inference the State Attorney is bad because all these number of years Mr. Adams has known just who it was, but he was just going to prosecute these two men and tuck them safely in death row.

Now, really what we're doing is baring the bones of what they are saying, why you should go back there and turn them loose.

Then they're saying that both of the attorneys are bad. David Carl Gaskin and Fred Turner were bad, and then they come right along down the line and they say the Judge is bad.

Mr. Hubbart. Your Honor, I object to that and move for a mistrial, there is absolutely no basis for that comment.

The Court. Motion for mistrial is denied.

Mr. Jones. By inference and think about it, they're saying Pitts and Lee were beat, beat, beat and yet he went before Judge Husband; he went before Judge Fitzpatrick four different times, and he finally went into open court and no judge and nobody else has done anything about it.

Isn't this the sum and substance of the whole argument?

And during about 15 minutes of [Hubbart's] argument, Leo Jones said this, Leo Jones said that, Leo Jones said this, let me tell you, Leo Jones is not perfect not by a far cry, but Leo Jones is not on trial. Judge Fitzpatrick is not on trial, Judge Husband is not on trial, Mr. Turner is not on trial, but you see this is the mode and method today, all police are bad, the system of justice is bad, judges are bad.

Gene Miller reported that the number twelve juror, A. J. Holley, nodded his head in agreement to this argument.[22] The rest of jury had their eyes glued on Jones. I vigorously objected.

> Mr. Hubbart. I'm going to object and move for a mistrial, this is a highly improper mischaracterization of my argument. I never at any time made such implications. I move for a mistrial.
> The Court. The motion for mistrial is denied.

Jones continued with his inflammatory argument:

> Mr. Jones. So in effect, what it is, is let's don't try the defendants, let's try the system. . . . Let me tell you two things about this argument and of course it's the argument all over nowadays, the police are bad, the criminal he's glorified.
> Mr. Hubbart. Your Honor, I'm going to move for a mistrial. This is an effort to whip up the emotionalism in this case and not an effort to discuss the facts and I move for a mistrial.
> The Court. Motion for mistrial is denied.[23]

During this highly emotional encounter, Judge Smith's face was flushed red with the strain of the trial. I was in full fighting form and relished this back and forth with Jones. Irwin Block was in the same mode. But I also feared that Jones's argument was terribly persuasive with this jury. Jones was in his element and he was at the peak of his down-home oratorical skills.

But if ever there was an improper, inflammatory, overreaching prosecutorial argument, this was it. We defense counsel never claimed that the entire Florida Panhandle was bad, that all the police were bad, that all the judges were bad, or that the entire system of justice was bad. Nor were we part of an alleged effort to upset the system of law and order in the country. That was pure demagoguery on Jones's part.

We were attacking certain Gulf and Bay County police officers who had physically abused Pitts and Lee. We were attacking Pitts and Lee's court-appointed lawyer for cooperating with the police in getting the defendants to confess in court and plead guilty. And we had a mountain of evidence to support our position.

But Leo Jones brushed all of that aside. He saw no need to call as rebuttal witnesses George Kittrell, Wayne White, Fred Turner, or any of the police officers who had abused Pitts and Lee. According to Jones, that would have been a total waste of the jury's time.

> Now the question comes up again, and I think it's important that we respond to it, why didn't you call this witness, why didn't we call George Kittrell . . . why didn't we call some of the other people that may have been around the jail, why didn't you call this and the other. It comes a point to where, as a trial lawyer or a State Attorney, you decide that to keep on putting on witnesses and putting on witnesses and putting on witnesses burdens the jury.
> * * *
>
> You know you could stand here and put on witnesses until the cows come home and you can say, "Ya, ya this, and ya that, and ya that," just keep right on and right on ad infinitum of the people that may have seen or may have done a lot of things.[24]

Jones had what he wanted to in order to obtain convictions. Why should he bother the jury with evidence that disputed our statements that Pitts and Lee had been physically abused and terrorized for the entire month of August 1963 both in and out of court? And why burden the jury by trying to explain the utter lack of forensic evidence in this case? Our whole case, in Jones's view, was a disgraceful attack on the Florida Panhandle, and it was not worth calling a single witness to dispute our statements. Jones no doubt was certain that this all-white southern jury would agree.

Jones also rambled on at great length about the trial testimony, discussed in excruciating detail the charges against the defendants and the judge's instructions on the law, praised Willie Mae Lee for being "a marvelous person,"[25] argued that the defendants' statements in court were voluntary and true, and tried to answer some of our positions. His closing argument filled sixty-two pages of trial transcript.[26] It was a long and exhausting experience that Jones seemed to apologize for as he ended: "Thank you and I hope I haven't overstayed my welcome but I figured it had to be said."[27]

* * *

After the court took a short lunch break, Irwin Block gave his final argument to the jury. He analyzed the evidence in detail, much as I had. But his most powerful arguments came when he answered Leo Jones's inflammatory attack against us as defense counsel. In fact, I had never seen Irwin so emotional in court as he poured out his heart in a case that meant so much to him:

Now, I take personal offense at being told that I am attacking the Panhandle, that I am attacking law enforcement. I did my best to see that a law enforcement officer would be on this jury to consult with you and I am going to attack law enforcement?[28] I worked many years with law enforcement and Mr. Jones knows it.

* * *

You've heard insinuations about Gene Miller, the *Miami Herald,* me, Warren Holmes. Ladies and Gentlemen, in 1968, Phil Hubbart, a friend of mine, came to see me about this case and I'm here for the same reason that Warren Holmes told you that he got involved, to prevent a miscarriage of justice.

I haven't been paid one cent, and I will not be paid one cent and I will not permit this so long as I am a lawyer under oath to go on. Not only haven't I been paid but it's cost me a pretty penny and it is my duty under my oath as a lawyer to come here and represent these people and tell you what the facts and the evidence is.[29]

* * *

As I told you when I interrogated you, I'm not asking you to change any opinions about the way you live, I'm from the old school. I don't go for many of these new things either. When I was seventeen, I enlisted. I didn't try to hide. I believe in God, and I'm upset over this case and you have seen me upset during the course of it and I was so upset last night that I didn't know what to do and when people came in to see me what I was doing, I was embarrassed. I was reading the Bible, trying to calm myself down.

How could this happen today? They talk about Willie Mae Lee and an outstanding young lady for Mr. Jones, a tormented soul, and I saw it last night as I looked and it said, "The truth will make you free," but she's not free because she's not telling the truth. She's tormented, she's owned body and soul.[30]

* * *

They say we're attacking the Panhandle, we're attacking law enforcement, I say they're desecrating my flag by this kind of case. I take great pride. I remember how I use to stand when stationed in Washington in Marine barracks and watch them raise the flag and I fight for my country and I fight for its system of justice. And they cannot accuse me of being insincere about this.[31]

* * *

We have an excellent relationship with [Jackson County] Sheriff

Gause and all his officers. We think well of them and we feel they think well of us. And I ask you not to be carried into the snake pit of passion and prejudice, not to permit the words of attack upon the Panhandle, no one has attacked the Panhandle.[32]

Irwin Block ended his argument with an eloquent plea. He touched the stars with this magnificent conclusion:

Can you imagine what has been going on in the minds of these two defendants on death row for a crime they did not commit? Do you know what torture that is? Can you imagine yourself in death row for a crime you did not commit, crying out, crying out, "Help" and no one listens.

We don't ask for compassion, we don't ask for sympathy, we ask for justice. Justice under the law, justice under our Constitution. . . . Ladies and Gentlemen, Freddie Pitts and Wilbert Lee are innocent.[33]

*   *   *

Leo Jones was the next to speak before the jury. He came roaring back with his old reliable us-against-them argument and once again argued that to acquit the defendants would be to indict the entire system of justice in Gulf and Bay Counties. His syntax may have been mixed, but his message was clear:

Now, let me, I believe we're right to the crux of this thing, they said that if you don't acquit these men or if you acquit these men, you can strike a blow for justice and a blow for right and a blow for this. On the basis of what they proved, on the basis of what they alleged, and only alleged, God help, if on that basis this jury would bring back a verdict of innocence. *The only thing you wouldn't do is to put a technical indictment on Judge Fitzpatrick, Judge Husband, Mr. Turner, and every law enforcement official in Bay and Gulf County,* because this is all—
Mr. Hubbart. I want to note our continuing objection to this highly inflammatory argument, they have no basis whatever which is highly improper, and I move for a mistrial.
The Court. Motion for mistrial is denied.
* * *
Mr. Jones. Your verdict is going to be an honest conscientious verdict on whether or not these men are guilty, but the last argument that was

made to you to say you can strike a blow for America and justice by freeing these two men.

You see how passion, because when you turn it around, if you quote it the other way on the basis of the allegations they've made against the court officials, the sheriff, the investigators, everybody else, turn it around what your verdict is done is indicted all of Bay and Gulf County.

Well that's not right, your verdict is going to be an honest, conscientious verdict from your heart.[34]

I followed as the last speaker. I began with the only argument I had made that day that might have given the jury some pause. I had the jury's attention, and the entire courtroom seem to come to a standstill:

I agree entirely with Mr. Jones that this case should not be decided on emotion nor on passion, it should be decided on the facts and on the evidence that you have before you and you know, throughout the entire argument, Mr. Jones, he has never once, not once, mentioned to you the sworn testimony of Willie Mae Lee before the State Attorney in 1968 in which she said these defendants are innocent. Not once did he comment on it.

Five years from now can the State, can Mr. Jones guarantee you that Willie Mae Lee won't come in again and say before the state attorney under oath: "What I told that jury in Marianna in 1972 was a lie." She's done it before, are you going to make an important decision in the life, in the very life of two other people on the word of a witness like that?

Not once has Mr. Jones seen fit to discuss the most important piece of evidence relating to Willie Mae Lee in this case.[35]

But in the end, who were we kidding? Nothing Irwin Block and I said that day had much to do with the outcome. In the battle of the final arguments, Jones had beaten us hands down before an all-white jury with his inflammatory but highly effective us-against-them argument. We were easy pickings for Jones with this jury, and he made the most of it.

Irwin Block and I, Pitts and Lee, and the entire defense team braced for the worst, which came swiftly that day after Judge Smith had instructed the jury on the law.

28

The Trial Concludes

After the final arguments of counsel, Judge Smith took a ten-minute recess. He then returned to the courtroom and announced:

> Ladies and Gentlemen of the jury, you have heard the evidence and the arguments of counsel. It remains for the Court to give you the law on the charge to which you are to apply the facts as you find them from the evidence. Under the law, I am required to read the charge rather than speak extemporaneously, so I shall proceed.[1]

The next twenty-two pages of trial transcript contain the prepared written instructions on the law that the judge read to the jury. The jurors gave the judge their rapt attention, and everyone else in the courtroom remained in respectful silence. The lawyers had copies of these instructions and followed along as the judge read them.

I always had my doubts about whether a jury understood or could follow a lot of the complicated jury instructions given in criminal cases. This was particularly true in this case in view of the adverse pretrial publicity about this case that had permeated Jackson County over the past six-and-a-half years. The judge began with an instruction that I knew the jury could not possibly follow.

> You are to decide this case solely on the evidence presented in the courtroom. You must completely disregard any press, television or radio reports which you may have read seen or heard. Such reports are not evidence and you should not be influenced by such publicity.[2]

There were other instructions the jury would have great difficulty following. One of the more problematic was this one:

> The defendant in every criminal case is presumed to be innocent, and such presumption remains and abides with him throughout every

stage of the trial unless and until the State has proven his guilt to your satisfaction by competent evidence to the exclusion of and beyond every reasonable doubt. If any one of the material allegations of the indictment is not so proven, you must give him the benefit of the doubt and acquit him.

The burden of proving the defendant guilty beyond a reasonable doubt rests upon the State. This burden never shifts throughout the trial. The law does not require the defendants to prove any material fact, either by guess or speculation or by conjecture, suspicion, or by a mere preponderance of the evidence.[3]

As a practical matter, however, the jurors almost certainly could not presume Pitts and Lee to be innocent of the Floyd-Burkett murders. Nor could they follow the instruction that the defendants were not required to prove their innocence. The jury had been exposed to too much adverse publicity to indulge in such legal fictions. Quite to the contrary, many of the jurors no doubt wanted the defendants to prove their innocence.

After Judge Smith read the two grand jury indictments charging Pitts and Lee with first-degree murder, he told the jury something else that the jurors would find hard to follow:

The indictment is no evidence of the defendant's guilt. It is merely the formal manner by which the State accuses persons of crimes in order to bring them to trial. The jury must not be prejudiced against defendants because an indictment has been returned against them, and must not consider this as any evidence of guilt.[4]

But, of course, in the real world rather than the world of legal fancy, this jury could not possibly disregard the indictment as no evidence of guilt. Their friends and neighbors in this small local community had indicted Pitts and Lee for murder, and that, no doubt, weighed heavily on the jurors' minds. In fact, no juror, in my view, could possibly think they could acquit these defendants and return to their community without being regarded as outright pariahs.

We nonetheless clung to the one jury instruction that we thought might save Pitts and Lee from an inevitable guilty verdict:

Your decision must be unanimous, that is concurred in by all of you before it may be brought back as a verdict except, of course, however, as the Court has already instructed you, that a recommendation of mercy need be concurred in only by a majority of your number.[5]

Earlier, Judge Smith had instructed the jury:

In capital cases where a jury convicts a defendant of murder in the first degree, a majority of their number may recommend him to the mercy of the Court and such recommendation reduces the punishment from death to life imprisonment.[6]

Maybe, just maybe, we thought, one or more of the jurors might hold out for a not-guilty verdict and hang the jury—or, failing that, the jury might convict but with a recommendation of mercy. That would require the votes of at least seven jurors, a majority of the jury.

Of course, there was also the remote possibility that the jury might reach a compromise verdict of guilty of second-degree murder, which would carry a sentence of life imprisonment. As is common in first-degree murder cases, Judge Smith instructed the jury on the three lesser included offenses that are legally embraced within the main charge of first degree murder: second-degree murder, third-degree murder, and manslaughter. Each of these offenses are lesser degrees of the main charge of first-degree murder. Under these instructions, the jury was allowed to acquit the defendants of first-degree murder and convict them of one of these three lesser included crimes. But in view of the premeditated nature of the Floyd-Burkett murders, which necessarily made them first-degree murder, we thought a conviction for second-degree murder or any of the other lesser offenses was a far-fetched possibility and never had any hope for it.

Judge Smith finally concluded with these words:

Nothing I have said in these instructions or at any time during the trial is any intimation whatever as to what verdict I think you should find. The verdict is the sole and exclusive duty and solemn responsibility of you, the jury, and neither the Court nor anyone else can help you in performing that duty.

Your first duty upon retiring will be the election of a foreman to preside over your deliberations and sign your verdict when you have arrived at one.

* * *

You may now retire, ladies and gentlemen, to the consideration of your verdict.[7]

The time was 4:27 p.m. as the twelve jurors filed into the adjoining jury room to decide this case. As they did so, the prosecutors, defense counsel, and the defendants stood as a measure of respect for the jurors' position. The fate of Pitts and Lee was now in their hands.

*   *   *

At this point, I was emotionally drained and greatly relieved. My work on this trial had virtually come to an end and the enormous strain that comes from trying any serious criminal case as a lawyer was finally over. I had lost a lot of sleep during our long stay in Marianna, working and worrying about this case. I was eating much less and losing weight. Irwin Block and I had used every skill we had to prevail in the case, and now it was in the jury's hands. Irwin and I shook hands and could only hope for the best.

We all then went into a defense conference room with Freddie Pitts and Wilbert Lee, where Irwin Block explained to our clients what to expect: that it would probably be a guilty verdict and that we would appeal until they got their freedom. Pitts and Lee both were resigned to the possibility that it would be a guilty verdict. Irwin and I mused together about who the jury foreman would be. We both felt that it would be either Billie Beck or A. J. Holley.

Judge Smith soon called the lawyers into his chambers for a conference. His face was flushed and he talked slowly, breathing heavily. The strain of the trial had taken a real toll on him. He said that he had made arrangements with the Florida Highway Patrol to protect Pitts and Lee regardless of the verdict.

The judge also said he was expecting a not-guilty verdict. Block and I were astounded. Could the judge be that out of touch with what had happened at this trial? We could only conclude that the judge must have believed—which, in my view, was correct—that the evidence established a reasonable doubt concerning the defendants' guilt or innocence and that an acquittal was legally required. Perhaps the judge himself had doubts about Pitts and Lee's guilt or innocence, having heard the one-and-a-half hour recording of Curtis Adams confessing to the Floyd-Burkett murders. We would never know what was really going on in the judge's mind, but clearly he was in some turmoil.

Soon thereafter, at 6:02 p.m., someone in the hallway cried out: "They've got a verdict." The jury had been out for a little over an hour, a mere seventy-five minutes, which was a bad sign for us. If the jury was going to hang, they would have to have been out for countless hours, even days. The short deliberations and fast verdict spelled nothing but disaster for us.

Quickly, everyone reassembled in the courtroom. I steeled myself for a guilty verdict and made every effort to hide my emotions. I rehearsed in my mind what I needed to say to the court if the jury returned with a conviction. This was my usual practice when receiving a jury verdict: expect the worst and know what needs to be done immediately thereafter.

Judge Smith then addressed the spectators in the packed courtroom with this solemn warning:

> The Court. I want to announce that at this time, the returning of the verdict in any case is a solemn occasion and I don't expect the audience to show any reaction to any verdict that may be returned. Under no condition shall you show any reaction. It is a serious business, it is not anything to be hilarious about or to be sad about actually, but when the verdict is returned or these verdicts are returned, I don't want any reaction from the audience. You may call the jury.[8]

The bailiff walked to the jury room, opened the door, and led the twelve jurors into the courtroom. As he did so, all the lawyers and the defendants stood until the jury was seated. I held my breath and my heart beat faster. None of the jurors had made any eye contact with any of us at the defense table, another bad sign for us.

The following scene took place:

> The Court. Ladies and Gentlemen, have you reached a verdict in this case?
> The Jury. We have, your Honor.
> The Court. You may deliver your verdict to the Court. The clerk will read the verdicts.

Billie Beck, the jury foreman, had in his hand four verdict forms that he handed to the clerk. The clerk began by reading the two verdicts relating to the defendant Freddie Pitts:

> The Clerk. The State of Florida versus Freddie L. Pitts, case no. 3-72-1. We the jury find the defendant Freddie L. Pitts guilty of murder in the first degree, as charged in the indictment. So say we all, the Fifteenth day of March 1972. Signed Billie Wayne Beck, [Foreman].
> The State of Florida versus Freddie L. Pitts, case no. 3-72-2, we the jury find the defendant Freddie L. Pitts guilty of murder in the first degree, as charged in the indictment. So say we all, the Fifteenth day of March 1972. Signed Billie Wayne Beck, Foreman.[9]

The clerk then read the two verdicts relating to Wilbert Lee. They were the same as the verdicts for Freddie Pitts: guilty of murder in the first degree. These four verdicts, covering the murders of Grover Floyd and Jesse Burkett, contained no recommendation of mercy. Under Florida law at that time, the judge had no discretion but to sentence the defendants to death.

Gene Miller later reported that as the verdicts were read, tears filled the eyes of Deputy Sheriffs Allen Rogers and Sonny Hughes, who had guarded and gotten to know Pitts and Lee over the past several months. The deputies were seated behind our counsel table. Several Black women in the audience quietly sobbed, including Louise Brooks, Freddie Pitts's mother, who was seated in the front row. Otherwise the courtroom was deathly silent.[10]

I then stood and addressed the court as planned:

Mr. Hubbart. We request the jury be polled and also to have a poll on the recommendation of mercy and also on innocence.
Mr. Jones. If the Court please—
The Court. I don't think a poll on recommendation of mercy, then you would know who voted for mercy and who doesn't.
Mr. Jones. The only question the members be polled if that is their verdict.
The Court. All right. Call their name and ask them if that is their verdict.[11]

The clerk then called out the names of each of the twelve jurors one by one and asked: "Are these your verdicts?" All twelve jurors answered individually in the affirmative.[12]

Judge Smith then addressed the jury, thanking them for their service, complimenting them for their conscientious consideration of the case, informing them of their entitlement to compensation for their service, and excusing them from the courtroom.[13]

After the jurors had filed out from the courtroom, I again addressed the court:

Mr. Hubbart. If Your Honor please, may we have fifteen days with which to file . . . a motion for new trial, an[d] [other] motions in this case?
The Court. Yes, you may have fifteen days. And will the defendants step forward please.

Pitts and Lee—and Block and I—stepped forward and stood before Judge Smith. Irwin was next to Pitts and I was next to Lee, who was shaking with fear.

> The Court. You, Freddie L. Pitts and Wilbert Lee, having been found guilty of murder in the first degree by a jury of twelve good and lawful citizens of Jackson County, Florida. The court does now adjudge you to be guilty of murder in the first degree in the Case Number 3-72-1, and 3-72-2. Is there anything you would like to say or any cause to show why judgment and sentencing of the Court should not be pronounced upon you?
>
> Mr. Block. On behalf of Freddie Pitts, the defendant is innocent. He did not receive a fair trial. He was denied due process of law, and we would respectfully request that we be given additional time and opportunity as Mr. Hubbart has requested for the filing of additional motions.
>
> Mr. Hubbart. On behalf of the defendant Wilbert Lee, we object to the imposition of any death sentence in this case on the grounds that the death penalty constitutes cruel and unusual punishment in violation of the Eighth Amendment and the Fourteenth Amendment to the United States Constitution. We furthermore object on the ground that the defendants did not receive a fair and impartial trial in this county for the reason and grounds stated throughout this trial. Wilbert Lee is completely and totally innocent of these murders.
>
> The Court. Well, I'm sorry but I can't agree with you and although I'm giving the fifteen days in which to file a motion for a new trial, I think the appropriate time to impose sentence is at this time.

Judge Smith, visibly trembling, then pronounced the death sentence in solemn tones. It was a macabre and chilling moment:

> You, Wilbert Lee and Freddie L. Pitts, having had a fair trial by a jury of your countrymen, and having been found guilty of the crime of murder in the first degree, the Court now adjudges you to be so guilty.
> * * *
>
> Saying nothing to preclude such sentence, it is thereupon the judgment of this Court and the sentence of the law, that you Freddie L. Pitts and Wilbert Lee, for the crime for which you have been and stand convicted be delivered to the Sheriff of Jackson County, Florida, to the proper officer of the State Prison of the State of Florida and be

by him safely kept until such day as the Governor by his warrant may appoint, at which time, as by said warrant directed, and within the walls of the permanent death chamber provided by law, you, Freddie L. Pitts and Wilbert Lee, be by the proper officer of said prison, electrocuted until you are dead; and may God have mercy on your soul.[14]

What occurred next I will remember for the rest of my life. Doris Block, Irwin Block's wife, and my wife, Martha, were seated near the aisle in the packed courtroom, having witnessed the entire trial. Both women were reserved and soft spoken. Doris, however, upon hearing the death sentences and outraged at the entire process, sprang from her seat, ran down the aisle in the courtroom past the low swinging doors and into the well of the court, pointed her finger at both Judge Smith and Leo Jones, and shouted at the top of her lungs: *"I hope you have this on your conscience till the day you die!"*

Judge Smith, red-faced and perspiring, rose slightly to his feet, stretched out his hands, and said: "Now, now," as if to calm her down. At that point, the judge appeared to be on the verge of a heart attack. In fact, he did have one a week later; he was in intensive care for five days but eventually recovered.[15] Doris then ran out the back door of the courtroom and disappeared. Irwin Block then turned to me and muttered in his usual sardonic style: "Good for her."

Needless to say, after this outburst, the courtroom was in an uproar for quite a while after the court adjourned, which was almost immediately. People milled around in the spectator section excitedly talking to one another, no doubt amazed at what they had just seen. The jurors soon disappeared from the courtroom. Two jurors, James Zeigler and Richard Tidwell, hid their faces to avoid a news photographer.[16]

*   *   *

Still, there was more to come. That night Jackson County Sheriff Barkley Gause drove Pitts and Lee safely out of Jackson County in his squad car, escorted by two Florida Highway Patrol cruisers. He drove the two men to the Leon County jail in Tallahassee for temporary custody and the next day delivered them to death row at Raiford Prison. Pitts and Lee, who were handcuffed, sat silently in the back seat while the sheriff and a deputy sat in the front seat.

On the way to Tallahassee, the sheriff finally spoke. He said he was disgusted with the way Pitts and Lee had been treated and called the state's case against them "trumped up evidence," likening the trial to a lynching in which the law was used as a cover to convict them.[17] Wilbert Lee reported that the sheriff was "stunned" and "hurt" by the verdict "because he had been with us every day."[18] Freddie Pitts's account of this encounter was similar, adding that the sheriff "stopped and bought us hamburgers and milk shakes with his own money, and I told him to thank everyone for the way they had treated us and all."[19]

Months later, Sheriff Gause summed up the case well:

> That Willie Mae Lee was behind the eight ball. She was lying to save her own neck; that's what it looked like to me. I think that Adams fellow should have been put before the jury.[20]

I remember thinking at the time how ironic the situation was—that of all people, white southern law enforcement officials in the midst of the civil rights upheaval in the South would be friendly to Pitts and Lee. But they were. The sheriff thought they had not been treated fairly. Two of his deputies wept upon hearing the verdict. I can only speculate that perhaps the sheriff had been chastened by his experience with the Cellos Harrison case in 1941–1943 and had grown, at least in part, into a more caring and decent person.

Both Pitts and Lee took the verdict and the sentence in their usual stoic manner. Freddie Pitts wasn't surprised at the verdict, as the best he had hoped for was a mistrial. Wilbert Lee agreed and expected the worst after the Klan rally on the eve of the trial.

When the defense team returned to Miami, Irwin Block issued the only press release we ever made in the case. He summed up our experience in Marianna well:

> Florida has witnessed the greatest miscarriage of justice in my life. Freddie Pitts and Wilbert Lee, although totally innocent, were convicted because they were black. Prior to the trial, every attorney I spoke to in the Panhandle told me we would never get an acquittal in Marianna. . . . . The attorneys certainly knew their people. Freddie Pitts and Wilbert Lee would have been convicted in Marianna if the twelve apostles testified for them.[21]

Almost immediately, we received an outpouring of support from many members of the Miami community. One of the most meaningful responses we got was a short handwritten letter from Leonard Mellon, a high-ranking executive state attorney in the Dade County State Attorney's Office. I had litigated against him in a major class action in the federal courts. Mr. Mellon wrote simply:

Dear Phil,

What little greatness there is in the Florida Bar is attributable to lawyers like you and Irwin.

Sincerely,
Len Mellon.[22]

Several months later after things had quieted down, Warren Holmes wrote this moving letter to Freddie Pitts and Wilbert Lee:

I haven't written to you because your conviction was the biggest disappointment of my life. Even today I can hardly believe that it happened. For three days after your conviction my senses were numb. Even writing to you is painful because it brings me back to the reality of this terrible blow.

As human beings do, I've been able to rationalize most failures and disappointments in my life. But in your case there is no rationalization. There is no excuse nor any justification for your conviction. If I didn't know the truth, maybe it wouldn't hurt so much.[23]

Despite this bitter setback, we defense lawyers weren't through with the case. Once again, a long struggle lay ahead of us as we prepared to appeal the convictions of Pitts and Lee.

29

The Appeal

In a process that dragged on for three and a half years, we appealed Pitts and Lee's convictions to two appellate courts: the First District Court of Appeal of Florida and the US Supreme Court. On March 27, 1972, I began this process by filing a timely motion for new trial in the Circuit Court for the Fourteenth Judicial Circuit in Marianna. The motion contained forty-seven grounds covering assorted judicial errors.

Over a year later, on April 6, 1973, Judge Smith heard the motion for new trial in his chambers in Ocala. I argued the motion at some length, after which Judge Smith announced that it was not necessary for Leo Jones to present any contrary argument. He then denied the motion, a result we fully expected.

Having fully recovered from his heart attack and no longer in turmoil over the case, the judge decided to josh me a little bit with a broad smile. He told me that he didn't think I really wanted a new trial anyway—meaning, I guess, that I really didn't want to go through the ordeal of another trial. When I assured the judge that we wanted a new trial, the judge asked with a skeptical grin whether I was really serious about Curtis Adams's confession. I assured the judge that I was.

Judge Smith, with his grandfatherly manner, seemed to be saying that all was well, that the right people had been convicted, and that our Curtis Adams evidence was a lot of nonsense. But the incident reinforced my belief that we lost this case because of Judge Smith's rulings denying our motion for change of venue, denying our motion to suppress the defendants' confessions, and denying our proffer of the voluminous evidence establishing that Curtis Adams had committed the Floyd-Burkett murders.

I nonetheless took the judge's ruling in stride with my usual professional manner by not responding in kind. I simply thanked him for his time, asked to be excused, and left his chambers. I never saw him again.

Under Florida law, we had thirty days from the denial of our timely motion for new trial to file a notice of appeal seeking review in the appropriate appellate court. On April 10, 1973, Judge Smith entered a written order denying our motion for a new trial, and on the same day we filed a notice of appeal with the circuit court in Marianna, stating that we were taking our appeal to the First District Court of Appeal.

Ordinarily, we would have taken the appeal to the Florida Supreme Court. That court has exclusive jurisdiction to review criminal convictions in which the death penalty has been imposed. But due to events that occurred after the trial, Pitts and Lee's death sentences had been vacated and they had been resentenced to life imprisonment. This meant that our appeal was to the First District Court of Appeal, which had jurisdiction over any appeal from a noncapital felony conviction entered within its district, including the Fourteenth Judicial Circuit of Florida.

A little background: on June 29, 1972, a few months after the defendants were convicted, the US Supreme Court ruled in *Furman v. Georgia* that the death penalty was unconstitutional because it constituted cruel and unusual punishment in violation of the Eighth and Fourteenth Amendments to the US Constitution.[1] The decision was made both prospective and retroactive. That is, the ruling applied to all future cases as well as all past cases, including the 1972 death sentences of Pitts and Lee. Remarkably, the Court reversed itself four years later and reinstituted the death penalty but only for all cases from that point forward.[2]

On September 21, 1972, Judge Smith entered an order resentencing Pitts and Lee to life imprisonment. While happy with this result, both men were also apprehensive about being released from their isolated cells on death row into the general prison population at Raiford, where they would come in daily contact with fellow prisoners.

Wilbert Lee, not realizing the irony, said "I'm not sure I want to be out there with all those murderers and robbers and everything."[3] Freddie Pitts was equally uncomfortable. Soon after they made the transfer, a fellow prisoner punched Lee in the face and broke his jaw. Another inmate stole Pitts's soap, watch, and shoes.[4] Although they eventually adjusted to their new status, they continued to suffer from their wrongful imprisonment in that maximum-security facility.

We defense lawyers were also apprehensive about this turn of events. We were now before the First District Court of Appeal, which had already issued two opinions against us. Based on this experience, we had zero

326 · Part III. The New Trial and Its Aftermath (1971–1975)

confidence that we could win before this appellate court and worse yet, we feared that the opinion of the court would distort the facts of the case in the state's favor when it dealt with our federal constitutional issues, similar to what Judge Rawls had done in the state's appeal from Judge Holley's new trial order. That would make it difficult for us to pursue these points in further appeals in the federal courts. Both state and federal appellate courts generally accept the facts stated in the opinion of the lower court from which the appeal is taken. Irwin Block was particularly adamant that we had to adopt an extraordinary strategy that would take into account that we were facing a hostile court in which we were bound to lose.

Consequently, on June 12, 1973, I filed a fifty-page brief with the First District Court of Appeal raising twelve otherwise solid points for appellate review but far more points than is usually advisable when prosecuting an appeal. Six of these twelve points were the federal constitutional claims that we intended to pursue in future appeals. The remaining six points, which we had no intention of pursuing further, were prominently featured in the brief, thus giving the impression, we hoped, that we thought less of our federal claims. This strategy was designed so that the court would be less concerned with these federal claims and less apt to distort the facts when rejecting them. I also confined my discussion of the facts to the procedural history of the case, to portions of the actual trial testimony, and to otherwise undisputed occurrences. It was a delicate balancing act.

On January 9, 1974, six months later, we argued the case before a three-judge panel of the First District: Judges Dewey Johnson, Tyrie Boyer, and Guyte McCord. The argument was uneventful and none of the judges asked any questions. Thereafter the court sat on the case for over a year.

On February 3, 1975, the First District finally issued an eleven-and-a-half-page opinion written by Judge Boyer affirming the defendants' convictions, as we expected.[5] Our strategy had worked: the court's discussion of our six federal constitutional claims contained no distorted facts and was primarily an analysis of the law. All in all, it was a palatable but unpersuasive opinion, one that we could safely pursue in further appeals to the federal courts.

I was also pleasantly surprised with the respect Judge Boyer paid to defense counsel at the end of the opinion.

> We do not intend the foregoing statements to be construed as criticism of appellants' counsel. On the contrary, our examination of the record and appellants' brief leads us to the inescapable conclusion

that appellants' counsel have ably represented their clients and have made the most advantageous use possible of the evidence and proceedings revealed by the record.[6]

But like the jury convictions in Marianna, an affirmance by the First District was a foregone conclusion. Any other result would likely have created a furor among the other judges on the First District and would have been received with outrage throughout the Florida Panhandle. Nonetheless, I appreciated the professional tone of Judge Boyer's opinion.

*   *   *

On May 1, 1975, I filed a timely 32-page petition for a writ of certiorari in the US Supreme Court, seeking review of the First District Court of Appeal's decision.[7] We decided to bypass the Florida Supreme Court on the grounds that it lacked jurisdiction to review the district court's decision and that the district court's opinion was the final decision in the case by the Florida courts.[8]

Jack MacKenzie, a longtime reporter for the *Washington Post* who was assigned to cover the US Supreme Court, was impressed with the petition. While doing a story on the Pitts-Lee case in July 1975, he interviewed a top prison official at Raiford. In the course of that conversation, MacKenzie remarked that he had read the petition and that it was "an extremely well-written document, a masterful job . . . one of the best written I've seen in a long time." He further stated that he thought the Court would grant the petition and hear the case.[9]

The petition was based on two federal constitutional grounds and addressed the many flaws in the district court's contrary decision. The first ground for review was our most important one; namely, that the exclusion at trial of all our evidence establishing that Curtis Adams had committed the Floyd-Burkett murders violated the defendants' constitutional right to call witnesses in their own defense, a right guaranteed by the Sixth and Fourteenth Amendments to the US Constitution, and their right to a fair trial, which was also guaranteed by the Fourteenth Amendment.

At issue was the admissibility of three confessions Curtis Adams had made to the Floyd-Burkett murders:

- The oral confessions Adams made to his girlfriend Mary Jean Akins on the night of the murders and the night after the murders;
- The tape-recorded confession Adams made to Warren Holmes at the Broward County Jail in December 1966; and

- The oral confession that Adams made to Broward County Deputy Sheriff Elihu Phares in January 1967 at the Broward County Jail.

Judge Smith had excluded all these confessions at trial as hearsay evidence.

Also at issue was the admissibility of all our evidence corroborating Adams's confessions. That evidence included the fact that two of these confessions had been obtained by agents of the state; namely, Warren Holmes, who had been hired by the Broward County state attorney to investigate the related Floyd McFarland murder case, and Broward County Deputy Sheriff Elihu Phares. These were not people of dubious reputation testifying to so-called jailhouse confessions; they were people occupying official public positions investigating criminal offenses.

In support of our petition, I relied heavily on the recent US Supreme Court decision in *Chambers v. Mississippi*.[10] That decision was announced on February 21, 1973, approximately one year after Pitts and Lee's trial. In that case, the Supreme Court reversed a state court conviction and ruled that the trial judge had committed reversible error when he excluded from evidence a corroborated series of confessions made by a third person to the murder for which the defendant was charged. This evidence, the Court held, was admissible in evidence based on the Sixth and Fourteenth Amendments to the US Constitution.

This was precisely the same type of evidence that we had presented to Judge Smith, evidence that tended to show that Curtis Adams had committed the murders the defendants were charged with. Judge Smith had erroneously excluded that evidence. As in *Chambers,* we argued, the corroborated Curtis Adams confessions were admissible in evidence under the Sixth and Fourteenth Amendments to the US Constitution.

This decision was a stunning breakthrough for us and the best case for the defendants that I ever discovered in my legal research.[11] Here is a critical part of the Supreme Court's opinion:

> Few rights are more fundamental than that of an accused to present witnesses in his own defense. [Citations omitted.] In the exercise of that right, the accused, as is required by the State, must comply with established rules and procedure and evidence designed to assure both fairness and reliability in the ascertainment of guilt or innocence.
>
> Although perhaps no rule has been more respected or more frequently applied in jury trials than that applicable to the exclusion of hearsay, exceptions tailored to allow the introduction of evidence which, in fact, is likely to be trustworthy have long existed.

The [third-party confession] testimony rejected by the trial court here bore persuasive assurances of trustworthiness, and thus was well within the basic rationale of the exception [to the hearsay rule] for declarations against interest. That testimony was critical to Chambers' defense. In these circumstances where constitutional rights directly affecting the ascertainment of guilt are implicated, the hearsay rule may not be applied mechanistically to defeat the ends of justice.[12]

In accord with this landmark decision, I announced our basic legal position in the argument section of my certiorari petition:

The [district] court below has mechanistically applied Florida's hearsay rule to defeat the ends of justice without any valid state purpose. The decision cuts the heart out of the Petitioners' defense in this case and the result is an incredible injustice.

The Petitioners have been precluded from establishing that Curtis Adams, Jr. committed the murders for which the Petitioners were charged by excluding at trial all of Adams's oral and tape-recorded confessions and all evidence in corroboration thereof. As such, the decision sharply conflicts in principle with *Chambers v. Mississippi*.[13]

I then pointed to a number of similarities between the Chambers case and our case—the first two of which were particularly compelling:

First the Court in *Chambers* noted that the [excluded] confessions were "made spontaneously to a close acquaintance shortly after the murder occurred." . . . Similarly, in the instant case, one of the confessions by Adams was made to a close acquaintance, Adams's girlfriend Mary Jean Akins, the night of the murders and was repeated [to her] the following night. . . .

In addition, the other confessions were voluntarily given by Adams and were obtained by the State pursuant to official State Attorney and police investigations in Broward County, Florida. Moreover, the tape-recorded confession was made under court order.

Secondly, the Court in *Chambers* noted that the [excluded] confessions were "corroborated by some other evidence in the case." . . . Similarly, in the instant case, Adams's confessions were amply corroborated by independent evidence.[14]

I then outlined the powerful pieces of evidence that corroborated all of Adams's confessions.[15]

The First District Court's effort to distinguish *Chambers* from our case was notably unpersuasive. The court's main argument was that Curtis Adams invoked his privilege against self-incrimination and refused to testify in our case, while the third-party confessor in *Chambers v. Mississippi* took the witness stand and repudiated his out-of-court confessions.[16] Here was my reply:

> Technically this is true. But should it make any constitutional difference? . . .
>
> Does it make any sense to deny to these Petitioners the vital constitutional right to call witnesses in their own behalf and place in evidence highly relevant, extremely trustworthy confessions by a third party, some of which were obtained by the State itself, because the third party has the intelligence to refuse to testify and invokes his self-incrimination privilege at trial?
>
> Surely this cannot be the law[,] else a guilty party like Curtis Adams, Jr. would hold within his power the decision on whether his damning confessions should be admitted in evidence to clear two innocent men.[17]

I closed this branch of the argument by addressing the district court's argument that while Curtis Adams's confessions were inadmissible in evidence, we were free to call Adams as a defense witness at trial.[18] Here is my reply:

> True, but small consolation to the Petitioners. Is it reasonable to expect a convicted, cold-blooded murderer like Curtis Adams, Jr. to take the witness stand in a court of law and confess to a capital crime for which he could be executed with no prior grant of immunity?
>
> Adams is no fool and the record shows he is motivated entirely by self interest. He has not and will not put himself in the electric chair by repeating his confession to the Floyd-Burkett murders without a prior grant of immunity.
>
> Adams should not be permitted to thwart the principle of the *Chambers* case by invoking his privilege against self incrimination and thereby preclude the Petitioners from proving the overwhelming case of guilt against him, including his repeated, detailed and highly trustworthy confessions.[19]

I then moved on to the second constitutional ground for our petition for certiorari; namely, that Pitts and Lee were subjected to a monumental denial of due process in violation of the Fourteenth Amendment to the US Constitution. I argued, with supporting legal authority and reasoning, five additional federal constitutional errors that further deprived Pitts and Lee of a fair trial:

- The defendants were indicted by a grand jury from which eligible Black jurors were systematically excluded.
- The defendants were tried, over our protest, in a small rural community that was prejudiced against them because of years of local adverse newspaper publicity and adverse conversations in the community.
- The defendants' confessions were improperly introduced in evidence at trial because those confessions were coerced and involuntary, given in an atmosphere of fear and terror.
- The prosecuting attorney systematically excluded every Black juror who survived a challenge for cause through the use of peremptory challenges.
- The prosecuting attorney made a grossly inflammatory argument to the jury appealing to white community prejudice against the petitioners.[20]

This part of the argument was absolutely essential to obtaining US Supreme Court review because it presented, in my view, the classic case of two Black men being legally lynched by a white power structure in the South, presenting yet another sad chapter in our nation's racial history. This argument, when combined with our first argument, made it a case of national importance—one worthy of Supreme Court review.

I ended the petition by asking the Court to assume jurisdiction and correct this gross miscarriage of justice. The Court, which was nearing the start of its summer recess (July–September 1975), did not immediately act on the petition and instead left the matter for the 1975 term, which began in October.

The Supreme Court, however, would never get a chance to rule on the petition because a series of events was simultaneously occurring outside the courts in the years 1972 to 1975 that would prove decisive in the case.

30

Freedom

After our expected but disappointing loss at trial in Marianna, we began to rethink our defense strategy. Perhaps, we thought, we should no longer focus solely on the courts to win this case. Maybe an additional approach was needed.

I was confident that the US Supreme Court would take jurisdiction in the case and reverse Pitts and Lee's convictions. But the best the Supreme Court or any federal court could do for the defendants would be to order a new trial in the Florida courts, directing that all our claimed errors at the first trial should not be repeated. And we, as defense counsel, would have to win an acquittal at the new trial. Everyone on the defense team was impatient with this glacial process and wanted more immediate results.

So after some discussion, it was decided that Miller and Holmes would concentrate on getting Pitts and Lee a full pardon from the state on the ground of innocence. Under Florida law, this meant convincing Florida's governor, Reubin Askew, and three other members of Florida's seven-person cabinet to vote for such a pardon. It was a delicate process because neither Miller nor Holmes occupied any official legal role in the case. Their efforts had to be indirect and behind the scenes while letting certain state officials take the leading roles.

We defense lawyers, on the other hand, would continue with our appeals. We would leave the pardon efforts primarily to Miller and Holmes while we remained in the background, ready to provide any help when required. Indeed, as defense counsel we were not permitted to file or pursue a formal petition for a pardon while our appeals were still pending. The Florida Cabinet had a long-standing practice of not entertaining petitions for clemency, such as a pardon, until all the appeals in the case had been exhausted.

These informal efforts all began when Gene Miller started corresponding with the governor's office to see if the governor might be interested in looking into the case. He got a favorable response. So Miller started sending the governor's office many of his long *Miami Herald* articles on the case while he continued to write about recent developments in the case.[1] Most important, Miller also began writing a book about the case entitled *Invitation to a Lynching*. When the book was finished but before it was published, Miller sent the governor the book's page proofs to read.

It should be noted, however, that Askew was not legally obligated to investigate the case. He could have easily declined to do so while our appeals were pending in the courts. Such a response would have mirrored the long-standing practice of past Florida governors. A simple letter from Askew's office reiterating this policy would have ended any quest for a pardon without any political cost to Askew.

But Reubin Askew was an unusual governor. He was a political moderate, he was sensitive to race issues, and he was part of a new crop of Democratic governors emerging in the South at that time that included Jimmy Carter in Georgia and, somewhat later, Bill Clinton in Arkansas. Askew was from Pensacola in the Florida Panhandle and was acquainted with many of the prominent people involved in the case. He was disturbed about the entire case and asked his assistant legal counsel, Donald Middlebrooks, to look into the matter.[2]

After getting permission from us as defense counsel, Middlebrooks went to Raiford Prison and interviewed Pitts and Lee. He was impressed with both men and decided to investigate further. He soon got in contact with Miller and Holmes, and on June 13, 1974, all three men went to Raiford Prison and interviewed Curtis Adams at length. The interview was taped, with Middlebrooks doing most of the questioning. Once again, Adams confessed to murdering Grover Floyd and Jesse Burkett.

Adams stated that he was living with Mary Jean Akins and her children in Port St. Joe on the night of the Floyd-Burkett murders and that he decided to rob the local Mo Jo station that night. He recounted the events that followed, concluding with the moment he shot and killed Floyd and Burkett in the woods.

Middlebrooks. Once you got there, what did you do then?
Adams. Made them lay down. . . .
Middlebrooks. On their stomachs?
Adams. One of them . . . on the side facing west.
Middlebrooks. Then what happened.
Adams. I shot them and left.

Middlebrooks. With the gun that you had?
Adams. The gun that they had.
Middlebrooks. And what kind of a gun was that?
Adams. A 38 revolver.
Middlebrooks. Do you remember which one you shot first?
Adams. Shot Floyd first. . . . After I left there, I took the gun and throwed it in the canal.

Warren Holmes then asked Adams:

What's it going to take for you to go before the Pardon Board and tell the real truth?
Adams. Well, sir. I don't want to be tried for it. I got about all the time I can do. I've got life and 40 years. That's going to be hard to do, isn't it?

Gene Miller asked:

Why are you telling us this now?
Adams. It's got to come out sometime. Something has got to be done.

And Middlebrooks asked:

How did you come to tell Mr. Holmes the first time?
Adams. I was trying to do what was right then. Things didn't work out.[3]

With Adams's taped confession in hand, together with Pitts and Lee's credible claims of innocence, Middlebrooks left the prison convinced there was something terribly wrong with this case. He conferred with Arthur Canaday, the governor's chief legal counsel, who soon joined the investigation.

Canaday tracked down and interviewed Mary Jean Akins, who was living in Tennessee. She fully corroborated Adams's account of the Floyd-Burkett murders including Adams's detailed confessions to her on the night of the murders and the night thereafter.[4]

Canaday and Middlebrooks next tried to interview Willie Mae Lee at her home in Beacon, New York. But she refused to discuss the case, saying with some remorse: "Yeah, I feel sorry for Freddie and Wilbert, but I feel more sorry for myself."[5] This was an odd comment. Why would she feel any compassion for these alleged ruthless killers unless she knew they were innocent? In the end, Willie Mae Lee was the only witness the governor's office contacted who refused to discuss the case.

Over a period of eighteen months, the governor or a member of his staff interviewed every other major witness connected with the case. Askew was a trained lawyer and reviewed many of the transcripts, pleadings, statements, and orders in the case, which we supplied him. At times, he would also telephone witnesses from the governor's mansion to discuss the case. No detail escaped him.[6] Askew also carefully reviewed Gene Miller's articles and his book on the case.

One aspect of the case particularly bothered him. Aubrey Branch, a young teenager, had testified at the 1972 Marianna trial that he was at the Mo Jo station on the night of the murders, that he had used the men's bathroom that night, and that no one had been inside.[7] This testimony contradicted Curtis Adams's repeated statements that he was hiding in the bathroom at that time. But when Askew telephoned Branch on September 7, 1975, Branch retracted his prior testimony and said: "At the time I testified, I honestly believed that to be true. But if I had to swear to it now, I don't believe I could." In Askew's mind, that may have been the final piece of evidence that clinched the case for recommending the pardon.[8]

As an aside, at the Marianna trial, Branch had also testified that he was first asked about this "remembrance" when a state investigator interviewed him in 1968, five years after the alleged event.[9] Branch further testified that he had been to the Mo Jo station many times over the years and had often used that bathroom.[10] He had no doubt conflated one of those visits with the night in question.

* * *

Meanwhile, our clients were going through hell. Although they had been outwardly stoic during their long ordeal, Freddie Pitts and Wilbert Lee were privately, at times, full of outrage, frustration, and bitterness, and their anger got even worse after our defeat in Marianna. They couldn't understand why they were still in prison when all the evidence needed to free them had been known since late 1966.

One letter Freddie Pitts wrote to Gene Miller during his time perfectly expresses the bitterness that both men felt:

I'm through crawling, begging and pleading and I'm tired of this stupid, silly little game. If this sounds bitter, it's because I am. If anyone thinks I'm going to sit here and rot and not be bitter, they've lost their marbles. . . .

Next month I'll be 30 years old with 10 and a half years of my life gone down the drain for nothing. If this isn't cause to be bitter, then I'll slit my throat as I'm no good to myself or anyone else. Things and times have changed and so have I. And in the end if I was right or wrong, a million angels shouting that I was right isn't going to make one damn bit of difference.

But some way, somehow, my voice, my feelings are going to be heard and listened to. A man can only take so much and still remain a man. A man has his limit which he will not be pushed. I've reached my limit.[11]

And how could anyone blame them for feeling that way when the best years of their lives had been stolen from them for nothing? "If you've ever been to Death Row," Wilbert Lee once said, "then you've been to Hell."[12] Regarding the three years they served off death row after the Marianna trial, confined in the maximum-security unit at Florida State Prison, Lee said, "This still does not lift the burden. To have suffered all these years for a crime we did not commit, well, we're still in a bad situation."[13]

Fortunately, however, both Freddie Pitts and Wilbert Lee were also men of remarkable good will, courage, endurance, and strength of character. Despite their inward bitterness, they never lost hope. They never fell into the pit of self-destructive hatred of their oppressors. "I never hated," Wilbert Lee said later. "When they locked me up, they had my body but not my mind."[14] And Freddie Pitts agreed, "I would be less than honest to say I was not bitter, but it was a bitterness that I controlled. I did not allow it to control me."[15]

*   *   *

Due to Gene Miller's continuous coverage of the case in the *Miami Herald* which revealed that Askew was investigating the matter, many people began contacting the governor. Jeanette Holston, an assistant professor at Florida Memorial College in Miami, organized a letter-writing campaign that produced over 600 letters to the governor protesting Pitts and Lee's convictions and calling for their pardon on grounds of innocence.[16] A group called the Ad Hoc Committee to Free Freddie Pitts and Wilbert Lee collected 6,000 signatures to a petition urging the governor to pardon Pitts and Lee.[17] A group in Miami, the Pitts-Lee Defense Committee, worked tirelessly in favor of the pardon and sent many petitions to the governor, as did many students at the University of Miami Law School and Florida Memorial College.

The campaign to free Pitts and Lee also got national and international attention. In April 1971, conservative syndicated columnist James J. Kilpatrick wrote a column strongly supporting Pitts and Lee's innocence.[18] And in the summer of 1974, Amnesty International—a highly regarded worldwide humanitarian group—took up Pitts and Lee's cause, concluding that our clients were the victims of injustice and that their imprisonment was a human rights violation. They bombarded the governor, the attorney general, and other members of the Florida Cabinet with literally thousands of letters, cards, inquiries, and leaflets protesting Pitts and Lee's imprisonment and supporting the pardon. This correspondence came from Amnesty International members in Europe and around the world.

I was in close contact with this group and had a year's worth of correspondence (1974–1975) with two of the group's leaders: Mrs. M. I. Houweling of the Netherlands and Mr. Thomas Werner of West Germany. I advised the group on American law, explained the status of the case, kept them advised about the progress of our appeals, and suggested how they should best proceed to support the pardon.

On January 18, 1974, a most unusual letter reached the governor's office. It was written by Chris Burkett, the eldest son of Jesse Burkett, one of the two men who was murdered in this case. Enclosing an investigative news article on the case, Chris Burkett wrote:

> Many years ago my father was murdered in the Mo-Jo station described in this article. For years, I had just assumed that those persons found guilty were in fact guilty. After reading this story, I am completely convinced otherwise.
>
> I think that you owe it to me, the State of Florida, and the interest of justice to correct this horrible injustice that has taken away so many years of two innocent human lives. I can think of no greater tribute to my dead father than to make sure that the blame is based on the right person and remove from [prison] Wilbert Lee and Freddie Pitts, now still on death row, for a crime I'm sure they did not commit.[19]

According to Arthur Canaday, the governor's general counsel, it was this letter that persuaded Askew that he should continue looking into the case.[20]

Chris Burkett had read about the case in an old copy of a five-page extensive article that appeared in the October 2, 1973, *Sunday Magazine* edition of the *New York News* entitled "Shadowy Justice in the Sunshine State," written by investigative journalist Kenneth Gross. At the time, Chris Burkett, who was 27 and lived in Freemont, California, worked in the circulation department of the *San Jose Mercury* in California. He later said that as he read the article, "I just got sick."[21]

Burkett knew many of the people involved in the case and knew full well what they were capable of. He knew the racism that infected both his family and many of the people of that area. As he told Gene Miller: "I dearly loved my family but I could never understand how they could preach the love of God and want to go to heaven and spent 30 per cent of their time in church—and not allow a Black person to step inside the church."[22]

After receiving news that the First District had affirmed Pitts and Lee's convictions, Chris Burkett again wrote to Governor Askew. This time Burkett was even more emphatic:

> Governor, I am still of the firm conviction that there were two crimes committed in Port St. Joe that summer so long ago. One in which my father was killed; the other committed by the State of Florida itself when it allowed a few over-zealous, political, ambitious small-town big wheels to arrest, beat confessions from, and wrongfully convict two innocent black men.
>
> You, as Governor, are the one man in the world that can convince your pardon board and ask [for] the pardon of Wilbert Lee and Freddie Pitts on grounds of innocence.[23]

As the time for the pardon drew near, Chris Burkett made a decision. He traveled from Southern California, saw his family in Port St. Joe, and then went on to Raiford Prison, where he personally visited with Pitts and Lee. At first, Freddie Pitts was extremely skeptical. He thought that Chris Burkett's story was a fraud. But soon he became convinced that Burkett was sincere. It was a cordial interview.

Chris Burkett then went to the governor's office and spent nearly an hour talking about the case with legal aides on the governor's staff, including Canaday and Middlebrooks. He later said:

> There is no doubt in my mind that [Pitts and Lee] are in prison for something they didn't do. The case against them is based on lies. It is a racial outrage. I know they didn't kill my father.

He added that Pitts and Lee had not gotten a fair trial in Marianna: "Marianna," he said, "was like holding the trial on my grandad's front porch."[24]

In all, the mail and telegrams sent to the governor's office ran about two to one in favor of the pardon, although the letters opposed to the pardon were far more passionate and bitter.[25] One Florida historian has stated that even "some of Askew's supporters found it hard to forgive him [for] his part in the pardoning of Freddie Pitts and Wilbert Lee."[26] Without question, the pardon was the most controversial decision that Askew made in his two terms as governor.

*   *   *

On September 10, 1975, at a meeting of the Florida Cabinet that was heavily covered by the media, Askew finally announced his intention to issue a pardon to Pitts and Lee. Askew made an extensive statement in support of his decision. He began with this preface:

> After personally reviewing every aspect of their case over a period of 18 months, I have become convinced that the case of Freddie L. Pitts and Wilbert Lee is . . . a special case. Members of my staff have interviewed the major witnesses in the case. I have spoken with attorneys from both the state and the defense. I have done my best to determine the truth.

Askew then carefully analyzed the case:

> There can be no ignoring the tragic fact that two brutal murders were committed in Port St. Joe in 1963. The senseless slaying of Grover Floyd and Jesse Burkett will forever be a reminder to all of us that violence cannot be tolerated. My heart and my prayers will remain with the families of these two men.
>
> I have decided, though, that substantial doubt exists as to the guilt of Pitts and Lee. A number of facts have led me to this conclusion.
>
> Basically, the evidence against Pitts and Lee consists of their statements to law officers after arrest and the testimony of Willie Mae Lee. Pitts and Lee contend that their statements were obtained under duress. Willie Mae Lee first accused Pitts and another soldier, Lambson Smith, for the murders. She later changed her account and said it was Wilbert Lee instead of Smith. At one point, Willie Mae Lee told investigators under oath that she knew nothing whatsoever about the murders. She said she named Pitts and Lee because she was afraid of being accused of the crime herself.
>
> Another person, Curtis Adams, has confessed several times that he murdered Floyd and Burkett. His confession is very detailed with information that would be very difficult to recount without knowledge of the commission of the crime.

Furthermore, the manner in which the confession came to light lends credence to his involvement. Adams was serving a sentence for armed robbery when a cellmate contacted the authorities concerning his belief that Adams had murdered a filling station attendant in Fort Lauderdale. During interrogation, Adams confessed not only to the Fort Lauderdale murder, but also to the murders of Floyd and Burkett in Port St. Joe. He had much to lose and nothing to gain by making such a confession. Later, he received a life sentence for the Fort Lauderdale murder.

The respective histories of Pitts, Lee and Adams are also persuasive. Curtis Adams has a long history of violent crime. He has been convicted twice for armed robbery, twice for escape and once for murder. Freddie Pitts was in the Army at the time of his arrest and had no criminal record. Wilbert Lee had been convicted once for auto theft, but completed his parole satisfactorily. They have not received any disciplinary reports during their 12 years in prison.

The testimony of Mary Jean Akins is very persuasive. She has been the most consistent witness in the case and has nothing to gain by her testimony. She has described in great detail how Curtis Adams left to rob a filling station in Port St. Joe and returned and told her he had murdered the attendants.

Askew then commented on the courts' handling of the case:

It would not be necessary, useful or appropriate for me as chief executive to attempt to pass judgment on the judicial history of this case. It should be pointed out, however, that at no time has a jury had an opportunity to weigh the confession of Curtis Adams that he and not Pitts and Lee murdered Grover Floyd and Jesse Burkett. Executive clemency allows me much greater latitude than the courts have had in considering all the circumstances and facts involved.

Askew then tried hard to downplay the racism that was implicit in this case:

This is the kind of case that pulls us apart as a people and is harmful to the fabric of our system of justice. It has been clouded by racial overtones. The Pitts-Lee case has been perceived by some as a symbol of oppression while others have viewed it as an attack on a fair system of justice. It is neither.

I hope that we can place the case behind us. I particularly hope that we can view the case in the context of the probability of the guilt or innocence of those concerned without emotionalism and burden of a cause. I can only ask that those who disagree with this action take time to carefully review all aspects and facts surrounding the case.[27]

But, of course, racism was at the heart of this case. It was the elephant in the room that no one wanted to acknowledge. I think this factor played a major, if unspoken, role in persuading the governor to grant this pardon.

Years later, on the twentieth anniversary of Pitts and Lee's 1963 death sentences, Askew stated:

I was personally convinced they didn't do it. I felt the entire system had malfunctioned. There was a gross miscarriage of justice in this case. At least in my mind, the preponderance of evidence indicated that they didn't do it, and the trials were clouded by great racial animosity.[28]

*   *   *

Another hero was Attorney General Bob Shevin. On September 9, 1975, the day before Askew's cabinet meeting, Shevin interviewed Mary Jean Akins at his office in the state capitol. Akins related to Shevin her basic testimony in the case, including her statement that on the night of the murders, Adams had confessed to her that he had killed the two attendants at the Mo Jo station and that he had repeated that confession in greater detail the next night.[29]

Later that day, Shevin and Warren Holmes traveled to Raiford Prison and interviewed Curtis Adams around 5:00 p.m. The interview was tape recorded. Once again, Adams confessed to the Floyd-Burkett murders.[30]

Shevin. Tell me in your own words what part, if any, you had with Burkett and Floyd in the murders that took place on the eve of July 31, 1963?
Adams. Well, it's hard to go back over that, I hardly know how to.
Shevin. Okay. Let me ask you this: Did you commit a robbery at the Mo Jo Station that night in Port St. Joe?
Adams. Yes, I did.
Shevin. And did you personally take the attendants at the service station out to the woods someplace and did you personally shoot these two men?

Adams nodded yes, and in half an hour related the same circumstances surrounding his robbery and murder of Floyd and Burkett that he had previously told Don Middlebrooks, the governor's legal aide.

Shevin. Why did you feel you had to shoot them?
Adams. Well, sir. They could identify me. They knew me.[31]

After hearing Adams's confession, Shevin told Holmes that he would vote for the pardon. He said simply: "If I had been on a jury and heard [Adams], I would have acquitted them."[32] The next day, during the Florida Cabinet meeting when Askew made his announcement, Shevin reiterated his intention to sign the pardon. And on September 11, 1975, he affixed his name to the pardon after Governor Askew had done the same.

Bob Shevin, in effect, threw away his political career in Florida, first by agreeing to a new trial for Pitts and Lee and later by voting to pardon them. When he ran for governor to succeed Askew in 1978, he was defeated by Bob Graham in the Democratic primary after overwhelmingly losing the Florida Panhandle and most of North Florida. His involvement in the Pitts-Lee case cost him the governorship. He retired from politics and returned to his law practice in Miami. He later served as a judge on the Third District Court of Appeal (1996–2005), thereby becoming one of the few Floridians to have served in all three branches of the Florida government.

On September 13, 1975, State Treasurer Phil Ashler signed the pardon, stating "I have come to the conclusion there is a reasonable doubt that Pitts and Lee committed the murders."[33] And on September 17, 1975, the pardon became official when Education Commissioner Ralph Turlington signed the pardon, stating, in effect, that he, too, had a reasonable doubt about Pitts and Lee's guilt or innocence: "I believe there is a good prospect of their innocence although I can't say that for a fact. . . . But I'm convinced I've done the right thing."[34] On September 19, 1975, after the pardon was officially filed in the state's records, Pitts and Lee were released from prison and made their triumphal trip to Miami.[35]

Gene Miller's and Warren Holmes's persistent efforts on behalf of the pardon had finally paid off. Broward County detective Elihu Phares put it best: "The wheels of justice turn slowly, I guess, but they turn."[36] He and Broward County detective Larry Lang had been the first law enforcement officers in Florida in 1966–1967 to develop evidence that Curtis Adams was the real killer in this case, not Pitts and Lee. They both welcomed news of the pardon.

On September 29, 1975, I also thanked Mrs. Houweling of Amnesty International by letter for their year-long effort to secure this pardon:

I was in the Governor's Office when the last signature [to the pardon] was affixed by Commissioner Turlington. Needless to say, we are all tremendously elated. . . .

Many, many thanks to you and your group for the vast letter writing campaign. It certainly paid off.[37]

In a strange twist, on September 19, 1975, the day Pitts and Lee were released from prison, Curtis Adams wrote a letter to Warren Holmes congratulating him for his long years of work on the case, stating at the end: "Again let me say you are one hell of a great man."[38] Holmes's reply to Adams is equally revealing. It shows the relationship of mutual respect that existed between these two men, a respect and understanding that had caused Adams to tell the truth and confess to Holmes in December 1966, nine years before.

I just received your letter, and I deeply appreciate your kind remarks. In fact, I'm very proud of your letter and have shown it to many people. Needless to say, Pitts and Lee would not be out of prison and pardoned if you hadn't stood up and told the truth. You might have done some wrong things in your life, but you are a man who possesses courage when needed.

I know it was a terrible ordeal for you to have to repeat your story before the different cabinet members. By doing so, you helped to balance the scale for those acts you shouldn't have committed in your life.

I want you to know that I respect the relationship we have had over the past nine years. Despite the difference in our life backgrounds, we have always gotten along on a friendly basis without trying to deceive one another. In fact, I've had a better understanding with you than with some of my so-called friends.[39]

Meanwhile, a cascade of events followed the pardon. On November 3, 1975, our petition for review in the US Supreme Court was dismissed because Pitts and Lee's convictions were now void and a new trial was unnecessary. On June 15, 1977, Freddie Pitts's dishonorable discharge from the army based on his murder convictions was rescinded and he was given an honorable discharge.[40]

344 · Part III. The New Trial and Its Aftermath (1971–1975)

And on May 3, 1976, Gene Miller was awarded a Pulitzer Prize for Local Investigative Specialized Reporting for his superb reporting in the Pitts-Lee case. The Pulitzer Award reads:

> For a distinguished example of general or spot news reporting within a newspaper's local area of circulation, preferably by an individual, giving consideration to alertness, resourcefulness and high-quality writing, One thousand dollars ($1,000).
> Gene Miller of Miami Herald.
> For his persistent and courageous reporting over eight and one-half years that led to the exoneration and release of two men who had twice been tried for murder and wrongfully convicted and sentenced to death in Florida.[41]

This was Gene Miller's second Pulitzer Prize for local reporting. He was one of eleven journalists in history at that time to win two Pulitzer Prizes and the only journalist to win twice in the local reporting category.[42]

Governor Askew applauded Miller's Pulitzer achievement with this tribute:

> While it took an act of government to ultimately free Freddie Pitts and Wilbert Lee, the man to whom they really owe their freedom is Gene Miller.
> His relentless pursuit of the truth over a period of years was in the finest tradition of journalism and it earned Gene Miller, rightfully, his profession's highest honor.[43]

Finally, on April 30, 1998, after twenty-two years of concerted effort on the part of Pitts and Lee, their counsel Ronald Lieberman, and many others, the Florida legislature awarded both men $500,000 apiece for their twelve years of wrongful imprisonment, nine of which were spent on death row.[44] The next day, May 1, 1998, Governor Lawton Chiles signed the measure into law in an emotional ceremony that both Pitts and Lee witnessed. Wilbert Lee broke down crying in the midst of Governor Chiles's remarks.[45]

I was not involved in this long struggle for reparations, as I had become a judge on the District Court of Appeal of Florida, Third District, in January 1977, where I served until February 1996. I greatly applauded this result, although I thought it a small atonement for all that Pitts and Lee had suffered.

Indeed, for the rest of their lives, Pitts and Lee would never fully recover from their death row experience. Pitts couldn't get the horror out of his mind. There wasn't a day that went by when he didn't think about his long ordeal.[46] At night, he would often walk from room to room at his home in Miami, wondering why his ordeal had happened to him.[47] Lee had nightmares. He would wake up in the middle of night shouting that he didn't want to die for something he didn't do.[48] This sounds a lot like post-traumatic stress disorder, a condition soldiers who have seen combat suffer from. The terror never goes away.

*   *   *

As I look back on the case now nearly half a century since Pitts and Lee's release from prison, my lasting memory of the entire experience was best expressed in my conclusion to the petition for a writ of certiorari filed in the US Supreme Court:

> The enormity of the injustice done to these petitioners is almost beyond belief. That such an event could happen in this country in this day and age is a reminder to all of us that injustice of enormous magnitude is still very much among us. No evasions, no rationalizations, and no highly skilled legal argument can quite obscure this simple truth.[49]

But my more visceral reaction to the case was quite different. It came out almost by accident in a talk I gave at a Dade County Bar Association luncheon. Shortly after the defense counsel team had returned to Miami from Tallahassee, having been present for the pardon, Irwin Block, Maurice Rosen, and I were invited to give a short talk on the case. When it was my turn, I related the basic facts in my usual professional manner, including an account of the dramatic days in Tallahassee that led up to the pardon. But when I came to the part when Ralph Turlington signed the pardon, making the pardon official, something came over me. I spoke in a way I have never spoken before or since in a public setting, using language I would never use publicly, expressing an emotion I had always kept to myself.

I began formally enough: "When I learned the pardon was now official, that Commissioner of Education Ralph Turlington had signed the pardon." I then paused for an instant, and an emotion came over me from the depths of my soul that I could not control. All my pent-up anger against J. Frank Adams, Leo Jones, Fred Turner, and all the law enforcement people involved in the case rushed to my mind. All of their stonewalling refusals to acknowledge the truth and do the right thing filled me with fury. I clenched my fist in front of me and said in an angry voice to thunderous applause: "I cannot begin to tell you the feeling I had that we beat those sonsabitches! We beat 'em!"

This rage remained with me for many decades, and it prevented me from writing about the case with any degree of objectivity. I gave lectures on the case to University of Miami law students and wrote bits and pieces here and there but could never bring myself to write a complete book about the case. The project was too overwhelming. It has only been in recent years that I have been able to shed this anger, to see the entire experience as a piece of history, and to write about it with both passion and understanding.

In my view, this entire shameful episode best reflects the times in which it arose: the civil rights era of the 1960s. Indeed, the case can only be understood as a product of that glorious but tragic era in our history. As Richard Rorty, professor of philosophy at the University of Virginia, expressed it:

> The civil rights movement was an expression of naked moral outrage at unnecessary human suffering. It was the great, inspiring moral event of our lifetime: the moment at which our country showed it was still capable of moral progress and of a national moral identity.[50]

The Pitts-Lee case was part of that movement: a long, drawn-out, twelve-year struggle against racism and mindless cruelty powered by a relentless fight to atone for this moral outrage. I hope this book has shed some light on this horrific miscarriage of justice, ever mindful of the ominous maxim by the Spanish philosopher George Santayana: "Those who cannot remember the past are condemned to repeat it."[51]

Acknowledgments

This book has been nearly a half-century in the making. I have many people to thank for their help and support in what turned out to be the most demanding work of my professional life.

I am deeply indebted to my wife Martha, a native southerner from outside Birmingham, Alabama, for her many creative ideas in shaping this project, for her expertise in proofreading the book, and for her steadfast support throughout the long ordeal of the Pitts-Lee case.

I am also greatly indebted to my brother-in-law Damon Nolin, also a native southerner, for reading and editing this book chapter by chapter as it was being written. Damon gave me many insights into the white southern mindset during the civil rights era of the 1960s and 1970s, having lived through those tumultuous times in both Montgomery and Birmingham, Alabama.

I am in awe of my sister-in-law Janice Nolin, Damon's wife and Martha's sister, for her expert Internet skills throughout this project. She tracked down the current whereabouts of many people involved in this case and the age and date of deaths of those who have passed away. She also secured photographs and useful background information about these people for inclusion in the book.

I thank my son Ted Hubbart for the photographs he took of the many scenes connected with this case and for his loyal support throughout this project. He was also able to solve the many computer problems I had while writing this work.

Dennis Ross and the members of his Creative Writing Workshop were an indispensable asset in developing this book. For nearly five years, I read the book to Mr. Ross's talented class, chapter by chapter, and received expert criticism on how to improve the writing.

I thank Caroline Heck-Miller, a retired assistant United States attorney in Miami, Florida, who is also Gene Miller's widow; Martin A. Dyckman, a retired associate editor of the *St. Petersburg Times;* and Kathie Klarreich, who succeeded Dennis Ross as the writing instructor of the Creative Writing Workshop, for their careful editing of the book's final draft and for their helpful suggested changes in the text.

Most important, I am indebted to Mitchell Kaplan, the legendary founder of Books and Books in Miami, for his unfailing support for the project and for connecting me with the University Press of Florida. I am equally grateful to Roy Black and H. T. Smith for their enthusiastic support of the book and for connecting me with Mitchell Kaplan.

I thank my friend Norman Rachlin for suggesting that I tell the story of this case mainly as an insider's account rather than entirely as a third-person narrative and for suggesting the title of the book. I am also most grateful to Sian Hunter, Kate Babbitt, and Carlynn Crosby at the University Press of Florida for their superb editing of the book.

Finally, many of my friends and family, too numerous to mention, encouraged me throughout this entire project. I thank them all for their support.

People Involved in the Pitts-Lee Case

Curtis Adams. Confessed to Warren Holmes and Broward County Deputy Sheriff Elihu Phares that he committed the robbery-kidnap-murders of gas-station attendants Grover Floyd and Jesse Burkett in Port St. Joe. Sentenced to life imprisonment for the robbery-kidnap-murder of Shamrock gas station attendant Floyd McFarland in Fort Lauderdale. No relation to J. Frank Adams. Died in prison on January 19, 1991, at the age of 59.

J. Frank Adams. State attorney for the Fourteenth Judicial Circuit of Florida; no relation to Curtis Adams. Prosecuted Pitts and Lee at the mercy trial in August 1963. Refused to reopen the Pitts and Lee case and fought all efforts to do so. Died on December 11, 1975, at the age of 66.

Mary Jean Akins. Curtis Adams's former girlfriend. Adams confessed to Akins that he robbed, kidnapped, and killed Grover Floyd and Jesse Burkett. Later, Akins separated from Adams, remarried, and eventually moved from Auburndale, Florida, to Tennessee in 1975.

Phil Ashler. Florida state treasurer. Voted to pardon Pitts and Lee in September 1975.

Reubin Askew. Governor of Florida from 1971 to 1979. Conducted an eighteen-month investigation into the murders of Grover Floyd and Jesse Burkett. Voted to pardon Pitts and Lee for those murders based on the ground of innocence. After serving two terms as governor, practiced law with the law firm of Greenberg Traurig. Served as US trade representative in the Carter administration (1979–1980). Tested the waters for a US presidential run for the 1981–1984 term but dropped out after the New Hampshire primary. Taught political science seminar courses at all ten Florida public universities; became a visiting professor at the University of South Florida in Tampa. Died on March 13, 2014, at the age of 85.

Cleve Backster. Controversial polygraph examiner in New York City. Conducted polygraph examinations of Mary Jean Akins and Willie Mae Lee. Continued working as a private polygraph examiner, testing plants and shrimp. Wrote *Primary Perception: Biocommunication with Plants, Living Foods, and Human Cells* (White Rose Millennium Press, 2003). Died on June 24, 2013, at the age of 89.

D. L. Barron. Chief of detectives in the Panama City Police Department. Part of the police team that interrogated Pitts and Lee in August 1963.

Doris Block. Wife of Irwin Block. Became enraged when Judge Smith sentenced Pitts and Lee to death at the 1972 Marianna trial. Ran into the well of the court, pointed at the judge and prosecutor, and shouted "I hope you have this on your conscience until the day you die!"

Irwin Block. Prominent practicing lawyer in Miami and pro bono lawyer with the ACLU. Served as chief defense counsel for Freddie Pitts and Wilbert Lee from 1966 to 1975. Continued his law practice in South Florida until his death on February 13, 2015, at the age of 87.

Tyrie Boyer. First District Court of Appeal judge. Author of the First District Court's opinion affirming Pitts and Lee's conviction at the 1972 Marianna trial. Continued serving as a judge on the First District Court until 1979. Practiced law thereafter in Jacksonville. Died December 17, 2013, at the age of 89.

Jesse Burkett. One of two service station attendants who was working at the Mo Jo gas station outside Port St. Joe, Florida, on the night of July 31–August 1, 1963. Was robbed, kidnapped, and murdered that night.

Arthur Canaday. General counsel to Governor Reubin Askew. Investigated the Pitts-Lee case for Askew to determine whether a pardon should be granted to the defendants. Later, served as general counsel for the Florida Power Commission. Retired and moved to Blowing Rock, North Carolina.

John Crews. Circuit judge from Gainesville, Florida. Presided at a pretrial hearing after Pitts and Lee were given a new trial. Dismissed the August 1963 grand jury indictment against the defendants on the ground that eligible Black voters in Gulf County were systematically excluded from the grand jury venire in violation of the Fourteenth Amendment. Later withdrew from the case.

M. J. "Doc" Daffin. Bay County sheriff. The major police investigator into the murders of Grover Floyd and Jesse Burkett in August 1963. Obtained confessions from Pitts and Lee that were later attacked in court for being false. Died while serving as sheriff on January 29, 1971, at the age of 68.

S. R. "Speedy" DeWitt. Investigator for the Florida Attorney General's Office. Investigated the Pitts-Lee case for the state in preparation for a weeklong hearing in Port St. Joe in September 1968. Took a sworn statement from

Willie Mae Lee in February 1968 in which Lee stated she had no knowledge of the Floyd-Burkett murders. Died on May 30, 1987, at the age of 59.

Earl Faircloth. Florida attorney general. Initially looked into the Pitts-Lee case beginning in 1967. Directed S. R. DeWitt, his top investigator, to conduct a complete review of the case. Thereafter, ran unsuccessfully for the US Senate. Practiced law in Broward County until his retirement. Died on May 5, 1995, at the age of 74.

W. L. Fitzpatrick. Circuit judge for the Fourteenth Judicial Circuit of Florida. Presided at the mercy trial for Pitts and Lee in August 1963 and sentenced both defendants to death. Retired in January 1980 and practiced law in Panama City. Died on April 25, 1999, at the age of 82.

Leonard Fleet. Attorney in Broward County, Florida. Represented Mary Jean Akins when she and Curtis Adams were indicted by the Broward County Grand Jury for the murder of Floyd McFarland in Fort Lauderdale. In 1982, elected circuit judge for the Seventeenth Judicial Circuit in Broward County, where he served for twenty-three years. Retired. Became a civil and family court mediator in Orlando.

Grover Floyd. One of two service station attendants who was working at the Mo Jo gas station outside Port St. Joe, Florida, on the night of July 31–August 1, 1963. Was robbed, kidnapped, and murdered that night.

Terry Furnell. Attorney practicing in Pinellas County, Florida. Represented Curtis Adams at a hearing in April 1969 at which Judge Holley granted a new trial for Pitts and Lee and at the March 1972 trial in Marianna. Continued to practice law in Pinellas County. Died on December 18, 2012, at the age of 75.

David Gaskin. Court-appointed lawyer for Pitts and Lee at the first appearance hearing in August 1963. Practiced law in Wewahitchka. Died on September 7, 2007, at the age of 81.

George Georgieff. Florida assistant attorney general. Lead counsel for the state in the weeklong evidentiary hearing in Port St. Joe in September 1968. Also served as counsel for the state in the state's appeal from Judge Holley's new trial order and in the appeal by the defendants from their conviction at the March 1972 trial in Marianna. Retired. Died on April 21, 1996, at the age of 73.

Michael Gilbert. Private psychiatrist practicing in Miami. Testified at the September 1968 evidentiary hearing in Port St. Joe concerning Willie Mae Lee's in-court hypnosis session. After the case was concluded, Gilbert testified to an innovative television intoxication diagnosis for the defendant in the Ronny Zamora murder trial in Miami in 1977, the first televised trial in

Florida. Practiced in Miami until he retired. Died on August 1, 2010, at the age of 94.

Israel Hanenson. Chief psychiatrist of the criminal ward at Florida State Hospital in Chattahoochee, Florida. Testified at the September 1968 evidentiary hearing in Port St. Joe concerning Willie Mae Lee's in-court hypnosis session. Died on October 11, 1969, at the age of 65.

Donald Hoag. Army CID investigator. Took a statement from Freddie Pitts in August 1963 that repudiated Pitts's prior confession to the police. Testified that Pitts had been beaten up by police.

Charles Holley. Circuit judge from Clearwater, Florida. Presided at the week-long evidentiary hearing in Port St. Joe in September 1968. Defeated for re-election as a circuit judge in Clearwater in 1972. Ran unsuccessfully for a seat on the Florida Supreme Court in 1976. Practiced law in Naples, Florida. Died on March 15, 1981, at the age of 56.

Warren Holmes. Private polygraph examiner in Miami. Obtained a tape-recorded confession from Curtis Adams to the murders of Grover Floyd and Jesse Burkett in Port St. Joe and to the murder of Floyd McFarland in Fort Lauderdale. Conducted over 70,000 polygraph examinations in a career that spanned nearly sixty years. Wrote *Criminal Interrogation: A Modern Format for Interrogating Criminal Suspects Based on the Intellectual Approach* (Charles C. Thomas, 2002). Died on April 25, 2013, at the age of 85.

Phillip Hubbart. Public defender for the Eleventh Judicial Circuit of Florida. Trial and appellate attorney for Pitts and Lee from 1965 to 1975. See also his biography on the last page of this book.

Sam Husband. Gulf County judge. Presided at the first appearance hearing for Pitts and Lee in August 1963.

Leo Jones. Assistant state attorney for the Fourteenth Judicial Circuit. Was the prosecuting attorney in Pitts and Lee's March 1972 trial in Marianna, Florida. Used his peremptory juror challenges at trial to get an all-white jury. Later became the state attorney for the Fourteenth Judicial Circuit until 1980. Left state service and practiced law in Panama City. Retired. Died on April 18, 2006, at the age of 79.

George Kittrell. Bay County Deputy Sheriff. Accused of inflicting a savage beating on Freddie Pitts in August 1963. After the case, became the Police Chief of the City of Springfield in the Florida Panhandle. Resigned in May 1976 after being cleared of loan sharking charges in an investigation conducted by Leo Jones. Died December 17, 1982, at the age of 61.

Larry Lang. Broward County deputy sheriff. Investigated the murder of Floyd McFarland in Fort Lauderdale and the murders of Floyd and Burkett in Port

St. Joe. Retired from police service and operated a private detective agency with his son Jeff Lang in Fort Lauderdale. Earned a bachelor's degree in legal studies from the University of Central Florida in 1994. Died on August 4, 2004, at the age of 76.

Ella Mae Lee. Wife of Wilbert Lee. Held in jail without a charge for nearly four weeks until Pitts and Lee were sentenced to death. Released for a few days during this period and re-arrested. Testified at the Marianna trial in March 1972 that Lee was home in bed with her at the time of the murders of Grover Floyd and Jesse Burkett. No relation to Willie Mae Lee. Lived in Pensacola, Florida, in 1968, and in Jamaica, New York, in 1972.

Wilbert Lee. One of the two defendants in this case. No relation to Willie Mae Lee. After he was pardoned, he settled in Miami, where he worked as a rehabilitation officer for the Miami-Dade County Jail until his retirement. Died on October 17, 2018, at the age of 83.

Willie Mae Lee. The state's chief witness against Pitts and Lee. No relation to Wilbert Lee or Ella Mae Lee. Lived in various places in New York state. Died in Panama City, Florida, on April 5, 2012, at the age of 68.

Joe McCawley. Licensed hypnotist in Orlando. Hypnotized Willie Mae Lee on the witness stand at September 1968 hearing in Port St. Joe. Continued his hypnosis practice until he retired. Died on April 15, 2014, at the age of 86.

Floyd McFarland. Shamrock gas station attendant in Fort Lauderdale. Was robbed, kidnapped, and murdered by Curtis Adams in August 1963.

Ray Markey. Florida assistant attorney general. Co-counsel for the state in the weeklong evidentiary hearing in Port St. Joe in September 1968. Continued working as a Florida assistant attorney general until resigning after more than thirty years of service. Later worked as an assistant state attorney for the Leon County State Attorney's Office. Died on January 17, 2006, at the age of 70.

Dorothy Martin. Sister of Wilbert Lee's wife, Ella Mae Lee. Argued with gas station attendants Grover Floyd and Jesse Burkett over the use of the white-only ladies restroom at the Mo Jo station in August 1963.

Virgil Mayo. Public defender for the Fourteenth Judicial Circuit of Florida, which includes both Port St. Joe and Marianna. Friend of Phillip Hubbart. Introduced Hubbart to various public officials in the circuit who were involved in the Pitts-Lee case. Declined any public role in the case. Twice elected president of the Florida Public Defenders Association. Retired after thirty-nine years of public defender service. Died on November 24, 2014, at the age of 90.

Donald Middlebrooks. Assistant general counsel to Governor Reubin Askew.

Investigated the Pitts-Lee case for Askew to determine whether a pardon should be granted to the defendants. After the case, practiced law in West Palm Beach, Florida, from 1977 to 1997. Appointed by President Bill Clinton in 1997 to serve as a judge on the United States District Court for the Southern District of Florida, where he currently serves.

Gene Miller. Pulitzer Prize–winning investigative journalist for the *Miami Herald* who covered the Pitts-Lee case for nine years (1967–1975). Author of *Invitation to a Lynching* (Doubleday, 1975), a pre-pardon comprehensive account of the case. Continued as an investigative reporter for the *Miami Herald* until he retired in 2001. Died on June 17, 2005, at the age of 76.

Willie Nicholson. Colorful retired Miami police officer and freelance investigator. Hired by the *Miami Herald* to conduct a short investigation of the Pitts-Lee case in Port St. Joe that yielded zero results, after which their relationship ended. Got involved in a crazed incident in Port St. Joe resulting in his arrest on various felony assault charges. Sent to the state mental hospital for an examination, following which all charges were dropped. Returned to Miami. Died on December 13, 1990, at the age of 64.

Jesse Pait. Fellow prison inmate with Curtis Adams. Informed on Adams to the Broward County Sheriff's Office. Stated that Adams confessed to having committed the murders of Floyd McFarland in Fort Lauderdale and Grover Floyd and Jesse Burkett in Port St. Joe. Died in prison on September 8, 1969, at the age of 45.

Byrd Parker. Gulf County sheriff. Participated briefly in the early stages of the police investigation in the Pitts-Lee case. Thereafter left the police investigation to his chief deputy sheriff, Wayne White. Served as sheriff until his retirement. Died on May 18, 1990, at the age of 63.

Elihu Phares. Broward County deputy sheriff. Investigated the murder of Floyd McFarland in Fort Lauderdale and the murders of Floyd and Burkett in Port St. Joe. Obtained a confession from Curtis Adams to the murders of Floyd and Burkett. Later became a captain of police at the Broward County Sheriff's Office. Retired. Lives in Fort Lauderdale.

Freddie Pitts. One of the two defendants in the Pitts-Lee case. A private in the United States Army at the time of his arrest. After being pardoned in September 1975, settled in Miami and worked as a trucker for his own firm. Lectured against capital punishment before various civic and law-related groups. Died on September 3, 2020, at the age of 76.

Bruce Potts. Army CID investigator. Took a statement in August 1963 from Freddie Pitts that repudiated Pitts's prior police confession. Testified that

Pitts had been beaten up. Eventually retired from the army and became a security officer for an Atlanta, Georgia bank.

John Rawls. Judge in the First District Court of Appeal of Florida. Author of the court's opinion reversing Judge Holley's order granting a new trial for Pitts and Lee. Served as judge until his retirement in 1977. Died on May 11, 1993, at the age of 72.

Maurice Rosen. Miami pro bono ACLU attorney for Pitts and Lee from 1966 to 1975. Practiced law in Miami until his death on October 8, 1991, at the age of 56.

Barry Semet. A lawyer with Irwin Block's law firm in Miami. Helped Phillip Hubbart write the brief and argue the case before the First District Court of Appeal on the state's appeal from Judge Holley's order granting Pitts and Lee a new trial.

Robert "Bob" Shevin. Succeeded Earl Faircloth as Florida attorney general in 1971. Confessed error on appeal before the Florida Supreme Court to give Pitts and Lee a new trial in 1971. Voted to pardon Pitts and Lee in September 1975. Ran for Florida governor in 1978 and lost in a runoff to Bob Graham in the Democratic Primary. Returned to Miami, where he practiced law. In 1996, appointed as a judge on Third District Court of Appeal in Miami. Died on July 11, 2005, at the age of 71.

D. R. Smith. Circuit court judge from Ocala, Florida. Presiding judge at Pitts and Lee's pretrial hearings in Port St. Joe and their trial in February and March 1972 in Marianna. Sentenced both defendants to death. Served as a circuit judge until he retired in 1978. Died on December 9, 1995, at the age of 82.

Lambson Smith. Army private initially accused of the Floyd-Burkett murders in Port St. Joe and held in jail. Later released. Continued serving in the army and was awarded the Purple Heart for his service in the Vietnam War. Died on January 12, 2003, at the age of 59.

Mike Tigar. Attorney in Washington, DC, with Edward Bennett Williams's law firm. Appeared briefly as part of the Pitts-Lee defense team at the September 1968 Port St. Joe hearing on the motion to set aside Pitts and Lee's convictions.

Joe Townsend. Polygraph examiner for the Florida Sheriffs Bureau. Polygraphed and interrogated Pitts and Lee in August 1963 and accused them of lying. Administered numerous polygraph tests to and questioned all the Black people arrested in this case as part of the police interrogation team. Continued working as a polygraph examiner for the Florida Department of

Law Enforcement in Tallahassee. Retired. Died August 14, 1992, at the age of 75.

Ralph Turlington. Florida commissioner of education. Voted to pardon Pitts and Lee in September 1975.

Fred Turner. Court-appointed trial and appellate lawyer for Pitts and Lee in 1963–1964. Conducted little or no investigation in the case. Accused of participating with the police in obtaining coerced confessions from Pitts and Lee. Pled the defendants guilty of first-degree murder with no prior plea agreement with the state. Refused to appeal the case until ordered to do so by Judge Fitzpatrick. Filed a three-page appellate brief before the Florida Supreme Court citing no legal authorities. Later became a circuit judge for the Fourteenth Judicial Circuit. Reprimanded by the Florida Supreme Court in October 1982 for "an arrogant, arbitrary and capricious abuse of his powers." Died on November 23, 2003, at the age of 81.

Wayne White. Gulf County deputy sheriff. One of two major investigators of the murders of Floyd and Burkett in August 1963. Accused of witnessing an all-night beating of Freddie Pitts administered by Bay County Deputy Sheriff George Kittrell. Later became the chief investigator for the state attorney for the Fourteenth Judicial Circuit until his retirement in April 1996. Died on April 21, 1997, at the age of 63.

John Wigginton. First District Court of Appeal judge. Author of the court's 1971 opinion denying the defendants' petition for a change of venue for their arraignment after Pitts and Lee had been granted a new trial. Served as judge until his retirement in 1973. Died on February 24, 1979, at the age of 70.

Edward Bennett Williams. Nationally known criminal defense lawyer practicing law in Washington, DC. Considered leading the Pitts-Lee defense team but ultimately declined.

Jack Winick. Army JAG lawyer. Interviewed Private Freddie Pitts on death row at Florida State Prison in 1964 and became greatly disturbed about the case. Tried unsuccessfully to get the army to intervene. Left the army, practiced law in Minneapolis, Minnesota, and joined the Pitts-Lee defense team. Later moved to San Diego and practiced law in California until his retirement in 2014. Died on October 24, 2019, at the age of 82.

Abbreviations

August 1963 arraignment transcript
Arraignment transcript, State of Florida v. Wilbert Lee, alias Slingshot Lee and Freddie L. Pitts, Case nos. 519 and 520, Wewahitchka, Florida, August 16, 1963, in author's possession

August 1963 hearing transcript
Court hearing transcript, State of Florida v. Wilbert Lee, alias Slingshot Lee and Freddie L. Pitts, Case nos. 519 and 520, Wewahitchka, Florida, August 12, 1963, in author's possession

August 1963 trial transcript
Trial transcript, State of Florida v. Wilbert Lee, alias Slingshot Lee, and Freddie L. Pitts, Case nos. 519 and 520, Wewahitchka, Florida, August 28, 1963, in author's possession

1966 Adams confession to Holmes
Tape-recorded and transcribed confession of Curtis Adams to Warren Holmes at the Broward County Jail, December 2, 1966, in author's possession

1967 Death Investigation
Joe Townsend, Death Investigation, Jesse L. Burkett–Grover Floyd/Victims, August 1, 1963 (date of investigation), Florida Sheriffs Bureau, March 1, 1967 (date of report), in author's possession

1968 Port St. Joe hearing transcript
Criminal Procedure Rule 1 Hearing Transcript, Freddie Lee Pitts and Wilbert (Slingshot) Lee v. State of Florida, Case nos. 519 and 520, Circuit Court for the Fourteenth Judicial Circuit of Florida at Port St. Joe, Florida, September 23–27, 1968, in author's possession

August 1971 Port St. Joe hearing transcript
Motion Hearing Transcript, State of Florida v. Freddie L. Pitts and Wilbert Lee, Case nos. 519 and 520, Circuit Court for the Fourteenth Judicial Circuit in and for Gulf County Florida at Port St. Joe, Florida, August 27–28, 1971, in author's possession

November 1971 Port St. Joe hearing transcript
Motion Hearing Transcript, State of Florida v. Freddie L. Pitts and Wilbert Lee, Case nos. 519 and 520, Circuit Court for the Fourteenth Judicial Circuit in and for Gulf County, Florida at Port St. Joe, Florida, November 18, 1971, in author's possession

January 1972 Marianna hearings transcript
Motion Hearings Transcript, State of Florida v. Freddie L. Pitts and Wilbert Lee, Case nos. 3-72-1 and 3-72-2, Circuit Court for the Fourteenth Judicial Circuit in and for Jackson County, Florida at Marianna, Florida, January 3, 1972, and January 21, 1972, in author's possession

1972 Marianna trial transcript
Trial transcript, State of Florida v. Freddie L. Pitts and Wilbert Lee, Case nos. 3-72-1 and 3-72-2, Circuit Court for the Fourteenth Judicial Circuit in and for Jackson County, Florida at Marianna, Florida, February 21, 1972–March 15, 1972, in author's possession

Notes

Prologue

1. Jack Greenberg, *Crusaders in the Courts: How a Dedicated Band of Lawyers Fought for the Civil Rights Revolution* (New York: Basic Books, 1994), 216.

2. "Inaugural Address of Governor George Wallace in Montgomery, Alabama," Alabama Department of Archives and History, https://digital.archives.alabama.gov/digital/collection/voices/id/2952/.

3. Diane McWhorter, *Carry Me Home: Birmingham, Alabama, The Climactic Battle of the Civil Rights Revolution* (New York: Simon and Schuster Paperbacks, 2001), 501–525.

4. Greenberg, *Crusaders in the Courts*, 338–340.

5. "John F. Kennedy, Civil Rights Address," June 11, 1963, American Rhetoric: Top 100 Speeches, accessed March 2, 2015, http://www.americanrhetoric.com/speeches/jfk-civilrights.htm. See also Theodore C. Sorensen, *Kennedy* (New York: Harper and Row, paperback edition, 1965), 556–557.

6. Taylor Branch, *Parting the Waters: America in the King Years 1954–63* (New York: Simon and Schuster, 1988), 824–827.

7. David R. Colburn, *Racial Change and Crisis: St. Augustine, Florida, 1877–1990* (Gainesville: University Press of Florida), 40–43, 48–49; William H. Chafe, *Civilities and Civil Rights: Greensboro, North Carolina, and the Black Struggle for Freedom* (New York: Oxford University Press, 1980), 71.

8. J. Michael Butler, *Beyond Integration: The Black Freedom Struggle in Escambia County, Florida, 1960–1980* (Chapel Hill: University of North Carolina Press, 2016), 53–54.

9. Diane McWhorter, *Carry Me Home: Birmingham, Alabama, The Climactic Battle of the Civil Rights Revolution* (New York: Simon and Schuster Paperbacks, 2001), 347–360.

10. Raymond Arsenault, *Freedom Riders: 1961 and Struggle for Racial Justice* (Oxford: Oxford University Press, 2006), 140–146, 209–220.

11. Gulf County Deputy Sheriff Wayne White, one of the top investigators in the Pitts/Lee case, made these statements in a conversation with Broward County Deputy Sheriff Elihu Phares on October 17, 1966, at the Gulf County Sheriff's Office in Port St. Joe, Florida. Detective Phares testified to this conversation at the 1972 trial in Marianna, Florida. 1972 Marianna trial transcript, 3853–3855.

12. Drew D. Hansen, *The Dream: Martin Luther King, Jr., and the Speech that Inspired a Nation* (New York: Harper Collins Publishers, 2003), 25–63.

Chapter 1. Introduction: The End of the Ordeal

1. Miller Epilogue, 3, unpublished manuscript in author's possession.

2. Mike Baxter, "Miller Captures a Pulitzer for His Pitts-Lee Stories," *Miami Herald,* May 4, 1976. Miller won the Pulitzer Prize for Local Investigative Specialized Reporting in May 1976 based on his voluminous newspaper articles on the Pitts-Lee case. Miller had won the same Pulitzer Prize in 1967 for his newspaper investigations that freed a man and a woman wrongfully convicted of murder.

3. Gene Miller, *Invitation to a Lynching* (Garden City, NY: Doubleday & Co., 1975).

4. Miller Epilogue, 3–4.

5. Miller Epilogue, 4.

6. James T. Wooten, "It's Over for 2 Wrongly Held 12 Years," *New York Times,* September 20, 1975.

7. Gene Miller, "Pitts, Lee Walk as Free Men," *Miami Herald,* September 20, 1975; Gene Miller, "'We'll Keep Our Plans To Ourselves,'" *Miami Herald,* September 20, 1975.

8. Patty Hearst was kidnapped in February 1974 by the Symbionese Liberation Army, a left-wing revolutionary group. Thereafter Hearst allegedly joined the group voluntarily and committed a series of federal bank robberies with them until she was finally arrested. "Patty Hearst Seized By FBI; Long Hunt Ends In San Francisco; Harrises and 3d Companion Taken," *New York Times,* September 19, 1975; "Patty's Twisted Journey," *Time Magazine,* September 29, 1975, 11–21.

9. In a paper delivered to the Southern Political Science Association, Askew was ranked as one of the ten most effective governors in America during the twentieth century. Askew shared this ranking with Robert Lafollette, who served as governor of Wisconsin, and Woodrow Wilson, who served as governor of New Jersey. See Martin A. Dyckman, *Reubin O'D. Askew and the Golden Age of Florida Politics* (Gainesville: University Press of Florida, 2011), 2–3.

10. Executive Order Number 75-49, remarks of Gov. Reubin O'D. Askew, September 11, 1975, filed with the Florida Secretary of State, September 24, 1975, in author's possession.

11. Bruce Smathers issued a two-page statement indicating that he had found "numerous contradictions, evidentiary gaps and unanswered questions" and that "these unanswered facts and circumstances prevent me from taking action at this time." Gerald Lewis similarly concluded that "it is impossible for me to arrive at the truth at this time." Doyle Conner issued a lengthy statement entitled "Dissenting Opinion" with attached documents that expressed his strong disagreement with the pardons and concluded that Pitts and Lee were guilty. Robert D. Shaw Jr., "Three Cabinet Members Refuse to Sign Pardon," *Miami Herald,* September 20, 1975.

12. "Burials at Raiford Cemetery, Union County, Florida," accessed June 15, 2018, http://files.usgwarchives.net/fl/union/cemeteries/raifordb.txt.

13. James Baldwin, "As Much Truth as One Can Bear," in James Baldwin, *The Cross of Redemption: Uncollected Writings,* ed. Randall Kenan (New York: Vintage Press 2011), 42.

14. As quoted in Raymond Lang, "Two Innocents Who Suffered on Death Row," *Ebony,* September 1983, 29.

Chapter 2. Curtis Adams and the Port St. Joe/Fort Lauderdale Murders

1. Port St. Joe had a population of 4,217 in 1960. "Table 7. Population of Counties, by Census County Division, 1960," in *1960 Census of Population,* vol. 1, *Characteristics of the Population,* part A, *Number of Inhabitants* (Washington, DC: US Department of Commerce, Bureau of the Census, 1963), page 11-12.

2. Richard Skipper testimony, 1972 Marianna trial transcript, 3055–3056.

3. Gene Miller, *Invitation to a Lynching* (Garden City, NY: Doubleday & Co., 1975), 213.

4. Gene Miller, "The Haunted Memories of Mary Jean Akins," *Tropic (Miami Herald* Sunday magazine), September 7, 1975, 10; Miller, *Invitation to a Lynching,* 42–43.

5. 1966 Adams confession to Holmes, 10–12; Mary Jean Akins testimony, 1968 Port St. Joe hearing transcript, 640.

6. 1966 Adams confession to Holmes, 13.

7. Freddie Pitts testimony, 1972 Marianna trial transcript, 3722–3723; Wilbert Lee testimony, 1972 Marianna trial transcript, 3789; Freddie Pitts testimony, 1968 Port St. Joe hearing transcript, 789–791.

8. Freddie Pitts testimony, 1968 Port St. Joe hearing transcript, 789–791; Ella Mae Lee testimony, 1968 Port St. Joe hearing transcript, 152–153; Wilbert Lee testimony, 1972 Marianna trial transcript, 3788, 3789–3791, 3795; Miller, *Invitation to a Lynching,* 85.

9. 1966 Adams confession to Holmes, 13.

10. Dorothy Martin testimony, 1972 Marianna trial transcript, 3647–3648, 3651–3652.

11. 1966 Adams confession to Holmes, 13–14.

12. 1972 Marianna trial transcript: Billy Versiga testimony, 3082–3090; Aubrey Branch testimony, 3188–3189.

13. 1972 Marianna trial transcript: Dorothy Martin testimony, 3647–3648; Ella Mae Lee testimony, 3666.

14. 1972 Marianna trial transcript: Freddie Pitts testimony, 3724, 3725–3726; Wilbert Lee testimony, 3790–3791; Ella Mae Lee testimony, 3667; Dorothy Martin testimony, 3649.

15. 1972 Marianna trial transcript: Wilbert Lee testimony, 3791–3792; Ella Mae Lee testimony, 3667; Dorothy Martin testimony, 3650–3651.

16. Freddie Pitts testimony, 1972 Marianna trial transcript, 3726–3729; Freddie Pitts Testimony, 1968 Port St. Joe hearing transcript, 792–795.

17. 1972 Marianna trial transcript, 3727–3728; Freddie Pitts testimony, 1968 Port St. Joe hearing transcript, 793–794.

18. Henry Hogue testimony, 1972 Marianna trial transcript, 3826.

19. 1972 Marianna trial transcript: Freddie Pitts testimony, 3729; William Versiga testimony, 3093.

20. Freddie Pitts testimony, 1972 Marianna trial transcript, 3729–3730.

21. 1966 Adams confession to Holmes, 15.

22. 1966 Adams confession to Holmes, 15; Miller, *Invitation to a Lynching,* 217

23. Mary Jean Akins testimony, 1972 Marianna trial transcript, 3633; Mary Jean Akins testimony, 1968 Port St. Joe hearing transcript, 640.

24. Miller, *Invitation to a Lynching,* 215–216. Mary Jean Akins gave a similar account when we proffered her testimony to the trial court at the 1972 trial in Marianna, Florida. See 1972 Marianna trial transcript, 3619–3634.

25. Miller, *Invitation to a Lynching,* 216.

26. Miller, *Invitation to a Lynching,* 216.

27. 1966 Adams confession to Holmes, 2, 56, 60–61.

28. Miller, *Invitation to a Lynching,* 217.

29. Miller, *Invitation to a Lynching,* 217. Mary Jean Akins testified, outside the jury's presence, to the same incident at the 1972 trial in Marianna, Florida. See 1972 Marianna trial transcript, 3635–3636.

30. 1966 Adams confession to Holmes, 62.

31. Miller, *Invitation to a Lynching,* 217–218.

32. Miller, *Invitation to a Lynching,* 218.

33. Miller, *Invitation to a Lynching,* 218.

34. Miller, *Invitation to a Lynching,* 218.

35. Miller, *Invitation to a Lynching,* 218; Mary Jean Akins testimony, 1972 Marianna trial transcript, 3635–3636.

36. 1972 Marianna trial transcript, 3636–3637.

Chapter 3. The Port St. Joe Interrogations

1. Gene Miller, *Invitation to a Lynching* (Garden City, NY: Doubleday & Co., 1975), 1.

2. Jimmy Barfield testimony, 1972 Marianna trial transcript, 3034–3038.

3. 1972 Marianna trial transcript: Jimmy Barfield testimony, 3038; Richard Skipper testimony, 3057–3064.

4. Wayne White's statement to Elihu Phares is in Elihu Phares testimony, 1972 Marianna trial transcript, 3854–3855.

5. 1972 Marianna trial transcript: Wayne White testimony, 3301; Aubrey Branch testimony, 3189–3190; William Versiga testimony, 3086.

6. Wayne White made these statements in a conversation with Broward County detective Elihu Phares on October 17, 1966, at the Gulf County Sheriff's Office in Port St. Joe, Florida. Detective Phares testified to this conversation at the 1972 trial in Marianna, Florida; see Elihu Phares testimony, 1972 Marianna trial transcript, 3853–3857. White virtually confirmed this conversation when he testified at the same trial. He stated it was "possible" that he had told Detective Phares that Curtis Adams was a "prime suspect" in the murders of Floyd and Burkett and didn't deny Phares's account of the conversation; Wayne White testimony, 1972 Marianna trial transcript, 3345.

7. Thomasina Stallworth testimony, 1968 Port St. Joe hearing transcript, 176–180.

8. Miller, *Invitation to a Lynching,* 134.

9. See Jeffrey Lickson, *David Charles: The Story of the Quincy Five* (Tallahassee: Mocking Bird Press, 1974), 16–111.

10. Freddie Pitts testimony, 1972 Marianna trial transcript, 3730; Freddie Pitts testimony, 1968 Port St. Joe hearing transcript, 796–797.

11. 1972 Marianna trial transcript: Freddie Pitts testimony, 3718–3721, 3730–3731; Richard Skipper testimony, 3050–3052, 3075.

12. 1972 Marianna trial transcript: Freddie Pitts testimony 3730–3731; Richard Skipper testimony 3053–3054.

13. Freddie Pitts testimony, 1972 Marianna trial transcript, 3730–3731.

14. Freddie Pitts testimony, 1968 Port St. Joe hearing transcript, 798; Freddie Pitts, statement to Warren Holmes, Florida State Prison, December 22, 1966, 41–42, in author's possession.

15. Freddie Pitts testimony, 1968 Port St. Joe hearing transcript, 798–799; Freddie Pitts, statement to Warren Holmes, 43–44.

16. Freddie Pitts testimony, 1972 Marianna trial transcript, 3732

17. Marianna trial transcript: Freddie Pitts testimony, 3732; Wilbert Lee testimony, 93.

18. 1972 Marianna trial transcript: Freddie Pitts testimony, 3732; Wilbert Lee testimony, 3793–3794.

19. 1972 Marianna trial transcript: Freddie Pitts testimony, 3732; Wilbert Lee testimony, 3793–3794.

20. Miller, *Invitation to a Lynching*, 92; Wilbert Lee testimony, 1972 Marianna trial transcript, 3794–3795.

21. Miller, *Invitation to a Lynching*, 92; Wilbert Lee testimony, 1972 Marianna trial transcript, 3796.

22. Wilbert Lee, statement to Warren Holmes, Florida State Prison, December 22, 1966, 24, in author's possession.

23. Miller, *Invitation to a Lynching*, 95.

24. Freddie Pitts testimony, 1972 Marianna trial transcript, 3732–3733.

25. Miller, *Invitation to a Lynching*, 95; Freddie Pitts testimony, 1972 Marianna trial transcript, 3733.

26. Miller, *Invitation to a Lynching*, 95; Freddie Pitts testimony, 1972 Marianna trial transcript, 3733.

27. Miller, *Invitation to a Lynching*, 92–94.

28. Miller, *Invitation to a Lynching*, 253–254. See the comprehensive investigative report on Townsend in "'Lie Detector' Man under Fire," *Tallahassee Democrat*, October 7, 1971. See also Martin Dyckman, "'The Polygraph Made a Big Mistake,'" *St. Petersburg Times*, October 10, 1971, for another comprehensive report on the subject.

29. 1967 Death Investigation, 2.

30. 1967 Death Investigation, 4, 14.

31. 1967 Death Investigation, 3, 7, 9, 11, 13.

32. 1967 Death Investigation, 4.

33. Wilbert Lee, statement to Warren Holmes, Florida State Prison, December 22, 1966, 24, in author's possession.

34. Wilbert Lee testimony, 1968 Port St. Joe hearing transcript, 351.

35. 1967 Death Investigation, 8.

36. Freddie Pitts testimony, 1968 Port St. Joe hearing transcript, 801–802.

37. 1967 Death Investigation, 7.

38. Freddie Pitts testimony, 1968 Port St. Joe hearing transcript, 803–804.

39. Freddie Pitts testimony, 1972 Marianna trial transcript, 3734–3736.

40. Wayne White testimony, 1972 Marianna trial transcript, 3354.

41. Wayne White testimony, 1972 Marianna trial transcript, 3317.

42. Wayne White deposition, April 29, 1968, Panama City, Florida, 3–4.

43. Bruce Potts testimony, 1972 Marianna trial transcript, 3918–3919. Potts identified Barron as the police officer who made this statement about Kittrell. The identity of Barron is found in Wilbert Lee's police confession, August 9, 1963, which lists "D.L. Barron, Chief of Detectives, Panama City Police Department" as a witness to this statement.

44. Wayne White deposition, 61.

Chapter 4. The Panama City Interrogations

1. Donald Hoag testimony, 1968 Port St. Joe hearing transcript, 3493–3494.

2. Wayne White was reluctant to admit all this but did so under the withering cross-examination of my co-counsel, Irwin Block. Wayne White testimony, 1972 Marianna trial transcript, 3357–3358.

3. See Equal Justice Initiative, *Lynching in America: Confronting the Legacy of Racial Terror*, 3rd ed. (Montgomery, AL: Equal Justice Initiative, 2017), 40, 45, 72. The National Memorial for Peace and Justice in Montgomery, Alabama, commemorates all the Black victims of lynching in America from 1877 to 1950. The names of the victims, the year, and the county and state where they were lynched are engraved on large stone slabs throughout the memorial.

4. Robert Sidwell testimony, 1968 Port St. Joe hearing transcript, 1226–1228.

5. Freddie Pitts testimony, 1972 Marianna trial transcript, 3737.

6. Wilbert Lee, statement to Warren Holmes, Florida State Prison, December 22, 1966, 24–25, in author's possession.

7. Robert Sidwell testimony, 1968 Port St. Joe hearing transcript, 1229.

8. Ludie Gaston testimony, 1972 Marianna trial transcript, 3104, 3108.

9. 1972 Marianna trial transcript: Ludie Gaston testimony, 3116–3117, James Graves testimony 3121.

10. Wayne White testimony, 1972 Marianna trial transcript, 3118.

11. Gene Miller, *Invitation to a Lynching* (Garden City, NY: Doubleday & Co., 1975), 99; W. L. Comforter testimony, 1972 Marianna trial transcript, 3138.

12. James Graves testimony, 1972 Marianna trial transcript, 3133–3134.

13. "Murder Suspects Held for Death of Two Gulf Countians," *The Star* (Port St. Joe, FL), August 8, 1963, 1.

14. "Murder Suspects Held."

15. Miller, *Invitation to a Lynching*, 109–110.

16. The Floyd autopsy report reads in relevant part as follows:

Diagnosis. Penetrating bullet wound entering scalp just to the left of midline at posterior-superior portion of the skull and exiting just behind the right mastoid area. . . . The only wound found is an entrance bullet wound, just above the lambda or the superior portion of the head in its posterior aspects. This entrance wound is slightly to the left of the midline.

The bullet evidently penetrated through the skull and through the posterior portion of the brain, crossing the midline, and exiting from the skull but not from the scalp just posterior to the mastoid portion of the right side of the head.

The lead pellet broke into three separate portions, the base of which was identified as being fired from a .38 caliber gun. There is only a small opening in the scalp in the exit area and the lead bullets were found beneath the skin. . . . The three separate pieces of lead were turned over to the sheriff of Gulf County.

Defendant's Exhibit 3, 1972 Marianna trial transcript, 3881.

The Burkett autopsy report reads in relevant part as follows:

Diagnosis. Bullet wound, entrance in right temporal area above right ear, no exit. Bullet found in left sphenoid bone. . . . Examination of the head shows an entrance bullet wound in the right temporal region. This entrance wound is very small. On removing calvarium it is noted that there is a fracture of the wing of the right sphenoid bone with the fracture extending down into the inner ear. There is a marked degree of destruction of the brain substance with liquefaction.

The bullet was found in the left wing of the sphenoid bone with fracture of this bone and fracture down into the left inner ear. There is no evidence of an exit. This bullet is thought to be a .38 caliber and was turned over to the sheriff of Gulf County.

The bullet, in traveling from the right to the left side caused a great deal of brain damage and I think was the cause of death.

Defendant's Exhibit 3, 1972 Marianna trial transcript, 3881.

17. J. Michael Butler, *Beyond Integration: The Black Freedom Struggle in Escambia County, Florida, 1960–1980* (Chapel Hill: University of North Carolina Press, 2016), 53–54.

18. Daffin had a checkered history. In 1961, Governor Farris Bryant removed him from office based on charges of corruption in the sheriff's office. The *News Herald* in Panama City had run a series of investigative reports written by W. U. "Duke" Newcome that showed that sheriff's deputies were taking bribes from moonshiners and owners of illegal gambling operations. In 1962, Newcome won a Pulitzer Prize for his exposé. However, Daffin was overwhelmingly reelected as Bay County sheriff in 1963 and served in that capacity until his death in 1971. "News Herald Pulitzer Prize Winner Dies," *News Herald* (Panama City, FL), September 27, 2012.

19. M. J. "Doc" Daffin testimony, 1968 Port St. Joe hearing transcript, 286–290, 292–293.

20. Willie Mae Lee, sworn statement to State Attorney J. Frank Adams and Florida Attorney General Investigator S. R. DeWitt, February 2, 1968, 3–4, 6. In author's possession.

21. Wilbert Lee testimony, 1972 Marianna trial transcript, 3798.

22. Willie Mae Lee, sworn statement to State Attorney J. Frank Adams, circa August

3, 1963, Petitioner's Exhibit D, 1968 Port St. Joe hearing transcript, 1; see Miller, *Invitation to a Lynching,* 101.

23. Willie Mae Lee, sworn statement to State Attorney J. Frank Adams, circa August 3, 1963, 2–3, in author's possession; see Miller, *Invitation to a Lynching,* 101.

24. Willie Mae Lee, sworn statement to State Attorney J. Frank Adams, circa August 3, 1963, 3; see Miller, *Invitation to a Lynching,* 101.

25. Henry Hogue testimony, 1972 Marianna trial transcript, 3826.

26. Willie Mae Lee, sworn statement to State Attorney J. Frank Adams, 3–9; see Miller, *Invitation to a Lynching,* 101.

27. Lambson Smith, statement to Warren Holmes, Fort Bragg, North Carolina, May 27, 1967, 14–17, in author's possession; Miller, *Invitation to a Lynching,* 105.

28. 1967 Death Investigation, 18–20; Miller, *Invitation to a Lynching,* 114–115.

29. Willie Mae Lee, sworn statement to State Attorney J. Frank Adams, 1; see Miller, *Invitation to a Lynching,* 111.

30. Willie Mae Lee, sworn statement to State Attorney J. Frank Adams, circa August 5, 1963, 2 et. seq.; see Miller, *Invitation to a Lynching,* 111.

31. Willie Mae Lee, sworn statement to State Attorney J. Frank Adams, circa August 5, 1963; Petitioner's Exhibit C, 1968 Port St. Joe Hearing, 3; see Miller, *Invitation to a Lynching,* 111.

32. Willie Mae Lee, sworn statement to State Attorney J. Frank Adams, circa August 5, 1963, Petitioner's Exhibit C, 1968 Port St. Joe Hearing 4–6.; see also Miller, *Invitation to a Lynching,* 111.

33. 1967 Death Investigation, 20.

Chapter 5. The Army CID Investigation

1. Bruce Potts testimony, 1968 Port St. Joe hearing transcript, 44; Gene Miller, *Invitation to a Lynching* (Garden City, NY: Doubleday & Co., 1975), 111.

2. Bruce Potts testimony, 1972 Marianna trial transcript, 3904–3905; Bruce Potts testimony, 1968 Port St. Joe hearing transcript, 42, 83; Donald Hoag testimony, 1968 Port St. Joe hearing transcript, 186; Miller, *Invitation to a Lynching,* 111.

3. Bruce Potts testimony, 1968 Port St. Joe hearing transcript, 116–117, 129.

4. Bruce C. Potts, CID Investigator's Statement, Military Police Company, Fort Rucker, Alabama, File No. 3-(92)-63-124, August 19, 1963, 1, in author's possession.

5. 1972 Marianna trial transcript: Bruce Potts testimony, 3906–3907; Donald Hoag testimony, 3482–3483.

6. Donald Hoag testimony, 1972 Marianna trial transcript, 3483; Bruce Potts testimony, 1968 Port St. Joe hearing transcript, 46.

7. Bruce Potts testimony, 1968 Port St. Joe hearing transcript, 46–47.

8. Bruce Potts testimony, 1968 Port St. Joe hearing transcript, 47–49.

9. Bruce Potts testimony, 1972 Marianna trial transcript, 3908–3909.

10. Bruce Potts testimony, 1972 Marianna trial transcript, 3909–3910; Donald Hoag testimony, 1972 Marianna trial transcript, 3484–3485; Donald Hoag, CID Investigator's Statement, August 18, 1963, 196, in author's possession.

11. Donald Hoag testimony, 1972 Marianna trial transcript, 3484–3486; Bruce Potts

testimony, 1972 Marianna trial transcript, 3909–3910; Donald Hoag testimony, 1968 Port St. Joe hearing transcript, 189–190; Miller *Invitation to a Lynching*, 109, 112.

12. Bruce C. Potts, CID Investigator's Statement, 1.

13. Bruce Potts testimony, 1972 Marianna trial transcript, 3485–3486, 3489–3490; Bruce Potts testimony, 1968 Port St. Joe hearing transcript, 49–50, Donald Hoag testimony, 1968 Port St. Joe hearing transcript, 192–193.

14. Bruce Potts testimony, 1972 Marianna trial transcript, 3912–3913; Bruce Potts, CID Investigator's Statement, August 19, 1963, 1.

15. Bruce Potts testimony, 1972 Marianna trial transcript, 3907–3908, 3912–3913; Donald Hoag testimony, 1972 Marianna trial transcript, 3485–3486, 3489–3490.

16. Bruce Potts testimony, 1972 Marianna trial transcript, 3907–3908.

17. Miller, *Invitation to a Lynching*, 112.

18. Bruce Potts, statement to Warren Holmes, Marriott Motel, Atlanta, Georgia, May 26, 1967, 29, in author's possession.

19. Bruce Potts testimony, 1968 Port St. Joe hearing transcript, 51–52; Miller, *Invitation to a Lynching*, 12.

20. Bruce Potts, statement to Warren Holmes, 32.

21. Bruce Potts, statement to Warren Holmes, 23–24; Miller, *Invitation to a Lynching*, 120.

22. Bruce Potts testimony, 1968 Port St. Joe hearing transcript, 59.

23. Bruce Potts, statement to Warren Holmes, 10.

24. Bruce Potts, statement to Warren Holmes, 8.

25. Bruce Potts testimony, 1972 Marianna trial transcript, 3910–3911. In an earlier statement to Warren Holmes, Potts had said, "He [White] said the way to interrogate the n——r gals down here was to tell them that you were going to shave their hair off and electrocute them. He said they'd tell you anything you want"; Bruce Potts, statement to Warren Holmes, 25.

26. Bruce Potts testimony, 1968 Port St. Joe hearing transcript, 199.

27. Donald Hoag testimony, 1972 Marianna trial transcript, 3492–3493.

28. Bruce Potts testimony, 1972 Marianna trial transcript, 3911.

29. Donald Hoag, CID Investigator's Statement, 2.

30. Bruce C. Potts, CID Investigator's Statement, 1.

31. Donald Hoag testimony, 1972 Marianna trial transcript, 3491.

32. Bruce Potts testimony, 1972 Marianna trial transcript, 3912.

33. Bruce C. Potts, CID Investigator's Statement, 1–2.

34. Bruce Potts testimony, 1968 Port St. Joe hearing transcript, 63.

Chapter 6. A Court Hearing

1. Freddie Pitts testimony, 1972 Marianna trial transcript, 3737.

2. Wilbert Lee testimony, 1972 Marianna trial transcript, 3799–4000.

3. 1968 Port St. Joe hearing transcript: Wilbert Lee testimony, 361; Freddie Pitts testimony, 812.

4. 1968 Port St. Joe hearing transcript: Judge Fitzpatrick testimony, 1160; David Gas-

kin testimony, 1187–1188; Sam Husband testimony, 1204. See also Gene Miller, *Invitation to a Lynching* (Garden City, NY: Doubleday & Co., 1975), 123.

5. David Gaskin testimony, 1968 Port St. Joe hearing transcript, 1189.

6. David Gaskin testimony, 1968 Port St. Joe hearing transcript, 1195.

7. 1968 Port St. Joe hearing transcript: Freddie Pitts testimony, 813, Wilbert Lee testimony, 361–362.

8. 1968 Port St. Joe hearing transcript: Freddie Pitts testimony, 813, Wilbert Lee testimony, 361–362.

9. Phillip Hubbart to David Gaskin, August 8, 1968, in author's possession.

10. David Gaskin to Phillip Hubbart, August 14, 1968, 3, in author's possession.

11. Gaskin to Hubbart, August 14, 1968, 1.

12. Gaskin to Hubbart, August 14, 1968, 1–2.

13. Gaskin to Hubbart, August 14, 1968, 2.

14. Gaskin to Hubbart, August 14, 1968, 2.

15. David Gaskin testimony, 1968 Port St. Joe hearing transcript, 1189–1191.

16. Miller, *Invitation to a Lynching*, 122–123.

17. Gaskin to Hubbart, August 14, 1968, 2.

18. Sections 902.01, 902.04 of the Florida Statutes (1963) required the magistrate to advise the defendant of his or her rights and to conduct a hearing in which testimony would be taken from witnesses. Section 902.13 of the Florida Statutes (1963) provided that "after hearing the evidence, if it appears that an offense has not been committed, or that, if committed, there is *not probable cause* to believe the defendant guilty thereof, the magistrate shall order that he be discharged." However, Section 902.14 of the Florida Statutes (1963) provided that "if it appears that any offense has been committed and that there is *probable cause to* believe the defendant guilty thereof, the magistrate shall hold him to answer" and if not admitted to bail, "the magistrate shall commit him to custody." Section 901.08 of the Florida Statutes (1963) provided that "all witnesses shall be examined in the presence of the defendant and may be cross examined."

19. Gaskin to Hubbart, August 14, 1968, 2.

20. Wilbert Lee testimony, 1968 Port St. Joe hearing transcript, 365–366.

21. Lambson Smith, statement to Warren Holmes, Fort Bragg, North Carolina, May 27, 1967, 19–20, in author's possession.

22. David Gaskin testimony, 1968 Port St. Joe hearing transcript, 1186.

23. David Gaskin testimony, 1968 Port St. Joe hearing transcript, 1197.

Chapter 7. Pitts and Lee Confess

1. Freddie Pitts Confession, 1:10 p.m., August 8, 1963, Panama City, Florida, in author's possession.

2. Bruce C. Potts, CID Investigator's Statement, Military Police Company, Fort Rucker Alabama, File No. 3-(92)-63-124, August 19, 1963, 2, in author's possession.

3. Bruce Potts testimony, 1972 Marianna trial transcript, 3914–3915.

4. Donald Hoag testimony, 1972 Marianna trial transcript, 3495–3496.

5. Bruce Potts testimony, 1968 Port St. Joe hearing transcript, 70.

6. Bruce Potts testimony, 1968 Port St. Joe hearing transcript, 70.

7. Donald Hoag testimony, 1968 Port St. Joe hearing transcript, 196–197.

8. Freddie Pitts, CID Statement, Bay County Jail, Panama City, Florida, Service No. RA-14-648-068, August 8, 1963, 2–3, in author's possession.

9. Donald Hoag testimony, 1972 Marianna trial transcript, 3496–3497; Donald Hoag testimony, 1968 Port St. Joe hearing transcript, 194–195; Bruce Potts testimony, 1968 Port St. Joe hearing transcript, 71–72.

10. Donald Hoag testimony, 1968 Port St. Joe hearing transcript, 204.

11. Bruce Potts, statement to Warren Holmes, Marriott Motel, Atlanta, Georgia, May 26, 1967, 35–36, in author's possession.

12. Freddie Pitts testimony, 1968 Port St. Joe hearing transcript, 817.

13. Wilbert Lee testimony, 1972 Marianna trial transcript, 3800–3801.

14. Scott Minerbrook, "The Stolen Years of Two Innocent Men," *Newsday Magazine,* August 21, 1983, 30.

15. Freddie Pitts Confession, 1:10 p.m. August 8, 1963, Panama City, Florida, 1, in author's possession; Sheriff M. J. Daffin testimony, 1963 Port St. Joe mercy trial transcript, 30, in author's possession.

16. Freddie Pitts Confession, 2.

17. Wilbert Lee Confession, 1:30 a.m. August 9, 1963, Panama City, Florida, 2, in author's possession.

18. Gene Miller, *Invitation to a Lynching* (Garden City, NY: Doubleday & Co., 1975), 119; Laboratory Report Re: 857-18, Freddie Lee Pitts and Wilbur [sic] (Slingshot) Lee, Death Investigation (Shooting) Jesse Burkett and Grover Floyd, Gulf County 7/31/63, Florida Sheriffs Bureau, August 27, 1963, 1, in author's possession.

19. Miller, *Invitation to a Lynching,* 119; Laboratory Report Re: 857-18, 2–3.

20. Laboratory Report Re: 857-18, 2–3; Laboratory Report Re: 851-1574, Freddie Lee Pitts and Wilbert [sic] (Slingshot) Lee, Death Investigation (Shooting) Jesse Burkett and Grover Floyd, Gulf County 7/31/63, Florida Sheriffs Bureau, August 26, 1963, 1–3, in author's possession.

21. Laboratory Report Re: 851-1574, 3.

22. Miller, *Invitation to a Lynching,* 119.

Chapter 8. The Initial Trial Court Proceedings

1. Judge W. L. Fitzpatrick deposition, Panama City, Florida, January 31, 1972, 30–31, emphasis added, in author's possession.

2. Fitzpatrick deposition, 7. Judge Fitzpatrick testified at a court hearing in September 1968 that he had asked Pitts and Lee during this chambers conference if they had been mistreated by the police and that they had said that they had not. Judge W. L. Fitzpatrick testimony, 1968 Port St. Joe hearing transcript, 3. But in his deposition testimony given in January 1972, the judge changed his testimony and said he couldn't remember making that inquiry. Miller and Holmes were concerned when they first learned of this supposed private meeting and went to Raiford to see Pitts and Lee. Pitts and Lee both said that they had had no such private conference with the judge. Gene Miller, *Invitation to a Lynching* (Garden City, NY: Doubleday & Co., 1975), 164. Miller also interviewed the clerk of court, George Core, in the clerk's office on September 18, 1968, concerning

this matter. Core told Miller, "I don't remember Judge Fitzpatrick taking Pitts and Lee into his chambers at any time." Gene Miller's notes of interview, 2, in author's possession.

3. August 1963 hearing transcript, 5, emphasis added.

4. August 1963 hearing transcript, 5.

5. August 1963 hearing transcript, 6.

6. Wilbert Lee testimony, 1968 Port St. Joe hearing transcript, 383.

7. August 1963 hearing transcript, 6.

8. Wilbert Lee testimony, 1968 Port St. Joe hearing transcript, 383.

9. August 1963 hearing transcript, 6.

10. Fred Turner deposition, Panama City, Florida, February 1, 1968, 21, in author's possession.

11. Fred Turner deposition, 11–12, 18; Miller, *Invitation to a Lynching*, 172.

12. Fred Turner deposition, 46. Turner said he notified the court and the defendants of his connection with Jesse Burkett. Turner testimony, 1968 Port St. Joe hearing transcript, 661–662.

13. Gideon v. Wainwright, 372 U.S. 335, 83 S.Ct. 792, 9 L.Ed.2d 799 (1963). Indeed, when Turner died in November 2003, he got a long obituary in the *New York Times;* "W. Fred Turner, 81, Defended Indigent in Key Trial," *New York Times,* November 28, 2003. And in 2013, the National Association of Federal Defenders created an award in Turner's name that is given annually to an outstanding federal public defender. *The Champion,* July–August 2014, 57.

14. Sheriff M. J. Daffin testimony, August 1963 trial transcript, 26–28.

15. Freddie Pitts testimony, 1968 Port St. Joe hearing transcript, 821–824. Also see Miller, *Invitation to a Lynching*, 140–141.

16. Wilbert Lee testimony, 1968 Port St. Joe hearing transcript, 376.

17. Wilbert Lee testimony, 1968 Port St. Joe hearing transcript, 375–376.

18. Wilbert Lee testimony, 1968 Port St. Joe hearing transcript, 379.

19. Sheriff M. J. Daffin testimony, August 1963 trial transcript, 27–31.

20. Miller, *Invitation to a Lynching*, 139–140. Turner testified in his deposition that Pitts and Lee denied their guilt at first but soon confessed when confronted by Willie Mae Lee. Fred Turner deposition, 34–46. We were never able to obtain Turner's Dicta-phone tape recording of his initial interview with Pitts and Lee. As I note in chapter 20, the tape mysteriously disappeared.

21. Fred Turner deposition, 155–158. Turner testified that he talked to both State Attorney J. Frank Adams and Judge Fitzpatrick about impaneling a jury to determine what sentence should be imposed on the defendants. But there were no discussions during these meetings about pleading guilty to first-degree murder in exchange for a sentence of life in prison. Turner did not have any discussions with Pitts and Lee concerning this issue.

22. See chapter 6.

23. Fred Turner deposition, 171–174.

24. Turner represented Pitts and Lee on appeal but apparently never read the trial transcript contained in the appellate record in the case.

25. Fred Turner deposition, 76–78.

26. Miller, *Invitation to a Lynching*, 175.

27. Fred Turner testimony, 1968 Port St. Joe hearing transcript, 703–704.

28. Fred Turner deposition, 34–46.

Chapter 9. The Death Sentence

1. Minutes of the Circuit Court for the Fourteenth Judicial Circuit, in and for Gulf County, Florida, August 15, 1963, 309, in author's possession.

2. *Merriam Webster's Unabridged Dictionary* defines "venire" as "a judicial writ ordering a sheriff to summon an indicated number of qualified persons to appear in court at a specified time for service as jurors." https://unabridged.merriam-webster.com/unabridged/venire.

3. George Core testimony, November 1971 Port St. Joe hearing transcript, 184.

4. Gene Miller, *Invitation to a Lynching* (Garden City, NY: Doubleday & Co., 1975), 248.

5. Defense Exhibit Read to Jury, 1972 Marianna trial transcript, 3871–3872, 3879.

6. J. Frank Adams testimony, 1968 Port St. Joe hearing transcript, 237–240.

7. See, e.g., White v. Ragen, 324 U.S. 760, 764 (1945); New York ex rel. Whitman v. Wilson, 318 U.S. 688, 689 (1943); Hysler v. Florida, 315 U.S. 411, 413 (1942). Also see Mooney v. Holohan, 294 U.S. 103 (1935).

8. Miller, *Invitation to a Lynching*, 141–142.

9. Fred Turner deposition, Panama City, Florida, February 1, 1968, 171–173, in author's possession.

10. August 1963 arraignment transcript, 11–12.

11. August 1963 arraignment transcript, 14–15.

12. Willie Mae Lee testimony, August 1963 trial transcript, 13–14, 19.

13. Willie Mae Lee testimony, August 1963 trial transcript, 13, 18–19.

14. Willie Mae Lee testimony, August 1963 trial transcript, 10.

15. "Sheriff Parker said the two men had no bruises or injuries other than the gunshot wounds." "Murder Suspects Held for Death of Two Gulf Countians," *The Star* (Port St. Joe, FL), August 8, 1963, 1.

16. August 1963 trial transcript, 26–50.

17. Freddie Pitts testimony, 1972 Marianna trial transcript, 3743–3745.

18. Wilbert Lee testimony, 1972 Marianna trial transcript, 3803–3805.

19. August 1963 trial transcript: Wilbert Lee testimony, 52–74; Freddie Pitts testimony, 84–91.

20. August 1963 trial transcript, 71, 82, 97.

21. James Graves testimony, 1972 Marianna trial transcript, 3133–3134.

22. "Murder Suspects Held For Death of Two Gulf Countians," *The Star* (Port St. Joe, FL), August 8, 1963, 1.

23. Defendant's Exhibit 3, 1972 Marianna trial transcript, 3881.

24. Wilbert Lee testimony, August 1963 trial transcript, 71.

25. Wilbert Lee testimony, August 1963 trial transcript, 75–76.

26. Freddie Pitts testimony, August 1963 trial transcript, 91–92.

27. Fred Turner deposition, Panama City, Florida, February 1, 1972, 100–101, in author's possession, emphasis added.

28. Minutes of the Circuit Court for the Fourteenth Judicial Circuit, in and for Gulf County, Florida, August 28, 1963, 329–332, in author's possession.

29. Miller, *Invitation to a Lynching*, 145.

30. Miller, *Invitation to a Lynching*, 12.

31. Martin Luther King Jr., "I Have a Dream," in *A Testament of Hope: The Essential Writings of Martin Luther King, Jr.*, ed. James M. Washington (San Francisco: Harper Collins 1986), 217, 219.

Chapter 10. The Appeal

1. Maurice Rosen quoted in Kenneth G. Gross, "Shadowy Justice in the Sunshine State: the Pitts-Lee Murder Case," *New York Sunday News*, October 1, 1972, 12.

2. Gene Miller, *Invitation to a Lynching* (Garden City, NY: Doubleday & Co., 1975). 16–17.

3. Miller, *Invitation to a Lynching*, 17.

4. Miller, *Invitation to a Lynching*, 17–18.

5. 42 U.S. Code §1983.

6. Freddie Lee Pitts, statement to FBI Special Agents John Page Jr. and Clark L. Newton, East Unit, Florida State Prison, October 24, 1963, 1–2, in author's possession.

7. Pitts, statement to FBI Special Agents John Page Jr. and Clark L. Newton, 2.

8. Fred Turner deposition, Panama City, Florida, February 1, 1972, 141; Miller, *Invitation to a Lynching*, 19.

9. Miller, *Invitation to a Lynching*, 18.

10. Miller, *Invitation to a Lynching*, 18.

11. Fred Turner deposition, February 1, 1972, 72.

12. Miller, *Invitation to a Lynching*, 20.

13. Brief of Appellants Wilbert Lee (Alias Slingshot Lee) and Freddie Pitts vs. The State of Florida, Florida Supreme Court, case nos. 32981 and 33022, filed November 2, 1963, 1, in author's possession.

14. See, e.g., Goodwin v. State, 751 So.2d 537, 544 n.8 (Fla. 1999).

15. Fred Turner deposition, February 1, 1972, 120–122.

16. See, e.g., Boykin v. Alabama, 395 U.S. 238 (1969); Koenig v. State, 597 So.2d 256 (Fla. 1992); Costello v. State, 260 So.2d 198 (Fla. 1972); Brown v. State, 92 So. 592, 109 So, 627 (1926); Pope v. State, 56 Fla. 81, 47 So.2d 487 (1908).

17. Fred Turner deposition, February 1, 1972, 124–125.

18. Legal Assistance Officer Jack M. Winick, 1st Lieutenant, JAGC, US Army Memorandum for Record, February 13, 1964, in author's possession.

19. Legal Assistance Officer Jack M. Winick, 1st Lieutenant, JAGC, US Army Memorandum for Record, February 28, 1964, 1, in author's possession.

20. Winick, US Army Memo for Record, February 28, 1964.

21. Legal Assistance Officer Jack M. Winick, 1st Lieutenant, JAGC, US Army Memorandum for Record, March 16, 1964, 1–6, in author's possession.

22. Legal Assistance Officer Jack M. Winick, 1st Lieutenant, JAGC, US Army Memo for Record, June 12, 1964, in author's possession.

23. Lee v. State, 166 So.2d 131 (Fla. 1964).

24. Fred Turner deposition, February 1, 1972, 136; Minutes of the Circuit Court for the Fourteenth Judicial Circuit, in and for Gulf County, Florida, August 28, 1963, 309, 333–336, in author's possession.

Chapter 11. Pitts and Lee Get a New Lawyer and the State's Case Begins to Collapse

1. Gene Miller, *Invitation to a Lynching* (Garden City, NY: Doubleday & Co., 1975), 33.

2. Gideon v. Wainwright 372 U.S. 335 (1963).

3. Lee v. State, 188 So.2d 872 (Fla. 1st DCA 1966).

4. Lee v. Florida, 386 U.S. 983 (1967).

5. Gene Miller, "'Two Face Death for Murders I Committed,'" *Miami Herald*, February 8, 1967; Miller *Invitation to a Lynching*, 29.

6. Terry Jones testimony, 1968 Port St. Joe hearing transcript, 655.

7. Miller, "'Two Face Death for Murders I Committed'"; Miller, *Invitation to a Lynching*, 30; Terry Jones testimony, 1968 Port St. Joe hearing transcript, 657.

8. 1966 Adams confession to Holmes, 48; Miller, *Invitation to a Lynching*, 30.

9. Terry Jones testimony, 1968 Port St. Joe hearing transcript, 655–656.

10. 1966 Adams confession to Holmes, 65.

11. Miller, *Invitation to a Lynching*, 30.

12. Miller, *Invitation to a Lynching*, 36.

13. Jesse Pait, statement to Warren Holmes, Belle Glade State Prison, March 3, 1967, 14–18, in author's possession; Miller, *Invitation to a Lynching*, 36.

14. Jesse Pait statement, March 3, 1967, 6–7; Miller, *Invitation to a Lynching*, 35–36.

15. Hank Messick, "The Strange Death of Floyd McFarland," *Miami Herald*, September 26, 1975.

16. "Herald Offers $15,000 Reward," *Miami Herald*, September 26, 1965.

17. Miller, *Invitation to a Lynching*, 33–34.

18. Pait statement, March 3, 1967, 19.

19. Pait statement, March 3, 1967, 19.

20. Miller, *Invitation to a Lynching*, 34.

21. The account of what happened during this interview is detailed in Miller, *Invitation to a Lynching*, 35–36.

22. Miller, *Invitation to a Lynching*, 40–41.

23. Miller, *Invitation to a Lynching*, 40–41.

24. Miller, *Invitation to a Lynching*, 40–41.

25. Miller, *Invitation to a Lynching*, 44.

26. Miller, *Invitation to a Lynching*, 44.

27. Elihu Phares testimony, 1972 Marianna trial transcript, 3858.

28. Actually, the Mo Jo station was located just outside Port St. Joe, not in the downtown area.

29. Elihu Phares testimony, 1968 Port St. Joe hearing transcript, 904–905, emphasis added.

30. Elihu Phares testimony, 1968 Port St. Joe hearing transcript, 905.

31. Elihu Phares testimony, 1972 Marianna trial transcript, 3859–3860.

32. Miller, *Invitation to a Lynching*, 45–46.

33. Miller, *Invitation to a Lynching*, 46.

34. Miller, *Invitation to a Lynching*, 47–48.

35. Miller, *Invitation to a Lynching*, 48.

36. Miller, *Invitation to a Lynching*, 48.

37. Miller, *Invitation to a Lynching*, 48; Gene Miller, "'Why This Injustice? Sloppy Police Work,'" *Miami Herald*, September 5, 1967.

38. Miller, *Invitation to a Lynching*, 48–49.

39. Miller, *Invitation to a Lynching*, 49.

40. Miller, *Invitation to a Lynching*, 49.

41. Gene Miller, "New Plea Fails, Adams Gets Life," *Miami Herald*, March 10, 1967.

42. Miller, *Invitation to a Lynching*, 253.

Chapter 12. Curtis Adams Confesses

1. The entire statement that Jesse Pait made to Detective Lang is quoted in Gene Miller, *Invitation to a Lynching* (Garden City, NY: Doubleday & Co., 1975), 37–38.

2. Miller, *Invitation to a Lynching*, 38–39; Gene Miller, "Pitts-Lee Prosecutor Was Aware of Adams Confession, Files Reveal," *Miami Herald*, February 21, 1972.

3. Miller, *Invitation to a Lynching*, 39.

4. Lang made this statement to the *South Florida Sun-Sentinel* at the time Governor Askew was considering the pardon for Pitts and Lee in 1975. "Larry Lang, 76, Detective. He Helped Two Men Wrongfully Convicted of Murder and Set Up His Own Detective Agency," *South Florida Sun-Sentinel*, August 6, 2004. This obituary highlighted Lang's work on this case as the major achievement of his career.

5. 1972 Marianna Trial, Elihu Phares testimony, 1972 Marianna trial transcript, 3857.

6. Miller, *Invitation to a Lynching*, 42; Elihu Phares testimony, 1972 Marianna trial transcript, 3853.

7. Miller, *Invitation to a Lynching*, 43.

8. Elihu Phares testimony, 1972 Marianna trial transcript, 3855–3857, emphasis added.

9. Miller, *Invitation to a Lynching*, 53.

10. Miller, *Invitation to a Lynching*, 53–54.

11. Miller, *Invitation to a Lynching*, 54.

12. Miller, *Invitation to a Lynching*, 76. All references to Adams's confession in this work are to a transcribed copy of the confession in book form that I have in my possession. This transcript was prepared shortly after the confession was given in December 1966.

This same confession can also be found in the transcript of the trial that was conducted in 1972 in Marianna (Curtis Adams Confession, 1972 Marianna trial transcript, 3514–3613). At this trial, we proffered the entire tape-recorded confession as evidence before Circuit Judge D. R. Smith. Judge Smith listened to the recording in open court outside the presence of the jury and the court reporter took down the entire confession.

Judge Smith ruled that the tape was inadmissible hearsay evidence, and accordingly, the jury never heard the confession.

13. Curtis Adams, confession to Warren Holmes, 12–15.

14. Curtis Adams, confession to Warren Holmes, 15–26.

15. Curtis Adams, confession to Warren Holmes, 36–39.

16. Curtis Adams, confession to Warren Holmes, 60–67.

17. Elihu Phares testimony, 1968 Port St. Joe hearing transcript, 907–911.

Chapter 13. The Struggle to Reopen the Case

1. Statement of Freddie Pitts to Warren Holmes, Florida State Prison, December 22, 1966, 76–79, in author's possession; Gene Miller, *Invitation to a Lynching* (Garden City, NY: Doubleday & Co., 1975), 77.

2. Statement of Wilbert Lee to Warren Holmes, Florida State Prison, December 22, 1966, 44–45, in author's possession; Miller, *Invitation to a Lynching*, 77–78.

3. The account that follows is taken from Miller, *Invitation to a Lynching*, 78–79; and from my conversations with Gene Miller.

4. Many years later the law changed, and today much of the Curtis Adams evidence would be admissible at trial. See Chambers v. Mississippi, 410 U.S. 284 (1973); §804(2) (c), Florida Statutes (2022).

5. Miller, *Invitation to a Lynching*, 151.

6. Miller, *Invitation to a Lynching*, 151.

Chapter 14. Dueling Newspapers in Miami and Panama City

1. Gene Miller, *Invitation to a Lynching* (Garden City, NY: Doubleday & Co., 1975), 78, 152.

2. Miller, *Invitation to a Lynching*, 78.

3. Miller, *Invitation to a Lynching*, 149–151.

4. Miller, *Invitation to a Lynching*, 80–81.

5. Gene Miller, "'Two Face Death for Murders I Committed,'" *Miami Herald*, February 5, 1967; Gene Miller, "'May God Have Mercy on Your Soul,'" *Miami Herald*, February 6, 1967.

6. Gene Miller, "'Why This Injustice? Sloppy Police Work,'" *Miami Herald*, February 5, 1967.

7. The following account is taken from Miller, *Invitation to a Lynching*, 152–153; Mike Darley, "Miami Man Attacks Officials in St. Joe," *News Herald* (Panama City, FL), February 10, 1966; and "Miami Man Charged in Gun Threat," *Miami Herald*, February 11, 1967.

8. See, e.g., Charles W. Eagles, *Outside Agitator: Jon Daniels and the Civil Rights Movement in Alabama* (Tuscaloosa: University of Alabama Press, 2000); Adam Parker, *Outside Agitator: The Civil Rights Struggle of Cleveland Sellers Jr.* (Spartanburg, SC: Hub City Press, 2018); Kent Spriggs, *Voices of Civil Rights Lawyers: Reflections from the Deep South, 1964–1980* (Gainesville: University Press of Florida, 2017).

9. Miller, *Invitation to a Lynching*, 163.

10. Mike Darley, "Miami Man Attacks Officials in St. Joe," *News Herald* (Panama City), February 10, 1966.

11. Mike Darley and Guy Middleton, "All Say Pitts, Lee Guilty," *News Herald* (Panama City), February 12, 1967, attached as Exhibit 3 to Defendants' Motion for Change of Venue, filed January 2, 1972, in State of Florida vs. Freddie Lee Pitts and Wilbert Lee, Case Nos. 3-72-1 and 3-72-2, Circuit Court for the Fourteenth Judicial Circuit in and for Jackson County, Florida, and as part of the appellate record in Freddie Lee Pitts vs. State of Florida, District Court of Appeal of Florida, First District, Case Nos. T-146 and T-147, 12–20, in author's possession.

12. The February 12, 1966, article written by Mike Darley and Guy Middleton includes the opinions of Fred Turner, Pitts and Lee's 1963–1964 court-appointed lawyer; William A. (Bill) Harris, a Panama City assistant prosecutor; Mrs. Jewel Poole, who lived near the Mo Jo gas station; George Core, the Gulf County clerk of the circuit court; Betty Gaskin Owens, the court reporter at Pitts and Lee's 1963 trial; Jimmy Barfield, a former Gulf County deputy sheriff; Gulf County Sheriff Byrd Parker; and Bay County Sheriff Doc Daffin. Darley and Middleton, "All Say Pitts, Lee Guilty."

13. Darley and Middleton, "All Say Pitts, Lee Guilty."

14. Fred Turner deposition, Panama City, Florida, February 1, 1968, 147–149, in author's possession.

15. Fred Turner deposition, February 1, 1968, 147–149.

Chapter 15. The Defense Prepares

1. Gene Miller, *Invitation to a Lynching* (Garden City, NY: Doubleday & Co., 1975), 258–259.

2. 373 U.S. 83 (1963).

3. Willie Mae Lee, sworn statement to State Attorney J. Frank Adams and S. R. De-Witt, Port St. Joe, Florida, February 20, 1972, 8, in author's possession.

4. I had read Williams's *One Man's Freedom* (New York: Atheneum Books, 1962) and was impressed with his account of the many cases he had handled.

5. Phillip Hubbart to Edward Bennett Williams, February 17, 1967, in author's possession.

6. The 1967 Pulitzer Prize for Miller reads:

> For a distinguished example of local investigative or other specialized report-ing by an individual or team presented as a single article or series, giving prime consideration to initiative, resourcefulness, research, and high quality of writ-ing, One thousand dollars ($1000). "Gene Miller of *Miami Herald*," The Pu-litzer Prizes, https://www.pulitzer.org/winners/gene-miller-0#:~:text=For%20 his%20persistent%20and%20courageous,sentenced%20to%20death%20 in%20Florida.

7. Robert Bolt, *A Man for All Seasons* (New York: Vintage Books, 1990), 66.

8. Miller, *Invitation to a Lynching*, 186.

9. Miller, *Invitation to a Lynching*, 186.

10. Irwin Block and Phillip Hubbart Statements, 1968 Port St. Joe hearing transcript, 513.

Chapter 16. The Port St. Joe Hearing Begins

1. Indeed, the case was still well known nearly fifty years later. In November 2016, I visited the office of the circuit clerk in Port St. Joe and spoke to one of clerks. I asked whether the office had a transcript in a case I was involved in many years ago. "Do you have the number of the case," the assistant clerk asked. "No," I said, "but the defendants' names were Freddie Pitts and Wilbert Lee." "Oh, everyone knows that case," she said and led me to the Pitts-Lee transcript in an adjoining room of the clerk's office.

2. Irwin Block statement, 1968 Port St. Joe hearing transcript, 264. Deputy Sheriff Wayne White later told the court that he had received no actual threats on the lives of Pitts and Lee but "tried to think before the public acts." He also said that "we felt like this was the best place to place these men." Wayne White statement, 1968 Port St. Joe Hearing, 1394.

3. Gene Miller, *Invitation to a Lynching* (Garden City, NY: Doubleday & Co., 1975), 185.

4. Mike Tigar later went on to a stellar career as a civil rights and criminal law litigator in many high-profile cases. He also became a law professor at the University of Texas.

5. 1968 Port St. Joe hearing transcript, 12–13. In a supplemental motion, I added three more grounds to our motion to vacate: (1) it was improper to appoint one lawyer to represent both defendants; (2) the death penalty was unconstitutional; and (3) jurors were excluded at the original trial solely because they were morally opposed to the death penalty. The law was against us on these grounds and I raised them only to preserve the issues for appellate review in the hope that the law would change. As expected, Judge Holley had ruled against us regarding these grounds in an earlier summary judgment hearing, so they were no longer issues at this hearing.

6. 1968 Port St. Joe hearing transcript, 3–4.

7. Miller, *Invitation to a Lynching*, 187.

8. See, e.g., Gene Miller, "Pitts, Lee Attract Top Trial Lawyer," *Miami Herald*, March 27, 1967; Gene Miller, "Pair Innocent, Petition Asserts," *Miami Herald*, May 21, 1967; Gene Miller, "Dusty File Beams New Light on Death Row," *Miami Herald*, August 20, 1967; Gene Miller, "Pitts Lee Guilty of Murder, Faircloth Aide Says," *Miami Herald*, September 1, 1967; Gene Miller, "Top State Court to Consider Pitts-Lee Murder Case," *Miami Herald*, November 20, 1967; Gene Miller, "Judge to Request Search for Murder Weapon," *Miami Herald*, August 23, 1967; Gene Miller, "Pitts-Lee Attorney Under Legal Attack," *Miami Herald*, September 16, 1968.

9. Gene Miller, "Fate of Two on Death Row May Hinge on a Memory," *Miami Herald*, September 9, 1968; Gene Miller, "Hearing Holds Hope for Two on Death Row," *Miami Herald*, September 23, 1968.

10. 1968 Port St. Joe hearing transcript, 17.

11. Willie Mae Lee testimony, 1968 Port St. Joe hearing transcript, 21.

12. Willie Mae Lee testimony, 1968 Port St. Joe hearing transcript, 22–23.

13. 1968 Port St. Joe hearing transcript: Bruce Potts testimony, 49–60, 64, 68, 188; Donald Hoag testimony, 189–192.

14. 1968 Port St. Joe hearing transcript: Bruce Potts testimony, 45–50, 60–64, 69–72; Donald Hoag testimony, 187–189, 194–196.

15. Ella Mae Lee testimony, 1968 Port St. Joe hearing transcript, 158–160, 166.

16. Wilbert Lee testimony, 1968 Port St. Joe hearing transcript, 367, 404–406.

17. Thomasina Stallworth testimony, 1968 Port St. Joe hearing transcript, 176–177, 179, 180–181.

18. Henry Hogue testimony, 1968 Port St. Joe hearing transcript, 138–39.

19. Dr. C. W. Ketchum testimony, 1968 Port St. Joe hearing transcript, 225.

20. J. Frank Adams testimony, 1968 Port St. Joe hearing transcript, 226, 229–231.

21. 1968 Port St. Joe hearing transcript, 242.

22. J. Frank Adams testimony, 1968 Port St. Joe hearing transcript, 237–240.

23. Related by Jack Winick in a telephone call with the author, August 11, 2016. I had telephoned Winick, who was living in San Diego, California.

24. Irwin Block statement, 1968 Port St. Joe hearing transcript, 1393.

25. Judge Holley statement, 1968 Port St. Joe hearing transcript, 1399.

Chapter 17. The Port St. Joe Hearing Continues

1. M. J. "Doc" Daffin testimony, 1968 Port St. Joe hearing transcript, 267–274.

2. Daffin testimony, 1968 Port St. Joe hearing transcript, 274.

3. Daffin testimony, 1968 Port St. Joe hearing transcript, 275–279.

4. Daffin testimony, 1968 Port St. Joe hearing transcript, 283.

5. Daffin testimony, 1968 Port St. Joe hearing transcript, 284–287.

6. Daffin testimony, 1968 Port St. Joe hearing transcript, 286–290, 292–293, emphasis added.

7. Daffin testimony, 1968 Port St. Joe hearing transcript, 293–309.

8. Wilbert Lee testimony, 1968 Port St. Joe hearing transcript, 350–84.

9. Wilbert Lee testimony, 1968 Port St. Joe hearing transcript, 1360–1361.

10. 1968 Port St. Joe hearing transcript, 450–453.

11. Warren Holmes testimony, 1968 Port St. Joe hearing transcript, 631.

12. 1968 Port St. Joe hearing transcript, 454–461.

13. Curtis Adams testimony, 1968 Port St. Joe hearing transcript, 467, 470–471, 490.

14. Adams testimony, 1968 Port St. Joe hearing transcript, 470–471, 486–488.

15. Adams testimony, 1968 Port St. Joe hearing transcript, 471, 490.

16. Adams testimony, 1968 Port St. Joe hearing transcript, 486–488.

17. Adams testimony, 1968 Port St. Joe hearing transcript, 477–478, 484–485, 491–492, 494–495.

18. 1968 Port St. Joe hearing transcript, 500.

19. 1968 Port St. Joe hearing transcript, 506.

Chapter 18. The Defense Rests

1. 1968 Port St. Joe hearing transcript, 508.

2. 1968 Port St. Joe hearing transcript, 509.

3. 1968 Port St. Joe hearing transcript, 510.

4. Warren Holmes testimony, 1968 Port St. Joe hearing transcript, 522–523.

5. 1968 Port St. Joe hearing transcript, 527, 535–603, 607–616, 617–618.

6. Holmes testimony, 1968 Port St. Joe hearing transcript, 624, 626.

7. Holmes testimony, 1968 Port St. Joe hearing transcript, 627–628.

8. Gene Miller, *Invitation to a Lynching* (Garden City, NY: Doubleday & Co., 1975), 181–182. See also Annie Jacobsen, *Phenomena: The Secret History of the U.S. Government's Investigations into Extraordinary Perception and Psychokinesis* (New York: Little, Brown & Company, 2017), 120–122.

9. Warren Holmes testimony, 1968 Port St. Joe hearing transcript, 519–590.

10. Mary Jean Akins testimony, 1968 Port St. Joe hearing transcript, 638–646.

11. Gene Miller, "Pitts-Lee 'Eyewitness' Said in '68 She Lied," *Miami Herald*, February 1, 1972, 8A.

12. Gene Miller, "The Haunted Memories of Mary Jean Akins," *Tropic* (*Miami Herald* Sunday magazine), September 7, 1975, 14; Gene Miller, *Invitation to a Lynching* (Garden City, NY: Doubleday & Co., 1975), 220–221; Gene Miller's notes on his interview with Mary Jean Akins, March 10, 1968, 2, 6, in author's possession.

13. Mary Jean Akins, sworn statement, Sheriff's Office, Bartow, Florida, March 6, 1968, 13–14, in author's possession. Also see J. Frank Adams testimony as proffered, 1968 Port St. Joe hearing transcript, 1255–1263, 1265.

14. Akins testimony, 1968 Port St. Joe hearing transcript, 646–647, 648.

15. Akins testimony, 1968 Port St. Joe hearing transcript, 649–650, 651–652.

16. Miller, "The Haunted Memories of Mary Jean Akins," 14; Miller, *Invitation to a Lynching*, 221.

17. Freddie Pitts testimony, 1968 Port St. Joe hearing transcript, 788–887.

18. Pitts testimony, 1968 Port St. Joe hearing transcript, 881–882.

19. Pitts testimony, 1968 Port St. Joe hearing transcript, 823–824.

20. Fred Turner testimony, 1968 Port St. Joe hearing transcript, 660–776.

21. Turner testimony, 1968 Port St. Joe hearing transcript, 672.

22. Turner testimony, 1968 Port St. Joe hearing transcript, 676.

23. Miller, *Invitation to a Lynching*, 177–178.

24. At the time of the hearing, Elihu Phares had been promoted to the rank of lieutenant in the Broward County Sheriff's Office. However, he was a detective at the time he investigated the murders in this case.

25. Elihu Phares testimony, 1968 Port St. Joe hearing transcript, 893–894.

26. Phares testimony, 1968 Port St. Joe hearing transcript, 903–906, 907–908.

27. Phares testimony, 1968 Port St. Joe hearing transcript, 912–913, 922.

28. Miller, *Invitation to a Lynching*, 190.

Chapter 19. The Port St. Joe Hearing Concludes

1. Gene Miller, *Invitation to a Lynching* (Garden City, NY: Doubleday & Co., 1975), 200; Joe McCawley testimony, 1968 Port St. Joe hearing transcript, 1065.

2. 1968 Port St. Joe hearing transcript, 987–989.

3. 1968 Port St. Joe hearing transcript, 1074–1078.

4. 1968 Port St. Joe hearing transcript, 1081–1115.

5. Miller, *Invitation to a Lynching*, 200.

6. Miller, *Invitation to a Lynching*, 194.

7. Willie Mae Lee statement under hypnosis, 1968 Port St. Joe hearing transcript, 1107–1112.

8. McCawley testimony, 1069.

9. Dr. Michael Gilbert testimony, 1968 Port St. Joe hearing transcript, 1134–1135.

10. Dr. Israel Hanenson testimony, 1968 Port St. Joe hearing transcript, 1144–1145.

11. Marion Knight testimony, 1968 Port St. Joe hearing transcript, 1237–1238, 1240.

12. David Gaskin testimony, 1968 Port St. Joe hearing transcript, 1184, 1186–1187.

13. Sam Husband testimony, 1968 Port St. Joe hearing transcript, 1203–1204.

14. Judge W. L. Fitzpatrick testimony, 1968 Port St. Joe hearing transcript, 1166–1167.

15. Wayne White testimony, 1968 Port St. Joe hearing transcript, 1329, 1334.

16. Robert Sidwell testimony, 1968 Port St. Joe hearing transcript, 1231.

17. Joe Townsend testimony, 1968 Port St. Joe hearing transcript, 1272–1273, 1312–1313.

18. George Core testimony, 1968 Port St. Joe hearing transcript, 1250–1253.

19. Thomas Arata testimony, 1968 Port St. Joe hearing transcript, 1213, 1220–1222.

20. 1968 Port St. Joe hearing transcript, 1368–1381.

21. 1968 Port St. Joe hearing transcript, 41.

22. 1968 Port St. Joe hearing transcript, 1384–1385.

23. 1968 Port St. Joe hearing transcript, 1389–1391. Judge Holley also directed that an order be prepared for his signature "directing that all and sundry attorneys, newspaper reporters, law enforcement officers . . . henceforth cease and desist and in no way molest, talk with, or interfere with Willie Mae Lee, with reference to any of the matters concerned in this hearing . . . except upon order of this court." 1968 Port St. Joe hearing transcript, 1381. This order was of dubious constitutionality under the First Amendment's guarantee of a free press and under the Sixth Amendment's guarantee of right to counsel. No such order involving any other witness in the case was ever entered.

24. 1968 Port St. Joe hearing transcript, 1393–1396.

25. 1968 Port St. Joe hearing transcript, 1397–1398.

26. Miller, *Invitation to a Lynching*, 210–211.

27. Frank Pate statement, 1968 Port St. Joe hearing transcript, 1396–1397.

28. Gene Miller, "Why 2 Innocent Men Can't Get Out of Jail," *Miami Herald*, October 5, 1969; Gene Miller, "Case Trapped in Quagmire of Legal Delay," *Miami Herald*, October 5, 1969; Miller, *Invitation to a Lynching*, 211.

29. Miller, *Invitation to a Lynching*, 211.

Chapter 20. The Ruling and the Appeal

1. On April 21, 1969, Holley entered an order directing that additional testimony be taken from Pitts, Lee, Willie Mae Lee, Bay County Sheriff Doc Daffin, and Fred Turner. This order sounded as if the judge wanted to focus on Pitts and Lee's confessions to Sheriff Daffin, which had been made in the presence of and with the participation of Fred Turner and Willie Mae Lee. However, this hearing never took place. J. Frank Adams claimed that Willie Mae Lee had left town for New York and that he didn't know where she was and Turner was excused based on his claim that there had been a death in his

family. The order was withdrawn. Gene Miller, *Invitation to a Lynching* (Garden City, NY: Doubleday & Co., 1975), 229.

2. Freddie Lee Pitts and Wilbert Lee vs. the State of Florida, Case No. 519, 520, April 22, 1969, 1–2 (motion for order directing the granting of immunity), in author's possession.

3. Judgment, Circuit Court for the Fourteenth Judicial Circuit in and for Gulf County, Florida, April 29, 1969, Freddie Lee Pitts and Wilbert Lee vs. The State of Florida, Case Nos. 519, 520, Record on Appeal, First District Court of Appeal, 33–34, opinion reported at 307 So.2d 473 (Fla. 1st DCA 1975), in author's possession.

4. Judgment, Circuit Court for the Fourteenth Judicial Circuit in and for Gulf County, Florida, April 29, 1969, 33–34

5. Judgment, Circuit Court for the Fourteenth Judicial Circuit in and for Gulf County, Florida, April 29, 1969, 33–34.

6. Judgment, Circuit Court for the Fourteenth Judicial Circuit in and for Gulf County, Florida, April 29, 1969, 33–34, emphasis added.

7. Daniel St. Albin Greene, "Charges of Wrongful Conviction Persist in Florida Double Murder," *National Observer*, August 12, 1972.

8. On April 27, 1972, Miami attorney James Kenny, a dear friend from Duke Law School, prepared a petition signed by him and ten other people asking Governor Reubin Askew "to reclassify Wilb[ert] Lee and Freddie Pitts from death row to the general population prisoners during the pendency of legal proceedings pertaining to the guilt or innocence of these men." The petition was sent to the governor under a cover letter on the letterhead of his law firm, Kelly, Black, Black & Kenny. Unfortunately the request was not granted and Pitts and Lee remained on death row, but I deeply appreciated the gesture.

9. Miller, *Invitation to a Lynching*, 230.

10. Editorial, "Faircloth for Law and Order?" *News Herald* (Panama City, FL), June 11, 1969, attached as Exhibit 3 to Defendants' Motion for Change of Venue, filed January 2, 1972, in State of Florida vs. Freddie Lee Pitts and Wilbert Lee, Case Nos. 3-72-1 and 3-72-2, Circuit Court for the Fourteenth Judicial Circuit in and for Jackson County, Florida, and as part of the appellate record in Freddie Lee Pitts vs. State of Florida, District Court of Appeal of Florida, First District, Case Nos. T-146 and T-147, 12–20, in author's possession.

11. "Faircloth States His Position," Letters to the Editor, *News Herald* (Panama City, FL), July 1, 1969, attached as Exhibit 3 to Defendants' Motion for Change of Venue filed in the Circuit Court for the Fourteenth Judicial Circuit in and for Jackson County, Florida.

12. Miller, *Invitation to a Lynching*, 233.

13. 369 U.S. 186 (1962).

14. For a comprehensive study of this decisive era in Florida politics, see Martin Dyckman, *Reubin O'D. Askew and the Golden Age of Florida Politics* (Gainesville: University Press of Florida, 2011).

15. State of Florida, Appellant, v. Freddie Lee Pitts and Wilbert Lee, Appellees, 241 So.2d 399 (Fla. 1st DCA 1970), 414 (hereafter *State v. Pitts*).

16. *State v. Pitts*, 414, emphasis added. The district court also concluded that Judge Holley had imposed the wrong standard of proof when he considered the four main grounds for postconviction relief (i.e., the standard of reasonable doubt). The correct

standard of proof was more demanding; namely, "a clear showing of a departure from essential requirements of law." But instead of sending the case back to Judge Holley so he could apply the correct burden of proof to the evidence received at the hearing and reach his findings of fact based on that standard, the district court decided to keep the case and pass on the merits of the appeal. *State v. Pitts,* 402.

17. See, e.g., F.B. v. State, 852 So.2d 226, 230 (Fla. 2003) (citing Tibbs v. State, 397 So.2d 1120, 1123 (Fla. 1981)).

18. Miller, *Invitation to a Lynching,* 234.

19. *State v. Pitts,* 402.

20. 1968 Port St. Joe hearing transcript, 41.

21. *State v. Pitts,* 413.

22. *State v. Pitts,* 409.

23. *State v. Pitts,* 400.

24. *State v. Pitts,* 412.

25. 373 U.S. 83 (1963).

26. Gene Miller "'I Believe the Court Is Wrong,'" *Miami Herald,* February 21, 1971.

27. Miller, *Invitation to a Lynching,* 237.

28. Miller, *Invitation to a Lynching,* 237.

29. Motion in Confession of Error, Memorandum, Freddie Pitts and Wilbert Lee vs. State of Florida, Case No. 40618, Florida Supreme Court, April 15, 1971, in author's possession.

30. Motion in Confession of Error, 8.

31. Ethics Governing Attorneys, Canon 5, 32 F.S.A. 606 (effective in August 1963).

32. Code of Professional Responsibility, D.R. 7-103(B), 32 F.S.A. (Supp.) 101–102 (1970).

33. *Pitts v. State.*

34. The First District Court of Appeal also receded from its earlier decision in the case in two material respects and held that (1) in all future cases, a claim that the state has suppressed evidence favorable to the defense may be entertained on a postconviction motion to vacate, even where the defendant has pled guilty; and (2) in all future cases, a claim that the state has suppressed evidence that goes to the credibility of a state witness may also be entertained on a postconviction motion to vacate. The court further receded from all of its prior decisions that were contrary to this holding. See *State v. Pitts.*

35. This investigator, Willie Nicholson, created a disturbance in Port St. Joe at the time, but he was mentally ill and gave himself up immediately. No one was ever hurt, and the charges against him were dismissed. Nicholson was never employed by the NAACP.

36. But these were just wild charges that Willie Mae Lee had made. J. Frank Adams, the local prosecutor, never filed any bribery charges against anyone.

37. "'In the Interest of Justice' Mr. Shevin Should Resign," Editorial, *News Herald* (Panama City, FL), April 28, 1971, attached as Exhibit 3 to Defendants' Motion for Change of Venue filed in the Circuit Court for the Fourteenth Judicial Circuit in and for Jackson County, Florida.

38. "Questions Need Answering 'In the Interest of Justice,'" Editorial, *News Herald* (Panama City, FL), May 9, 1971, attached as Exhibit 3 to Defendants' Motion for Change

of Venue filed in the Circuit Court for the Fourteenth Judicial Circuit in and for Jackson County, Florida.

Chapter 21. Phase I of the Pretrial Proceedings

1. Bruce Giles, "Pitts, Lee Plead Not Guilty at Arraignment; Trial Set for August 16," *Miami Herald,* July 8, 1971.

2. Freddie Lee Pitts and Wilbert Lee, Petitioners, v. Hon. Robert L. McCrary, 251 So. 2d 694, 696 (Fla. Dist. Ct. App. 1971) (hereafter *Pitts v. McCrary*).

3. *Pitts v. McCrary,* 697.

4. W. Somerset Maugham, *The Razor's Edge* (1944; repr., London: Mandarin Paperbacks, 1990), 141.

5. Gene Miller, *Invitation to a Lynching* (Garden City, NY: Doubleday & Co., 1975), 242. See also Willie Mae Lee testimony, August 1963 hearing transcript, 2–25.

6. Miller, *Invitation to a Lynching,* 242.

7. Leo Jones testimony, August 1971 Port St. Joe hearing transcript, 58–59.

8. Miller, *Invitation to a Lynching,* 243.

9. Miller, *Invitation to a Lynching,* 242.

10. Mary Jean Akins testimony, 1968 Port St. Joe Hearing, 649–650, 651–652; Mary Jean Akins, sworn statement, Sheriff's Office, Bartow, Florida, March 6, 1968, 13–14.

11. Miller, *Invitation to a Lynching,* 243.

12. Miller, *Invitation to a Lynching,* 243–244; "New Judge Sought for Murder Trial," *Miami Herald,* July 4, 1971.

13. Miller, *Invitation to a Lynching,* 244; Gene Miller, "Myths Die Hard in the Pitts-Lee Case," *Miami Herald,* October 24, 1971.

14. Hershel T. Dean testimony, August 1971 Port St. Joe hearing transcript, 41; David Helman testimony, August 1971 Port St. Joe hearing transcript, 67–68; Miller, *Invitation to a Lynching,* 245.

15. August 1971 Port St. Joe hearing transcript, 230–231.

16. Miller, *Invitation to a Lynching,* 245; Leo Jones testimony, August 1971 Port St. Joe hearing transcript, 55–56.

17. George Core testimony, August 1971 Port St. Joe hearing transcript, 184.

18. August 1971 Port St. Joe hearing transcript, 187, 189.

19. Order, Appellate Record at 30, Freddie Lee Pitts and Wilbert Lee, Appellants, v. State of Florida, 307 So. 2d 473 (Fla. Dist. Ct. App. 1975).

20. August 1971 Port St. Joe hearing transcript, 344.

21. August 1971 Port St. Joe hearing transcript, 330. Mr. Core later amended his testimony in a letter to the court stating that that in 1959, one Black voter had served on the Gulf County Grand Jury. Miller, *Invitation to a Lynching,* 248.

22. August 1971 Port St. Joe hearing transcript: George Core testimony, 192–196; Mrs. Parker testimony, 209–215.

23. August 1971 Port St. Joe hearing transcript, 383–384.

24. Order at 30–31, *Pitts and Lee v. Florida,* 1971, 30–31.

25. November 1971 Port St. Joe hearing transcript, 4.

26. November 1971 Port St. Joe hearing transcript, 5.

27. November 1971 Port St. Joe hearing transcript, 6–7.

28. November 1971 Port St. Joe hearing transcript, 37.

29. November 1971 Port St. Joe hearing transcript, 79.

30. Miller, *Invitation to a Lynching*, 271.

31. James Smith testimony, August 1971 Port St. Joe hearing transcript, 62.

32. Miller, *Invitation to a Lynching*, 250.

33. November 1971 Port St. Joe hearing transcript, 88–92.

Chapter 22. Phase II of the Pretrial Proceedings

1. January 1972 Marianna hearings transcript, 120.

2. Phillip Hubbart to Alyne Pittman, March 21, 1972, in author's possession.

3. Summary of Registered Voters and Jury Roll Lists by Race for Jackson County, Florida (1963–1971), State of Florida v. Freddie Lee Pitts and Wilbert Lee, Circuit Court for the Fourteenth Judicial Circuit of Florida in and for Jackson County, Florida, case nos. 3-72-1 and 3-72-2, January 21, 1972, in author's possession.

4. Motion to Dismiss at 35, Freddie Pitts and Wilbert Lee v. State of Florida, 307 So. 2d 473 (1st D. Ct. App. Fla. 1972), in author's possession.

5. Eubanks v. Louisiana, 356 U.S. 584, 585 (1958). And according to the Court, proof of that exclusion can be established by a statistical showing of a long-standing disparity between the number of eligible Black voters on the voting rolls and the number of Black voters that were placed on the jury rolls. Alexander v. Louisiana, 405 U.S. 625 (1972).

6. January 1972 Marianna hearings transcript, 198–199.

7. January 1972 Marianna hearings transcript, 209.

8. Motion to Suppress in Appellate Record at 41–42, Freddie Pitts and Wilbert Lee v. State of Florida, T-146, T-147 (1st D. Ct. App. Fla. 1972), in author's possession.

9. January 1972 Marianna hearings transcript, 212.

10. January 1972 Marianna hearings transcript, 212.

11. January 1972 Marianna hearings transcript, 214.

12. Motion for Change of Venue, Freddie Pitts and Wilbert Lee v. State of Florida, 1972, T-146, T-147, First District Court of Appeal of Florida, Appellate Record, 12.

13. Motion for Change of Venue at 16.

14. Motion for Change of Venue at 13.

15. January 1972 Marianna hearings transcript, 129–130.

16. January 1972 Marianna hearings transcript, 150–151.

17. January 1972 Marianna hearings transcript, 140–142.

18. January 1972 Marianna hearings transcript, 157.

19. The lynching of Claude Neal in Marianna, Florida, on October 19, 1934, was particularly brutal. After murdering Neal, a white mob mutilated his corpse, burned it with hot irons, drove over it with cars, shot it multiple times, and hung it on a tree on the courthouse lawn. A mob also burned down the homes of Neal's family. Equal Justice Initiative, *Lynchings in America: Confronting the Legacy of Racial Terror*, 3rd ed. (Montgomery, AL: Equal Justice Initiative, 2017), 40, 45, 72.

20. January 1972 Marianna hearings transcript, 164–174.

21. January 1972 Marianna hearings transcript, 174.

22. January 1972 Marianna hearings transcript, 249–250.

23. January 1972 Marianna hearings transcript, 250.

24. Gene Miller, *Invitation to a Lynching* (Garden City, NY: Doubleday & Co., 1975), 258; see 258–260 for an account of this entire incident.

25. State of Florida v. Freddie Lee Pitts and Wilbert Lee, Case Nos. 3-72-1 and 3-72-2, Circuit Court for the Fourteenth Judicial Circuit in and for Jackson County, Florida, and as part of the appellate record in Freddie Lee Pitts v. State of Florida, District Court of Appeal of Florida, First District, Case Nos. T-146 and T-147, 57–60.

26. Miller, *Invitation to a Lynching*, 269.

27. 1972 Marianna trial transcript, 66–68, 74.

28. 1972 Marianna trial transcript, 84–85.

29. 1972 Marianna trial transcript, 76–78.

30. 1972 Marianna trial transcript, 90.

Chapter 23. Phase I of Jury Selection

1. 1972 Marianna trial transcript, 290.

2. Gene Miller, *Invitation to a Lynching* (Garden City, NY: Doubleday & Co., 1975), 267.

3. Gene Miller, "Justice Faces Test in Panhandle," *Miami Herald*, February 20, 1972.

4. See, e.g., Gene Miller, "Pitts-Lee Prosecutor Was Aware of Adams Confession," *Miami Herald*, February 3, 1972; Gene Miller, "Lifer Seeking Chance to Aid Pitts and Lee," *Miami Herald*, February 2, 1972; Gene Miller, "Pitts and Lee 'Eyewitness' Said in '68 She Lied," *Miami Herald*, February 1, 1972; Gene Miller, "Investigator Employs Pitts-Lee Witness," *Miami Herald*, January 30, 1972; Gene Miller, "Refusing to Take Testimony. Jury Re-Indicts Pitts, Lee," *Miami Herald*, January 5, 1972; Gene Miller, "New Grand Jury to Get Pitts-Lee Case," *Miami Herald*, December 16, 1971; Gene Miller, "Pitts-Lee Murder Trial Moved from Port St. Joe to Marianna," *Miami Herald*, November 19, 1971; Gene Miller, "State Supreme Court Asked to Bar Pitts-Lee Case Judge," *Miami Herald*, November 2, 1971; Gene Miller, "Pitts-Lee Judge Denies Bid to Disqualify Him," *Miami Herald*. October 27, 1971; Gene Miller, "Pitts-Lee Defense Seeks Trial Shift," *Miami Herald*, July 4, 1971; Gene Miller, "Shevin Asks Court for New Pitts-Lee Trial," *Miami Herald*, April 16. 1971.

5. Miller, *Invitation to a Lynching*, 278.

6. Miller, *Invitation to a Lynching*, 267.

7. Miller, *Invitation to a Lynching*, 276.

8. Gene Miller, "The Unending Trials of Pitts and Lee," *Tropic* (*Miami Herald* Sunday magazine), September 7, 1973, 54.

9. Rob Elder, "Three Flee Cell Next to Pitts' and Lee's," *Miami Herald*, February 25, 1972; Miller, *Invitation to a Lynching*, 279.

10. For a detailed account of the Cellos Harrison case, see Tameka Bradley Hobbs, *Democracy Abroad, Lynching at Home: Racial Violence in Florida* (Gainesville: University Press of Florida, 2015), 68–120.

11. 1972 Marianna trial transcript, 137, 138.

12. 1972 Marianna trial transcript, 148.

13. 1972 Marianna trial transcript, 178, 180.

14. 1972 Marianna trial transcript, 181.

15. 1972 Marianna trial transcript, 156, 157.

16. 1972 Marianna trial transcript, 455–456.

17. 1972 Marianna trial transcript, 302, 306. Billy Hay Williams, whose husband worked for the State Beverage Department, confirmed that this case had been a general topic of conversation "of this whole area." 1972 Marianna trial transcript, 240. Robert Pforte, an automobile dealer and member of the Marianna City Commission, testified that the case had been a topic of conversation "for years" in Jackson County. 1972 Marianna trial transcript, 1069.

18. 1972 Marianna trial transcript, 2383.

19. 1972 Marianna trial transcript, 1902.

20. 1972 Marianna trial transcript, 2636.

21. Paul McFarlin, an employer with a local peanut plant, said that he had heard the names Pitts and Lee before coming to court ("I read it in the paper, headlines") and had heard people expressing the opinion that it was a waste of time to try the case again. 1972 Marianna trial transcript, 2247, 2249.

John Williams, who was in the feed and farm supply business, confirmed that in all his conversations with others, no one ever said that Pitts and Lee were innocent and that all who expressed an opinion said that they were guilty. 1972 Marianna trial transcript, 1408–1409.

Linda Herndon, whose husband was an electrician for the city of Chattahoochee, had a similar experience; many people she knew said that Pitts and Lee were guilty. She also said that she knew that Pitts and Lee had been tried before and convicted. She said that she would try to put all that out of her mind but admitted that "I cannot be positive" that she could do so. 1972 Marianna trial transcript, 1023–1025, 1035.

Homer Fowler, a local resident, said he couldn't presume that the defendants were innocent because "I have read about it in the paper quite a bit and heard it from sources and I feel they had a fair trial to begin with." 1972 Marianna trial transcript, 1023–1025.

Harry Olive, a retiree on disability, said that he thought the defendants were guilty "up until I hear different evidence" and that it would take evidence in court to the contrary to change his mind. 1972 Marianna trial transcript, 1743, 1747.

James Harrell Foran, another local resident, said that he had a fixed opinion about the defendants and that "it would have to be pretty strong evidence otherwise" for him to think any different. 1972 Marianna trial transcript, 1720.

George D. Hilton Sr., a retired grocer, said that "I have heard a lot of talk about the evidence, seen it on television, and read about in the news press." He said he would require the defendants to produce evidence of innocence or he would have to vote to convict. 1972 Marianna trial transcript, 675. 683.

22. 1972 Marianna trial transcript, 1447.

Chapter 24. Phase II of Jury Selection

1. State v. Neil, 457 So. 2d 481 (Fla. 1984); Batson v. Kentucky, 476 U.S. 79 (1986), overruling Swain v. Alabama, 380 U.S. 202 (1965).

2. 1972 Marianna trial transcript, 337.

3. 1972 Marianna trial transcript, 337.

4. 1972 Marianna trial transcript, 1606–1607.

5. 1972 Marianna trial transcript, 2208.

6. 1972 Marianna trial transcript, 1583–1584.

7. 1972 Marianna trial transcript, 369, 1048.

8. The state eventually closed this institution, the Arthur Dozier School for Boys, in 2011 after the governor ordered an investigation amid allegations that countless boys had been beaten and tortured by the school staff over the school's 111-year history. Some boys were probably murdered; unmarked graves of boys were found on the grounds of the institution. See, e.g., Lizette Alvarez, "At Boys' Home, Seeking Graves, and the Reason," *New York Times,* February 10, 2019.

9. 1972 Marianna trial transcript, 253, 788.

10. 1972 Marianna trial transcript, 1138–1142.

11. 1972 Marianna trial transcript, 1142.

12. 1972 Marianna trial transcript, 1143.

13. 1972 Marianna trial transcript, 551.

14. 1972 Marianna trial transcript, 506–507.

15. 1972 Marianna trial transcript, 507.

16. 1972 Marianna trial transcript, 702, 722–733.

17. 1972 Marianna trial transcript, 698–723.

18. 1972 Marianna trial transcript, 722–723.

19. 1972 Marianna trial transcript, 762–763.

20. 1972 Marianna trial transcript, 765–766.

21. 1972 Marianna trial transcript, 2790.

22. 1972 Marianna trial transcript, 2785–2786, 2789–2780.

23. 1972 Marianna trial transcript, 2786.

24. 1972 Marianna trial transcript, 2787–2788, emphasis added.

25. 1972 Marianna trial transcript, 2731, 2735.

26. 1972 Marianna trial transcript, 2732–2733, 2737.

27. 1972 Marianna trial transcript, 2738.

28. 1972 Marianna trial transcript, 2736, 2737.

29. 1972 Marianna trial transcript, 2699, 2704, 2708, 2711.

30. 1972 Marianna trial transcript, 2443, 2447.

31. George B. Williams said that he had heard the case being discussed "a little bit" at work and knew that the defendants had been charged with a murder that had been committed in Gulf County; 1972 Marianna trial transcript, 590, 589. William Tyus said that he had overheard conversations about the case in passing but had not participated in them; 1972 Marianna trial transcript, 369. James Fears said that he had glanced at the headlines in the newspaper and had heard the names Pitts and Lee from passing conversations with people in the community; 1972 Marianna trial transcript, 2597. Richard Tidwell said that he had heard the names Pitts and Lee in similar conversations and thought he had seen the KKK motorcade that had recently gone through the Black residential section of Marianna; 1972 Marianna trial transcript, 2334–2335. Florence M.

Jordan said that she had read about the case in the *Jackson County Floridan* but that her mind was not oriented to legal matters and she didn't concern herself with such things; 1972 Marianna trial transcript, 477, 486. "I have read the paper but I haven't kept up on it," she said; 1972 Marianna trial transcript, 473.

32. Larry Nichols, "2 Jurors Accept Pitts-Lee Pardon," *Florida Times-Union,* September 13, 1973, B2.

33. 1972 Marianna trial transcript, 1045.

34. 1972 Marianna trial transcript, 2855, 2856, 2861, 2864, 2868, 2871.

35. 1972 Marianna trial transcript, 2074.

36. 1972 Marianna trial transcript, 2875.

37. 1972 Marianna trial transcript, 2875–2889.

38. Gene Miller, *Invitation to a Lynching* (Garden City, NY: Doubleday & Co., 1975), 280.

39. Miller, *Invitation to a Lynching,* 280.

40. 1972 Marianna trial transcript, 2880.

41. 1972 Marianna trial transcript, 2882.

42. 1972 Marianna trial transcript, 2890.

43. 1972 Marianna trial transcript, 2901–2954.

44. 1972 Marianna trial transcript, 2954.

Chapter 25. The State's Case

1. 1972 Marianna trial transcript, 2958.

2. 1972 Marianna trial transcript, 2958–2959.

3. 1972 Marianna trial transcript, 2959.

4. 1972 Marianna trial transcript, 2959–2960.

5. 1972 Marianna trial transcript, 2960.

6. 1972 Marianna trial transcript, 2960–2961.

7. 1972 Marianna trial transcript, 2962.

8. 1972 Marianna trial transcript, 2930.

9. 1972 Marianna trial transcript, 2981–2982.

10. "Pitts-Lee Jury Favors Wallace, 11–1," *Miami Herald,* March 13, 1972. Gene Miller reports that this account came from *Washington Post* reporter Stu Auerbach, who was traveling with the Wallace campaign. A Florida state trooper who had heard about the trial from a court bailiff told Auerbach about the vote. Gene Miller, *Invitation to a Lynching* (Garden City, NY: Doubleday & Co., 1975), note on p. 273.

11. Richard Skipper testimony, 1972 Marianna trial transcript, 3049–3053.

12. 1972 Marianna trial transcript, 3053–3054.

13. 1972 Marianna trial transcript, 3075.

14. Judge Smith also barred from evidence the testimony of Marion "Bart" Knight, a former state senator from that area, concerning certain incriminating statements Pitts and Lee had allegedly made; 1972 Marianna trial transcript, 3384–3394. Knight claimed that the defendants had made these statements to him one day in court during a court recess, but he was so confused about when this event allegedly happened and the circumstances surrounding it that Judge Smith excluded the testimony as being incredible.

1972 Marianna trial transcript, 3392, 3404. Pitts and Lee both denied ever talking to Knight at any time.

15. Willie Mae Lee testimony, 1972 Marianna trial transcript, 3181.

16. Willie Mae Lee testimony, 1972 Marianna trial transcript, 3201.

17. Gene Miller to Willie Mae Lee, August 21, 1967, in author's possession.

18. 1972 Marianna trial transcript, 3203.

19. Willie Mae Lee testimony, 1972 Marianna trial transcript, 3163–3175.

20. 1972 Marianna trial transcript, 3164–3165, 3166.

21. Willie Mae Lee testimony, 1972 Marianna trial transcript, 3165, 3167, 3170, 3172, 3173.

22. 1972 Marianna trial transcript: Willie Mae Lee testimony, 3209–3212; Wayne White testimony, 3344–3345.

23. Willie Mae Lee testimony, 1972 Marianna trial transcript, 3165, 3221–3222.

24. Willie Mae Lee testimony, 1972 Marianna trial transcript, 3262–3163.

25. Willie Mae Lee testimony, 1972 Marianna trial transcript, 3166, 3167–3168, 3223–3224.

26. Willie Mae Lee testimony, 1972 Marianna trial transcript, 3174, 3243.

27. 1972 Marianna trial transcript, 3273–3274.

28. Willie Mae Lee testimony, 1972 Marianna trial transcript, 3271–3272.

29. 1972 Marianna trial transcript, 3272

30. Willie Mae Lee testimony, 1972 Marianna trial transcript, 3272–373.

31. Willie Mae Lee testimony, 1972 Marianna trial transcript, 3277–3278.

32. Willie Mae Lee testimony, 1972 Marianna trial transcript, 3280–3281.

33. 1972 Marianna trial transcript, 3407–3408.

34. 1972 Marianna trial transcript, 3418–3472.

35. 1972 Marianna trial transcript, 3475.

36. 1972 Marianna trial transcript, 3476.

Chapter 26. The Defense Case

1. 1972 Marianna trial transcript, 3476.

2. 1972 Marianna trial transcript, 3478.

3. 1972 Marianna trial transcript, 3514–3515.

4. Robinson v. Pepper, 116 So. 2d 4 (Fla. 1928); Sullivan v. McMillan, 26 Fla. 543 (1890). See also Section 90.804(4), Florida Statutes (2017), which codifies the declarations against interest exception to the hearsay rule and extends this exception to declarations against penal interest where "corroborating circumstances show the trustworthiness of the statement." This statute was not in effect in 1972.

5. 1972 Marianna trial transcript, 3515–3519.

6. 1972 Marianna trial transcript, 3521.

7. 1972 Marianna trial transcript, 3524.

8. 1972 Marianna trial transcript, 3525. Jones, citing no case authority, also argued that Adams's tape-recorded confession was inadmissible under the best-evidence rule. The best evidence, he argued, was the testimony of Curtis Adams, whom we had subpoenaed as a possible witness. 1972 Marianna trial transcript, 3520, 3522. But the best-

evidence rule relates solely to written documents or their equivalent (i.e., electronic recordings) and generally bars the admission of oral testimony that describes the contents of a document or recording. The best evidence is generally the document or recording itself. Williams v. State, 386 So. 2d 538, 540 (Fla. 1980); Liddon v. Bd. of Pub. Instruction for Jackson County, 175 So. 806, 808 (Fla. 1937); Sun Bank of St. Lucie County v. Oliver, 403 So. 2d 583, 584 (Fla. 4th DCA 1981). Jones's argument that the best evidence was the oral testimony of Curtis Adams turned the best-evidence rule on its head. The state did not use this meritless argument in later proceedings, including trial and appeal.

9. 1972 Marianna trial transcript, 3527.

10. 1972 Marianna trial transcript, 3534–3537.

11. 1972 Marianna trial transcript, 3541–3613.

12. 1972 Marianna trial transcript, 3613.

13. 1972 Marianna trial transcript, 3614.

14. 1972 Marianna trial transcript, 3616.

15. Warren Holmes testimony, 1972 Marianna trial transcript, 3698–3707.

16. Mary Jean Akins testimony, 1972 Marianna trial transcript, 3617–3639.

17. 1972 Marianna trial transcript, 3862–3868.

18. 1972 Marianna trial transcript, 3868–3869.

19. Williams v. State, 110 So. 2d 654 (Fla. 1959) (similar crimes evidence is admissible at trial if it shows a common scheme or plan with the crime for which the defendant is charged). I argued that the robberies, kidnappings, and murders Curtis Adams had committed at gas stations in Port St. Joe and Fort Lauderdale within a period of sixteen days were similar crimes because they showed a common scheme or plan, thereby making evidence of the Fort Lauderdale gas station robbery, kidnap, and murder admissible at trial against Adams as similar crimes evidence.

20. 1972 Marianna trial transcript, 3843–3852.

21. 1972 Marianna trial transcript, 3849–3850.

22. 1972 Marianna trial transcript, 3533.

23. Elihu Phares testimony, 1972 Marianna trial transcript, 3857–3859.

24. 1972 Marianna trial transcript, Freddie Pitts testimony, 1972 Marianna trial transcript, 3725–3770.

25. Wilbert Lee testimony, 1972 Marianna trial transcript, 3791–3792.

26. Ella Mae Lee testimony, 1972 Marianna trial transcript, 3667–3668.

27. Ella Mae Lee testimony, 1972 Marianna trial transcript, 3670.

28. Ella Mae Lee testimony, 1972 Marianna trial transcript, 3667–3668.

29. Ella Mae Lee testimony, 1972 Marianna trial transcript, 3684–3685.

30. Ella Mae Lee testimony, 1972 Marianna trial transcript, 3689.

31. Ella Mae Lee testimony, 1972 Marianna trial transcript, 3690.

32. Ella Mae Lee testimony, 1972 Marianna trial transcript, 3691.

33. Ella Mae Lee testimony, 1972 Marianna trial transcript, 3692–3693.

34. Ella Mae Lee testimony, 1972 Marianna trial transcript, 3693.

35. 1972 Marianna trial transcript: Freddie Pitts testimony, 3733–3750; Wilbert Lee testimony, 3796–3809.

36. 1972 Marianna trial transcript: Donald Hoag testimony, 3480 et seq.; Bruce Potts testimony, 3904 et seq.

37. Dorothy Martin testimony, 1972 Marianna trial transcript, 3646 et seq.

38. Henry Hogue testimony, 1972 Marianna trial transcript, 3831.

39. Ella Mae Lee testimony, 1972 Marianna trial transcript, 3669.

40. Wilbert Lee testimony, 1972 Marianna trial transcript, 3820–3822.

41. 1972 Marianna trial transcript, 3935.

42. 1972 Marianna trial transcript, 3938.

Chapter 27. The Final Arguments

1. Rule 3.250 of the Florida Rules of Criminal Procedure for 1972 provided that "a defendant offering no testimony in his or her own behalf, except the defendant's own, shall be entitled to the concluding argument before the jury."

2. 1972 Marianna trial transcript, 3969.

3. 1972 Marianna trial transcript, 3969–3970.

4. 1972 Marianna trial transcript, 3970–3971.

5. 1972 Marianna trial transcript, 3975–3990.

6. 1972 Marianna trial transcript, 3976.

7. 1972 Marianna trial transcript, 3976–3980.

8. 1972 Marianna trial transcript, 3980.

9. 1972 Marianna trial transcript, 3981.

10. 1972 Marianna trial transcript, 3982–3983.

11. 1972 Marianna trial transcript, 3965–3866.

12. 1972 Marianna trial transcript, 3986.

13. 1972 Marianna trial transcript, 3133.

14. 1972 Marianna trial transcript, 3987.

15. 1972 Marianna trial transcript, 3990–3991.

16. 1972 Marianna trial transcript, 3991–3992.

17. 1972 Marianna trial transcript, 3994.

18. 1972 Marianna trial transcript, 3994–3995.

19. 1972 Marianna trial transcript, 3996–3997.

20. 1972 Marianna trial transcript, 4007.

21. 1972 Marianna trial transcript, 4008.

22. Gene Miller, *Invitation to a Lynching* (Garden City, NY: Doubleday & Co., 1975), 294.

23. 1972 Marianna trial transcript, 4013–4017.

24. 1972 Marianna trial transcript, 4057–4058.

25. 1972 Marianna trial transcript, 4022.

26. 1972 Marianna trial transcript, 4009–4072.

27. 1972 Marianna trial transcript, 4072.

28. James Zeigler, the number ten juror, was a US Treasury revenue agent. 1972 Marianna trial transcript, 2699.

29. 1972 Marianna trial transcript, 4074.

30. 1972 Marianna trial transcript, 4077.

31. 1972 Marianna trial transcript, 4081–4082.

32. 1972 Marianna trial transcript, 4093.

33. 1972 Marianna trial transcript, 4093–4094.

34. 1972 Marianna trial transcript, 4104.

35. 1972 Marianna trial transcript, 4107.

Chapter 28. The Trial Concludes

1. 1972 Marianna trial transcript, 4119.

2. 1972 Marianna trial transcript, 4120.

3. 1972 Marianna trial transcript, 4124.

4. 1972 Marianna trial transcript, 4127.

5. 1972 Marianna trial transcript, 4142–4143.

6. 1972 Marianna trial transcript, 4139.

7. 1972 Marianna trial transcript, 4143–4144.

8. 1972 Marianna trial transcript, 4146.

9. 1972 Marianna trial transcript, 4147.

10. Gene Miller, *Invitation to a Lynching* (Garden City, NY: Doubleday & Co., 1975), 297; Rob Elder, "Pitts and Lee Get the Chair Again," *Miami Herald*, March 16, 1972.

11. 1972 Marianna trial transcript, 4148.

12. 1972 Marianna trial transcript, 4148–4149.

13. 1972 Marianna trial transcript, 4149–4150.

14. 1972 Marianna trial transcript, 4152–4153.

15. Miller, *Invitation to a Lynching*, 301.

16. Gene Miller, "The Unending Trial Transcripts of Pitts and Lee," *Tropic* (*Miami Herald* Sunday magazine), September 9, 1973, 17.

17. Miller, *Invitation to a Lynching*, 300.

18. Miller, *Invitation to a Lynching*, 300.

19. Miller, *Invitation to a Lynching*, 300.

20. Miller, *Invitation to a Lynching*, 300.

21. Miller, *Invitation to a Lynching*, 300–301.

22. Leonard Mellon to Phillip Hubbart, March 15, 1973, in author's possession.

23. Warren Holmes to Freddie Pitts and Wilbert Lee, May 3, 1972, in author's possession.

Chapter 29. The Appeal

1. 408 U.S. 15 (1972).

2. Gregg v. Georgia, 428 U.S. 153 (1976).

3. Gene Miller, *Invitation to a Lynching* (Garden City, NY: Doubleday & Co., 1975), 303.

4. Miller, *Invitation to a Lynching*, 303.

5. Freddie Lee Pitts and Wilbert Lee, Appellants, v. State of Florida, 307 So. 2d 473 (Fla. 1st DCA 1975).

6. *Pitts and Lee v. State*, 487.

7. A writ of certiorari is an order issued by an appellate court to review a decision of

a lower court. The Latin word "certiorari" means "to be more meaningfully informed." Bryan Garner, *A Dictionary of Modern Legal Usage*, 2nd ed. (New York: Oxford University Press, 1995), 143.

8. The Florida Supreme Court has review jurisdiction over only a select class of District Court of Appeal decisions. The court has no jurisdiction to review district court decisions that do not fit into this category, and ordinarily a district court's decision is the final decision in the case. Under Article V of the Florida Constitution, the Florida Supreme Court has review jurisdiction over district court decisions that conflict on the same point of law with the decision of another district court district of appeal in Florida or with a Florida Supreme Court decision. We saw no such conflict in this case.

9. Suzi Wilson to Phillip Hubbart, July 22 1975, in author's possession. Ms. Wilson was the public information director for the Florida State Prison System. In this letter, she recounted a conversation she had with Mr. MacKenzie, who at the time was doing a story on the Pitts-Lee case. Ms. Wilson quotes Mr. MacKenzie in this letter as it appears in the text. For Mr. MacKenzie's comprehensive article on the Pitts-Lee case, including my 1975 petition for a writ of certiorari with the US Supreme Court, see John F. MacKenzie, "Complex 1963 Murder Case Raises Major Legal Questions," *Washington Post*, August 4, 1975.

10. 410 U.S. 284 (1973).

11. The Florida Evidence Code currently reflects the holding of the *Chambers* decision: "A statement tending to expose the [third party] declarant to criminal liability and offered to exculpate the accused is inadmissible, *unless corroborating circumstances show the trustworthiness of the statement.*" Fla. Stat. 90.804 (2)(c) (2022), emphasis added.

12. Chambers v. Mississippi, 410 U.S. 284, 302 (1973).

13. 410 U.S. 284 (1973). See Petition for a Writ of Certiorari, Freddie Pitts and Wilbert Lee v. State of Florida, US Supreme Court, May 1, 1975, 20–21, in author's possession.

14. Petition for a writ of certiorari, 22.

15. Petition for a writ of certiorari, 22–23.

16. *Pitts and Lee v. State*, 485.

17. Petition for a writ of certiorari, 24.

18. *Pitts and Lee v. State*, 485.

19. Petition for a writ of certiorari, 26.

20. Petition for a writ of certiorari, 27–32.

Chapter 30. Freedom

1. See, e.g., Gene Miller, "New Trial Sought for Pitts and Lee," *Miami Herald*, March 26, 1972; Gene Miller, "U.S. Supreme Court Is Urged to Review the Pitts-Lee Case," *Miami Herald*, May 4, 1975; Gene Miller, "Victim's Son Visits Pitts, Lee—'I Know They Didn't Kill My Father,'" *Miami Herald*, September 6, 1975; Gene Miller, "'I Shot Jesse and Floyd,' Adams Admits to Shevin," *Miami Herald*, September 10, 1976; Gene Miller, "Tape Clearing Pitts, Lee 'Forgotten'?" *Miami Herald*, September 14, 1975; Gene Miller, "Convict Repeats Confession to Mo-Jo Murders," *Miami Herald*, September 18, 1975.

2. Many years later, in 1997, President Bill Clinton appointed Donald Middlebrooks as US district court judge for the Southern District of Florida.

3. Transcript of Curtis Adams confession to Donald Middlebrooks, Florida State Prison, Raiford, Florida, June 13, 1974, in author's possession.

4. Gene Miller, "Believing Pitts, Lee Innocent, Askew Plans to Seek Pardon," *Miami Herald,* September 9, 1975; Gene Miller, *Invitation to a Lynching* (Garden City, NY: Doubleday & Co., 1975), 307.

5. Miller, *Invitation to a Lynching,* 307.

6. On one occasion, Askew telephoned a Port St. Joe bank official to verify one aspect of Mary Jean Akins's testimony, namely that she had cashed her last telephone company paycheck in Winter Haven, Florida, on August 3, 1963. Robert D. Shaw Jr., "How Askew Reached His Decision on Pardon," *Miami Herald,* September 11, 1975.

7. Aubrey Branch testimony, 1972 Marianna trial transcript, 3190.

8. Shaw, "How Askew Reached His Decision on Pardon."

9. Aubrey Branch testimony, 1972 Marianna trial transcript, 3196, 3197–3198.

10. Aubrey Branch testimony, 1972 Marianna trial transcript, 3197–3198.

11. Miller, *Invitation to a Lynching,* 302.

12. Raymond Lang, "Two Innocents Who Suffered on Death Row," *Ebony,* September 1983, 29.

13. Miller, *Invitation to a Lynching,* 303.

14. Lang, "Two Innocents Who Suffered on Death Row," 30.

15. Lang, "Two Innocents Who Suffered on Death Row," 29.

16. Miller, *Invitation to a Lynching,* 305–306.

17. "6000 Petition Askew to Free Pitts, Lee from Death Row," *Miami News,* January 8, 1975. Joseph Waller, a leader of the group, later called Askew "a demagogic fraud." As explained in chapter 1, Askew was infuriated with this group and later got assurances from me that we as defense counsel had no connection with these people.

18. James J. Kilpatrick, "Pitts And Lee at Port St. Joe: A Case of Southern Injustice," *Miami Herald,* April 20, 1971. Kilpatrick also wrote a congratulatory column after Pitts and Lee were pardoned and released from prison; James J. Kilpatrick, "Happy Ending for Pitts and Lee," *Miami Herald,* September 30, 1975.

19. Miller, *Invitation to a Lynching,* 306.

20. "Askew Aide to Interview Witnesses in Pardon Probe of Pitts-Lee Case," *Miami Herald,* October 9, 1974.

21. Miller, *Invitation to a Lynching,* 306.

22. Miller, *Invitation to a Lynching,* 306.

23. Miller, "Victim's Son Visits Pitts, Lee."

24. Miller, "Victim's Son Visits Pitts, Lee."

25. Mary Ann Lindley, "Pitts-Lee Pardon Favored by 2–1, Askew Mail Shows," *Miami News,* September 25, 1975.

26. Charlton W. Tebeau, *A History of Florida,* rev. ed. (Miami: University of Miami Press, 1980), 469.

27. Executive Order Number 75-49, Remarks of Reubin O'D. Askew, Governor of Florida, September 11, 1975, filed with the Florida Secretary of State, September 24, 1975, in author's possession.

28. Scott Minerbrook, "The Stolen Years of Two Innocent Men," *The Newsday Magazine,* August 28, 1983, 30.

29. Miller, "'I Shot Jesse and Floyd.'"

30. Miller, "'I Shot Jesse and Floyd.'"

31. Miller, "'I Shot Jesse and Floyd.'"

32. Miller, "'I Shot Jesse and Floyd.'"

33. Robert D. Shaw Jr., "Ashler Signs Pardon: Turlington's Signature Will Make It Official," *Miami Herald,* September 13, 1975.

34. Robert D. Shaw Jr., "Turlington Adds Fourth Signature," *Miami Herald,* September 17, 1975. Warren Holmes and Detective Elihu Phares spent nearly three hours in closed session with Ralph Turlington and Secretary of State Bruce Smathers discussing the case. Robert D. Shaw Jr. and Steve Franklin, "Turlington Still Checking, Says He'll Still Sign Pardon for Pitts, Lee," *Miami Herald,* September 16, 1975.

35. During this time, Curtis Adams once again confessed to the Floyd-Burkett murders at Raiford Prison to two other members of the Florida Cabinet: Secretary of State Bruce Smathers and State Comptroller Gerald Lewis. But by that time it was academic, as the pardon had already become official. Gene Miller, "Convict Repeats Confession to Mo-Jo Murders," *Miami Herald,* September 18, 1975. Smathers and Lewis were both sympathetic to Pitts and Lee but declined to sign the pardon because they didn't feel they knew enough about the case. Only Doyle Conner, the commissioner of agriculture, was adamantly opposed to the pardon.

36. W. D. Luening, "Justice Dragged for Pitts, Lee," *Fort Lauderdale News,* September 12, 1975.

37. Phillip Hubbart to M. I. Houweling, September 29, 1975, in author's possession.

38. Curtis Adams to Warren Holmes, September 19, 1975, in author's possession.

39. Warren Holmes to Curtis Adams, September 25, 1975, in author's possession.

40. Of Proceedings in the Case of Pitts, Freddie L., Army Board of Corrections, June 15, 1977, in author's possession.

41. "Gene Miller of *Miami Herald,*" The Pulitzer Prizes, https://www.pulitzer.org/winners/gene-miller-0#:~:text=For%20his%20persistent%20and%20courageous,sentenced%20to%20death%20in%20Florida.

42. Mike Baxter, "Miller Captures a Pulitzer for His Pitts-Lee Stories," *Miami Herald,* May 4, 1976.

43. Baxter, "Miller Captures a Pulitzer for His Pitts Lee Stories."

44. Karen Branch and Tom Fiedler, "Nightmare Ends for 2 Wrongfully Accused," *Miami Herald,* May 1, 1998.

45. Karen Branch, "Chiles Signs Bill for Pitts, Lee," *Miami Herald,* May 2, 1998.

46. "Pitts and Lee Can't Forget, Won't Forgive," *Vero Beach Press Journal,* July 31, 1983.

47. Dorothy Gaiter, "Pitts and Lee Wait for Justice . . . and Legislators," *Miami Herald,* May 2, 1985.

48. "Pitts and Lee Can't Forget, Won't Forgive."

49. Petition for a Writ of Certiorari, Freddie Pitts and Wilbert Lee v. State of Florida, US Supreme Court, May 1, 1975, 32, in author's possession.

50. Richard Rorty, "Color-Blind in the Marketplace," *New York Times Book Review,* September 24, 1975, 9.

51. George Santayana, *The Life of Reason; or, The Phases of Human Progress,* 2nd ed. (New York: Charles Scribner's Sons, 1922), 284.

Index

Williams, George, 275
Winick, Jack M., 96–98, 163, 169
W. P. Comforter Funeral Home, 35

Zeigler, James A., 274

Phillip A. Hubbart served as a judge on the Third District Court of Appeal in Miami, Florida, from 1977 to 1996. For two and a half years (1980–1983), he was chief judge of that court.

Before that, he served as the elected public defender of Miami-Dade County, Florida, from 1971 to 1977; as an assistant defender in the Office of Public Defender from 1965 to 1969; and as a lawyer for the Legal Aid Agency for the District of Columbia (now the Public Defender Service) from 1962 to 1963.

He holds a BA degree from Augustana College, Rock Island, Illinois; a JD degree from Duke University Law School; and an LLM degree from Georgetown University Law Center, where he was an E. Barrett Prettyman Fellow.

He is the author of *Making Sense of Search and Seizure Law: A Fourth Amendment Handbook,* 2d ed. He edited and commented on his great-great grandfather's Civil War letters in *An Iowa Soldier Writes Home: The Civil War Letters of Private Daniel J. Parvin.* He is the lead editor of *To Form a More Perfect Union: An Anthology of American Values and the Debate on Wealth and Income Disparity.*

He practiced appellate law as a founding member of the law firm of Wetherington, Klein & Hubbart in Miami from 1996 to 2016. He is now retired.